Of Islands and Women

1. MADEIRA *Susanna Hoe*
2. CRETE *Susanna Hoe*


*forthcoming*

TASMANIA *Susanna Hoe*
SRI LANKA *Susanna Hoe*
SINGAPORE *Paula Kaplan*
HAWAII *Betty Wei*
POLYNESIA: Tahiti, Easter Island, Cook Islands *Susanna Hoe*
CARIBBEAN: Jamaica, Barbados, Haiti *Susanna Hoe*
HONG KONG and MACAU *Susanna Hoe*

# Crete

## Women, History, Books and Places

SUSANNA HOE

HOLO BOOKS
THE WOMEN'S HISTORY PRESS
OXFORD

Published in 2005 by The Women's History Press
A division of HOLO Books
Clarendon House
52 Cornmarket, Oxford OX1 3HJ

www.centralbooks.co.uk

British Library Cataloguing in Publication Data
A catalogue record for this book is available from the British Library

ISBN-10   0–9537730–7–8
ISBN-13   978–0–9537730–7–7

10   9   8   7   6   5   4   3   2   1

Designed and produced for HOLO Books by
Chase Publishing Services Ltd, Fortescue, Sidmouth EX10 9QG, England
Printed and bound in the European Union

For Anna and Ros
and to mark five years

# Contents

**Contents**                                              **ix**

# Illustrations

# Preface

## Crete

Parents are often surprised by how their children differ one from the other. I would like to extend the slightly cliched analogy of producing a book and a child. When I envisaged this series – which is described below – I saw little books (livrets) marching along the shelf all much the same. But, for a start, Crete has turned out rather fatter than Madeira (about which I first wrote). That is the fault of the Minoans who, gallivanting in 'palaces' several millennia before the Portuguese arrived in Madeira, have muscled in and tried to dominate the story. I hope I have not let them overwhelm the other women of Crete.

In the nineteenth century, Madeira was visited by many foreign women who left accounts. I have found only one in Crete – Mary Walker who lived in Istanbul for thirty years or so. Two other women of the late Ottoman period stand out by name, one a native – Elizabeth Kontaxaki, sometimes known as Elizabeth of Crete, leader of a political movement – the other a long-time foreign resident – Baroness Schwartz, supporter of insurgents, philanthropist, correspondent of Liszt, mistress of Garibaldi. She travelled but left no published account. Their contribution, particularly that of Baroness Schwartz, is unrecognised. There is more to be found out about all three women and I take this opportunity to ask for help. Such elusiveness will draw me back to Crete, and I hope my struggle to give women their due in history will help you to enjoy your visit more fully.

As for the early twentieth century, because of the Minoans, Crete was well-visited by pioneering women archaeologists, of whom the first and most renowned was Harriet Boyd. Their work, and particularly their lives in Crete, were a great asset to my research, and they are very much a feature of the book. But what accounts they left cannot be found in bookshops or local public libraries. Archaeology is not a major feature of Madeira, where remains of indigenous habitation before the fourteenth century are still being looked for. The two islands do have in common plenty of rocky mountains.

I have managed to start both livrets with a woman arriving unconventionally on the shores of the island: Anna d'Arfet in Madeira, the goddess Europa in Crete. I think I can maintain this self-generated convention for the next livret, Tasmania, and even Tahiti. But, in the end, each livret will be its own own book.

## Series – 'Of Islands and Women'

The places most alluring to travellers or holiday makers are often islands. But even the small ones may have too much to see in one visit. Over the years I have, therefore, refined a stratagem that begins to overcome that problem. And, since I assume that others, particularly women, may like to travel as I do, I put forward the following proposition: the most rewarding way for a woman to visit an island is to read books by women who have travelled there, or by or about women who have been part of its history, and to visit the places they describe or where they had their being. Happily, the novelty and excitement of the chase seems to appeal as much to my husband, Derek Roebuck, as to me.

Guide books, and those travelling companions which include extracts from travellers to a particular place, offer essential or pleasing information about many aspects, but seldom much about women. I have to do much of my own research from scratch and, with Derek's help, find the places. Since we have now travelled our way so often, it seems natural to write about it – to fill a gap. Hence this series and, as the books are intended to be quite short and portable, I have revived the word 'livret'.

The subtitle common to each, 'Women, History, Books and Places', combines the essential elements of the series. There are suggestions for which books to read, as well as a flavour of them, and where to go. A historical background, concentrating as far as possible on women, is followed by itineraries. Most of the information comes from women's accounts or studies and our own experiences.

You may feel that what follows is sufficient for your reading needs about the island in question. But for those who share, or would like to share, my book obsession, this is my method. Some of the books I read before I go, some I read there, and some I read on my return. As far as possible, I like to have my own copies. This has become much easier now that you can buy secondhand books on the internet, and I have suggested which books should be easy to come by and which not. That is not to say that I don't visit bookshops: to do so invites serendipity.

A list of future livrets – about islands that have already been visited – is in the front of this one. If you have ideas for them that you think should be included, please let me know; I hope that your story, properly acknowledged, might form part of the text. In that way we can extend the boundaries of what is known about women's past and have some fun.

Oxford
February 2005

# Author's Note

The place where I first landed in Crete can be spelt in English Chania, Khania, or Hania. Well into the twentieth century, writers were still calling it Canea, the name used by the Venetians, even though they had not been the occupying power there since 1646. This example highlights the problems of transliteration from the Greek alphabet into the Roman over time, between languages, and across disciplines. I have decided to use Chania and to apply the same rule to other names with the same Greek letter.

Saint can be translated and transcribed (in the feminine) as Hagia, Agia, Aghia, or Ayia; once again, I have plumped for a traditional English version, Hagia. I have made an exception with Agios Nikolaos. The capital of Crete is commonly written Iraklion today. Many quotations use its Venetian name, Candia, and many modern texts simplify the traditional to Heraklion, which was tempting; but I have stuck to Herakleion.

There are different systems of transliteration but no source seems to follow one consistently. I have, thereafter, after worrying away over many months, decided that the main consistency should be within my own writing. My transliterations may not always be those you will find in guidebooks or on the road signs (where those are in English). Modern Greeks have their own system which does not necessarily fit with what foreign classicists have been used to. So be alert! Taking advantage of the confusion, I have differentiated two places: the archaeological cemetery near Archanes is Phourni; and I have called the village near Chania by the transliteration used in a modern quotation, Fourne.

Because of Crete's long prehistory, the reconstruction of its twentieth century history has a considerable archaeological component; the biographical details of visiting women scholars who flourished between 1900 and 1970 are given in chronological order in chapter 14 at the end of the history section. Where I think it helpful, other mentions of these women refer you to that entry. Other women, including legendary ones, are in **bold** in the text where their fullest details occur, or where they are just mentioned once, and a bold page number in the index corresponds for most of them. As usual in my writing, I tend to be familiar and use first names.

Many archaeological artefacts mentioned in the history section are in Crete's museums, particularly the Herakleion Archaeological Museum. The Herakleion itinerary has a section devoted to the museum with these artefacts detailed under their room number which also appears in brackets in the historical text; and the artefacts are appropriately mentioned in the relevant itinerary. The Chania, Agios Nikolaos and Siteia archaeological museums are treated similarly but more simply. Artefact, history and place are also cross-referenced.

Guidebooks are not consistent or necessarily up-to-date on which archaeological sites are open to the public when. If you are keen to visit a site, often your only recourse is to go there. You will obviously be discreet and responsible whatever the formal situation.

The bibliography is divided into sections: Women's Works (general reader); Women's Specialised Works; Unpublished Material; General Reference; and Guides. Some visitors to Crete just want to have fun and do some idle reading; some plan to spend time going round ancient sites and want to receive straightforward and comprehensible information about what they are seeing, and how they can best appreciate Crete's long history and its contemporary women. Then there are those who really know their onions archaeologically and care about every argument. I hope I have not been too ambitious in trying to cater for all those in the text, and the bibliography reflects the differences. A glossary defines unfamiliar terms.

Regarding the use of precise references to quotations or specific theories, I decided that the general reader might be more comfortable without. Because of this, and because I wanted to include as many women engaged in work on Crete, or pertinent women's issues, as possible, I have tried to make it clear in the text whose voice I am using and from where. The names can be married to the bibliography.

This book has no pretensions to be a complete guide to Crete, nor indeed, to cover everything to do with women, history, books and places. It is the result of three visits over three years totalling seven weeks, and as much darting about as was physically possible, together with years of reading and picking the brains of scholars. Ultimately, it is an entirely personal exploration by a complete outsider who does not speak the language, accompanied by a husband who reads ancient Greek. You will also need a good guidebook, or two – I have mentioned in the bibliography those I have used; in the text I have mostly recommended Pat Cameron's 2003 *Blue Guide*. *The Rough Guide to Crete* is also useful, particularly for general information and sometimes sharp asides. There are several large format, illustrated guides available in Crete, nice to have but, unfortunately, often undated and, therefore, possibly outdated. You will also need an up-to-date map – the creation of good roads is a continuing process.

In case of a future edition, anything you would like to add would be warmly received.

## Acknowledgements

When you roam around the world in the recreation of women's history, you are laying yourself open to trouble with experts on a particular place or of a particular discipline, nowhere more so than Crete with its complicated prehistory and archaeology. I have, therefore, been warmed by the sympathetic response I have received from scholars of the island. It is impossible to convey here the time and trouble they have taken to answer queries, lend me material in advance of publication, and direct me towards sources, some of them over several years, nor to adequately thank them. Several have also read relevant parts – but, of course, I am responsible for the result. Family members of my characters have also been generous and, as usual, I have imposed on friends; several have translated from Greek for me. If I list names alphabetically without apportioning degrees of thanks, they are no less warm. I include those who have given personal permission to use their or their family's material (more formal permissions are given below or in the list of illustrations).

Annie Allsebrook, Colin Allsebrook, Maria Andreadaki-Vlasaki (Chania Archaeological Museum), Ashmolean Museum, Oxford (Evans Archives), Ann and Graham Bacon, Cassandra Balchin, Rosemary E. Bancroft-Marcus, Elizabeth W. Barber, Felicity Barker, Staff of the Bodleian Library, Staff of the British Library, Gerald Cadogan, Lucy Cadogan, Malcolm Chapman, (Manchester University), Getzel Cohen, Nicola Coldstream, Jo Day, Sue Donnelly (London School of Economics Archives), Alexandre Farnoux, Enrica Fiandra, Christine Finn, Maria Fiotodimitraki, Michalis Gerontis, Geraldine Gesell, David Gill, Lucy Goodison, Sonia Greger, Frejä Gregory, Nicolas Hawkes, Barbara Hayden, Judith Herrin, Mary Hiscock, Rachel Hood, Sinclair Hood, Patricia Kyritsi Howell, Helen Hughes-Brock, Zeynep Inankur, Stelios Jackson (Hellenic Bookservice), Elizabeth James (London University Library), Maria Kafetzaki (Istron Bay Hotel), Amalia Kakissis (British School at Athens), Tonia Karindinou (The Balcony, Siteia), Katerina Kopaka, Ann Lum (Natural History Museum), Sally McKee, Rebecca McKenzie-Young, Michalis Maniadakis, Nicoletta Momigliano, Sir David Money-Coutts, Vivienne Monk, Marianna Nikolaidou, Lucia Nixon, AnnCharlotte Nordfeldt, Anna Pafitis, Brother Paisios (Faneromeni Monastery), Holly Parton, Alex Pezzati (University of Pennylvania Museum), Lefteris Platon, Sosso Platonos, Harriet Pottinger, Ivor Powell, John Prag, Paul Roebuck, Staff of the Sackler Library, Oxford, Efi Sakellarakis, Elizabeth Schofield, Sarah Searight, Sophia Seiradaki, Susan Sherratt, Anne Thomson, (Newnham College), Marjorie Theobald, Molly Travers, Metaxia Tsipopoulou,

Henri van Effenterre, Micheline van Effenterre, Staff of Villa Archanes, Emmanuel Voyiakis, Elizabeth Warren, Peter Warren.

Ray Addicott has exercised his usual kindness, patience and acuity in the production.

Readers of this book will get some hints of the part played in its research by my husband, Derek Roebuck. They are only a small part of his contribution. He is integral to all my writing.

## Permission to use

Dorothea Bate's 'Journal Kept in Crete', by permission of the Trustees of the Natural History Museum; *The Life of Ismail Ferik Pasha*, Rhea Galanaki, Peter Owen Ltd, London; University of Pennsylvania Museum of Archaeology and Anthropology, published and unpublished letters of Edith Hall; Extracts from *A Quest of Love* and *Dawn of the Gods*, by Jacquetta Hawkes are reproduced by permission of PFD on behalf of the Estate of Jacquetta Hawkes; The Principal and Fellows, Newnham College, Cambridge, Jane Ellen Harrison letter; From *The King Must Die* by Mary Renault, published by Arrow, reprinted by permission of the Random House Group Ltd; Reproduced with permission of the British School at Athens, unpublished letters, Hilda Pendlebury White; Every effort has been made to secure necessary permissions.

WESTERN AND CENTRAL CRETE

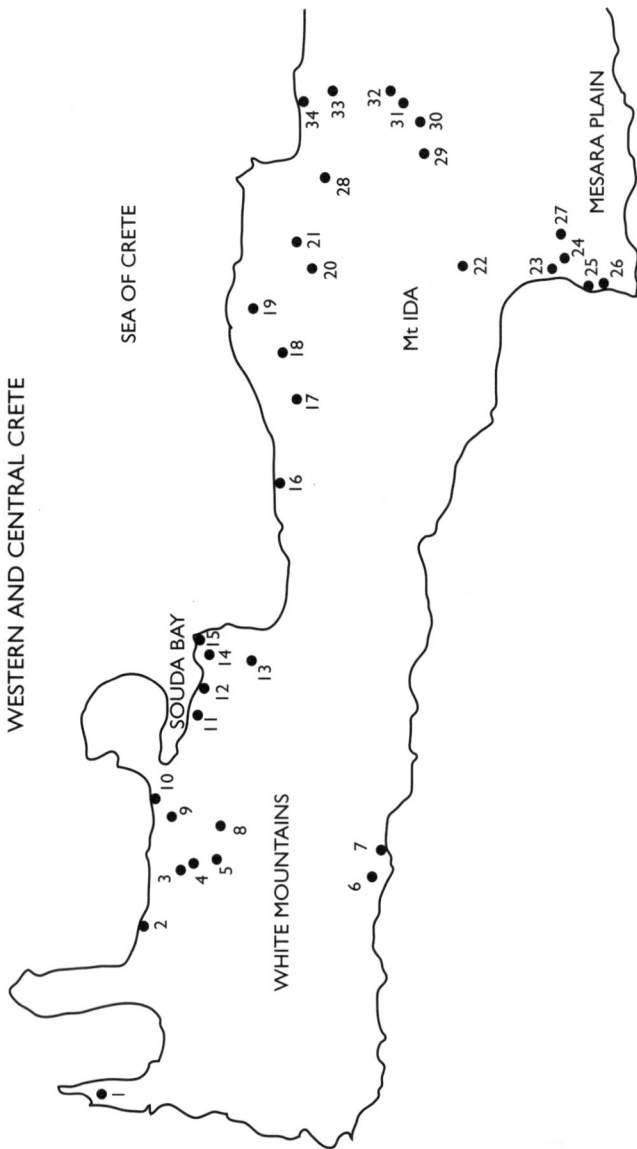

SEA OF CRETE

SOUDA BAY

WHITE MOUNTAINS

Mt IDA

MESARA PLAIN

LIBYAN SEA

EASTERN CRETE

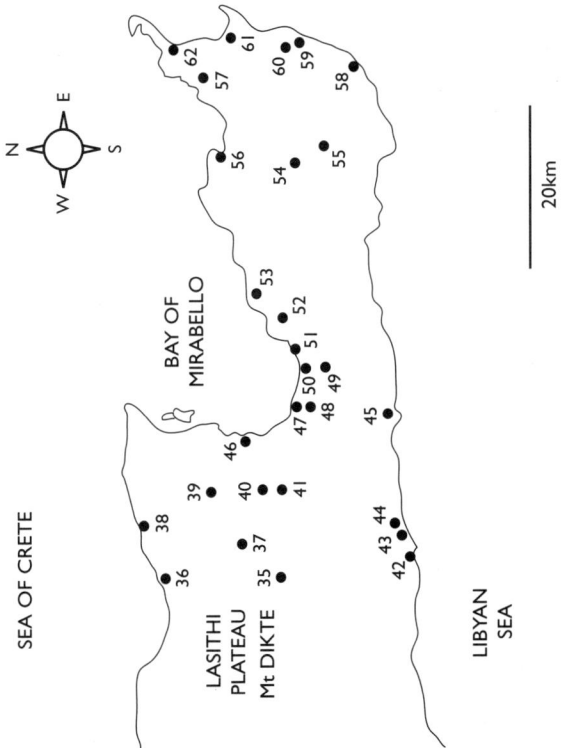

SEA OF CRETE

BAY OF
MIRABELLO

LASITHI
PLATEAU
Mt DIKTE

LIBYAN
SEA

20km

N
W — E
S

1 Gramvousa
2 Maleme
3 Alikianos
4 Fourne
5 Meskla
6 Lissos
7 Sougia
8 Theriso
9 Mournies
10 CHANIA
11 Aptera
12 Kalyves
13 Kalamitsi Amigdali
14 Gavalochori
15 Kokkino Chorio
16 RETHYMNON
17 Arkadi
18 Eleutherna
19 Melidoni
20 Anogia
21 Kamariotis
22 Kamares cave
23 Hagia Triada
24 Phaistos
25 Kommos
26 Matala
27 Gortyn
28 Tylissos
29 Paliani
30 Prophitis Ilias
31 Vathypetro
32 Archanes

33 Knossos
34 HERAKLEION
35 Psychro
36 Mallia
37 Tzermiado
38 Milatos
39 Neapoli
40 Lato
41 Kritsa
42 Myrtos
43 Pyrgos
44 Phournou Koriphi
45 IERAPETRA
46 Agios Nicolaos
47 Istron
48 Vrokastro
49 Vasiliki
50 Gournia
51 Pacheia Ammos
52 Kavousi
53 Sphaka
54 Praisos
55 Voila
56 SITEIA
57 Toplou
58 Xerokampos
59 Zakro
60 Ano Zakro
61 Palaikastro
62 Itanos

# Crete

# Glossary

*apotheke* – archaeological pot shed, for storing, sorting, mending etc.

*chiton* – full length Minoan dress made in three lengths in sheer linen or silk

Daedalic – used to describe an artefact from the Archaic/Classical period; term created from the name of Daedalus, Minos and Pasiphae's master-craftsman and inventor

faience – pottery with a glass-like finish

*horta* – mountain greens and herbs gathered from Minoan times to today

Kamares ware – Protopalatial pottery, sometimes eggshell thin, found in the cave of that name above Phaistos

*kampos* – the Lasithi plain which is divided into individual agricultural plots

*katholikon* – chapel

*kouros* – a youth

libations – liquid offerings to a deity

MGUA – Minoan goddess with upraised arms

*pithoi* – huge jars

polo – Daedalic divine headdress, rather like a pill-box, on hair like a judge's wig

Tanagra – terracotta figurine in the style of Tanagra in Boeotia on the Greek mainland

Tholos – circular vaulted building, as in Tholos Tomb, Archanes

Vasiliki ware – Prepalatial pottery, mottled red and black, first found at that site

# Women's History

## Introduction

Once upon a time, a white bull clambered ashore at what is now Matala on the south coast of Crete. Overlooking the sandy beach on the left was a long, tapering cliff face; it was not then pitted with caves as it is today. Clinging to the bull's back was the Phoenician princess Europa.

The bull was the god Zeus who, passing near the Mediterranean city of Tyre, had espied the young woman gathering flowers by the shore and taken a fancy to her. Turning himself into a handsome bull, he inveigled Europa onto his back and swam out to sea until he reached Crete (where he was born). From Matala, Zeus carried Europa to nearby Gortyn. There, under a plane tree, he seduced her.

In the autumn of 2001, I walked along the beach at Matala. It is as well to have somewhere to stay when you are driving from the north-west of the island to visit the ancient sites of Phaistos, Hagia Triada and, of course, Gortyn. Somehow as I walked, I broke a bone in my foot. The next day at Gortyn, as yet undiagnosed but sore and swollen, I hobbled from the car as far as the famous Code inscribed on stone, with its suggestion of women's position in society some 2,700 years ago. But it was all too much to try and find the descendant of that special kind of plane tree which, in honour of Europa, has remained evergreen ever since. That incident is very much a part of following in the footsteps of women who have gone before.

But did Europa exist? Of course not, in one sense; but nor can she be entirely dismissed as an idea. Europa and the god Zeus are said to have been the founders of the Cretan people. Their son conceived at Gortyn was Minos, after whom a whole civilisation lasting nearly two thousand years has been named, one which is seen as the forerunner of Ancient Greece, foundation of today's Western civilisation. It is difficult to think of Knossos without seeing there Ariadne, daughter of Minos and Pasiphae, falling in love with the Athenian prince Theseus and helping him to defeat the dreaded half-man, half-bull Minotaur, progeny of Pasiphae and a bull. It was presumably Europa's earlier experience that led to bull worship in Minoan Crete but, more lasting, the continent of Europe is named after her and to visit Crete today is to realise how important the concept of Europe is perceived there.

1. Europa abducted by Zeus, 5<sup>th</sup> century BC, Tarquinia Archaeological Museum

But Europa and Zeus and their descendants face the writer trying to present a concise, accessible, chronological history of Crete with huge problems. For the Olympian deities, of which Zeus was the most important, probably came to be worshipped during the Mycenaean civilisation which prevailed in Ancient Greece and was extended to Minoan Crete by 1450 BC. In reality, neolithic people, predating even the Minoans, had starting inhabiting Crete from at least 4,500 years before.

The chronology is further distorted by the fact that the Mycenaean civilisation, both in Crete and mainland Greece, came suddenly to an end, giving way to a period known as the Dark Ages where previous methods of writing were no longer used. If memory of Mycenaean and earlier times survived, it was relayed orally generation after generation, constantly respun, until it was written down, then mostly lost again with retrieved fragments being incorporated into even later writing. By then women had an inferior position in the society of the (Greek) writers. The result of this time lag and proliferation of sources is, therefore, not only a skewed perception but also a bit of a hotchpotch: myths vary in detail, so that, for example, not everyone would agree that Europa came ashore at Matala and some say that at Gortyn Zeus changed into an eagle and raped Europa. Nor, as you will see in the itineraries, is there agreement on whereabouts the goddess Rhea gave birth to Zeus.

To look to myths for historical fact is to become dizzy, for they evade scholarship. But myths often have a function, however tenuous the reality, and the story of Cretan Ariadne and mainland Theseus may reflect how Minoan civilisation in Crete gave way, probably through force, to Mycenaean, a transfer of culture not yet fully understood. The myth of Europa suggests how the Greeks saw the Cretans as foreign, she being Phoenician.

That hiatus in time and culture is just one of the puzzles that archaeologists have been working on for over 100 years and it is to them that we have to look for some idea of the early history of Crete. But, in spite of the hundreds of archaeological sites in Crete (with more still emerging), scholars have comparatively little to go on and, in spite of much work, digging, retrieving artefacts, improving methods through science, technology, and rigour, interpreting and cross-referencing, they are not certain about much.

One reason is the lack of decipherable written records before Mycenaean times, and only fragments thereafter. Another is that many of the sites were inhabited for millennia so that there are multiple layers of habitation. Over that time, buildings were destroyed more than once, often by earthquakes. In the destruction, walls toppled and crumbled and fires – accident or arson – wreaked further havoc so that storeys became jumbled. Picture an underground mille feuille when you cut into it with a fork, or a triple-decker sandwich filled with small shrimps and peas from which you have taken a bite. Then, of course, you have to remember that the most recent habitation was on top and might have been built using material from a building beneath it.

A major puzzle, one which particularly concerns women, is the position of our ancestors in neolithic and Minoan times. Of all the controversies surrounding Crete's ancient past, this one has probably produced the most paper. How woman-centred was Minoan religion? What was the place of the goddess or goddesses and of priestesses? Was there once a matriarchal society, one ruled by women – not to be confused with matriliny, inheritance through women? Did a woman sit on the 'Throne of Ariadne' at Knossos? And, given that Minoan civilisation lasted so long, how did the position of women change over time?

For many years, scholarship tended to ignore both women's position generally outside religion, and their day-to-day activities. Now there are more women archaeologists, often interested in women's matters. Increasingly, there is discussion about the part women played in, for example, textile production and pottery. We cannot, however, make assumptions based on our own time and places – that way can lie anachronism. There are even problems with relating Minoan society to other ancient peoples: it does seem, in many ways, to have been unique. And, even the question of who wore particular excavated jewellery, women or men, can be at issue.

The more uncertainty there is, the more scope there is for interpretation and disagreement; indeed, the shifting of interpretations across the decades of the twentieth century, and continuing now, gives almost as much an impression of the history of ideas in our time as of the pre-history of Crete. This is so marked that it has become the subject of a doctoral study – 'The Role of Women in Minoan Crete: A Historiographic Approach' by **Rebecca McKenzie-Young** (1999). As she has noted, changes in theories on specific themes in Bronze Age Crete 'have often been based not upon changing evidence, but changing social beliefs concerning women'.

In the end, I have had to read a lot – conference papers as much as books – then steer a course gently round controversies and through uncertainties to provide a manageable, and necessarily sketchy, historical framework for the itineraries that follow it. Try not to be irritated by a liberal sprinkling of the words 'perhaps' and 'probably'; I would mislead if I omitted them.

Traces of the unresolved issues will find their place within the chronology and the itineraries. For example, sometimes I will go along with a use of 'goddess' or 'goddesses'; at others, I will introduce some discussion. I cannot burden you with all the arguments but feel you would appreciate a flavour of them.

Perhaps I need to make clear here that I am not setting out to write a guide for Goddess tours, a feature of what is known as the Goddess Movement. And, much though it might suit me to revel in an ancient Cretan matriarchy, the evidence does not allow me to do more than poke a nose down that path either.

There is, however, an engaging feature of attempting to pull together sometimes conflicting threads and arguments: it is often the women archaeologists and other scholars, starting with Harriet Boyd in AD 1900 (see p. 162), who provide, through their lives and work in or about Crete, a story about the island that illuminates its mostly unwritten, ancient past. And it is archaeological sites, particularly those excavated by women, or which have other women connections, such as artefacts found there, that are among the most fascinating places to visit. The earlier women scholars will have a separate place of their own later in this historical section.

Inevitably, by making this book women-centred, by concentrating for the early millennia on women finds, myths and archaeologists, I am presenting a slightly partial picture (while trying to right a general historical and travel guide imbalance). I hope this does not mislead, but you will need to take it into account when you draw your own conclusions.

Ironically, we begin to know more about Minoan and Mycenaean women than we do about those who followed. The Gortyn Code reveals a later, general and legal framework but, thereafter, before the fourteenth century AD, sightings of women under Byzantine and Saracen (Arab) rule are rare. With the Venetians came the written records of administrators and lawyers which throw light on women's lives in particular areas, such as commerce.

Under two centuries of Ottoman rule, starting in 1669, Crete had little importance outside that empire, and indigenous women (Muslim and Christian) led constrained, almost invisible lives, except where they emerge, mostly as victims, during frequent uprisings against the occupying power. Unlike many other places, accounts by women travellers in the nineteenth century are rare; I have found only one – Mary A. Walker. With little infrastructure and much blood-letting, the island was obviously considered too obscure and insecure for the growing band of women extending their horizons through travel; visitors of the early twentieth century, however, capture a lingering whiff of life under the Ottomans. These are supplemented by the writing of a handful of men travellers with a scientific background who visited Crete earlier. They had some appreciation of the ancient past but, until the Ottomans gave up their rule in 1898, it was not possible to begin discovering it systematically or meaningfully.

With that introduction, I will now attempt to flesh out chronologically the periods into which scholars have divided Crete's history (see contents page for a skeleton). The earlier years can be looked at four different ways; the easiest is technologically: Stone, Bronze and Iron Age, and I have incorporated these changes of technology into chapter headings. Secondly the periods can be determined by changing styles of pottery found among the different layers of habitation: Neolithic, Early, Middle, and Late Minoan. Scholars have then divided these major Minoan sections into even smaller ones – LMIIIb (Late Minoan IIIb) – is an example; on the whole, only the major ones appear in the text. The third system divides the Minoan era according to the historical development of the 'palaces' and uses terms such as Prepalatial (before the palaces), Protopalatial (First Palaces), and so on. They are sub-chapter headings. More obviously, the periods are divided by date, about which there is continuing discussion.

From knowing nothing, I have had to get my mind round these different systems, which do not neatly correspond one with the others, and I am conscious that some readers will not wish to be blinded by science. I have tried to make the main chapter headings of these earlier times immediately accessible, while at the same time giving the technical terms and dates in elaboration. If all this is not for you, just enjoy the broad sweep!

# I

## Stone Age Women

### Neolithic – 7000–3000 BC

The low hills of Kephalia, where the remains of several palaces of Knossos now stand (on top of each other), have been inhabited from the earliest times – in fact, Knossos is the earliest known neolithic settlement on an Aegean island. When you stand there, you can throw your mind back seven or eight thousand years and linger there 3000 years. If you squint into the sun, you will be less distracted by the later remains of Minoans and Mycenaeans (see also itinerary pp. 195–213).

Those earliest people probably migrated from south-west Anatolia (now Turkey). They were long-headed, dark-haired, and short. Gradually, they made permanent homes in hamlets, their houses built of mud brick with flat roofs, their implements, stone or bone, with (imported) obsidian which they chipped into blades. They grew crops such as wheat and legumes and tended domesticated animals such as goats and sheep. Eventually, as suggested by clay spindle whorls found at Knossos, they spun and wove wool. Their rough earthenware pottery had first burnished decoration and, in later layers, geometric patterns filled with red or white paste. Harriet Boyd talks of 'incisions like the marks on a cottage tart or pie'. There is some evidence that women were not only weavers but also potters, the latter craft being connected with both food and medicinal plants and their potency. It is fair to assume that they were also involved in agriculture. We should think, too, of the place of domestic water in all societies where it is not on tap, and women's common role in its collection.

Unrefined female figurines with big bums (steatopygous) made of clay or stone, more common than male, have been found apparently near hearths, for example at a neolithic site at Phaistos; they may have been part of a house cult or used in initiation. There is also evidence of living, worshipping and burial in caves. The cave known now as the Eileithyia cave or sanctuary near Amnisos, not far from Knossos, is one of these. It was here that the goddess of childbirth, Eileithyia, daughter of Zeus and Hera (Europa was just one of many flings) was born. She inherited her role from an earlier, neolithic goddess – sometimes called the Great Goddess or **Mother Goddess**.

This is the deity about which Jacquetta Hawkes (see p. 175), an archaeologist but outsider to Crete, wrote in her vivid and feminised *Dawn of the Gods* (1968) that 'In the lands and islands of the Aegean the goddess and her worship were introduced with the earliest farming' and transferred to Crete. Jacquetta was building on the work of others, in particular the Cambridge classicist, Jane Ellen Harrison (see p. 164) who, with her teaching at Newnham College and writing, influenced more than a generation of women scholars. Jane Harrison wrote in her sketch of reminiscences (1925) how, after a visit to Knossos in 1901, where Arthur Evans showed her various seals, she was inspired to write her first important book *Prolegomena* (1903) for 'Here was this ancient ritual of Mother and Son which long preceded the worship of the Olympians.'

Sometimes this lesser deity is a consort who, it has been held, died and was reborn each year to signify the regeneration of vegetation and life. Some archaeological evidence has been found to support this suggestion, though both women's views have generally been questioned. Even Harriet Boyd was, earlier, ambivalent – she believed the smaller figure was a later import. For the general reader, Mary Renault (see p. 174) brings this process to life in a pocket of the old religion on mainland Greece in her novel *The King Must Die* (1958).

It is so easy to be beguiled by the image of a Great Goddess and a matriarchal society. The later classicist **Sarah B. Pomeroy** tackles the Mother Goddess and the attractiveness of the idea to women head on in *Goddesses, Whores, Wives and Slaves: Women in Classical Antiquity* (1975; 1994):

The existence of the mother goddess in prehistory has been seriously challenged by scholars in recent years. In a study of anthropomorphic figurines from late neolithic Crete — the period postulated for the dominance of the mother goddess — it was discovered that 37.3. per cent were female, 9.2 per cent male, 40.7 per cent sexless, and 12.8 per cent indeterminate. Some scholars claim that to attempt to connect a hypothetical earth mother of prehistory to mother goddesses of classical mythology is fallacious. Modern anthropology has also demonstrated that anthropomorphic figurines emphasizing buttocks and breasts in ways similar to prehistoric figurines can be used for pubertal rites, rather than as representations of goddesses.

As Sarah ends that chapter, 'The impartial scholar will be forced to confess that the question is open and may never be answered.' But in the caves (if you like caves), the visitor can dream.

In the sloping entrance to the Eileithyia cave is a stalagmite with a moulded shape said to resemble a pregnant woman and, as a fertility symbol, has been worn smooth through the urgent rubbing of worshippers probably dating back to neolithic times. This has also been seen as a sacred pillar for later Minoans. In the Herakleion Museum are a highly stylised figurine with incised decoration instead of anatomical detail and others that are more obviously rounded. They were found in the cave and may represent the early goddess.

Another goddess figure, found at Kato Chorio north of Ierapetra and now in the Herakleion Museum (Giamalakis Collection, room XVIII), is quite marvellous, with its flat head/topknot of hair merging into a beaky nose, merging into a long, fat neck, sloping down to shoulders and pointy breasts; her broad arms rest on a spreading belly which balloons out into vast bum and thighs, becoming stubby, incised legs, for all the world like French loaves, which curl round each other. It is difficult from such figures to imagine what the women of the day might have looked like.

Another cave, this time Lera on the Akrotiri Peninsula north of Chania, has also been recognised as a neolithic site. In later Minoan-

Mycenaean times, an idol said to represent **Acacallis**, another daughter of Minos and Pasiphae and mother of King Cydon, legendary ruler of Cydonia (Chania), was to be found there, illustrating again how the importance of some sanctuaries crossed millennia. (Acacallis is also to be found later at Tarra, see p. 78.) Have you noticed how easy it is to let myths intrude when they are the only individual names we have? With a name and a figurine we can begin to imagine a real woman.

In later neolithic times, new settlements were established on the Lasithi Plateau. The migrants took shelter and left evidence of burials in the Trapeza cave there (see itinerary, p. 298). Women archaeologists of the 1930s, such as Hilda Pendlebury (see p. 169), and Mercy Money-Coutts (see p. 170), will add another dimension to the cave when we visit it in the Lasithi itinerary.

Discoveries continue to be made, often by women – now in charge rather than in a subsidiary role. Lucia Nixon and Jennifer Moody, for example, have made an archaeological survey of the previously neglected Sphakia region in the south-west and have found evidence of late neolithic settlement.

The Neolithic Period lasted 3,000 or so years and not only did obvious development take place but also the continuing proliferation of settlements. One of the late changes was the use of bronze instead of stone, which leads us conveniently from one age to another.

# 2

## Early Minoans and the Bronze Age

### Prepalatial – 3000–1900 BC

Around 5,000 years ago, further developments in Crete led to a period with largely corresponding scholarly names: Early-Middle Minoan, Prepalatial, and the beginning of the Bronze Age. Although it predated the palaces of which Knossos is the most famous, its people had similar characteristics to those who were to follow for the next 2,000 years or so. Those early Minoans may have migrated to Crete once again from the east and they brought with them the knowledge and use of copper.

During this period of 1,000 years, the sea increasingly played a role, not just for fishing but also for the trade of such items as tin to turn copper into bronze. This influence was to lead, it has been suggested, to Minoan domination of the Aegean Sea. The growing importance of the sea also led to the gathering together in settlements on the coast towards the east of the island. The houses had more rooms and were more substantial than in neolithic times. Tools were increasingly made of bronze. The pottery was still handmade, but better fired and painted and differently shaped.

A unique example of this pottery was found in the early 1960s at Myrtos Phournou Koryphi, a settlement on the south-east coast overlooking the Libyan Sea housing perhaps as many as 100 Early Minoans. From what seemed to be a shrine there emerged the long-necked vessel known as the 'Myrtos Goddess'. In *The Minoans* (2002), **Lesley Fitton** of the British Museum, writing for the serious general reader, engagingly describes how the goddess 'cradles her water jug in the crook of her arm like a baby'. (Interestingly, though, representations of mother and child are lacking.) Other, similar, goddess vessels from that period have been found. Typical is one from Mochlos (on the north-east coast) holding breasts which form spouts; another, from Koumasa (near Gortyn), has patches for breasts and a spout carried like a bouquet against her left shoulder and a snake worn as a stole. This seems to be the first sign of a snake, so much associated with the Minoans.

Another pottery development, showing advanced technical skills, was named Vasiliki ware when it was found at a site of that name in 1904 – it was not necessarily made there. The American archaeologist Edith Hall (see p. 163), who was handed one of the first pieces warm from the soil, described it in a letter as 'early hard polished red and black pottery which was not known in Crete before [the Early Minoan period]'. Her colleague Harriet Boyd, then overall director of the sites in the area, added to the moment they shared, in her little book *Crete: The Forerunner of Greece* (1909), 'It was brilliantly mottled red and black ware.' And, although similar pottery had been found in a wide area from Turkestan to Spain, it was 'nowhere of such unusual quality and form as at Vasiliki'. At the time, Harriet Boyd was excavating nearby Gournia for which she became renowned and where she found some evidence of habitation during this early period, though the main town of Gournia is later (see pp. 32 and 338).

The first gold jewellery and ivory carving were to be found, too, from this early period and fine seal stones (the engraving of which represents a very early form of writing in Europe). Harriet Boyd describes how the ancient seals (discovered by peasants in their fields) were worn as charms by the Cretan women she knew at the beginning of the twentieth century. They were called milkstones and were believed to increase the flow of a mother's milk. Again, it is not possible to know who, women or men, crafted them.

In spite of the riches displayed, there is no evidence of the hierarchical social structure that was to follow; indeed, the architecture of Myrtos Phournou Koryphi – 90 or so rooms without apparent separate houses or alleys – suggests a large clan living communally. It is tempting to conclude that egalitarianism covered gender. Because this settlement was destroyed by fire before the next phase of Minoan society emerged, and was never rebuilt or re-inhabited, interpretation is particularly interesting and less contradictory.

Weaving continued to be important and textiles were, perhaps, traded. The best evidence, exemplified by dozens of loom weights, also comes from Myrtos. The villagers grew olives and grapes on the nearby slopes (the earliest evidence found) and from them produced oil and wine which were stored in the *pithoi* (huge jars) found there. Seal stones indicate the keeping of records. They also grew and stored barley and wheat, kept sheep, goats, pigs and cattle and caught fish. They undoubtedly gathered wild green plants. This early diet has remained basic to Crete, including the gathering of mountain greens and herbs (*horta*). There can be no certainty about the part women played but it is easy enough to speculate.

The French archaeologist Micheline van Effenterre (see p. 173) introduces us to the problems of speculating about women's work when she writes of Myrtos in '*Le Travail Professionnel des Femmes dans la Crète Antique*' (Women's Professional Work in Ancient Crete', 1999):

The methodical excavation of a dwelling has revealed, beside a potter's workshop, a series of little rooms devoted to the production of textiles. Workshops, certainly, and for women. It is likely. But the little village of Myrtos is the site of a communal life so strange that one does not know if what we really have here is women's work. What is the role of a woman or of women in this context? What use is production that exceeds the needs of the community, in an economy which is still at the pre-monetary stage?

(Myrtos, and its two sites, Phournou Koryphi and the later villa at Pyrgos, will be further discussed and in itinerary, pp. 325 and 330.)

Increasingly the dead were buried in tombs as well as caves. One of the best known burial areas is that of Phourni, near Archanes, not far from Knossos. The site was excavated in the 1960s by the wife and husband team Efi and Yannis Sakellarakis (see p. 177). They discovered tombs, some dating back as early as 2400 BC. Among the finds in the earliest (Tholos Tomb C) were precious jewellery and 15 figurines (female and male), the most important of which is a woman in ivory, which came from the Cyclades (islands north of Crete) – one of the confirmations of interchange between Crete and the outside world. Copper and silver probably also came from there, and Cretan settlements exchanged goods such as pottery among themselves. (Phourni is discussed in more detail on p. 61 and itinerary p. 221.)

In *Minoan Religion* (1994) **Nanno** (Ourania) **Marinatos**, an archaeologist following a family tradition, discusses both tombs and the goddess vessels from Mochlos, Koumasa and Myrtos. The first two vessels were found outside tombs and these communal tombs were, Nanno Marinatos suggests, scenes of community cult practices to do with reburying bones, with the goddess and other vessels being used for libations (liquid offerings to a deity) or toasting rituals connected with fertility and regeneration. She ascribes a similar function to the Myrtos Goddess found on a shelf in a shrine – the oldest domestic shrine known in Crete.

These goddess vessels apparently leave the only traces of the goddess or goddesses of the time. Figures of animals and birds, often found in the same places, suggest the deity already had strong ties to nature; indeed, the goddess vessels have also been called Mistress of Animals and Nature or fertility goddesses. But such interpretations are constantly open to scholarly discussion and reassessment. **Lucy Goodison** (scholar of early religions) and **Christine Morris** (archaeologist) provide them in 'Beyond the Great Goddess', a chapter in *Ancient Goddesses* (1998) of which they were joint editors. For them, 'females are important, but the focus of attention seems to be the natural world: sun, animals and plants'. And they write of the 'goddess vessels',

The small platform at Fournou Korifi does not seem strong enough grounds for interpreting this class of objects as goddesses, although their jugs or pierced breasts do seem significant, suggesting the importance of liquids and rituals of pouring. Overall the finds from Koumasa point towards a variety of religious concerns and ritual acts, but none of them indicate an overriding concern with a female deity.

Edging us away from our need 4,000 years later to identify a vessel as a deity, female or not, they also suggest, based on the orientation of the tombs, that 'Early Cretan religion may have included a cult of the sun, apparently practised by women.' They go on to explain that we today 'may have been missing evidence of a very different experience and very different concerns, one to do with bones and heat, life and the dead, animals and plants, the weather and the passing of time'. (See also p. 212.)

Their propositions are both provocative and accessible but where does it leave those of us seeking something more cut and dried when we visit Crete and gaze at its artefacts? The vessels themselves,

2.   Myrtos Goddess, 3000–1900 BC, from Phournou Koryphi,
Archaeological Museum, Siteia

whatever they represented, or whatever their function was, are certainly female and marvellously quirky; they set your imagination racing about Early Minoan women, whether your see the pottery figures illustrated in books, in the 'flesh' in museums, or stand on the site where they were found. I have done all three where the Myrtos Goddess is concerned, scrambling up a gully to stand as victorious as if I had just discovered the ancient ruins, and ending up in the archaeological museum in Agios Nikolaos (see pp. 320 and 330). There she gleams, alone in a glass case, leaving her image, with its snakelike head and neck, indelible on your mind.

# 3
## The First Minoan Palaces

### Protopalatial – 1900–1700 BC

Around 4,000 years ago, a unique phenomenon began to emerge on Crete – what today archaeologists call 'palaces'. A string of them, dotted around the island, mostly on the coast, was built at Knossos, Mallia, Phaistos, Zakros, Archanes, Chania, and other places still being discovered. Scholars are rather stuck with the term 'palace', bequeathed by Sir Arthur Evans at the turn of the twentieth century and so, therefore, are we.

It is now generally acknowledged that these multistorey complexes, built round a large open space, had several functions: the home, perhaps, of a ruling family and their 'court', an administrative, cultural and religious centre, a storehouse for produce brought in from the surrounding countryside – some as offerings (to the deity) or tribute (to the ruler) – and the site of large-scale textile and pottery production.

The palace complexes – of which only limited remains have been found – were architecturally uniform, suggesting the beginnings of a state, with a certain equality among the centres, though Knossos was probably the grandest and, therefore, most powerful. How far there was resistance to this centralisation is uncertain but Metaxia Tsipopoulou has found fortifications at Petras, near Siteia, which she regards as evidence of a period of social stress leading to the emergence of the palatial system (see pp. 56 and 365).

Surrounding the palaces, the settlements that had existed there from earlier times became thriving towns and there is evidence of both pipes and drainage systems within, providing bathrooms (including water closets) and drinking water, and irrigation without. Perhaps the most extraordinary evidence for the architecture is a terracotta model house of two storeys, a flat roof, balcony and columns found at nearby Archanes (Herakleion Museum, room V). Knossos town may have had as many as 12,000 inhabitants and the surrounding area provided labour of some 15–20,000.

The dominant pottery of this period, red and white paint on a glossy dark background, is known as Kamares ware. It was named after the cave (dating back to neolithic times and probably dedicated to the goddess of fertility, later Eileithyia) on Mount Ida, above Phaistos, where it was first found by archaeologists. As the period progressed, so pottery was produced for the first time on a wheel, with swirling designs, often abstract. A particularly fine and large haul of Kamares ware was found at Phaistos at the level of the first palace (even though little of the palace itself remained). It was much sought after and widely exported. It could be made so thin that it was termed 'eggshell' and Jacquetta Hawkes devised the caption for an illustration in *Dawn of the Gods*, 'pretty eggshell cups ... strongly feminine in taste'.

The art historian who wrote under the name **Mrs Groenewegen-Frankfort** notes in *Art of the Ancient World* (1971) that the technical advances and inventiveness seen in Kamares ware marked 'a true birth of civilization', and that with its colourful and gay decoration it proved that 'Cretans were born painters'.

No one can be sure what part women played in any of the pottery processes. The Linear A tablets of the period – found particularly at Phaistos – which might enlighten scholars about many craft aspects (as later Linear B tablets have done) have not yet been deciphered. Once again, seal stones, with their hieroglyphic or pictographic information, have been found in abundance. Though they, too, are indecipherable, we cannot rule out the possibility that women were involved in their making and, certainly, their wearing – often on a bracelet.

The famous Phaistos disc (now in the Herakleion Museum, room III) dates from the cusp of this period and the next (its date is still debated: perhaps as late as 1600 BC). It, too, tantalisingly refuses to reveal its meaning, in spite of much scholarly brainpower devoted to cracking the pictographic script which is different from the others. There have even been arguments about whether or not it is Cretan. The woman image on the disc – hair flying back in the breeze, breasts more neolithic than 'snake goddess' – is rather different from the normal run of Minoans but two c.1750 BC figures found at Phaistos are identical.

Of the efforts to decipher the script, of particular interest are those of **Melian Stawell**, which I discovered, with the help of **Sue Sherratt** of the Ashmolean Museum, Oxford, among files of letters written to Sir Arthur Evans (for many years Keeper there). Although I have been able to discover no evidence that Melian ever went to Crete, she devoted at least 20 years to the task and, as she set out in *A Clue to the Cretan Scripts* (1931), thought she had succeeded.

She saw the disc as a hymn to the Mother Goddess whom she called **Rhea**, later to be the mother of the Olympian god Zeus. She even came up with a transcription, part of which reads:

> Be swift, Mother of water, Holy One!
> I offer sacrifice. Put forward thy strength, Saviour!
> Warrior, Rhea, rise!

Unfortunately, other scholars do not accept her results. These Minoan scripts may be indecipherable but they show that literacy had developed. How far women were included in that intellectual progress it is impossible to deduce, but easy enough to speculate.

At Mallia town, in the Quartier Mu, French archaeologists found four house-workshops which must have produced pottery. Lesley Fitton describes how

They have storage areas and living rooms to support a household, and seem to have been family homes. The specialist workshop areas were usually somewhat separate from the living room, often with their own access, but still the craftsmen seem to have been working as a family unit.

More interesting to us than the word 'craftsman' is the term 'family unit'. It is unlikely that women had no part in one or more of those processes. Indeed, Micheline van Effenterre who, with her husband Henri, continued the earlier French excavations at Mallia (see itinerary p. 303), is prepared to push the frontiers of speculation as far as she dares in her exploration of women's professional work:

The women worked there without doubt but, like the children, to help in the making of seals, pots, metal casts and other products by the qualified specialist who lived in each dwelling and depended doubtlessly on the [output] of the whole [Quartier] Mu. What you had was a family workshop.

Micheline also looks beyond Mallia: 'When a figure, clearly feminine, appears in the middle of pots, as on a prism in the Evans Collection, undoubtedly excavated at Knossos, it is probable that this is a representation of a woman potter, perhaps with the responsibility of adding handles to vases.' The layperson, looking at the purely practical, has to ask, can you really see a male hand coping with the painting on an 'eggshell' cup?

**Marianna Nikolaidou** pulls several scholars' threads together in her chapter 'Palaces with Faces in Protopalatial Crete' (2002). Previously there had been suggestions that 'ceramic knowledge and practice shifted from female to male hands with the invention of the fast wheel ... and the resulting transformation of pottery from household to palace-dependent industry'. She and others dispute this; the situation is far more complicated involving use, access to resources, knowledge and status.

At Mallia, potters deviated deliberately from the Kamares fashions of Knossos and Phaistos in favour of local decorative styles as valid as the better-known ones. From my own observation elsewhere, craft styles and patterns are the sort of lore passed on from one generation of women to the next. (This is by no means the end of discussion about women and pottery; see p. 33.)

As for jewellery, the most striking piece of gold-work from this period was found in the Chrysolakkos funerary building at Mallia. It is known as the Bee Pendant (to be seen at the Herakleion Museum, room VII, and reproduced on the front of the Mallia site's leaflet). Who made it? Who wore it? Who was it buried with? A queen, a princess, a nobleman? How far had social ranking progressed? Had elite families evolved into rulers? Is royalty – queens, kings, princesses – an anachronistic concept? And, most controversial, what part did gender play? These questions cannot yet be answered with any certainty, though scholars have attempted to do so.

The pendant is so unusual and so fine that inevitably it has attracted particular attention from scholars. They even debate if the two insects are bees, hornets or wasps. I latch onto bees for their womanly association with, for example, Melissa (Bee), one of the daughters of Melisseus, mythical king of Crete, who may have been worshipped there later. The priestesses of the Crete-born goddess Demeter were also known as bees, and the first part of the name of the pre-Greek goddess Britomartis has the meaning 'to remove honey from bees'. The circular disc around which the two insects curl may be a honeycomb. Sosso Platonos and Nanno Marinatos, in their travel guide *Crete* (1984), suggests that bees are a symbol of regeneration and fertility and are usually associated with spring and vegetation. For these reasons, the purchase of honey comes into an itinerary (see p. 283).

Whatever the answers to the questions the pendant raises, it is another of those artefacts that has an intrinsic and timeless beauty removed from its context. How it would turn heads, hung against a long, black, silk crepe dress cut on the bias!

The palace walls of this period were decorated but not yet with the famous frescoes of bold-eyed women that we know from later years. But we do at least begin to conclude better how Minoan women then looked.

One of the most interesting clues comes from the Petsophas sanctuary on the peak above Palaikastro in the east. Of all the images I could have stuck beside my desk as I write, I have chosen the stylised drawing of a Petsophas figurine. There is something ineffable

3. Drawing of votive figurine from Petsophas,
courtesy of Marianna Nikolaidou

about the way her high collar tilts back, and the bodice becomes a
décolletage to the waist. The tip of her conical hat (viewed from the
side) looks like a wind sock tilted jauntily forward. (Seen from the
back the cone is flat and, from the front, a high, stiff turban.) Her
skirt balloons out from her slim waist, encircled with a thick cord,
and the whole, head to toe, is black with white zebra stripes.

It is a little disappointing to discover that the drawing has, in order
to record clearly, taken artistic licence. The reality – the real figurine
that is – is a bit different. Six or seven of them – 10–14 cm tall, in
painted terracotta – have been found whole. There are a further eight

without heads. The detail is less sharp, more as if fashioned by a child from plasticine. (Examples can be seen in the Herakleion Museum, room II, and see itinerary p. 371.)

4.   Photograph of votive figurine from Petsophas,
Archaeological Museum, Herakleion

Efi Sakellaraki who, at Archanes, has had perhaps more experience than most in determining how Minoans looked, describes them more generally in this period in an article, 'Hair Styles in the Minoan Era':

The women are seen to have favoured the most eccentric fashions. They wear mantillas, bonnets, tall tiaras, wide hats with turned-in brims and medallions as well as tall hats with successive ribbons or bands. Whenever the head is shown uncovered, wisps of hair fall across the forehead or locks are set on the crown with horsetails or buns as a variation. The hair is also seen done up on top or bound with wide ribbon or in loose locks falling on the neck and shoulders. Numerous buns interspersed with small curls are another variation. Again, there are occasions when the hair is done in long plaits covering all the back of the head or set to flow over tall hats, reminiscent of the XVIIIth [AD] century coiffures.

The average height of women then was 1.55 m (5 ft 1 in); (of men 1.67 m – 5 ft 3¾ in); life expectancy for women was 30 (for men, 35). These facts are somehow more telling than fashion.

The sanctuaries such as that on Petsophas peak were for worship but the high caves such as the Kamares, and the ones mentioned in the earlier periods, seem to have had more than one function over the millennia: sometimes for habitation, sometimes for burial, sometimes for worship. Deities could be more easily imagined in high, wild places. And the artefacts found within them might be to do with the dead or be votive, an offering to a deity. Harriet Boyd wondered 'what motive of gratitude impelled the grand dames of Palaikastro, to offer images of themselves [at Petsophas] in fashionable dress and hats of modern size'.

As well as whole female and male figures at Petsophas, and broken ones, there were many body parts that were obviously made as such – they too were offerings, a very early Lourdes. Archaeologists such as Geraldine Gesell, who has continued Harriet Boyd's work at her earliest site of Kavousi, suggests that they show the healing function of a fertility goddess.

Four different texts discuss another aspect of religion using two objects, both in the Kamares style and both found at Phaistos. Their different approaches show once again the attempts by scholars to get it right with little to go on. One piece is a heavily reconstructed pedestal 'offering table' 30 cm in diameter. It shows three stick females in spotted bell-skirts dancing; the middle one, slightly bigger, holding a flower in each upraised hand. Around the base are several more with arms akimbo.

Geraldine Gesell talks simply (1983) of the central figure as a goddess holding lilies which identify her as 'a vegetation goddess concerned with the fertility of plants'. The writing of Anne Baring and Jules Cashford draws its influence from the Goddess Movement which was given impetus by the work of the Lithuanian scholar Marija Gimbutas, starting with *Goddesses and Gods of Old Europe* (1974). In *The Myth of the Goddesses* (1991) they suggest that the two images are involved in 'going down' and 'coming up'. In the bowl, the two figures are bending down, drooping, mourning, as the third moves downwards into the earth. On the stand, all three are 'gesturing upwards together as in a celebration'. The scene has the feeling of 'rising movement, such as a return from below the earth.' They suggest that these images foreshadow the later Harvest Goddess Demeter, her daughter Persephone and a Mycenaean ritual.

Nanno Marinatos is both straightforward and certain; she writes in *Minoan Religion* (1994) of what she calls a 'fruit stand', that 'two dancing women flank the goddess ... on the stand she has a human form, looms large, and has raised arms displaying lilies'. And she writes of the lily that 'it is a typical spring flower, and can thus be best regarded as a seasonal determinative.'

You might expect the next interpretation chronologically to be even more sure. But Lucy Goodison and Christine Morris, writing of the stand in their chapter 'Beyond the Great Mother'(1998), do not simply add another layer of paint: typically, they go back to basics:

The size of the object, and the effort and skill involved in producing it, all suggest that it was no ordinary secular object carrying trivial decoration. Several features of the design itself also suggest more than an everyday scene of people dancing. The all-female cast suggests a special dance performed by a particular group. The repeated bending gesture around the rim shows no practical purpose; since repetition can be a defining feature of ritual action, this repeated gesture may be symbolic. Moreover, the heads of the figures seem to have beaks like birds — a feature noticeable in other Cretan designs, perhaps indicating a bird-mask or some other ritual headgear. Lastly, the gesture of the central figure, with two arms raised, is one which in later images usually indicates a goddess. Here there is nothing to mark this figure out conclusively as divine. She is central and larger, but otherwise not different from the figures around her; and they seem to be dancing, not holding their hands in a gesture of worship towards her. Whether she is a priestess or a goddess, the scene seems clearly focused both on her and on what she is holding up in her hands; two pieces of vegetation in flower.

The second object is a bowl depicting another dance by beak-faced females, a flower overseeing the action. Geraldine Gessel is clear that the central figure is a goddess, and she is specific about which one: the 'serpentine loops along her dress' identify her as a snake goddess. In doing so, she harks back to the much earlier goddess figures, particularly the one from Koumasa with the snake around her shoulders (see p. 15), and she looks forward in time to the famous Snake Goddess found at Knossos (see p. 39). But Lucy Goodison and Christine Morris are tentative in their interpretation of what is going on: 'Perhaps the dance is celebrating the growth or flowering of a particular plant at a certain time of year (Spring?).'

Looking at these objects in the Herakleion Museum (room III) and trying to decide what we see, we are left with several choices. But, whatever shades or differences of interpretation scholars reach, based on the available evidence and their paths of deduction, we are free to use our imagination. And, in any case, we will be hard-pressed to hide a smile because the figures, thousands of years old, could have been drawn this morning by a cheeky artist, perhaps as a logo, or advertising something, or on a paper napkin one day selling for thousands.

The image that puts the most flesh on Minoan women of this period, and on their religion and, indeed, brings the period to a close, was found near Archanes, at the sanctuary of Anemospilia, by Efi Sakellarakis and her husband. (With Efi's help I will describe the scene and, particularly, the priestess, in more detail in itinerary p. 216.) There, on Mount Juctas, overlooking Knossos as well as Archanes, the Minoans constructed a temple. Sometime between

1750 and 1700 BC, intimations of a seismic catastrophe must have been received. In one of the rooms of the sanctuary, surrounded by religious artefacts, we meet our first real Minoans as individuals. A priestess and a priest had just carried out the ultimate sacrifice to persuade the deity to spare the community: they had killed a young man.

The skeletons of all three participants in the ritual were found buried beneath the rocks that came crashing down around them – an earthquake which may also have shattered the other buildings, including the grand palaces, throughout the island.

# 4
## The New Palaces

### Neopalatial; Second Palaces – 1700–1450 BC

Whatever caused the destruction of the First Palaces – and scholars are still not certain, though fire seems to have been a factor – the inhabitants managed to survive; the absence of skeletons in that archaeological layer is marked. So, very soon, new palaces – larger, grander, and more technologically advanced – began to rise up on the same sites. The palace at Zakros may date from this later period. If some sort of resistance to the continuing centralisation of power was involved in the destruction, there was no significant break in Minoan culture. One theory has it that the New (or Second) Palaces had less storage room devoted to the redistribution of produce, and more areas for ceremonial activities, with entry apparently more restricted than previously. These changes have been attributed to such factors as provision of, and access to, prestige activities, such as banquets, and goods, ranging from grain to artefacts.

It is the remains of these New Palaces that we mostly see when we visit the best known Cretan sites and, at Knossos, the reconstruction that Arthur Evans undertook there is his vision of the architecture and way of life. Because so much more remains of this period, so much more is known, and the debates become increasingly complex.

One suggestion is that it is more appropriate to speak of these 'palaces' as 'regional centres', there being little evidence for them being seats of authority for a ruler, woman or man. And, often, confusingly, there are large complexes with central courts, and other palatial characteristics, built near each other; the most obvious examples are Archanes not far from Knossos and Hagia Triada near Phaistos.

Two other types of centre developed. One is self-contained towns such as Gournia (also with its little palace) which Harriet Boyd started to excavate in 1901. Her discovery made her name as well as causing excitement in the archaeological world. On the Bay of Mirabello, she unearthed the remains of streets with, cheek by jowl, two-storeyed artisans' workshops and the stores and houses of tradespeople, all their tools and trappings still in place. The town climbed up the hill to a larger building containing a shrine. In front was an open space – a town square – for meetings and ceremonies (see itinerary p. 338). A similar town, even bigger, is Palaikastro, further to the east (see itinerary p. 366).

The other phenomenon of the period is what archaeologists call 'villas' (and argue about the name and function). They may have taken on some of the functions previously carried on in the palace complexes, such as storage and distribution. One of these was at Myrtos Pyrgos (on the south-east coast). Like its neighbour, Myrtos Phournou Koryphi, the settlement of Pyrgos had been inhabited earlier and destroyed by fire; unlike Phournou, it was rebuilt and, when villas (also called town mansions or country houses) became the fashion, one was built there.

Pyrgos is of particular interest because the wife of the director of excavations, Lucy Cadogan, wrote a novel, *Digging* (1987), giving essential, if wicked, information to the general reader not about Minoans but about what goes on among scholars with trowels in their hands. How much of it applies to Pyrgos I will explore in the itinerary see p. 325.

But the villa most accessible to the uninitiated is Vathypetro, not far from Archanes. Because it is rather difficult to picture the lives of women so many years ago from the bare bones of stubby ruins, and artefacts in museums, I am grateful to the archaeologist Jacquetta Hawkes for her idiosyncratic novel *A Quest of Love* (1980). It is at Vathypetro that her heroine, Ianissa (Jacquetta in a previous life), starts out.

5. Jacquetta Hawkes, courtesy of Mark Gerson, photographer

Ianissa's father is the 'lord' or 'squire' of the manor with its comfortable country house and outbuildings where wine and olive oil production, pottery making and weaving are carried out. Fields of crops or animals stretch into the distance. Archaeological evidence for all these activities has been found, though there was not, necessarily, a lord (male) of the manor. (There may have been a village or town, too, round about, that has not yet been found.)

One of the widowed heroine's main delights – pottery painting – leads us back to women and pottery. It was she, indeed, who put me on the trail of the subject – one I happily discovered scholars are now exploring. Jacquetta starts this chapter of her novel – which has her leading different lives throughout the millennia, up to her own time: 'I put down my brush, straightened my back and my cramped fingers. Then for the first time I could see the jug as a whole thing. It was good. As well as the pattern of the grasses, I heard their rustling and saw them bending in the wind.' A little later that day, she continues that, since her widowhood,

I had not been idle. I had tended the shrine, arranged the flowers, supervised the hives and honey, and helped my mother to manage the house – and sometimes even with the weaving – much though I disliked it. I had mastered the art of vase painting, an unheard of thing for a woman of the nobility.

Life at Vathypetro will be explored more fully, partly through Ianissa's eyes, in itinerary p. 225.

**Katerina Kopaka** is one of those who have given thought to women and pottery, as she sets out in a series of questions in a conference paper, 'Women's Arts – Men's Crafts' (1997); to quote at some length is to show, again, the intricacies of Minoan scholarship:

An example from pottery production can be used. To start with art depictions, are all the males, but sometimes also females depicted with pots, 'potters' – on the MM [Middle Minoan] Malia and Phaistos seals? Would some of them be just 'handle attachers'? Who actually shaped, finished and painted the vessels in these specific workshops? Who carried water for the potter? Who fired and, eventually, who supervised? Who was in charge of the distribution or the exchange of the products? ...

Moreover, what can literary evidence add? Remember, *ke-ra-me-u* ... constituted an apparently male craft in Pylos [mainland Greece]. Yet, the feminine *ke-ra-me-ja* ... on KN Ap 639, could have corresponded to a woman potter, and, perhaps, not to a mere, individual coincidence. Would this particular name also imply a reminiscence of some, former, female 'art', related to the Minoan pottery production? Could it mean a foreign skill in potting? or does it, simply, connote, in a more biased way (?), a potter's wife?

A considerable amount of information could furthermore be added by investigations of the fingerprints on pots, the interpretation of decorative motifs, the study of potmarks, potter's wheel discs and other tools or implements in households, sanctuaries or tomb contexts.

Could we not bear in mind, at least, some questions of this type, while excavating or interpreting a pottery workshop. The definition of the gender of craftsmen and craftswomen still eludes us, although so decisive in order to evaluate human participation in the complexity of prehistoric societies.

Micheline van Effenterre also looks at Ke-ra-me-ja and feels sure that it refers to 'a woman potter and not a potter's wife'. 'As to where she had her workshop,' she adds, 'it is still too early to suggest.'

The pottery over this Late Minoan period of two and a half centuries was simpler and less colourful than earlier Kamares ware and had three main types of design: flowers and grasses, marine life, and those which included what are called double axes and sacral knots – said to be symbols of the goddess. One vase from Knossos combines flowers and double axes.

Katerina Kopaka raises more specific and essential questions than Jacquetta Hawkes, but reading a novel, the way it more readily engages the imagination, makes it easy to picture, at the very least, craftswomen bending over their exquisite objects, hour by hour, paintbrush in hand, eyes squinting, back aching, painting flowers and grasses. If it was not done as a 'hobby' but out of economic necessity in a palace or villa workshop under pressure for distribution or export, they may even have gained little satisfaction. If it was a home craft it may have been more rewarding.

In her more serious work, *Dawn of the Gods*, Jacquetta sums up her opinion on the subject:

The extraordinary skill and sensibility of [the] potters arouses curiosity as to their sex. It is very likely that, as in most simple societies, Cretan women had been the potters in the days before the first palaces were built. But often it happened elsewhere that with the coming of civilisation and the adoption of the wheel, the old feminine craft was taken over by the men. Had this transfer already taken place in Crete before 1700 BC?

Flowers, such as crocuses and lilies, play a key part in frescoes, too, but now, for the first time, human figures appear as well. It is from this period that we have the famous images, particularly of women, such as La Parisienne, the Ladies in Blue, and the Bull-leapers.

In an effort to understand exactly what and who they depict, scholars have decided – particularly where there is doubt – to follow the ancient Egyptian and Near Eastern convention that the pale-skinned figures are women, the ruddy ones men. However revealing these entrancing images apparently are, we have to keep reminding ourselves that often only a small part of the frescoes (now mostly in the Herakleion Museum) remained when excavated. Considerable reconstitution has taken place, mostly in the time of Arthur Evans, so that it is sometimes difficult to know if the twentieth century artist involved felt contemporary artistic influences, such as Art Nouveau, or if it was the other way round.

Confirmation of the problem concerning La Parisienne comes from Micheline van Effenterre's *Les Minoens* (1991) which has not been translated and is not easy to come by, but a couple of extracts are contained in a little, easily found book, *Knossos: Unearthing a Legend* (A. Farnoux, 1993). Micheline writes:

As her title suggests, the elegant lady of Knossos had been completed somewhat imaginatively, to resemble an urban coquette of the Belle Epoque. But Platon [Nicholas, director, then, of the Archaeological Museum, Herakleion], after studying painted fragments collected at the same time as the Parisienne, produced a reconstruction in a much more serious vein. The young woman was seated, just as Evans had assumed, but she was neither a lady of rank nor an elegant commoner. She was a goddess who, along with others, received the homage and offering of a series of young men and women ... Wisely, the curator did not touch this image, which had become so popular since Evans's time. He decided only to place beside her a small graphic reconstruction of the work as it must have looked to Minoans viewing it on the wall.

La Parisienne's identity has, as Rebecca McKenzie-Young notes, changed over 100 years from 'superficial socialite to a Goddess Impersonator'. (Some place this fresco in the following period.)

Priestesses and even divinities were sometimes represented in 'court' dress. These frescoes therefore allow us to form an image, however misleading in some aspects, of a high-class Minoan woman of the day (we know nothing of working women, urban or agricultural). She is elaborately coiffed – long black tendrils escape from strands of gold and beads; her profile is aquiline, though the nose is sometimes a bit tip-tilted; and she is bold-eyed (usually painted in profile so that one eye dominates her face). Eyebrows were probably plucked; tweezers have been found among pins, and other jewellery, and mirrors existed. Pins were probably used to attach some item to clothing, the more delicate of them to fasten a veil to the hair.

Our Minoan is beautifully dressed and bejewelled, her breasts perhaps exposed or the decolletage filled with gauze. Skirts are best judged by the faience figure known as the Snake Goddess. There the gently flared skirt falls to the ground in a series of flounces.

It is difficult to go past the structure of this skirt without including women and weaving. Scholars are fairly comfortable in assuming that it was, in large part, women's craft at this time because the Linear B tablets – from the period following this, which have been deciphered – record women as weavers (though men were also involved in some processes). There are, of course, also ethnographic parallels.

**Elizabeth W. Barber** was the first textile expert I came upon, particularly her lively book *Women's Work, the First 2000 Years: Women, Cloth and Society in Early Times* (1994). She describes the women depicted watching a spectacle at Knossos:

The men in the paintings sit together in one area, gesticulating with their arms and the women sit in another section, largely in front of the men, in animated conversation – perhaps over the performance, their own splendid jewelry and gracefully piled hairdos, and their elegant dresses.

The plainest dresses are merely striped; the fanciest ones display a mind-boggling array of all-over patterns: grids of tiny diamonds filled with various little squiggles, complex figures of three- and four-pronged interlocking shapes (petals, stars, lobes, or crosses), as well as spirals, 'yo-yos' and rosettes. Bright tassels and patterned edgings replete with zigzags, spirals, rosettes, wavy lines, and simple bars trimmed the outfits, along with thick sashes, sculpted aprons, and colourful hair bands.

She goes on to describe the process of producing fabric; she even tells us exactly what dyes were used and how they were obtained – saffron from crocuses, for example, which was also used for women's menstrual pain. Indeed, there are Minoan frescoes showing women collecting saffron which Lucy Goodison and Christine Morris, and

Micheline van Effenterre, suggest might have been part of women's economic activities. Nanno Marinatos has suggested that saffron was part of a rite of passage – puberty. (In Venetian times, women in Crete used saffron as a hair dye (see p. 105); did Minoan women too?)

Bernice Jones, in a conference paper, 'The Minoan "Snake Goddess": New Interpretations of her Costume and Identity' (2000), builds on Elizabeth Barber's work, disputing details the while. She describes how the three pieces of the costume might have been made because she has experimented by deconstructing and reconstructing the 'dress', building it on a model whom she photographed during each stage of the experiment: 'Thus "the bodice" is actually a full-length dress which I call the Minoan chiton. Since the figure's legs are visible through the fabric, it is sheer, either linen or silk.' As she proceeds with making and fitting the chiton, she concludes that 'the fabric was not cut on the bias as Barber has suggested, but was cut on the straight. The chiton was thus made of 3 lengths of cloth: two for the front and one for the back.'

We begin to form a vivid picture of a whole process. There is evidence of silk – a Minoan cocoon found at Akrotiri – which is almost as early as that found in China. In Crete today, you can see enough of women involved in silk, from cocoons onwards, to throw your mind back. (I have some cocoons which I was given when I bought a rug woven from silk from a women's co-operative; see p. 286.) Then the spinning, dyeing, weaving. Writing of the palace at Archanes, Efi Sakellarakis adds to our information:

The most important natural dyes used crocuses, saffron, pomegranate, myrsine and walnuts. Also used, amongst other materials, was the blood of various insects, murex shell, indigo, mineral colours and perhaps iron oxides. A group of conical cups found mostly in Area 19 played some role in textile production (possibly as containers for dyes) since they were found with loom weights and coloured mineral substances (yellow, red, grey-blue). The abundance of weights shows that this area housed an industrial installation with many upright looms. The rock-crystal, steatite and ivory whorls found in Area 3 indicate that spinning also occupied the more refined classes. Embroidery, which we know must have existed because of the complex motifs employed on textiles depicted in frescoes, would have constituted a separate activity. Weaving, therefore, must have constituted a major industrial activity, and indeed the end product may have been exported since we know of the existence of textiles made by the Minoan Keftiu from Mesopotamian sources. What we do not know, however, is whether a specific class undertook the sewing of the complex garments with their fringes, complicated belts, and feathers, and the construction of masks for certain ceremonies. It is not impossible that this may have been the work of private handicrafts.

The dressmakers now have the fabric; they can start making the parts of the costume until, finally, the woman for whom it is made sallies forth, flaunting the latest Minoan fashion.

The Snake Goddess wears an apron over the seven tiers of her skirt, an embellishment rather than to keep her clean. Bernice Jones concludes her article with the suggestion that the apron might have 'marked the office of the Minoan High Priestess and possibly was associated with sacrifice'. This leads neatly from Minoan women's finery to their religion.

There is, however, an immediate link between women's dress and religion. Found in the same place as the Snake Goddess were several faience costume plaques that look for all the world like fashion designs. It is uncanny to see replicas hanging on the wall of a showcase in the Ashmolean Museum, Oxford, as if they had come straight from some modern-day dress designer's folio. According to Elizabeth Barber, there was a tradition of women offering sacred clothing to their patron goddess. And these were the physical manifestation.

As for the figure commonly called the Snake Goddess, there are two of them, slightly different, and fragments of a third figure. The term used for their finding place is the Temple Repository (a name given by Evans) but it is not usually spelt out in guidebooks what that means or its significance. Lucy Goodison and Christine Morris usefully do so:

It is clear that these important objects were deliberately and permanently buried since the cists [stone-lined temple repositories] were sealed under the floor of the new, second palace, perhaps as a ritual offering (following the earthquake destruction of the first palace).

These figures were, it should be remembered, also found in pieces and reconstituted, particularly the missing head and one arm of the Snake Goddess, with her arms outstretched, a snake brandished in each hand, a small feline perched on her head. (There is some evidence that at least one figure was broken before it was buried.) Both figures have prominent breasts exposed, their waists cinched above a decorative apron. The taller figure in the stovepipe hat has snakes curling round her body and arms, framing her open bodice and round her hat. She had her face, left arm and body below the hips replaced. It is the figure with arms outstretched that one sees most often replicated, unflatteringly, in shops in Crete; there is a rather nicer copy in the Ashmolean Museum. Apart from the fact that the Snake Goddess is an icon for today's Goddess Movement, her other functions in Minoan times are still the subject of discussion; there is disagreement, for example, about whether or not the two figures were different facets of one goddess, or several goddesses, or if one was a goddess, the other a priestess.

Harriet Boyd saw her as worshipped in domestic shrines as 'Mother of the Living and the Dead'. The names, Mistress of the Animals and Household Goddess (or House-mother) have common currency. She has also been described as a temple snake charmer. Then there is the suggestion that the snakes and, therefore, the goddess, were connected with health and healing. Some see the Snake Goddess as the forerunner of the Greek goddess Athena. This fits in with another suggestion, that, because of her wisdom, the priestess was involved in dispute resolution (see p. 195). Lyn Webster Wilde takes quite another line in *On the Trail of Women Warriors* (1999): she links the Snake Goddess, with her snakes and thrust out breasts, and the female bull-leapers – particularly the figure that Arthur Evans dubbed Our

Lady of the Sports – and decides that 'Crete being one of the sources of the Amazon image should not be discounted'.

So important was the unique find of the faience figures that a significant number of fakes of slightly different goddess figures came into circulation, starting in 1914. Unfortunately, Our Lady of the Sports – with her thrusting breasts and codpiece, purchased by the Ontario Museum in 1931 and used by Arthur Evans on the cover of one of his volumes – was another.

The figure known as the Fitzwilliam Goddess – a stone carving with a tall hat and flounced skirt clutching her breasts in both hands – is a third. The questioning of its provenance must have been a searing experience for the person largely responsible for its acquisition in 1926. It seemed at first a coup on the part of the honorary keeper of Greek and Roman Antiquities of the Fitzwilliam Museum in Cambridge, the archaeologist Winifred Lamb (see also p. 201). But, in spite of continuing support, particularly from Arthur Evans, triumph – 'she will make our dept. world famous' – became humiliation. Gradually, the figure was considered less authentic and given less prominence until, by 1991, it had been removed from display.

Another Evans discovery at Knossos was the seat which he dubbed, as it emerged from the earth, the Throne of Ariadne. Soon, however, partly because it was too small for a woman's ample bottom, he decided that it belonged to a priest/king and that was his published view, one adhered to for many years.

By 1958, the German scholar **Helga Reusch** suggested that, since the throne was framed by two griffins, which elsewhere appear with female figures, the throne's occupant was more likely to be female, perhaps a high priestess enacting epiphany – revelation of the goddess. This would change the whole tenor of the Throne Room. Her theory appeared to fall on stony ground but has since been further developed.

Looking again at where the throne was found, which way it faced, how the sunlight connected at certain times with that space and object, Lucy Goodison suggests how a priestess, using tricks of light to intensify the drama, appeared to worshippers in the form of the goddess; she became the goddess. Her description of her experiment to explore this possibility is particularly interesting; indeed, the details of her own experience are worth recounting in their own right, as I hope you will agree (see itinerary p. 213). As so often, women archaeologists and other scholars have a place of their own in the continuing story.

If the goddess, or goddesses, were so important in late Minoan religion, and the priestess who stood in for her had a commensurate position, where did that leave ordinary mortal women? There is some suggestion that, while women held high rank in religion, it was men who dominated temporal power. Another suggestion put forward is that women represented in the frescoes of crowds and ceremonies appear larger and in more prominent positions physically, thus implying their importance.

That seems reasonable enough but, as **Cynthia Eller** remarks in *The Myth of Matriarchal Prehistory: Why an Invented Past Won't Give Women a Future* (2000), 'Though the frescoes show an unprecedented intermingling of the sexes and significant freedoms for women, they are no more than what we are accustomed to in our own culture, one which, according to feminist matriarchalists, is patriarchal.'

Micheline van Effenterre cuts across discussion of gender, and yet adds to it, when she notes that the depiction of crowds is, in itself, unusual. Even in Roman times, while you would have a mosaic of a gladiator in the arena, the crowd was not deemed worthy of inclusion; and yet, in the Late Minoan period, frescoes of crowds, as crowds (often of women), are normal.

However prominent the women appeared in frescoes, and whatever conclusions can be drawn, this has not traditionally equated with the living space in the palace precincts accorded by archaeologists to women. There, the larger rooms at the centre are deemed suitable for men (the male ruler and his suite) and the smaller ones, more isolated, beautifully decorated, of course, with dolphins swimming on the walls, for the 'queen' and her 'court'. At least it is they who were given the lavatory. But, as AnnCharlotte Nordfeldt has logically put forward (1987), 'The attribution of smaller rooms to women and larger ones to men is somewhat arbitrary. There is no evidence of Minoan women having been either smaller, or fewer, or less important than Minoan men.' Indeed, she regards the rooms not as residential but as ceremonial.

A complete reallocation, and feminisation, is made of the rooms at Knossos by Rodney Castleden in his little book *Knossos: Temple of the Goddess* (1997) – one of those publications most available to visitors to, for example, the Ashmolean Museum. His work does not appear to be picked up by scholars.

When it comes to identifying the image of the ruler, the fresco of the Priest/King (or Prince with Lilies) has become, since Arthur Evans' day, an object of controversy. After he had transferred it to the Herakleion Museum, he gave a copy a particularly prominent place in the reconstruction of Knossos. But Micheline van Effenterre, for example, sets out evidence of a fitting together of disparate bits of fresco to form a whole male image that has become popular with the public but which ultimately represents little more than imagination.

Sue Sherratt, in a slender, accessible Ashmolean Museum publication, *Arthur Evans, Knossos and the Priest-King* (2000), details and illustrates the chronology of each part of the discovery and reconstruction of the parts of the figure and its background. She concludes that it 'is arguably one of the most inventive of all the fresco images with which Knossos has been retrospectively adorned through the power of Evans's and his assistants' imaginations'.

The off-white figure with a hint of red in the torso has also been dubbed a crowned girl athlete, a princess in bull-leaping costume, perhaps leading a bull, or a priestess/queen having herself depicted as a male.

While Jacquetta Hawkes accepts the male designation in *Dawn of the Gods*, she does note the young man's un-warrior-like demeanour and regards the fresco as a marked exception, continuing,

The absence of these manifestations of the all-powerful male ruler that are so widespread at this time and in this stage of cultural development as to be almost universal, is one of the reasons for supposing that the occupants of Minoan thrones may have been queens.

Jacquetta's idiosyncratic interpretations have been somewhat disregarded, for more than one reason: to begin with, although an archaeologist, she was not a Crete specialist; then, her interpretations often have femininity and sexuality, even instinct, as their base. Scholars sometimes write as if she had never spoken, which is partly because she gave up engaging with her fellows and appealed direct to the public. Her certainty is engaging and the book is easy to read and come by, and finely illustrated; it is also very much part of the history of ideas on Minoan life and culture.

Seven years after its publication, Sarah B. Pomeroy was to write of the Minoans in 'A Classical Scholar's Perspective on Matriarchy' (1975),

The material remains of Bronze Age Greek societies do not, thus far, provide sufficient evidence concerning the relative status of males and females. We feel we have contributed to feminist scholarship merely by criticizing the traditional assumption that men enjoy the higher status unless proven otherwise. On the basis of the current archaeological evidence available, it is prudent to withhold judgement.

It is possible that religious officials were also the ruling class. This is spelled out by **Helen Waterhouse** in a 1981 elaboration of a 1974 conference paper published in 2002, after her death, by admirers. She suggests that,

If a predominantly female [religious] pantheon, why not a theocratic state, with at its apex the priestesses who alone could claim to be the incarnations — in ritual — and mouthpieces of the divine? ... To suggest that at the highest level Minoan centres were directed by high priestesses is not to deny the co-existence of male hierarchies, in charge, perhaps, of shipping and overseas trade.

In case that seems a bit of an unsubstantiatable put-down of men, remember that the richness of Minoan culture depended on its wealth and that, in turn, depended not only on trade but on the fact the Minoans were at the centre of trading crossroads and may have had some control of the seas. A former theory that they ruled the waves is now tempered: their influence was probably more cultural and commercial than one of political power.

Frescoes are not the only artistic evidence of women's position: there are also gold signet rings (perhaps worn round the neck as pendants), and impressions left on clay sealings, depicting what appear to be scenes of worship not only of one goddess but perhaps more than one and, in addition, of figures that could be gods – male figures that do not appear to be 'consorts', as suggested by earlier scholars for earlier times. The best known clay sealing image (impression of ring or seal stones) is the Master Impression (found at Chania).

Lucy Goodison and Christine Morris very clearly left the question of women's power still open when they wrote in 1998:

Is there, however, perhaps a hint of modern sexual asymmetry in interpretations which now admit males to the world of divine power, but still exclude females from temporal power, distancing them in the realm of the transcendent as goddesses or priestesses? In the absence of recognizable 'ruler iconography' in Minoan Crete the question of who held authority in the temporal sphere remains unresolved.

Someone writing about the site at Palaikastro on the information board there suggests that the 'genders lived as equals', and suddenly the Minoans seem even more interesting (see p. 370).

Yet another question has hung over the position of women, though not necessarily of those in power, in the Bull-leapers fresco. There, while one figure is ruddy, two are white and for some time it has been more or less accepted that females were also involved in this 'sport'. It has, unfortunately, been brought to my attention that some scholars, including women, now suggest that pale skin denotes youth as well as women; they therefore conclude that women were not bull-leapers. I cannot yet accept that!

Mary Renault is a historical novelist rather than a scholar, but most archaeologists have a certain respect for the research that went into *The King Must Die* (1958) and the conclusions she drew about Minoan life and religion. In telling the story of Ariadne, high priestess to the goddess, and Theseus, the Athenean prince who came to Knossos with seven young women and six other young men as tribute to Minos and the Minotaur, she presents a totally convincing scenario for the Bull-leaper fresco. She also cleverly evokes, through the bull-leapers and their reasons for being in Crete, the foreign relations of a powerful Minoan society.

I shall discuss both Mary Renault and the story of Ariadne and Theseus in more detail (see p. 50) but, for the moment, here is a flavour of the bull-leapers as Theseus recollects:

The dancers circled again. A girl paused on tiptoe, arms lifted, palms outspread; an Arabian, the colour of dark honey, with long black hair. She was straight as a spear, with the carriage of women used to carrying their burdens on their heads; big discs of gold hung from her ears and threw back the sunlight. Sometimes in the Bull Court I had seen her white teeth flashing. She was a haughty, mocking girl, but she looked grave now, and proud.

She grasped the horns, and pressed upward. Perhaps something had been going on in the bull's dull mind; or perhaps her balance was less true than the Corinthian's. Instead of tossing up his head, he shook it sideways.

The girl fell across his forehead. Yet she had somehow kept her hold upon the horns. She hung on them like a monkey, riding the bull's nose, her feet crossed on his dewlap. He started to run round and round, shaking his head. I heard a deep mutter from the men's seats, and from the women's a high breathless twittering. I looked up at the pillared shrine. But the golden goddess [Ariadne dressed up to represent her] sat unmoving, and her painted face was still.

So far as I can tell, no work has been done to suggest the smell at such an event, presumably held in the sun – bodies packed together, excitement, fear, and the pungent whiff of the bull relieving itself.

I don't think I will be giving the story away if I say that the climax of *The King Must Die* is a great earthquake and an uprising at Knossos against some parts of the ruling class, aided and abetted by Theseus and his fellow bull-leapers (and Ariadne). Mary Renault is more certain of how the Second Palace period came to an end than are scholars.

# 5

## The Coming of the Mycenaeans

### Final Palatial and Postpalatial – 1450–1050 BC

At one time the theory that the New (Second) Palaces were destroyed by volcanic eruption was most attractive. But recent research has shown that the eruption on Santorini (Thera) and the end of the New Palace period in Crete, which was caused by a widespread destruction throughout the island, accompanied by fire, were two separate events. It is likely, however, that the eruption, and the resulting tsunami, somehow weakened Cretan power.

Recent scientific ability to give a more precise date to that event – which certainly took place – and other evidence in the centres on Crete have reopened discussion of what happened between about 1490 and 1450 BC. While many important buildings around the Knossos palace, as well as the palace at nearby Archanes, were destroyed, the Knossos palace complex itself was not. The palaces at Mallia, Phaistos and Zakros were destroyed. The villa at Myrtos Pyrgos burnt down, but not the surrounding town. The whole of Gournia town fell. These events probably did not take place at the same time.

Palaces had been destroyed before, but this time they were abandoned and not rebuilt. Only the palace at Knossos continued, probably as strong as before, but it was not the Minoans who held power there, it was the Mycenaeans, Achaean people who had become powerful on mainland Greece, particularly at Mycenae, during the previous period.

Did the Myceneans invade Crete? Did they simply take advantage of cataclysmic natural events there? Were rival administrative centres particularly targeted and Knossos specifically spared? Did Knossos itself institute the destruction? Had there already been a Mycenaean infiltration there? Did the earlier eruption on Thera cause crop failure over time in eastern Crete, leading to an uprising? Certainly, it must have caused a shift in trade routes and, therefore, in the regional balance of power. Was there one event, or gradual destruction over time? There is no unanimous answer.

You may have noticed that I have so far barely touched on Minos, after whom the Minoans were called – a coinage popularised by Evans. It is assumed that Minos may have existed, but that the name was a dynastic title, that there was more than one of them. Another theory has it that the title was not gender specific. What we know about Minos is mythical, stories passed down over centuries, lost, refound, embellished. The first Minos was said to be the son of the god Zeus and the Phoenician princess **Europa**; she later married 'King' Asterios of Crete. Idomeneus, who took part in the Trojan War, probably of the twelfth century BC, and described by Homer in the eighth century BC as bringing forces from Crete, was said to be the grandson of Minos. **Aerope**, mother of Agamemnon (of Mycenae) and Menelaus (of Sparta), the main Greek protagonists, seems to have been a Cretan princess, granddaughter of the first Minos.

While myths may not give us historical fact, their memory will not go away. Many scholars tend to steer clear of them, but you can hardly go to Knossos without being conscious of Minos, his family and their exploits, and their parentage is that of the Olympian gods coming into prominence on the mainland at that time. What is more, Mary Renault's *The King Must Die* is the most accessible account of this period for the general reader, and she presents a rational explanation of the myths.

It may be that Mary Renault's earthquake and uprising refer not to c.1450 BC when all but Knossos fell, but to c.1380 BC, the end of Knossos itself after a Mycenaean-dominated phase – certainly some scholars place the Bull-leaper fresco in this later period. Helen Waterhouse was not afraid of engaging with Minos; she wrote:

Minos II, the oppressor, was surely the last Achaean ruler of Knossos before its fall, a king in the mainland manner who, having usurped the old title, was able to exploit the maritime skills of his Cretan subjects ... and the resources of the whole island ... to extract tribute from the Aegean land.

The family tree (opposite) tries to give an impression most directly of some of these Minoan-Mycenaean mythical characters and their parentage, part deity, part mortal; sources differ on detail. (The deities themselves were not so much myth as enduring figures of worship.) At the time of our story – which I shall tell only briefly, for it is often repeated – Minos and his wife **Pasiphae** daughter of Helios, the Sun, and Perseis, an ocean goddess, ruled at Knossos. **Ariadne**, one of their daughters, was priestess to the goddess. Pasiphae had, giving in to unnatural desire, been covered by a bull and given birth to the Minotaur who was kept in the labyrinth at Knossos. Theseus arrived as one of the 14 young Athenians who were required as a sacrifice to the Minotaur because the Athenians had killed one of Minos' sons.

Ariadne, in love with Theseus, or as part of a power struggle at Knossos, gave him the means to defeat the Minotaur. The baddies were defeated; the goodies, including Ariadne, escaped; the regime at Knossos fell. New rulers took over. Perhaps that story – which comes from several sources over time – was an attempt by the Mycenaeans to make sense of, to explain or to rewrite a Cretan past or, perhaps, it was the same attempt by peoples who followed. Helen Waterhouse reflects:

The overthrow of such a Minos by Theseus (if he existed!) would make good historical sense; no wonder too that Theseus had Cretan support, symbolised by his alliance with Ariadne, and no wonder either that the alliance was short-lived, as 'Theseus' was probably an adventurer of the same kind.

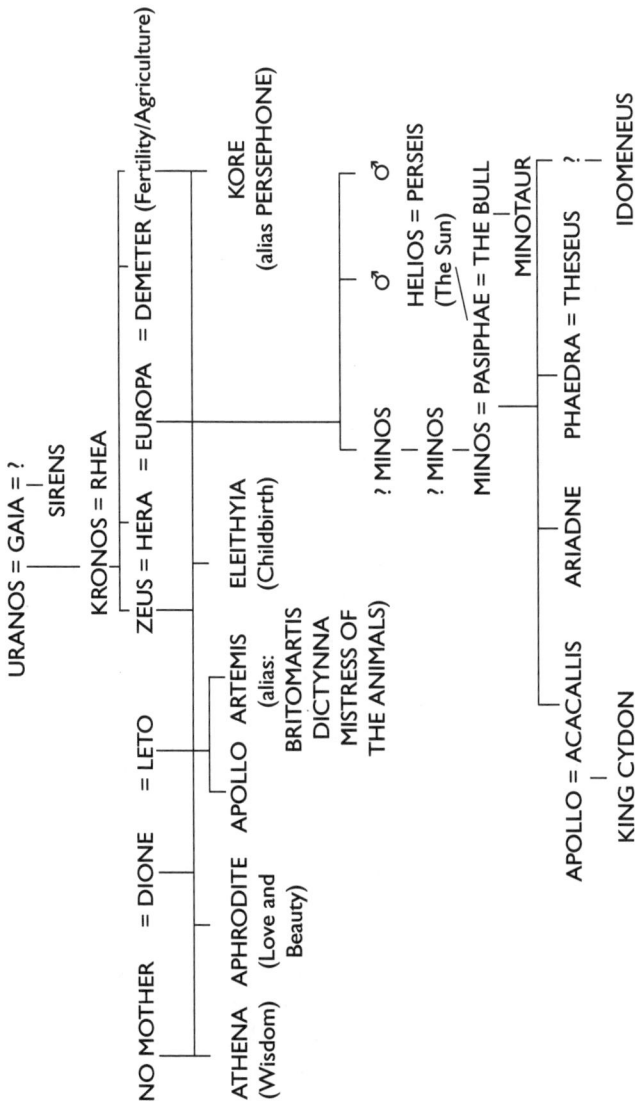

6. Family tree of the Olympian deities

URANOS = GAIA = ?
SIRENS
KRONOS = RHEA
ZEUS = HERA

NO MOTHER = DIONE = LETO

ATHENA (Wisdom)   APHRODITE (Love and Beauty)   APOLLO   ARTEMIS (alias: BRITOMARTIS, DICTYNNA, MISTRESS OF THE ANIMALS)

ELEITHYIA (Childbirth)

EUROPA = DEMETER (Fertility/Agriculture)

KORE (alias PERSEPHONE)

? MINOS
? MINOS
MINOS = PASIPHAE = THE BULL

HELIOS = PERSEIS (The Sun)

MINOTAUR

APOLLO = ACACALLIS   ARIADNE   PHAEDRA = THESEUS   IDOMENEUS   ?

KING CYDON

It is worth following Ariadne and her sister **Phaedra** a step further, since they are Cretan women. The story of Ariadne being dumped by Theseus on the island of Naxos is well known in literature, art and opera. Mary Renault suggests that it happened because Theseus caught her indulging in grisly Minoan practices of the past to do with the murder each year of the Goddess' consort. And that's fair enough. But I prefer the proposition put forward in the poem 'From Knossos to Naxos' by Sonia Greger in her easily obtainable and portable book *Ariadne: A Cretan Myth* (1992):

> We came together to Naxos.
> Then even as we dreamed together by the sea or among
> the olives, he told me of his life to come in Athens: of
> his gods and his plans for the future.
> Eagerly I questioned him about the household, and told
> him of the forms I would bring to order it and keep it
> functioning well.
> And what of Society? How would they receive a
> princess and a priestess who was called goddess?
>
> The more we talked, the more there came a space between
> us, until it became a chasm I knew we could not bridge.
> 'Ariadne', he said to me, 'In Athens you will be as
> Athenian women are. I owe you my life and I love you;
> but I owe to myself as a Greek that my wife shall serve me
> in loving humility. You will be neither goddess nor
> matriarch in Athens, and if you love me you will forget
> the conceits of Minos' court and learn to be a natural woman.
> Only thus can you be happy in Athens.
> We talked on. The gods know we tried. I think even in
> the end, when I stayed here and let him go, he could not
> see that I was anything other than obstinate, so sure
> was he that it is the woman's nature to be subordinate.
> He thought my priestly training had taught me lies.

'How was it I saved you from the labyrinth if I did
not hear the truth from my goddess?' I asked him.
'You loved and needed me as I then was. If I permit you
to change me now — even if it were possible — you will
neither love me, nor gather the good I can give you.
Better we part now, while the thread remains strong,
and our love can live on in each of us, though separate.'
I could see he was surprised to hear such reasoning from
a woman. He expected me to beg and embarrass him with my pleas.
Instead, he left with sorrow yet relief, and I stayed
with grief yet a still soul. So it has remained.

Ariadne consoles herself with the god Dionysus (Bacchus) (does she, perhaps, simply take to drink?). The Athenian prince goes back to Athens, becomes king and falls in love with the Amazon queen Hippolyta, by whom he has a son, Hippolytus. When Hippolyta is killed, he marries Ariadne's sister, Phaedra. She is rather third best which does not improve her character, nor her fate. Mary Renault continues the story in *The Bull from the Sea* (1962).

Rebecca McKenzie-Young, rather mischievously, in a throw-away, personal line in the Conclusion to her doctorate, writes, 'Perhaps Ariadne and Phaedra were not originally the daughters of Minos, but his equals or superiors, a concept unacceptable to later Greek thought.' None of the mythical Minoan women come out of it well: Pasiphae, Ariadne, Phaedra – perhaps a later attempt to put uppity Cretan women in their place.

Homer does not mention Theseus but he does write of 'the dancing floor which once Daedalus created in broad Knossos for beautiful-tressed Ariadne'. Two dancing circles have been found at Knossos (in the Stratigraphical Museum extension site) which point to a connection. Although it should be said that Evans had earlier found another dancing floor, which makes rather a lot of originals.

Terracotta figures found at Palaikastro – three women dancing round another playing a lyre – add to a picture of the continuing importance of ritual dancing. (The figures are in the Herakleion Museum, room X; see also p. 369.) And we came across this Minoan tradition with the beaky stick women dancing on the offering stand and bowl found at Phaistos.

One of today's Cretan dances, the Kritikos Syrtos, is not uncommonly led by a woman and is said to be the symbolic recreation of the Cretan myth in which Theseus and those he rescued are led out of the labyrinth by Ariadne.

Given that dancing and music should be considered inextricable, it is a pity that there seem to be no clues left about the music of Minoan times; it should not be assumed that it resembled the Ancient Greek music which has been pieced together, notated and even played. At least there is evidence of women playing a musical instrument.

Certain stereotypes about the Minoan character and way of life have existed even among scholars. Minoans were decreed at one time in the twentieth century to have been peaceful, charming, carefree, feminised, beautiful people. The Mycenaeans, or Achaeans, on the other hand, were masculine, bearded, women-in-their-place, sword-in-the-hand sort of people. Put crudely, the epitome of matriarchy and patriarchy.

In fiction, Mary Renault was very much an advocate of these images. Theseus' first sight of Cretan men, even before he reached the island, left him almost speechless:

They picked their way daintily about, their waists nipped in like wasps', their kilts embroidered; some had found fresh flowers to stick in their long hair. From their wrists hung carved seals on bracelets of gold or beads; and the scents they wore were strange and heady.

The aromatic and therapeutic herbs of Crete are still famous; and some apparently still bear their Minoan names. There is said then to have been a class of artisans who specialised in perfume-making and pharmaceuticals. They may also have imported perfumes from Cyprus.

Mary Renault implies the difference between Minoans and mainlanders when Theseus recalls:

These young lords and ladies were full of nonsense, having almost their own language, like children's games. And they held their honour as light as they held their gods. The deadliest insults passed for jest among them; and if a husband would not speak to his wife's seducer, it was considered something great. Once, when alone with a woman, I asked her how long it was since any of them had washed out a slight with blood. But she only asked me how many men I had killed myself; as if, through two wars and a journey overland, I should have kept a tally.

The next day he was insulted, and erupted inside: 'If I had my Companions here, and a few thousand warriors, I could sweep Crete from end to end. These people are in second childhood, fruit for the plucking; finished, played out.'

Jacquetta Hawkes also followed the peaceful Minoan/violent Mycenaean line, not only in *Dawn of the Gods* but also in the Minoan chapter of her novel *A Quest of Love*. Ianissa (Jacquetta herself) is a typical Minoan lady. After that beginning at Vathypetro (see p. 32), she travels from the family country home to the court of 'Lord Minos and the Queen' at Knossos where her father has finally accepted a diplomatic appointment: he is to go to Amnisos, the port for Knossos, and meet an Achaean prince. Ianissa accompanies him. As the ship docks, it is not only a typical scene from a romantic novel but also aptly distinguishes between the two peoples:

Two of the men leapt on to the quay and stood facing the ship, hands on their sword hilts, while their lord disembarked with one immense stride. The rest followed close behind him. As they approached our easy-standing, courtly-dressed little party, it seemed to me that eagles were descending on my flock of pretty doves. My father counts as a tall man among us, but when he stepped forward and introduced himself in the simplest of styles he had to look up into the Achaean's face.

When he then presented me, the prince bowed stiffly and said he had not expected the honour of being received so soon by a noble lady. He spoke our tongue no better than a child, but his voice was deep and full. Heard against it, even my father's voice seemed suddenly womanish ... As for what came from the Prince Alectryon's blue eyes at that moment, it could best be called contempt. He looked at me as he would have looked at a horse offered to him by some outlandish client. It was not hidden from me either, that when he said 'he had not expected' to be received by a woman his meaning was a scornful rebuke that such a thing should be inflicted upon an Achaean.

You can begin to guess what happens, but don't be totally put off – it's quite well done and does give a rich flavour of the place and time – just before the Mycenaeans took over, or as they were doing so.

The peaceful nature of the Minoans has, however, been called into question. Lucia Nixon, for example, in doing so, remarks (1983): 'I merely wish to point out that we may have been over-influenced by the lack of what *we* might think of as solid fortification to assess the archaeological evidence properly.' Certainly, the palaces show little obvious evidence of fortification, but most of them are by the sea which may have been their protection, or the Minoans may have ruled the waves. Some early settlements, such as Myrtos Phournou Koryphi, were built on a hill – presumably with defence in mind; what is more, that whole settlement was destroyed by fire – by whom? Why? More telling, the archaeologist **Stella Chryssoulaki** recalls what she noted when as a young girl after the Second World War, she travelled round Crete with her father, an engineer building new roads: she saw plenty of strong walls and is convinced that, in the early palace period at least, the countryside was controlled by small forts.

Recent work has revealed real fortification, particularly at the palatial complex of Petras, near Siteia. Metaxia Tsipopoulou, director of the excavation, 1989–91 and 1991–96, suggests that defensive work – a raised platform, substantial walls, three rectangular towers, and a massive bastion – took place during a period of social unrest that led to the emergence of the palace system, when resources were becoming centralised in places such as Petras which developed from a settlement to a palace.

Having questioned certain assumptions about the Minoans, Lucia Nixon concludes: 'I submit that these ... ideas reveal far more about ourselves than they do about the Minoans.' And she adds later, 'We use analogy constantly and often unwittingly.'

However peaceable, or not, the Minoans turn out to have been, what seems clear is that, following c.1450 BC, Minoan culture became heavily influenced by Mycenaean. One of the confirmations of mainland Greek inroads into Minoan life comes from the deciphering of the Linear B script in 1952: it was revealed as an early form of Greek (whereas the earlier Linear A script is still undeciphered and does not resemble Greek). The inscribed tablets only survived because they were baked in destructive fire.

The cracking of Linear B turned Minoan scholarship upside down. Previously it had been thought that Minoans colonised, or at least heavily influenced, the mainland; now it seemed that, instead, Mycenaeans ruled at Knossos or, as Dilys Powell was memorably to describe 1380 BC in *The Villa Ariadne* (1973), her often firsthand description of life and scholarship at Knossos in the years surrounding the Second World War: 'It might have been the Minoans themselves, the subject people, who rebelled against their Greek overlords and set fire to the palace.'

The Linear B tablets cannot tell us how the Mycenaeans came to be at Knossos because they are not chronicles or literature. But they are records, probably temporary, so did open up other areas of scholarship. We do know, for example, a little more about ordinary women and their work at Knossos. The tablets confirm that women were involved in the wool industry, though not clearly in which processes. Women textile workers, some old, some young, some children, outnumber men two or three to one; they seem in some way to have lacked freedom, either to be indentured or slaves. They were probably allocated raw material from a central palace authority from which to make cloth. The tablets record production targets and receipt of final products. They were also allocated food. Some women, living outside the palace, specialised in high-class varieties of cloth, others in fancy borders. These may have been made as prestige gifts, which then went the rounds, or ritual offerings.

Helen Hughes-Brock, in her exploration of Mycenaean beads (1999), wonders whether women had some hand in palatial bead-making; she suggests that beadwork on cloth, woven or sewn in, 'was probably a sub-department of textiles and thus likely involved women'. She does not assume, however, that only women wore beads, most usually found in tombs, without their cloth or string; frescoes show that men, occasionally did, too. It is women, however who were sometimes depicted holding or fingering their beads, perhaps to show their value if it was to be an offering. Beads are often found in shrines.

The Linear B tablets can be used for purposes other than obvious conclusions about women's work. In 'Women, Children and the Family in the Late Aegean Bronze Age' (1998), **Barbara B. Olsen** looks at the tablets and notes that of 22 occupations or statuses of women at Knossos, only two are shared with men – religious functions and slave. Occupations are segregated. Family units are apparent only where they were regulated. Children were itemised and divided into girls, boys, older and younger. Even older boys are grouped with their mothers. Women are, therefore, responsible for childcare in the palace workplaces at Knossos. But she goes on to compare two centres – Knossos and Pylos on the mainland where Linear B tablets were found – and concludes that other evidence gives another picture of society. Whereas, on the Mycenaean mainland, mother and children images proliferate in iconography, or works of art and craft, on Crete, even Mycenaean Crete, this is not so. She goes as far back as the Goddess of Myrtos in Prepalatial Crete 'who', she notes, 'reserves the space in her arms not for children but for a miniature terracotta juglet resembling those found in excavations at Myrtos' (see p. 14). Motherhood may have been seen as the primary function of mainland Mycenaean women, but not of Minoan-Mycenaeans. She writes: 'This might seem surprising in light of the allegations of a matriarchal and goddess-centred Minoan culture and the patriarchal nature of Mycenaean culture.'

But she concludes from this that Mycenaeans were not so much interested in women as mothers but in keeping them in the home, out of the public sphere. Images of Minoans, on the other hand, seem to place their women in public life. 'Above all, emphasis is on the social rather than the biological, the public rather than domestic.' She wonders about the place of a 'Minoan Mother Goddess', ending with the assertion, 'There is simply no evidence for the celebration of motherhood, divine or human, among the Minoans.'

The Linear B tablets present evidence in another sphere, this time showing both Minoan-Mycenaean diversity and connections. The tablets record offerings of olive oil and honey to deities, female and male. But these were Olympian (the deities of Ancient Greece), even if some of their roots were Minoan. Potnia (Lady, or Mistress) Athena, Damata (Demeter), Artemis, Hera and Eileithyia are examples. (Their genealogy is given on p. 51, and places where they were worshipped are suggested later.)

For the Minoans, **Athena** is assumed to have evolved from the Snake Goddess with household or civic attributes; for the Mycenaeans she might have been connected to a warrior goddess.

**Demeter**, Crete-born, was Goddess of the Earth, agriculture and fertility in general.

**Eileithyia**, born in a cave in Crete and worshipped in caves throughout the island, was associated with women and birth and sometimes identified with the goddess Artemis.

**Artemis** was, in turn, identified with the Cretan goddess **Britomartis Diktynna** (born at Kaino in the Samaria Gorge) and with the Minoan goddess known as Mistress of the Animals. Artemis was primarily Goddess of the Chase – she could wound but she could also heal, using Crete's legendary dittany herb (*origanum dictamum*) which was also called artemidion, after her (see pp. 186 and 235).

Images of Eileithyia are sometimes garlanded with dittany, which is thought, even today, to ease the pains of childbirth. Not far from the Eileithyia cave at Amnisos, is the site known, because of its fresco, as the Villa of the Lilies – a flower assumed to be a symbol of the goddess.

There is also mention of a Mistress (Potnia) of the Labyrinth. The word labyrinth and its meaning to us today may be a red herring – in spite of the complicated architecture of Knossos and the myth of the Minotaur. There is some speculation that it comes from a word meaning 'place of the double axe' – that being a symbol of the goddess.

A linking together of the goddesses, old and newer, seems to be indicated by the garland frescoes found in a Knossos house, probably destroyed c.1450. Careful analysis (by Peter Warren) of the plants and flowers in the garlands – papyrus, poppy, dittany, rose, lily, olive – may show the connection between fertility, dance, women, plants, life, death and goddessses. Britomartis Diktynna, Eileithyia, Ariadne and Europa were to become part of a chain unbroken through time.

Assumptions can be made about the part women played in herbal knowledge and preparation of medicines, perfumes and cosmetics from these links between goddesses and plants, the frescoes of women gathering crocuses for saffron, and what is known from other places and times. As for the use they made of the products, Micheline van Effenterre, having consulted a specialist in the island's botany and the origins of words, rhapsodises about the 'universe of scents, perfumes, rouges and tints' of which their dreams were made.

There is mention in the tablets of offerings to the Diktaian Zeus who was to become the most important of the ancient Greek gods. If he started at this time to become important, some suggest it was because of disillusionment with the ability of the Goddess to protect the people from natural disaster. **Hera**, his wife (as opposed to other mothers of his children), was also his sister; their marriage was sacred and part of later rituals, in spite of being one long row.

There seems much support here for the suggestion that the Greek deities of post-Minoan Crete spent their formative years on the island. The only priestess mentioned in the tablets is the Priestess of the Winds.

One of the most obvious changes in Mycenaean times was the decline in the quality of art, both manufactured and crafted. An example of the change in depiction is the absence of women on thrones, or landscapes with women (goddesses or worshippers) and animals, birds, plants and trees. These images had been a feature of earlier times. In spite of that, many aspects of Minoan religion still prevailed, as suggested by an elaborate Mycenaean sarcophagus excavated at Hagia Triada (which had been substantially rebuilt). It is not known who was buried in it but the scenes depicted on the outside suggest traditional rituals with much involvement of women as goddess or priestess. On the ends are pairs of female figures in chariots; one is pulled by goats, the other by griffins – the latter suggesting that the driver and passenger are goddesses. The side panels have women apparently performing religious rites such as pouring liquid, presumed bull's blood, from vessel to vessel. (The sarcophagus is in the Herakleion Museum, room XIV, and interpretations of its frescoes are further discussed in the itinerary that includes Hagia Triada; see p. 258.)

The bull connection was clarified by the even more striking evidence found by Efi Sakellarakis and her husband in a tomb at the Phourni cemetery near Archanes in 1965. Tholos Tomb A, the best preserved, is in the Mycenaean beehive style. Efi (and her husband) write in *Crete: Archanes* (1991), 'The deceased's identity as a queen-priestess is most powerfully attested by the sacrifices made in her honour, in particular that of a bull.'

The woman had been buried in a long, gold-trimmed gown, with a full panoply of jewellery and domestic items. Her footstool had boar's tusk handles in which had been carved Mycenaean warrior heads. The ivory inlay was a succession of miniature shields. The depictions on her several seals and rings indicate that she was connected with the highest administration at Knossos, while the place of her burial suggests an involvement with the nearby peak sanctuary on Mount Juctas. This find was made in time for it strongly to strike a chord with Jacquetta Hawkes in *Dawn of the Gods* (1968). She felt that there had been queens in Crete earlier, with their continuing priestess function now supported by the find.

Not content with that discovery, the Sakellarakis team found the slightly later (1350–1300 BC) skeleton of another woman of substance – 'a person of royal blood' – in Tholos Tomb D at Archanes. The tombs of these two women – rich and powerful at a time of what appears to have been an increasingly masculine society – are, so far, the richest and most important burials found. (Both women will find their place in itinerary, p. 221.)

Also from Archanes, from the Small Cave of Metochi, comes a terracotta figure of a woman sidesaddle (facing sideways, both legs hanging down) on a horse (Herakleion Museum, room X). The caption below the illustration in Efi's book reads 'riding goddess' but she's wearing stripy trousers, not a skirt. Is she a warrior goddess? Warrior or not, the woman on horseback, and those in chariots on the sarcophagus from Hagia Triada, give some indication of modes of transport, and that women were active, rather than passive, in getting themselves about. You can still see women on country roads today sitting in the same improbable position on donkeys.

The cemetery at Phourni was probably in use until 1200 BC, but somewhat earlier, around 1380 BC, the Final Palace at Knossos fell. Although people continued to live there in individual houses or rooms, with its fall came the end of another era. The period following it is known as Postpalatial and sees a distinct decline of the Minoan civilisation that we have been following.

One of the most common features of Postpalatial Crete religion was shrines in which were found figures made of terracotta known as the Goddess with the Upraised Arms. She comes in all shapes and sizes – from 10 cm (4 in) to 85 cm (31½ in) – and is as quirky in her own way as some of the earlier goddess figures.

Apart from upraised arms, the figures tend to have big heads lacking delicacy, funny pointy little stuck-on breasts and a body that, after the waist, ends in a sort of barrel base. This makes some of them reminiscent of those old-fashioned, hand-held children's

toys of a wooden figure on a barrel which jerks around when pressed from the bottom.

The best known sanctuary of this period is the Shrine of the Double Axes south of what has been described as the Domestic Quarter of the destroyed palace at Knossos. This goddess has a dove on her head and is accompanied by female figures with hands on their breasts. At Gournia, the goddess found by Harriet Boyd has snakes on her arms and around her body. One from Archanes stands in the doorway of a cylindrical sanctuary, like a stripy tent, with two worshippers and a dog on top (Herakleion Museum, Giamalakis Collection, room XVII; others are in rooms XX and XI).

The goddesses are usually more simple, though often with a crown of flowers, such as poppy heads, or birds, or small animals. The vertically-slit capsules indicate the extraction of juice for opium, probably for its visionary or medicinal properties, and there is a suggestion that this use of opium in ritual later re-emerged in the 'cult of Demeter which was taken from Crete to Eleusis [on the mainland]'. Evidence of Demeter in Crete is found in places such as Knossos, Aptera and Gortyn, as you will see in the itineraries.

The terracotta goddesses tended to be placed in numbers, standing on bench-like shelves in shrines, accompanied by tubular offering vessels with multiple-loop handles commonly called snake tubes; the offerings were probably poured into the tubes in front of the goddess.

The period known as Postpalatial lasted from the fall of Knossos in about 1380 BC until about 1100 BC. During those years, according to mythology and the epics of Homer, the Trojan War took place. This event, some evidence for which has been excavated at Troy, has been dated to 1250–1100 BC (the Homeric account is dated to the eighth century BC). Cretan forces took part in the war on the side of the Mycenaeans, but more interesting to our story is one of its footnotes.

Homer talks of a Phaeacian realm ruled by **Queen Arete** and King Alcinous. It was visited by his hero Odysseus on his way home to his wife Penelope from the Trojan War. The whereabouts of Phaeacia is one of those subjects that engage the attention of classicists. Often it is said to be Corfu but, just sometimes, Minoan Crete is put forward – that would be in the time of Idomeneus, Minos' grandson. Homer also writes of Odysseus visiting Crete by name on another occasion, but don't let that worry you, Homer had various sources from different times.

The scholar most convincing about Arete being a Minoan is Elizabeth Barber in *Woman's Work*. When, after reading her dissection of Homer's text in support of her theory, I asked her where in Crete she thought Arete (and her husband) might have ruled, she drew back a little – the scene was Minoan, not necessarily in Crete but another area of the Aegean that was under Minoan influence. Nevertheless, other scholars have also hinted at Phaeacia being in Crete: one has Arete at Knossos, another on the southern shore, perhaps Hagia Triada.

Assuming that Knossos Palace was finally destroyed in 1380 BC (some scholars put its destruction as late as the thirteenth century), another northern, and still-thriving coast city seems a more likely place to find Arete. Chania in Mycenaean times had emerged as a centre of increasing importance to the new order; indeed, it can be seen as an intermediary between Crete and the mainland. As a complete outsider, who has visited Crete looking for Arete, I see the court there. Driving along the coast to the east, I picture Odysseus coming ashore where a stream trickles into Souda Bay opposite the islands which are said to be the final resting place of the mythical Sirens. There he was befriended by Arete's daughter. In the itinerary (see p. 284), it is at Chania and its environs that I shall put Arete, knowing I am being slightly mischievous. Homer writes of her: 'The people think she is divine and shout their greetings to her as she goes through the city. She has plenty of decent common sense, so that – if she feels like it – she arbitrates their disputes. Yes, those of the men as well.'

By 1050 BC, Minoan-Mycenaean administration had petered out. Chania, having had a period of expansion, then a fire, then reconstruction and reoccupation, was abandoned without evidence of destruction. Knossos left tombs but little else to be found by then. The making of artefacts had dried up so that often it is heirlooms from earlier periods that were interred with the dead.

Perhaps it is with the aftermath of the ten-year-long Trojan War and the resulting internal struggles on the mainland that the power of the Myceneans, and of the Minoans, came to an end. New people, probably a Greek tribe descended from the north, began to assert themselves with the new technology of iron.

# 6

## The Last Minoans and the Iron Age

### Sub-Minoan, Geometric and Orientalising – 1050–700 BC

There are no records about the arrival of the Dorians in Crete. There are no signs of major destruction. Did they trickle in? No conclusive details exist about their presence over the next 300 or so years, nothing resembling the Linear B tablets, or even the yet undeciphered Linear A; indeed, scholars still debate when they were present; it might have been in the next period.

There are, however, archaeological remains of what seem to have been the last vestiges of the Minoans, known as Eteocretans, or true Cretans. A link between their past and their continuing life was the shrines containing (Minoan) goddesses with upraised arms (archaeologists call them MGUAs which is neat, but not very respectful).

An increasingly common place for such shrines was the remoter reaches of eastern Crete. Among the best-known of these is Kavousi, where Harriet Boyd first started excavating in 1900. Many years later (1978 onwards) her work was continued there by Geraldine Gesell and Leslie Preston Day. Indeed, the best place to picture such a shrine is Vronda, the ridge leading up behind Kavousi to the Kastro (citadel). There, the bench on which the goddesses stood (fragments of 25 have been found) is still intact and the location, looking down over the Bay of Mirabello and upwards to the Kastro, allows the imagination full range. Geraldine describes the making of the goddess figures in a delightfully practical and enlightening way in a conference paper (1997):

The statues of the goddess and her ritual equipment were probably made in the summer when the clay would have dried quickly, allowing the potter to finish the work on the same day. They would then have needed to dry an additional day and a half before firing. In other seasons when there was more moisture in the air, a longer drying time would have been required ... Now it is clear that the craftsman or craftswoman was a potter who used the same potting skills needed for cooking pots, jars and pithoi.

The goddess figures were made in two pot shapes fitted together, with limbs and breasts modelled separately.

Geraldine and Leslie describe the settlement at Vronda in *Crete 2000* (2000), a rather magnificent publication to mark the centenary of American archaeological work in Crete (starting with Harriet Boyd). Dating from the twelfth to eleventh centuries BC, Vronda consisted of 12–15 houses in clusters on and around the summit. Each house had a large room with benches along the walls for storage, and a flat roof.

After the settlement's abandonment in the middle of the eleventh century BC, the site was used for burials. The bodies were at first interred in tombs but later (eighth and seventh centuries BC) cremated – a feature of Dorian culture. Tombs contained pottery, iron weapons and tools, and bronze jewellery.

Presumably the inhabitants of Vronda moved up to the Kastro, not an obviously comfortable or convenient move. Excavation of that settlement revealed the pottery styles of the period, named by archaeologists Proto-geometric (or Sub-Minoan), Geometric and Orientalising. The slopes of the Kastro were covered with narrow terraces supporting houses, often large and elaborately constructed. The Kastro settlement was at its largest in the eighth and early seventh centuries BC, but was then abandoned. (See itinerary pp. 334–8.)

A decade after Harriet Boyd's work at Kavousi, her junior colleague, Edith Hall (see p. 163), then directing an excavation of her own (1910–12), unearthed the refuge sanctuary and settlement at Vrokastro, a steep limestone spur above and to the west of Gournia.

She wrote up her finds in *Excavations in Eastern Crete Vrokastro* (1914, now reprinted). Her work is being continued by Barbara Hayden who brings the site up to date in *Crete 2000*.

The Vrokastro settlement was founded in the twelfth century BC, and inhabited until the seventh. Edith found only a few traces of the earliest settlement and some pottery; the buildings on the summit and north slope date to the eighth century. The houses were, as at Kavousi Kastro, terraced into the steep terrain and rather crowded on the summit. To climb up there today is to wonder how it was big enough for even one dwelling, and the wind must have howled round it and sent you reeling if you ventured outside. It is a long way down.

As well as finding Geometric pottery, Edith Hall discovered much earlier Minoan Kamares ware. Shrines have been found containing terracotta figurines in what may have been the house of the headman and his family.

Edith Hall also found Sub-Minoan tombs with burials in jars and the usual artefacts such as iron age tools and weaponry and bronze jewellery including pins and beads and, what I always like because it brings those ancient people so close, tweezers. There is also evidence of cremated remains in Geometric tombs. Barbara Hayden notes that in the early seventh century BC, with the arrival of a more stable period, the coastal zone, what is now the Istron area, was once more inhabited. The itinerary pp. 350–4 describes Edith's work more personally through her unpublished letters and a lively article.

In the late 1930s, under the direction of her husband John, Hilda Pendlebury, with Mercy Money-Coutts, excavated the refuge settlement on the Kastro at Karphi above the Lasithi Plateau. A settlement of 150 stone-built houses was revealed, together with a network of narrow streets and a cobbled public square. They found tombs on the slopes below. The settlement was abandoned during the eleventh century BC. One of the questions that remains is how did the inhabitants manage in the winter when today the site can be covered in snow and very cold? Today, people living in the Lasithi

Plateau, below Karphi but still above what is called the olive line, decamp to winter quarters lower down. No similar settlement has yet been found for the ancient Karphiots. Karphi is described as the best preserved site of the Dark Ages in the Aegean. (See also itinerary pp. 300–1.)

At least two of these settlements lasted several centuries, the first century usually called Sub-Minoan, suggesting the last refuge of the Minoans before their descendants mingled with the incomers. But Karphi seems only to have lasted for that one century. Did the people move down because the location was so inhospitable, or was it a last redoubt? The shrines in all three were independent since religion was no longer controlled from centres – though the traditional Minoan rituals and symbols were common.

Where previous periods have ended in something of a bang, the Minoans finally left the stage unobtrusively. Two thousand extraordinary years simply drifted to a mysterious close. The abiding images for me are of stupendous views and rows of terracotta figures – goddesses or Eteocretan women – with upraised arms standing on benches facing open doors looking out to sea, zonked on opium.

Life went on elsewhere, mostly in separate communities often called city states of which Gortyn was the most important. The different city states were likely to be at loggerheads with their neighbours. They will be elaborated on in the next period, for which there is more information.

People also continued to live at Knossos and pottery has been discovered there dating from the eleventh to seventh centuries BC. It is their tombs that have been most successfully excavated, though the Geometric pottery there is of rather poor quality, as if cut off from the mainstream of artistic inspiration. These pots were placed as grave gifts with cremated remains in rock-cut or stone-built family tombs.

The most important find was a collection of tombs behind the hill on which the village of Fortetsa stands, between Knossos and Herakleion – part of what is now known as the North Cemetery. The excavation was started in 1935 by two archaeologists, one of whom was Humfrey Payne, husband of Dilys Powell. Payne and his colleague Alan Blakeway both died before they could finalise and write up their excavation of early Iron Age, Geometric and Orientalising finds up to the seventh century BC. This task was taken up by their young colleague James Brock.

Brock and his wife Ursula and their two younger sons returned to Knossos for two winters after the war (1950–51), staying at the Villa Ariadne, built by Evans but made famous by Dilys Powell's incomparable book about the history of the house, *The Villa Ariadne* (1973). The result of their work was *Fortetsa* (1957), financed by Brock's mother. **Ursula Brock** (1913–1993), daughter of Art Nouveau gold- and silversmith John Paul Cooper, was a silk weaver, an early user of the Jacquard loom which was worked using geometric grids. She wove to her own designs, influenced by Greek patterns. This training and facility enabled her to draw tomb plans and analyses of patterns of the Geometric pottery.

Also involved in recording the finds was the artist **Audrey Petty** (soon to be Corbett) who had been at the British School at Athens before the war. The work of both women forms an important part of Brock's book.

Among the finds was a ninth century urn with figures reminiscent of the Minoan Snake Goddess under the handles. To see this figure is to understand the term 'geometric': her body is a rectangle filled with square boxes with a spot in the centre of each; her chest is an inverted triangle; her arms are at angles and striped; her long, striped neck is at an angle to the base of the triangle and her snaky head is topped by a striped, brimless kepi.

Another and later find from elsewhere in the North Cemetery has a nature goddess arriving on a chariot in spring on one side and on the other one leaving in autumn. These images were drawn for publication by a later archaeological wife, Nicola Coldstream. It begins to grow obvious that drawings by women, sometimes wives, have been quite a feature of archaeological records.

A piece of jewellery completes the explanation of terms Geometric and Orientalising. It is a gold pendant – a rounded crescent enclosing a cross and four birds, ending in two female heads wearing crowns (a bit like the geometric snake goddess's kepi), worked in oriental cable pattern (found at Tekes Knossou and to be seen in the Herakleion Museum, room XII)). This style was probably introduced into Crete by a Near Eastern artisan. These styles are not necessarily Dorian; more likely, both come from the East.

Three artefacts from this period, to be found in room XII of the Herakleion Museum but excavated from different places, have an unexplained common theme: Ariadne and Theseus. The most engaging image, on a wine jug (from Arkades/Aphrati), shows the two meeting: he puts his hand to her chin; she touches that wrist; he puts his second had on her thigh; she puts her hand on top of his. From the Idaian cave comes a tripod cauldron: oarsmen row a boat; in it are Theseus armed and helmeted and Ariadne raising her arms protectively (see p. 234). From Fortetsa comes a small urn: Theseus again in a helmet.

In the gap left between goddesses and twentieth century women archaeologists, the skeleton of a real woman who lived 3,000 or so years ago emerged in 1959 from a tomb at Hagios Ioannis near Knossos. She was found by Jacquetta Hawkes' student son, Nicolas, and she has proved difficult to place because of the large bronze pins she still wore on each shoulder – she does not fit Minoan or Mycenaean culture in dress, but rather that of peoples from north of Greece. She may have represented a movement of peoples, a change in fashion, or an element of trade. She was about 60 years old and may have used the pins to fasten a Doric peplos (shawl hanging in loose folds).

The North Cemetery was abandoned in about the seventh century BC and nothing further seemed to happen at Knossos for the next 100 or so years – a time sometimes known as the Period of Silence.

# 7

## Living with Zeus and the Gortyn Code

### Archaic/Classical – 700–330 BC

Among the centres that began to develop from the ninth century BC were Aptera, Lissos and Cydonia (Chania) in the west; Gortyn, Eleutherna and Rizenia (Prinias) in the centre, and Dreros, Lato and Itanos in the east. By the eighth century, old Minoan sites such as Phaistos, Hagia Triada and Mallia had been resettled. They prospered particularly in the seventh century but, by a century later, had entered a period of decline, partly because of inter-communal warring. In the fifth century, Crete was cut off from the short-lived flowering of Athens and wars in the region.

Following the arrival of the Dorians, each of Crete's city states (about 150 of them) lived under an oligarchy similar to that of Dorian Sparta on the mainland; the system was hierarchical, rigid and military. Dorians were the elite; indigenous Cretans (what was left of the Minoan-Mycenaeans) could partly own their own land and paid taxes to the Dorians; slaves had been mostly taken in war or were Minoans who had refused to knuckle under.

Women and men were segregated; men's lives revolving around military training in groups, warfare, and the initiation of young men into the system. There is evidence that relations between a youth and an older man, sometimes starting with a ritual abduction, were part of attaining adulthood. Marriage, when it came, was controlled. Each city had a special men's hall where men ate and talked together (the food prepared by women and slaves). As time progressed, and their military skills were valued, Cretan men also acted as mercenaries.

While the men were thus occupied, the women were very often managing both home and property.

Lucia Nixon suggests other occupations in 'Gender Bias in Archaeology' a chapter in *Women in Ancient Societies* (1994):

In Iron Age Greece, we know that in the Orientalising, Archaic, and Classical period women should be seen as active patrons of the arts rather than passive consumers. But what about women as producers, that is as artists? The representation of a woman painting a vase has long been known: there is also a vase-painter's name, Douris, which could well be a variant of a common Greek woman's name, Doris. These two points suggest that sometimes women took part in the production of vases, just as they are known to have participated in other professions.

One of the most important of the city states was Gortyn, and the reason we know so much about it is the discovery, starting in AD 1857, of the Gortyn Code – inscribed in the Dorian dialect of Crete onto twelve large limestone columns forming a semicircle, most of it still in Gortyn (see itinerary p. 251). It is thought that this remarkable law document dates from the fifth century BC, but probably refers to the situation in the seventh to sixth centuries BC. It is so early and unique a record of laws (the oldest and most important of Greek antiquity) that it has been called the Queen of Inscriptions.

The groundwork allowing later scholars to explore the Gortyn Code was laid by the Italian classicist Margherita Guarducci (see p. 168) who published four volumes of inscriptions between 1935 and 1950, parts of which were based on the work of the archaeologist who had found and reassembled the code.

The Code is usefully revealing about the position of women. Sarah B. Pomeroy sums up varying opinions of the implications in *Goddesses, Whores, Wives and Slaves*:

Some scholars believe that the Gortynian code represents a stage in the evolution of increasing freedom for women. Others, including those who believe in the existence of matriarchal and matrilineal systems in Bronze Age Crete, suggest that the code documents a gradual restriction of female freedom but retains traces of the earlier patterns.

The Code's main provisions deal with the personal freedom of citizens, the distinction between classes of free citizens and slaves, civil and criminal offences (including rape and adultery), family law (divorce, distribution of paternal property, legal recognition of offspring, relations between parents and children, adoption, and so on). Typical of the provisions reads:

> If a man and his wife separate, (then) the wife should take back all that belonged to her when she married, plus half of the produce (income) if this produce is from her own land; and she shall keep half of all the cloth she has woven, plus five gold staters if the husband is the cause of the divorce. If, however, the husband maintains that he is not responsible for causing the divorce, the judge will decide on the matter after making the husband take an oath.

Even though free women had the right to possess, control and inherit property, the inheritance of a daughter was less than that of a son.

Punishment tended to be by fine for crimes such as rape (of women or men), higher if a slave raped a free person, but there was also a penalty for raping a household slave. This raises questions about issues such as rape, divorce and adultery in Minoan times – questions which cannot be answered.

While Sarah Pomeroy goes into further intricacies concerning women, those about slaves are of particular interest. We know nothing about slavery in Minoan Crete, apart from an unclear suggestion of slave weavers in the Linear B tablets found at Knossos. Does that mean that earlier there were none? Was the introduction Mycenaean, or were the Dorians, with their even more warlike society, the real instigators of a phenomenon which was to beset Crete in one way or another until modern times?

Under the Gortyn Code, some adulteries were more serious than others, but there was no penalty for adultery between a free man and an unfree woman. If a free woman married an unfree man and lived in his house, their children were unfree; but she might have free children from another union. When slaves with different masters married, the woman's children belonged to her husband's master. But she could have possessions and, on divorce, would return to her previous master. If a slave mother was unmarried, her children belonged to her father's master.

Another inscription of this period indicates that the loom, like the plough, could not be mortgaged, and one from Prinias suggests that a woman's work, and its value to the community, was recognised: on a funeral stele a female figure wearing a long chiton stands holding a spindle, with a half-filled distaff nearby (Herakleion Museum, room XIX). We may be able to assume that working women of the time were similarly dressed.

Prinias, the site of the ancient city of Rizenia – on a hill, half-way between Gortyn and Knossos – has notable ruins of the seventh and sixth centuries BC that introduce us to religious practices. One is a small temple harking back to Minoan times; indeed, Rizenia was probably another refuge of the Eteocretans – like Karphi, Kavousi and Vrokastro. A goddess figure with upraised arms, and her snake accoutrements, were found on the site.

The temple was devoted to the goddess Rhea (mother of Zeus) and has been reconstructed in the Herakleion Museum (room XIX). Above the lintel of carved animals, on either side are seated goddess figures. Their headdress consists of pillbox hats (polos) on long curls and their shawl, belt and embroidered dresses are similar to other figures of the period. They are said to represent a continuation of the earlier Mistress of the Animals, in Archaic times transferred to Artemis or her alter ego Britomartis. A miniature ivory plaque, probably of the Mistress of the Animals, slender and dressed in an ornate chiton, was found in the Idaian cave (see itinerary p. 234).

At Eleutherna (see itinerary p. 240), to the west of Knossos, was found a large stone goddess, probably Athena, with the same shawl and belt but with luxuriant, wig-like hair (Herakleion Museum, room XIX). This style, Egyptian inspired but locally developed, is termed

Daedalic art and reached its peak between 650 and 500 BC. The goddess figures may give us some idea of how elite women looked. A typical figure, with her rigidly frontal posture and hair like an English judge's wig, is that known as the Lady of Auxerre (650–600 BC) which you can see in the Louvre. Other terracottas can be seen in the museums of Siteia and Agios Nikolaos. Wood was also used for statues at this time – one of Britomartis/Artemis still existed in the second century AD at Elounda (Olous) on the Bay of Mirabello where the goddess had her festival.

The second Prinias temple was more like that found at Dreros (near Neapoli), dedicated to the god Apollo Delphinios (of the Dolphin) and dating from the second quarter of the eighth century BC. It is one of the earliest temples to have survived in Greece. In it were three small bronzes, probably depicting Apollo, his twin sister Artemis, and their mother, the demi-goddess Leto; they are known as the Triad of Dreros and can be seen in the Herakleion Museum (room XIX). The two women, robed and wearing pillbox hats, stand rather small and subdued beside a large and cocky Apollo in a beret. They are the earliest examples found of hammered bronze, and are later than the temple – c.650 BC. (Elounda/Olous was probably the port for Dreros, but the site is now under water and has not been excavated.)

South of Dreros (and north of Kritsa) is the seventh century BC site of Lato – a Cretan Doric version of Leto's name. Eileithyia was the patron goddess here, as coins found suggest (see itinerary p. 318). Coins depicting the goddess Artemis have also been found at Lato (and at Elounda of her alter ego Britomartis). At Gortyn a famous coin series portrays the sacred marriage of Europa and Zeus (forget poor Hera!). One silver stater, for example, has Europa on one side sitting under a willow tree; on the reverse is the bull (Zeus) licking his flank (see itinerary p. 251). Coins have been found at Knossos of Demeter, goddess of earth, agriculture and general fertility, sister of Zeus and another of his amours (their daughter was **Persephone**, also known as **Kore**). Demeter is sometimes also identified with Rhea, her mother.

A sanctuary dedicated to Demeter has been found on the Gypsades hill, to the south of the Minoan palace at Knossos. The offerings date from the seventh to second centuries BC; there was a marked revival of the cult in the fifth century BC. Among the figurines offered to the goddess are seated goddesses and girls carrying waterpots (hydriai) – to symbolise Demeter's concern with watering the crops. Among the animal figurines are the goddess' favourite – pigs. There are also silver rings inscribed Damatri – her name in Doric dialect.

Worship of Demeter appears to have been carried out primarily by women and associated with the cult were plants of particular use to women and human reproduction. One of these was pennyroyal – a variety of mint – which was used as an anti-fertility drug. The archaeologist **Lucia Nixon**, who grows it in her Oxford garden to show that it can be done today, notes in her work on Demeter and Kore (on the mainland), from sources of antiquity, that it was used for 'opening the uterus for various reasons: preconceptual purgation, hysteria, emmenagogue [bringing on periods], expulsion (of foetus/afterbirth) and stimulation of the lochia [afterbirth]'. Other sources call it an abortifacient. Demeter herself was a skilled practitioner of herbal medicine. Other common attributes of Demeter in post-Minoan centuries were snakes, trees, poppies and small animals – harking back to those earlier times.

Diktynna, a goddess associated with Britomartis and Artemis of the wild countryside, mountains and hunting, also had her coins on which she is portrayed in hunting dress with a bow and quiver. She had a temple at Lissos (south-west coast) and another, more famous, at Cydonia (Chania) one of the most powerful city states. An inscription of the sixth century BC shows its financial accounts. These suggest that the temple's revenues came from slaves and cattle let out for hire, and sale of cattle, wool and cheese. How far women were involved in that process is not made clear by my source; was it raw wool or spun, for example? Were the men who might have been concerned in business away training or fighting, leaving women in charge?

Cydonia – which covered the area from Chania to the south coast – is said to have been founded by King Cydon which leads us on a merry chase. Ancient Tarra, an independent city state, is now in the National Park of Samaria. There, Apollo and Artemis went to be purified. Some say there was then a temple there to Artemis/Britomartis, others that there was a cult of Apollo. Yet another myth has it that Apollo made love there to Acacallis, a daughter of Pasiphae and Minos. Minos so disapproved that he banished his daughter to Libya but, too late, she had already conceived Cydon (see p. 261).

Minos was a fine one to talk. There was a seventh century BC temple dedicated to Diktynna at Kap Skala in the far west. It is from here that she leapt into the sea to escape the attentions of Minos. She was saved from drowning by fishermen catching her in their net. The ruins of the temple there today are those of one built in the second century AD, following a visit by the Roman emperor Hadrian to Crete – showing that Diktynna continued to be of consequence in Roman times.

**Aphrodite**, goddess of love and beauty, was another of Zeus' daughters, this time by his aunt Dione (whom he ravished). It was Aphrodite who caused Pasiphae (Minos' wife) to crave sexual relations with the bull. One of the goddess's lovers was Hermes, another of Zeus' children, messenger of the gods, patron of land travel and commerce, and inventor of the lyre. Aphrodite had a son by him, tellingly called Hermaphroditus and there was a peak sanctuary dedicated to them high above the village of Kato Syme (south of Mount Ida).

The open air sanctuary, which harked back to the Minoan First Palaces period, was still in use in the Hellenistic and Roman periods which follow, as shown by remarkable bronze cut-out plaques (in the Herakleion Museum), offerings, graffiti on roof tiles, and stone inscriptions.

Aphrodite was to inspire **Sappho** (born about 613 BC), who some rank among the greatest poets, to write about Crete (from her home at Mytilene on the island of Lesbos). In the 'Prayer for Aphrodite's Presence', only a fragment of which remains because much of her work was lost during the Dark Ages, she wrote, 'Leave Crete and come to me now ...' And, in another fragment that, for us, recalls Ariadne and links her to Athena and Artemis in their love of dancing, she wrote:

> And their feet move
> Rhythmically, as tender
> feet of Cretan girls
> danced once around an
> altar of love, crushing
> a circle in the soft
> smooth flowering grass

The preponderance of temples dedicated to Archaic and Classical goddesses in Dorian Crete may tell us something about religion – that the goddesses were important to the wellbeing of the worshippers – but it does not necessarily add anything about the position of women to what is suggested in the Gortyn Code. Quite apart from how ambiguously frescoes and paintings of the Virgin Mary and other female saints have reflected attitudes in Christian centuries, legislation, including inscriptions, can be misleading: after all, we have had equal pay legislation in Britain for many years but it is certainly not yet fully implemented.

And it seems clear that, of all the deities, the most powerful was Zeus, lover of several goddesses, father of many of the others. The most instructive information comes from Palaikastro – a town in the east that had been similar to, but bigger than, Gournia in Minoan times and resettled in the Postpalatial period. Here, in 1904, Robert Carr Bosanquet made an important find. He wrote to his wife Ellen on 25 May:

On Friday we began trenching there, and yesterday came on a fragment of a marble slab inscribed on both sides with a hymn in honour (almost certainly) of Dictaean Zeus. In the afternoon we found another piece, and hope for the rest. It's a most exciting find, for this must be the Dictaean Temple for which we have long hunted.

It is disappointing that Ellen Bosanquet (see p. 105) was not there to write home herself about this find. Her husband was Director of the British School at Athens and she had been persuaded by a diplomatic wife there that she would be happier not undergoing the vicissitudes of archaeological life in Crete. (She paid at least one short visit but Palaikastro was certainly not, then, the place to take small children.) But at least Ellen made sure, following her husband's death, that his letters to her were published.

The Hymn to Zeus had been inscribed in Christian times but, from its dialect and vocabulary, it was apparently a copy of a panegyric composed, it is thought, in the fourth to third centuries BC. In the hymn, the young god is summoned by his guardians, the Kouretes, to return to Dikte, his birthplace, where his sacred altar stood. But the sanctuary itself, probably in use from Archaic to Roman times, has not been found at Roussolakkos, the site at Palaikastro (see itinerary p. 368); some suggest that it was destroyed by Christians, rather than by time.

Jane Ellen Harrison (see p. 164), the Cambridge classicist, who had been inspired by finds at Knossos in 1901 to write *Prologemena*, tells us in her reminiscences 'Then when some years later I again visited Crete, I met with the sequel that gave me the impulse to *Themis* [(1913)], the *Hymn of the Kouretes* found in the temple of Diktaean Zeus.' **Annabel Robinson**, in *The Life and Work of Jane Ellen Harrison* (2002), analyses this inspiration in some detail, and the two books about the origins of the Greek religion, with modern introductions, are not difficult to come by.

Much later, a partly burnt gold and ivory statuette of a young god was found at Palaikastro. It is about half a metre high, the left foot slightly forward, as in the Archaic kouroi (young men figures). The sandals and perhaps the sword sheath were of gold sheet and the top of the head is serpentine. It is unique and is given pride of place in the Siteia Museum (see itinerary p. 364).

So exciting is all this that no one mentions the trials of his mother, Rhea, surrounding the birth of Zeus; I will elaborate on these in the itineraries (see pp. 234 and 295). I use the word in the plural deliberately because there are claims for more than one cave sanctuary as the birthplace.

By now, the mainland god Zeus had not only been absorbed into the religion of Cretans but even appropriated by them. Alone of the classical Greeks, they believed that Zeus was not just born in Crete but died there too. And not only was he buried on Mount Juctas, south of Knossos and above Archanes, but he was reborn and died again annually. This was blasphemy to the Greeks because Zeus was immortal, he could not die. It is from this difference of opinion that slurs were cast against the honesty of Cretans thereafter. As for this Zeus, some see him as a surviving form of the son or consort of the Minoan Mother Goddess.

# 8

## More Influences from Abroad

### Hellenistic – 330–67 BC

The significance of the term 'Hellenistic' given to this period in Crete stems from its more general use as a description of an enlarged, cosmopolitan Greek world 300–150 BC. This in turn was a result of the conquests of Alexander the Great who continued those of his father Philip of Macedon. Cretan archers served in Alexander's army (336–23 BC) and one of his generals was Cretan. As the whole region seethed, so manipulation and aggression from outside affected Crete. Ptolemy II of Egypt (whose new rulers, from 323 BC, descended from another of Alexander's Macedonian generals) set up a naval base at Itanos in the far east of Crete and a protectorate over the whole of that area lasted for 200 years (see p. 374). One Cretan city (now unknown) was named Arsinoe, after the Queen of Egypt, wife and sister of Ptolemy II.

In addition, internal hostilities caused significant disruption and misery, particularly those between Knossos and Gortyn. We can catch glimpses of what life was like for women. In 220 BC, while Lyttos' army was away campaigning against Hierapytna (Ierapetra), Knossos sacked it, enslaving its women and children. On their return to find their families gone, the Lyttos men were so demoralised that they did not have the heart to rebuild – taking refuge instead elsewhere. Gortyn destroyed nearby Phaistos and captured its port Matala (where Europa came ashore).

Hierapytna, the principal Dorian town in the east, was by 201 BC controlled by Rhodes as that island tried to protect its trade routes. Crete was notorious as a hotbed of profitable piracy. Hierapytna was responsible in 145 BC for razing to the ground its nearby rival

Praisos, the last stronghold of the Eteocretans (see itinerary p. 380). They now disappear from history, or did the men send their women and children away to safety as so often happened later when danger threatened communities? There is evidence, at the beginning of the third century BC, that when Sparta (on the mainland) was threatened by invasion, there were plans to send women and children to safety in Crete; several Cretan cities had Spartan inhabitants or were friendly towards that Dorian state.

Around Praisos, there are archaeological remains dating from neolithic to Hellenistic times. It had also been a rival of Itanos, over control of the Zeus sanctuary at Palaikastro, or an earlier Minoan shrine; indeed, that was one of the reasons that Itanos was glad of Egyptian protection. These rivalries are usually revealed through treaties that brought the warring to an end, often arbitrated from outside.

Artistic influences also came from abroad. The rather lovely remains of a terracotta Tanagra figurine of a woman was an offering found in the nine-chambered tomb of the Mathioulakis family in Chania – the head, a swanlike neck and a sliver of a shoulder and arm. It is typical of the ancient Greek statues we are used to. (Its influence was from Alexandria, seat of the Greek Ptolemies of Egypt and a cultural centre of the time.) It can be seen in the Chania Museum (see p. 262).

A similar figure, this time all the pieces, was found at a site at the far end of the beach at Xerokampos just south of Zakros in the far east. Described as a Hellenistic Tanagra, she stands looking to one side, arms slightly bent backwards, a double skirt draped over one knee bent slightly forwards. She is tiny and so different from the Daedalic figures of the previous period – graceful instead of rigid; she is light years away from Minoan figures. She can be seen at the Siteia Museum (see p. 364 and itinerary p. 379).

At Lissos, on the south coast, are the remains of an Asclepeion, named after Asclepius, the mythical Greek physician hero eventually worshipped as god of medicine. This early sort of hospital grew up

7. Hellenistic *Tanagra* figurine from Xerokampos,
Archaeological Museum, Siteia

round medicinal springs. Asclepius' daughter **Hygeia** (sometimes called his wife) was the Goddess of Health (mental and physical). Her mother was **Epione**, also a healer. Hygeia's symbol was a serpent. A statue of her, found in the Asclepeion, is in the Chania Musuem, as is that of a graceful little girl clutching a ball to her chest also found there (see pp. 262 and 279).

Hygeia was also worshipped in the Asclepeion at Lebena near Gortyn and it is from here that we have evidence about a real woman:

thanks offered to Asclepius are inscribed on a stone in the temple. In the first century BC, the woman was cured of an ulcer on her little finger by the application of shell of oyster ground down with rose ointment, and an anointing of compound of mallow and olive oil. The treatment took place while she was asleep in the temple and part of it was to remember her dreams which should be of the remarkable deeds of the god.

An Aphrodision dating from the second century BC has been found on high ground between Elounda and Agios Nikolaos. This temple to Aphrodite and Ares (God of War, son of Hera and Zeus, adulterous lover of Aphrodite and slayer of her lover Adonis) was built on top of a Geometric temple of 'ancient Aphrodite' according to an inscription. Since the Hellenistic Aphrodision was on the boundary between Olous (Elounda) and Lato, there was keen rivalry over who controlled it – which was not resolved until an arbitration in Roman times in favour of Lato.

In the Chania Museum, there is a lissom second century BC statue of Aphrodite, handless (but otherwise repaired) and naked save for a shawl knotted above her knees and falling in folds to her feet.

Some exquisite gold jewellery, from the third century BC, is also in the Chania Museum. It came from a woman's tomb excavated during work on the drainage system of the city. One piece is of dozens of gold and garnet (?) drops hanging from rosettes attached to a thick knitted gold collier; earrings have large rosettes with dangling, heavenly figurines (see itinerary p. 262).

Cydonia (Chania) at this time was one of the most powerful city states, prosperous through trade and ever-ready to throw its weight about.

# 9
## The Romans

### Greco-Roman – 67 BC–AD 330

Roman involvement in Crete became serious in 196 BC. After Rome's defeat of Sparta over its use of piracy, leading to Sparta's withdrawal from its bases in Crete, Rome began to find pretexts to intervene in the island's affairs. Piracy, however, increased. When a Roman fleet sailed to Crete to release Roman women and children of noble family taken in a pirate raid on Ostia (Rome's seaside), the fleet was defeated and the prisoners hanged en masse.

Only Gortyn cooperated with Rome, thus becoming the centre of pro-Roman sentiment on the island. Knossos and Cydonia (Chania) were particularly intransigent. In 171 BC Cydonia attacked nearby Apollonia; as the (Roman) records recount, 'They slew the men, they seized all goods and property, and the women and the city were shared out and taken possession of.' These glimpses suggest the continuing experience of women during these warring centuries.

Mainland Greece had become part of the Roman empire in the middle of the second century BC; now, Rome finally had had enough of the problems Crete caused and conquered it in 68 BC. Gortyn, having behaved so well earlier and thus prospered, was made the capital and seat of the Roman pro-consul when, in 27 BC, Crete became part of the Roman province of Cyrene (Libya) with a provincial council and magistrates. Other important centres included Lyttos, Aptera, Hierapytna (Ierapetra) and Knossos. Many other sites were inhabited again for the first time since the Bronze Age.

Pax Romana now prevailed and, for the first time for many years, Crete became stable and prosperous. By this time, the province had a population of some 300,000. In spite of the fact that Latin was the language of government, Greek otherwise continued to be used, and Greek culture to flourish. Some Roman customs were introduced, such as public baths. In the city of Arkades (modern Ini, central south Crete) an inscription mentioned the timetable, separate hours for women and men. Public works such as roads, aqueducts and irrigation schemes were very much a feature of Roman Crete.

Religious influences continued eclectic: ancient Cretan goddesses such as Britomartis/Diktynna were worshipped as well as Olympian Demeter. Until Roman times, Cydonia controlled the important sanctuary of Diktynna (sometimes called Diktynnaion Artemis) on the Spatha promontory in the Bay of Menies Rodopau in the far west. Then Polyrrhenia gained control. The rich centre was protected by trained dogs and its income was used for public works.

To the north of Polyrrhenia was its foe Phalasarna, named after a nymph or a local heroine **Phalasarne**. The city was destroyed by the Romans in the first century BC as they tried to clear the Mediterranean of pirates. But a third century BC stone found at the lesser sanctuary of Diktynna here was inscribed with a treaty between the two foes guaranteed by the Spartans. This information is contained in *The County of Khania Through its Monuments* (2000) by the director of the Chania Museum, Crete-born **Maria Andreadaki-Vlasaki**, and most easily found at the marvellous museum itself (see itinerary p. 260).

Maria Vlasaki does not suggest that the famous Throne of Phalasarna, hewn into the rock and still there, might have belonged to the high priestess of Diktynnaion Artemis, but another source does. Changes in sea level, probably because of earthquakes, mean that the remains are now far from the sea.

Mosaics were noteworthy in Roman times and a fine one found in Chania, now in the museum, and illustrated by Maria Vlasaki, shows the nymph Amymone (daughter of Europa) being rescued from a satyr by the god Poseidon (third century AD) (see p. 262).

There is a Roman statue of Aphrodite from Gortyn in the Herakleion Museum (room XX), but rather more modest than the

Hellenistic one in the Chania Museum: this time a basin on a stand in front of her reaches carefully up to the pubic line (see itinerary p. 253).

There was a temple to Athena Polias at Itanos in the far east of the island (known now as Erimoupolis, or the Deserted Village), which is interesting enough, but Itanos has another claim to fame during this period: in 37 BC, at the height of Cleopatra's relations with the Roman joint-ruler Mark Anthony – relations which estranged him from Rome – he appointed her ruler of several parts of the Roman Empire around the Mediterranean, including Eastern Crete and in particular Itanos, where there had been a Ptolemaic garrison in Hellenistic times (see p. 82). **Cleopatra** (69–30 BC) was to be the last of the Ptolemaic (Macedonian) rulers of Egypt. I can't help being fanciful and imagining Cleopatra setting foot in Crete at Itanos, just to have a quick look at one of her possessions (see itinerary p. 374).

It is not so far-fetched. The temple to Athena at Itanos was a Samonian one and Cleopatra, according to her biographer, Lucy Hughes Hallet, sailed to the island of Samos more than once. And, in 32 BC, Cleopatra and Anthony moved to Patrae, 'distributing their fleet between half a dozen sites on the western seaboard of the Greek Archipelago from Corfu to Crete'. After the Battle of Actium, where Cleopatra and Anthony were defeated by Octavian (who became Emperor Augustus), Itanos reverted to the Roman Empire. A lingering legacy at Itanos was, perhaps, a dedication to the Egyptian goddess **Isis** in her guise as the Roman goddess Fortuna Primigenia.

Isis and Fortuna (luck) were introduced to Crete in Roman times and were interchangeable; they were worshipped noticeably at Gortyn. Then, Crete was one of the first places to receive Christianity when St Paul landed at Gortyn in AD 58. Persecution of Christians started early, in the period of the Emperor Decius, AD 248–51. There is no evidence of early women martyrs.

Christians were ready to pull down signs of pagan religion: at Lissos, the remains of Hellenistic statues, including Hygeia, found in a pit, were probably broken by Christians.

At least three women survive by name in Crete from Roman times. **Flavia Philyra** describes in an AD first to second century inscription on the architrave of the Isis and Serapis temple at Gortyn how, with her children, she rebuilt it from its foundations (see itinerary p. 253). The earlier one may have been pulled down, or it may have fallen in an earthquake; the town suffered severely from one in AD 46, and they continued destructively in the centuries that followed.

In the North Cemetery at Knossos there is a first century AD funerary plaque for G. Kanpanios Philephebos and his wife (?) **Kanpania Kledon**. A first or second century AD Roman woman, **Noyia Ancharia**, set up a statue of Demeter's daughter Kore at Knossos. And Crete's history was familiar to the Romans; indeed, Sara Paton tells, in the chapter 'Roman Knossos' (1994), how one Roman emperor claimed to be descended, through his mother's family, from Pasiphae.

In the Chania Museum there is a grave stele found at Aptera lamenting the death in AD third century of 'a young lady from Libya' named Sumpherousa. In spite of being a foreigner, she was much honoured by the citizens of the town, but it was her grief-stricken husband who had composed the moving inscription (see p. 263 and itinerary p. 283).

The further away from the Minoans Crete's history has moved, the less interesting it has seemed to archaeologists. Roman times, however, benefitted in the early 1970s from the commitment of Ian and **Janet Sanders**. Sara Paton, following in their footsteps and writing of Hellenistic and Roman Crete in Davina Huxley's series of essays *Cretan Quests: British Explorers, Excavators and Historians* (2000) describes their work:

In the autumn of 1973, after a year's preparatory work in libraries [Ian Sanders] and his wife Janet (also an archaeologist) set out on ten months systematic exploration of the island, to check known sites and add new ones to the list. They had one student grant to share between them, and an elderly Landrover in which they travelled and also lived; they were young and enthusiastic, and luckily that winter was a mild one.

From time to time they returned to the Taverna at Knossos for a breather and to prepare the next stage of the campaign, but even there they could not afford the meals and continued to cook for themselves on a camping stove in their room in the Annexe. In 1975 they returned to Crete for three weeks to check a few last details, but by then Ian was already ill. He finished his dissertation only weeks before his death, and his doctorate was awarded posthumously. Janet saw to the publication of the thesis as a book; it is the foundation on which all subsequent studies of Crete in the historical period of antiquity are, and will continue to be, built ...

*Roman Crete: An Archaeological Survey and Gazetteer of Late Hellenistic, Roman and Early Byzantine Crete* (1982) draws together the scholarship of many fields and nationalities; it is a gazetteer of 429 sites and has chapters on the history, administration, economy, art, architecture and religion of Crete. It also follows a precedent set by John and Hilda Pendlebury who, in the 1930s, tramped over Crete for his book *The Archaeology of Crete* (1939) (see p. 375). These are books for the initiated; their interest for us is the part the women, both archaeologists in their own right, played in seminal works by their husbands.

Sara Paton also writes about how an early Christian tomb came to be found in the North Cemetery at Knossos in 1978:

This tomb was excavated by Jill Carington Smith, who is an unsung heroine of Hellenistic and Roman Knossos. During her years as Knossos Fellow she carried out innumerable rescue digs of all periods, often under very difficult conditions and with minimal backup. While excavating at the North Cemetery she had, for example, no transport, and was once obliged to hire a taxi to ferry six Early Christians back to the Stratigraphical Museum, first prudently disguising them as groceries since four is the maximum number of passengers allowed in a taxi.

Rome had converted to Christianity in the third century, so Christian Crete was not, after that, subject to repression. And there is no evidence of revolt against Roman occupation during the 400 years that it lasted.

In AD 330, the capital of the Roman state was transferred to ancient Byzantium (renamed Constantinople after its first Christian emperor), and Crete came under the eastern Roman Empire becoming, in AD 395, a separate province with a Byzantine general as its governor; Crete's Roman days came naturally to an end.

# 10
## Byzantines and Saracens

### AD 330–1204

When Rome fell in AD 476, what was left of it became the Byzantine Empire with Constantinople as its capital. Subsequently riven by religious factionalism, the empire regained stability with the crowning in 527 of Justinian, famous for his legacy of codified law. His wife Theodora (497–548) ruled as his partner, which is particularly interesting not so much because a stable empire should be good for Crete but because at least one source suggests that the daughter of a bear trainer who became an actress (synonymous then with being a prostitute) was Cretan. It may be unscholarly to push this point, but I am unable to resist doing so. (Other sources suggest Cyprus or Syria as Theodora's birth place; scholars have now decided that it was probably Constantinople itself.) Theodora later converted to Christianity and became a wool spinner; but she must have caught Justinian's eye earlier. They were married in 525 and she was crowned with him in 527.

Theodora was not only to have influence on policy generally but she was also particularly concerned with women's rights. She is believed by more than one source to have had some say on laws concerning prostitution and procuring women for the stage, laws more favourable to women in marriage and inheritance, and protection of women charged with offences. There is no evidence that any reforms that bear her fingerprints affected Crete (and no evidence that they did not). Indeed, details about Crete during these centuries are sparse.

Christianity seems to have flourished, with bishoprics in as many as 22 cities. Remains of basilicas have been found, for example, at

Gortyn, Knossos, Siteia and Phalasarna. The best known then and now is St Titus at Gortyn. The name of the Paliani Convent enters the records in AD 668 – perhaps the earliest such institution. It was later to become associated with the bravery of its nuns and, today, is known for their handicrafts and a sacred myrtle tree. The convent will appear again in Crete's history (see pp. 127, 133 and 139 and in itinerary p. 228).

Signs of individual women are few and far between. On a list of 'persons of Cretan origin or active in Crete during the Byzantine period' (fifth to twelfth centuries) only one woman is mentioned – **Anna**, a nun – on an inscription from Eleutherna (fifth to seventh centuries) (see itinerary p. 240). On another list of 'persons with no office or title', **Anastasia** is on an inscription from Gortyn (sixth to seventh centuries). Then there is **Juliane**, mother of St Gregory of Akrita (eighth century), and **Theodore**, a girl from Kisamos (fourth/ fifth century). From the same period from a Kisamos inscription comes one which seems to read **Sophia**, from Gortyna, an elder of the convent of Kisamos.

These were not easy years for Crete: not only were there devastating earthquakes, such as those in 365 and 415, but there were also major outbreaks of plague, for example in 542 and 746. In 623 Slavs from the north landed on the island. Then, from the mid–seventh century, there were threats from piratical Arabs.

In 656, Abd Allah bn. Sa'd launched a major attack. What is fascinating is that his wife, Qayla bint Umar, apparently accompanied him on raiding expeditions. There was another Arab raid in 671 and, in 674, two Arab commanders wintered in Crete. The raids gathered momentum until, in 824, the raiders took control of the island.

The Arabs, or Saracens, who conquered Crete had started out in Spain and been forced out of Andalusia following friction between different Islamic dynasties on the peninsula. The refugees, perhaps 10,000 of them, landed in Egypt in about 813 and captured Alexandria in 818. But they were expelled from there and Crete became their destination.

By this time, Byzantium had returned to unstable days and its navy was unable to protect its island possession. The intruders razed Gortyn, so that it was never to recover, and built a new capital surrounded by thick walls and a moat, Rabdh al Khandaq (today's Herakleion). The island once more became a hotbed of piracy and a centre for slavery.

In spite of these general claims, a scholar on the Arabs and Crete suggests that the influx of Muslims from various places during the 130 years of Arab rule brought fewer ethnic and social changes than might be expected. He argues against the view that there were many mixed marriages between indigenous women and conquerors on the grounds that elsewhere Muslim soldiers took their families with them and even sailors were accompanied by their wives (as Qayla bint Umar has demonstrated). Examples from Spain show how slow the Arabs were to marry outsiders because of the strength of traditional blood ties and tribal solidarity.

It is also suggested that the Arabs were more interested in levying taxes than in converting the natives to Islam. However, the imposition of taxes from conquerors would hardly be comfortable and, certainly, much wealth (presumably from piracy, slavery and trade, as well as taxes) was found at al Khandaq when finally the Arabs were ousted.

Not a single cultural monument appears to have survived from Arab times, suggesting that nothing was ploughed back into the occupied island, though the claim that St Titus in Gortyn was desecrated is now suspect. Among the few Arab place names to survive is Souda (Bay).

Byzantine rulers tried several times, unsuccessfully, to regain Crete. The attempt of most interest to us was in 843. Then, another Empress Theodora (r.842–56), regent to her son, appointed Logothete Theoktistos to command a large naval force. He managed to gain, and briefly maintain, a foothold on Crete. According to one (perhaps unreliable) source, the Arabs spread the rumour that the Empress Theodora had, meanwhile, elevated a new emperor; Theoktistos hurried home to reassert his own position as co-regent and his deserted army was wiped out.

Another Byzantine commander set out for Crete in 960 and landed near al Khandaq. There, Nikephoros Phokas set siege to the fortified Arab town – a siege which was to last several months and to be exacerbated by famine in the surrounding countryside. The siege was finally lifted on 7 March 961 and the Byzantine forces looted the town and massacred its Arab citizens. Their commander's instruction to leave women unharmed was ignored.

Crete was once again taken under the wing of Constantinople. To wipe out the past and ensure its future stability, Christianity was positively restored with the help of the Byzantine Church and its missionaries who founded monasteries and built churches. The population had dwindled under the Arabs, but this was soon remedied when Nikephoros Phokas, who had become emperor, settled many of his soldiers on the island; other colonists came from mainland Greece.

The new regime, under a military governor, attempted to set up a new capital (at what is today Prophitis Ilias; see itinerary p. 227) but, when that was found to be unacceptable, they reverted to the one the Arabs had built, which they called Khandakas.

From this new era, and over the next two and a half centuries, the economy of Crete picked up, linked as it was to an international trade system. Some evidence for its finances comes from coin finds; a good haul, 16 coins, is from the reign of yet another Empress Theodora (b. c.981) who ruled in 1042 and 1055–56. Under her, according to one source, the empire 'prospered and its glory increased'.

Towards the end of the twelfth century, twelve important Byzantine families came by grants of land in Crete. They were to be called the Archontopouli (aristocrats or lordly ones, sometimes shortened to archontes). Among the family names was **Agiostephanites** (otherwise known as Argyropoulos). According to a list of names, **Anna** was the wife of Stephen. Their bequests give some idea of the place they created for themselves, otherwise nothing remains of Anna. In 1206, the family donated a number of vineyards in the vicinity of the village of Varvaroi to the Monastery of Patmos. They were one of several benefactors of Patmos. Such records show that these families had landholdings then, that they were benefactors, and that the monasteries must have prospered as a result.

Nine members of the Skordylis family owned land in an immense crescent which contained three-fifths of today's eparchy of Sphakia. But there is some question historically about the authenticity of the imperial sanction given to these families to own their lands. Whatever the truth, they were to dominate Cretan society henceforward and, because of encroachment on their lands and privileges, to play a major part in uprisings against the next regime, the Venetians.

Many of the small churches that these families built on their estates still survive. It was also a period of portable icons such as the Panagia Kardiotissa (Holy Virgin of the Heart). The convent just below the Lasithi Plateau which takes its name from that icon may date from that period (see itinerary p. 301).

There is little archaeological evidence yet available for the Byzantine years and nothing apparently written about women's lives. I approached **Judith Herrin**, an expert on Byzantium, for help and she was forced to reply: 'I have written a lot on Byzantine women, but never found much evidence for women from Crete until the Venetian occupation.'

It would give a false picture to suggest that life for women in Crete, with their distinctive history and culture, resembled that of their sisters in Constantinople, but some inkling of it surely emerges from Judith Herrin's chapter 'Public and Private Forms of Religious Commitment among Byzantine Women' in *Women in Ancient Societies* (1994), edited by Leonie J. Archer and others.

For some time Crusaders had been on expeditions to the Holy Land. At first they were an attempt to rescue Christianity's holy places from Islam; latterly they had become more of a tussle between European centres of power. By 1204, because of the strains between Latin and Byzantine factions resulting from the Great Schism of 1054, the Fourth Crusade had been directed towards taking Constantinople.

# 11
## The Venetians

### AD 1204–1669

In 1204, the armies of the Fourth Crusade sacked Constantinople; the Byzantine state, including its overseas lands, was divided up. Manipulations behind the scenes had ensured that, in the parcelling out of territory, Crete was to go to Boniface of Montferrat. But as Boniface was ill-equipped then to take over the island, the Doge of Venice took advantage of his opportunities and made Boniface a financial (5,000 gold ducats) and political offer he could not refuse.

Crete was ceded to the Most Serene Republic of Venice (*La Serenissima*) and became an integral part of its geopolitical strategy and trade route system in the eastern Mediterranean. Venice then put Crete on the back-burner with the result that a Genoese pirate and rival of Venice seized the initiative and a large part of the island. Quickly, Enrico Pescatore refortified Khandakas, Siteia and Rethymnon. It took the Venetians until 1212 to get rid of the Genoese, and some pockets held out until 1217.

Throughout its rule of four and a half centuries, Venice was unable to relax its guard, for the indigenous Greek Orthodox Cretans, usually led by the not-so-indigenous twelve noble Byzantine families, constantly struggled to shake off the Roman Catholic (or Latin) colonial yoke.

Under the Venetians, Khandakas became Candia; indeed, that name was attached to the whole island. Administration was modelled on that of Venice with a Venetian duke as colonial, military ruler. Most of the surviving information comes from the area of the capital, Candia (Herakleion), because when the Ottomans took over in 1669, they allowed those archives to be taken back to Venice, whereas when other centres, such as Chania (which the Venetians called Canea) and Rethymnon, had fallen some years earlier, their records were destroyed.

The records consist of those kept by the Venetian administration, giving details of, for example, Council meetings, court reports and the numerous revolts, and wills and marriage and business contracts drawn up by Greek notaries – notaries public and lawyers being the only two official positions open to Greeks.

Happily for us, one of the most energetic scholars in the field is a woman, **Sally McKee**, and much of her work has consisted of mining the notarial papers for information about women. She sums up the effect of this material in 'Women Under Venetian Colonial Rule' (1998):

> If the government's records of its deliberations, proclamations, and court records provide a moving image of Candia, notarial records furnish the soundtrack of the city's bustle, thus bringing the scene closer to life than either set of sources would do on their own.

Dovetailing with that article, another and a book by Sally McKee is an examination of literary sources at a time of literary flowering in Crete. In 'Women in the Cretan Renaissance (1570–1669)' (1983) and 'Attitudes to Women in the Drama of Venetian Crete' (2000), **Rosemary E. Bancroft-Marcus** explores the lives of women mostly through the way they were depicted in the plays and poetry of the time. For a general outline, without special concentration on women, there is 'The Historical and Social Context', an introductory chapter by **Chryssa Maltezou** to another literary study (1991). For the first time in Crete's history, there are some facts to go on though, for the thirteenth century, the beginning of Venetian rule, details of women are still sparse.

Venice's false start in Crete led to the creation of a system of military fiefs within six districts, combined with a central administration answerable to the Senate of the colonial power. Lands were granted to Venetian settlers in return for military duties and obligation to provide military service from their feudal tenants – indigenous

Cretans – who also contributed by their labour to the land taxes. During the first century of occupation, as many as 10,000 settlers and their families arrived, at a time when Venice itself had a population of only 60,000. Society was divided into classes: Venetian nobles; Cretan nobles; the bourgeoisie; and free and unfree peasants.

Another means of controlling the Cretan population was to remove the top echelons of the Byzantine Church and replace them with Latin. Increasingly, over time, Cretans would turn to their church for sustenance, and the monasteries which were established, such as Faneromeni (c. 1293), Kardiotissa (c. 1333) and Kroustallenia (c. 1241) would be ready to assist rebellion. (These three have women connections which will become clear later; see itineraries pp. 301, 311 and 391).

It was at this time that now suspect documents surfaced relating to the landholdings of the twelve noble Byzantine families in Crete, the archontes, proving title to their lands then under threat from incomers. Venetians muscling in on the previous Byzantine order, lands and privileges led immediately to revolt – the first was in 1211 led by the Agiostephanites family in the Lasithi district. Over a period of two centuries, 27 uprisings are recorded. The Cretan noble families leading the revolts were often split between rebels and those loyal to the regime who hoped thus to gain an advantage.

I shall not detail these rebellions, except where there are facts or impressions about women, but it is easy to imagine the effect that such instability would have on family and community life, even when women were not under direct threat from the authorities because of the activities of their menfolk. I have found no evidence of women taking up arms, as some were to do later against Ottoman and German invaders.

The Lasithi Plateau, so often involved in uprisings because of its isolation and the insubordination of its Cretan landowners, was declared out of bounds to habitation in 1284, following the revolt under the most powerful archonte Alexios Kallergis, that started in 1282 (see also p. 290). The treaty signed between the Venetians and rebels in 1299, known as Pax Alexii Callergi, obtained several concessions and privileges for the archontes, particularly Kallergis himself – autonomy, and unprecedented Venetian nobility for his son, in return for an oath of allegiance. It is significant to us for the clause stating that marriage between Venetians and Cretans was to be allowed. Previously it had been prohibited so that Venetian property would not end up in Greek hands. Wills suggest that such marriages had taken place nevertheless; and sexual relations were commonplace, from the highest to the lowest.

In 1319, the son of an unfree peasant woman, **Herini Xerokalichea**, was able to prove that his father was not a man of the same status but Giacomo Tiepolo, Duke of Candia, at the time of his conception. A Latin father made him a free man because Latins could not be unfree. There appear to be no recorded cases of a Greek woman proving that, by birth, she was Latin and therefore free.

It also seems that if a Latin man had a child by a Greek peasant who was not his property, the child could not claim freedom. Sally McKee writes of a 1353 will, 'Nicolaus Habramo left money to a daughter whom he had by a slave belonging to another. He states "I leave to Maricoli, my natural daughter whom I had by the late slave of the sister of Iohannes Suriano, 15 *perperi*, if her mistress wishes to free her".'

Care for a natural daughter suggests that such fathers 'were inclined to endow them with sufficient dowries to attract men of moderate means'. But the mothers of their children fared less well. Nicolaus Habramo could not have left Maricoli's mother anything because she was dead but, when his widow, Marchesina, drew up her will in 1340, her apparent generosity stopped at leaving bequests to the natural children of her sons; there was nothing for their mothers.

Sally McKee's research among the marriage contracts and wills of upper class women in the fourteenth century, not only shows increasing intermarriage between Latin and Greek noble families but also emphasises continuing marriage and joint enterprises among Latin noble families. There is no evidence of moving between classes through marriage, and nearly all the noble marriages across ethnic groups were Latin men marrying Greek women; Greek dowries being a major incentive one way and Latin privilege the other.

In spite of the Kallergis settlement, there was virtually no change politically then and, in 1319, revolt broke out in Sphakia – an area which had never been tamed and had a certain autonomy. The pretext was that the Venetian garrison commander had 'offended the honour' of a Skordylis daughter. After killing the commander and his men, the Sphakiots declared rebellion. This time Kallergis intervened on behalf of the Venetians.

A revolt over taxation by the village of Margarites and the inhabitants of nearby provinces under Vardas Kallergis broke out in 1333. The Venetians were helped by sons of Alexios Kallergis and the revolt was ended by the burning down of Margarites. The Venetians exiled the families of the rebels and ruled that the children and brothers of Vardas should remain in prison for life. Accounts do not mention the women involved – no Kallergis or other women appear by name; we have to guess their suffering, including how the extended family coped with divided loyalties.

Seven years later (1341) a new rebel movement was started in the Apokoronas area (see itinerary p. 285) by Leo Kallergis; once again the family was on both sides. The revolt was finally crushed in 1347 when the Venetians, increasingly frustrated and vengeful, having killed the ringleaders, sent their women and children to Venice and tortured anyone else who may have been involved.

But the most convoluted revolt took place between 1363 and 1366. The pretext for the St Titus revolt was a plan to increase taxes, including those paid by the Latin settlers. Two important Venetian families, the Gradenigo and the Venier, allied themselves with two Kallergis brothers and declared the setting up of an independent republic under St Titus, the island's patron saint. This union was to show how close Latin and Greek noble families had grown over a century and a half. The Venetians had, in effect, gone native. Or, as

Sally McKee expresses it more elegantly, 'In reality, the Latin colonists had to coexist with the Greeks, not the Venetian Senate.'

Thanks to Sally McKee and her further research in their wills for *Uncommon Dominion: Venetian Crete and the Myth of Homogeneity* (2000), we finally have some named women affected by rebellion and its suppression. Her purpose on this occasion was not to highlight particular women but to show the intermarriage and breaking down of ethnic barriers between noble Latin families (originally Venetian) and noble Greek families (Cretan archontes). From diffuse information, I have tried to establish precise relationships but, since they were like a cat's cradle, I may have made some slips. My concern is to give particular women who went through hell their place in history.

We start with **Elena Dandolo** (née Cornaro), who was in some way connected to Marco Gradenigo, declared head of the new republic. Her daughter, **Marizoli** (sometimes written Maricoli), was married to the other ringleader, Tito **Venier**. Venier's Latin father, Bartholomo, had married both a Latin woman, Tito's mother, and a Greek woman, in order to get his hands on Greek lands; she also had a son. Another rebel, a Greek, Michael **Ialina**, had three daughters; each was married to a Latin rebel: **Elena** to Pietro **Muazzo** (sometimes written Mudacio), **Frangula** to Giovanni **Ghizi**, and **Anica** to Andrea **Pantaleo**. Frangula Ialina and Giovanni Ghizi's daughter, **Nicolota**, married into the **Da Vigoncia** family, also implicated in the cause.

The rebellion was crushed, Marco Gradenigo and Tito Venier were executed, and rebel lands confiscated. How many others died is unclear, but three sons of Elena Ialina and Pietro Muazzo were massacred after they had left the rebels. Some accounts suggest that the rebel families were broken up and the women and children expelled from all Venetian territories in the Mediterranean. All were declared persona non grata within the Venetian nobility and lost their fiefs and rights. The original concessions dating from 1211 were annulled and the remaining Latins had to swear an oath of loyalty to Venice. Victory over the rebels was marked by grand celebrations and a special day entered the calendar.

In spite of all the punishments directed against the rebel families, Sally McKee's research suggests that when Elena Dandolo, mother of rebels, died, the court appointed her daughter, Marizoli Dandolo Venier, wife of rebel Tito Venier, guardian of Elena's orphaned grandson (Marizoli's nephew). Sally McKee concludes, 'Either they never left the island or the regime granted them clemency and allowed them to return.' Perhaps, after all, she adds, only male kin were expelled.

Expelled or not, those three years of revolt and the grisly and inhumane aftermath must have been hard to cope with. What the revolt also shows is how society, and the initial divisions between Latin and Greek noble families, had changed over time.

Although over those first two centuries of Venetian rule the archontes eventually regained much of their land as a result of revolt, it did not affect their lack of political status. And traditional Cretan (Byzantine) nobility was broadened by the Venetian authorities who rewarded with noble status those Greeks who supported them, financially, militarily, or in some other way. Those with this status are sometimes called, loosely, 'archon', distinct from the superior 'archonte'.

Greek women married into Latin families under Roman rite tended to continue an attachment to the Orthodox Church. In another study – 'Greek Women in Latin Households of Fourteenth Century Venetian Crete' (1993) – Sally McKee gives as an example **Agnes Cornaro**, daughter of Alexios Kallergi. She made her will in 1331 and left many bequests to Greek churches in Crete and abroad, in spite of having married into one of the most important Venetian families and in spite of Latin control over the Greek Church.

Agnes also bequeathed small amounts to several people with obviously Greek names, suggesting that she still had strong ties to her original Greek community. Her servants would have been Greek and her new Latin family probably spoke Greek as well.

Accounts of revolts and research in wills give us some facts, and we can use our imagination about life during and just after revolts, but what about day-to-day life for noblewomen? There seems to be little to go on for the fourteenth and fifteenth centuries, but Rosemary Bancroft-Marcus had gleaned enough for her earlier study of the sixteenth and seventeenth to paint quite a picture. While it is dangerous to assume that society was static and, while most of the material is from the period generally or from Venice rather than Crete, we are left with too many bare bones not to catch at any possible glimpse of flesh.

In public, a woman had to be modest, discreet, virtuous, accompanied, her honour and that of her family all important; her father or brothers would defend her honour, and punish her if necessary. She married the man chosen for her and moved from her father's authority to her husband's.

So much for the public face. Mostly a woman's life was secluded but, within that seclusion, all was not gloom, as Rosemary Bancroft-Marcus shows in an irresistible reconstruction:

When relaxing in private, Veneto-Cretan women took the air on discreet balconies and roof-top terraces shaded by potted plants and shrubs. There they lounged in loose chemises and comfortable high-soled slippers, drying their hair over wide-brimmed crownless sun-hats. Hairstyles evolved from a simple style with central parting, a little height over the temples and soft curls, to a frizzed and high-piled style, and later back to a more natural look with high braided buns and perhaps a short curled fringe. Married women often wore some kind of head-dress, and widows, of course, wore black.

It is interesting what she then writes about dress on formal occasions:

A fashionable young woman appeared in a beautiful dress of stiff, heavy fabric such as brocade, with a smooth deep-pointed bodice, a skirt opening in front over a rich contrasting underdress, sleeves elaborately puffed and winged, and a dainty transparent partlet coquettishly veiling the decolletage. Jewels of every kind were worn as diadems, necklaces, and rings, and worked into embroidery; pearls became especially popular in the later part of the period [seventeenth century].

I say interesting because Chryssa Matzou describes how earlier Candia women dressed according to foreign fashion with damasks and gold and silver brocades imported from Venice and Lombardy. But so extravagant did all this become that the authorities issued an edict in 1339, affecting Venetians as well as 'Cretans and Jewesses', which prohibited 'the wearing of velvet or gold brocade dresses, and the use of embroideries, gold or silver ribbons, tassels, pearls and other decorative attachments'.

There is evidence from as early as 1444 that no one took much notice because, in the only mention I can find of a noblewoman in the fifteenth century, **Quirina Kallergi** asked her uncle Francisco Dandolo to 'bring back from Venice a gold-embroidered dress and a cloak (*pelanda*) of purple silk velvet'.

Chryssa Maltzou also notes that, by the seventeenth century, a Dutch traveller to Crete remarked, 'The women wear aprons of silk and very fine lace. Their fingers are full of diamonds, while they themselves are adorned with pearls which they wear round their necks, on their heads and on their sandals.' Such finery comes into sharper focus when Rosemary Bancroft-Marcus comments on women of the period more generally:

Within this beautifully bejewelled, embroidered, padded, lined, slashed and lace-trimmed vision of splendor, sad to relate, there was confined a plump and rather grubby body itching in a tight corset and burdened by a heavy hoop or farthingale. In this unhygienic age, a pomade was a desirable adjunct to a lady's costume, performing the triple function of perfume, deodorant and disinfectant; and she might toy with a pretty flea-fur of sable, to attract vermin away from her delicate person.

Elsewhere, Rosemary adds to this picture that pale skin was much admired and saffron might be used to dye hair.

Records surviving in the archives in Venice show a completely different aspect of women's lives and, indeed, women of a different status. Another of Sally McKee's studies from notarial records concentrates on the economic activities of Greek women – with only glimpses of noblewomen. She starts by observing that they laboured under two drawbacks: they were Greek and they were women. It is clear that this did not necessarily hold them back at any level: nobility, bourgeoisie or peasant. Most women of all classes had legal guardians – their fathers or husbands – and the men's names often appeared on the contracts that the women signed; but female economic activity was essential to the city of Candia.

Women were involved in 'service, trade, industry, credit and investment and the wine trade'. The most obvious service jobs were servants. They were not well paid, food, clothing and shelter making up most of their reward. Wet-nurses fared better, though **Sofia Moussourena** was told that if her milk was insufficient for the little girl for the whole two years of her contract, it would be dissolved and she would only be paid for the time she had suckled.

**Maria de Negroponte** is an example of a worker in the retail trade but her employment was more diffuse. In early 1320, she managed Palmerio de Veronas' wineshop and sold his wine. But she was also contracted as nursemaid to his child when his wife was expecting. During that time, Maria and her daughter received shelter.

**Fingenu Calergi** was a shoemaker, taught the craft by her boss's wife, **Agnes Ghisi**. **Maria Brixiano** was a furrier, and **Agnes Balneo** a physician or surgeon. We need to imagine them living and working in those Venetian parts of Herakleion or, indeed, other places, that still exist.

Clothmaking was a common craft for both Greek and Latin women and, in their wills, they customarily left relevant items to other women. For example, **Pliti**, the Greek widow of Leo **Cavartora,** left to another her 'silk thread'. Much spinning and weaving was done at home and a woman of the Latin elite, such as **Marizoli**, wife of Niccolo **Pantaleo**, might have her thread made by a woman from a village outside Candia. We know this because Marizoli left the woman a bequest in her will. Sally McKee speculates that the threadmaker may have been one of the Pantaleo dependent peasants.

Girls might also enter a clothmaker's home as apprentices. Sally McKee describes an instance of how that worked:

In 1321, Maria de Policandro, resident of the village of Pendimodhi, contracted with Herini Lastudhena, a Greek resident of Candia, for Maria's daughter Cherana to work for Herini 'in the service of your trade' and provide other household services for ten years. During that time Herini was to teach Cherana the skill of clothmaking and provide her with food and clothing.

There is also evidence of clothmaking as a commercial enterprise, with contracts showing several Greek women, such as **Maria Gavrilopula** and **Cali Fradelena**, providing cloth to a particular male distributor. These women may or may not have been those who made the cloth for, in the contract, they were called *mercatrix* (merchant). Some of those whose husband's names were not included in the contracts may have been widows; they tended to regain control of their dowries and property and therefore to have economic freedom.

Greek women also seem to have been moneylenders and acted as pawnbrokers and investors; sometimes that may have been within their community of women, but **Helena**, widow of Iohannes **Sachlichi**, made a large loan to two Latin men from eastern Crete. Some loans were apparently interest free, known as *causa amoris*, typically within an extended family. Maria, a tavernkeeper and former servant of Michael Panteleo, lent money to Pietro Pantaleo, presumably his relative. Perhaps the strangest lenders expecting interest, given Christian attitudes towards usury, were nuns in their religious houses. Here is an example:

Calinichi Samea, a *monacha* [nun] in the city of Candia, lists in her will all outstanding debts owed her and the pawns she took in surety of those loans. Apparently at least some of these loans were not made 'causa amoris' because she instructs her executors to investigate the profit from the investment made by her debtors.

In fact, even *causa amoris* was often a technique to avoid restrictions on taking profit in the form of interest. We do not know the name of Calinachi's convent in Candia, but you could picture her while visiting, for example, the Paliani Convent.

Wine was then, as now, an important part of Crete'economy, for local consumption as well as for export, and women were much involved. They tended to be from villages outside Candia, and may have been growers of grapes and producers of wine as well as sellers. **Herini Vastarchena**, for example, bought 116 *mistati* of wine for eleven and a half *perperi* from **Sophia Fruliadhena**. But the most outstanding example is **Cali**, widow of Andrea **Agapito** (a goldsmith, like so many of the husbands cited).

Cali appears in 54 notarial contracts between 1345 and 1347, the last just before she died. They show that she was not only involved commercially in buying wine, though that was her major interest; she also lent money to merchants and sold livestock and silk. She was already a widow by 1339, when she made her first contract, and she had a daughter, **Anica**, and a son, Andrea. Combing her will, as well as her contracts, Sally McKee finally deduces that Cali was a Greek Cretan woman with female relatives married to both Latin and Greek men and, by the time of her will, no matter her origins, she was rich – her bequests equalling the dowries of noblewomen.

From her research into women's activities, Sally McKee concludes that 'In general, women very possibly played a significant role in the local distribution of the island's products, serving as intermediaries between the producers in the villages and the exporters in Candia.'

As for the oldest profession in the fourteenth century, one source mentions prostitutes in passing, in the same sentence as gambling, as being a matter of concern to the authorities because of its appeal to 'the dissolute young'. It does not, however, seem as if only men were involved in gambling because a decree of 1325 forbade Leonardo, a cloth shearer, and the wife of the cobbler Marcus Rapacinus from using their houses as gambling clubs.

Another source, detailing dissolute activities among the orthodox clergy in the fourteenth century, talks of the old custom of *syneisakton*, whereby women were brought into the homes of monks 'for supposedly spiritual and ethical reasons', a practice which had apparently become an excuse for concubinage or sexual exploitation.

The Greek Orthodox clergy continued to have a reputation for moral laxity; a mid-sixteenth century case was reported (by a Latin priest) of a *protopapas* of Candia who abandoned his family, and his church duties, to live with his mistress.

Those are just snippets from historical sources; literary ones are more revealing. In the same volume as Chryssa Maltezou's historical overview (Holton, 1991), is a chapter, 'Literary Antecedents'. Arnold van Gemert introduces us to the first Cretan poet, Stefan Sachlikis, and, in doing so, gives rather more than a hint of prostitution in fourteenth century Crete.

Sachlikis was imprisoned in about 1370 for debauchery and, blaming it on the whores he frequented, wrote remarkable poems and an autobiography naming over 80 real women of Candia. We learn of five female brothel keepers: 'And what I wrote in jail about expert madames, even the schoolchildren often sang.' The main character of *The Council of Whores* is **Koutagiotaina**, wife of Koutagiotis, the woman whom Sachlikis most wants to vilify in revenge.

Koutagiotaina is prioress of the Council of Whores, but she is part of a chain:

> Koutagiotaina is screwing while her dog barks
> and her little children cry, but she laughs her head off.
> The widow Kapsampelaina is her protectress
> and eats her to the bone, exploiting her.

Among the sisterhood, or guild of whores, is Nikoletta 'the wife of Noufri who did it for a *grosso* [coin]'. 'Frantziskina who spoke churchy and Jewish', and 'the niece of Pilataina who specialised in Roman Catholic monks'. Koutagiotaina visited Sachlikis in prison, intending to offend his wife, and succeeded.

Sachlikis also reveals that when women were suspected, or were guilty, of adultery, they were led through the streets to the pillory.

Rosemary Bancroft-Marcus describes, from literary sources, how little had changed by the sixteenth and seventeenth centuries:

The industry of selling love for money was administered entirely by women; there were no male pimps or brothel-owners. Like Venetian banking, the prostitution business seems to have required an incredible number of intermediaries. Clients were put in touch with prostitutes by a kind of mafia of *ruffiane*, madams, procuresses or go-betweens, who took a large share of the profits. Some procuresses became immensely wealthy and controlled the activities of several fashionable courtesans and well-stocked brothels. Go-betweens might also supplement their income with freelance liaison work for loose-living servant-girls and hypocritical widows, a line of work which presumably afforded many opportunities for blackmail. At the turn of the sixteenth century, however, there appears to have been a trend away from the use of the go-between. Prostitutes appeared outside the brothel, standing openly in the streets soliciting passersby for custom; amorous widows were conducting their own affairs by letter.

Prostitutes lived precariously; they might, for example, be denounced by ill-wishers and subjected to a public whipping. And it was especially dangerous for Jews, to whom only few professions were open. Giacomo Foscarini, proveditor generale 1574–77, imposed severe penalties on Christians consorting with Jews and, to set an example, publicly burnt the corpses of two Jewish prostitutes who had been executed.

A Scot (William Lithgow), visiting Crete in 1610, alleges that its women, undifferentiated, were 'insatiably inclined to *venery* [probably sex, not hunting], such is the nature of the soyle and climate'. An observation that may reflect equally on the visitor who seems to have been a bit of a lad.

Another option for women outside regular commercial life in a superstitious society was to be a 'wise woman' or witch. Rosemary Bancroft-Marcus explains that 'There was a brisk trade in dreams, omens, prophecies, horoscopes, love-potions and beauty ointments, and a certain amount of experimentation with devil-conjuration and profaning of the sacraments.' But then you might be denounced to the Inquisition.

All visitors noted the abundance of medicinal herbs, particularly on Mount Ida, not specifying who collected or used them, but it is fair to assume that they were in the armoury of wise women and witches (see itinerary p. 235).

Greek courtesans led a different, more social, life. Apparently they were 'notoriously greedy, unscrupulous, mendacious and unfaithful'. They did not necessarily sleep with their clients but played them off one against the other. When a courtesan finally chose who she would give her favours to, it might be because her lover was particularly generous, had proved his military prowess (in a macho society), or could be an ally in a vendetta. She was in many respects more free than a noblewoman.

If life for a prostitute, as opposed to a courtesan, in Candia was hard, it had some advantages over that of the dependent peasant in a village outside. Feudal work was compulsory for men aged between 14 and 60 and women of all ages. Manning the warships was undoubtedly the most gruelling work for men. Their women were obliged to make huge supplies of ships' biscuits, but they were also left to undertake all the farmwork – remembering that there were feudal dues of farm labour as well – often as widows, as well as bringing up their children, if they survived childbirth and the epidemics and plagues which fell regularly upon Crete.

The Scottish visitor of 1610 gives an impression in passing of those countrywomen: They 'generally weare linnen breaches as men do, and bootes after the same manner [white leather], and their linnen coates no longer than the middle of their thighes'. And a compatriot a year later (George Sandys) suggests a different village under different circumstances: 'The women only wearing loose veils on their heads, the breasts and shoulders perpetually naked, and dyed by the sun into loathsom tawny.' Two pieces of mosaic which show nothing of women's life but allow us a small physical insight.

Another glimpse, of a different class of woman away from the main urban centres, is given by the 1518 frescoes of donors to the church of Hagios Giorgios at Voila near Chandras in the Siteia area. On the

8.  Donors to Hagios Giorgios, Voila, 1518, from Matton, *La Crète*

right is the mother and father, on the left, the daughter-in-law, son
and grandson. The mother is wearing a lilac-coloured dress and a
scarf to tone covering her head. (The ruins of the medieval village
of Voila can still be seen, dominated by the fifteenth century double-
naved church; see itinerary p. 380.)

In the plague of 1521, 26,000 people may have died all over Crete.
At least five major plagues followed over the next century, killing
thousands and devastating villages. An earthquake in 1508 – 'the
great disaster of Crete' – was said to have killed 30,000 (though
historians query that figure left by a traveller), mainly in the areas
of Candia, Siteia and Ierapetra. Figures for the population of the
island were not reliable until the seventeenth century, but may
have fluctuated between 50,000 and 300,000 during four and a half
centuries of Venetian rule. In 1644, there were 136,425 women and
150,742 men.

In 1453, Constantinople fell to the Islamic Ottomans and all
hopes of Crete becoming once again part of the Byzantine Empire
disappeared. In some ways, however, Crete benefited because Greek

refugees flooded into the island, resulting eventually in a creative renaissance. Painting, plays, poetry, all flourished and, indeed, the Cretan School of painting of the sixteenth and seventeenth centuries became famous throughout Europe. (The Cretan who became known as the painter El Greco made his way to Spain during that period.) Artists might be commissioned by convents to paint icons; for example, **Evgenia Trapezondiopoula**, a nun at the Convent of St John Mesambelitis, paid the balance of the fee for an icon by Francesco Kavertsas in market produce.

There is no evidence of women artists or writers, but they did inspire fine work and had plays written specially for them, either as a particular tribute or as suitable entertainment for delicate women in a louche age. Indeed, the creation of a necessary literary ambiguity, as well as the exploration of women's feelings, was part of the style's universal appeal. The famous heroic poem *Erotocretos* (probably written 1646; published 1715) is the only writing to have an educated (self-educated) heroine, Princess Arethousa, though the style of speech of women characters in plays would lead the audience to conclude that they were cultured. The houses of the nobility often possessed extensive libraries. Nuns provided elementary education, implying their own education.

A much later piece of Cretan literature, *The Cretan Weddings* (published 1871), has made it difficult to clarify the facts of the last major revolt against the Venetians – the Kandanoleon uprising of 1526–28 which took place in the region stretching from Canea (Chania) to Sphakia. George Kandanoleon, elected governor of an independent authority by the rebels, set up his headquarters at Meskla in the White Mountains, supported by Cretan families claiming descent from archontes such as the Pateros and Mousourios. The rebels collected taxes and administered the surrounding area.

For some reason, and at some stage – dates as well as facts are in dispute – Kandanoleon proposed to heal the breach by suggesting a marriage between his son Petros and **Sophia**, daughter of Francesco **Molino** (or Damolino), a Venetian noble who had an estate at nearby

Alikianos. Molino accepted, the betrothal took place, the marriage was set to go ahead. Hundreds of guests from both families turned up but, while the Cretans drank to their hearts content, the Venetians only feigned drunkenness. Troops summoned by Molino arrived, arrested the rebels and, thereafter, many were executed in different places, villages were razed, and women and children fled to caves in the mountains; some pregnant women were horribly murdered near Mournies in a later punitive raid.

Another source says that Molino proposed the marriage and that the wedding guests were slaughtered in their drunken stupor (all the women as well?). Names and dates do not always tie up and not everything can be true.

There certainly was a revolt around 1527, probably caused by taxes and administrative injustice. Kandanoleon was the leader, but the marriage may have been fictitious, even if the usual aftermath of a failed revolt was not. Rebels were executed, villages destroyed, inhabitants of other villages evicted and the villages left desolate. At least one whole clan was exiled and others put under indefinite suspicion. (Meskla and the environs will be visited in itinerary p. 276.)

In spite of this, tensions had begun to ease between Venetians and Cretans; from 1500, Cretans were able to hold official positions in the administration. There was another influx of Greek refugees in the mid-sixteenth century when families whose grandparents had fled Constantinople a century earlier had to flee Venetian Peloponnese as a result of continuing Veneto-Ottoman conflict. The Venetian authorities in Crete took advantage of the empty Lasithi Plateau and failures elsewhere in the grain harvest to settle many of the newcomers there.

Among the families was that of Francis **d'Anassi** who had two daughters, **Pallantia** and **Theokliti**. They had been mother superiors of convents in the Peloponnese and were, therefore, given 300 hectares of land on the plateau on which to build two religious houses.

The Kroustallenia had existed from at least 1241 but, when the plateau was forcibly evacuated in 1284, it fell into disrepair. Pallantia rebuilt it and became its mother superior (see itinerary p. 291). Traces of Theokliti's convent, if it was ever founded, seem to have disappeared.

In 1522, during a pirate raid on Ierapetra, many inhabitants were taken prisoner. As the sixteenth century progressed, such raids against Crete emanating from the Ottoman Empire increased. Piracy was by no means a new phenomenon in Venetian times; indeed, there is some evidence to suggest that Cretan harbours were used as slave entrepots in the fourteenth and fifteenth centuries and, in the sixteenth, thousands of Cretans were taken captive and sold in slave markets on the Barbary Coast.

Women living near the sea were vulnerable whatever their class; they had to be ready to take refuge at a moment's notice. A remarkable document of 1562 was found in a notarial register in Candia and used in *History of Crete* (Theochoris E. Detorakis, 1994) (the most easily found and comprehensive history for visitors to Crete):

Two years ago Turkish corsairs took captive the wife of George Tzabanis, son of Stergios, brother of me Konstantis Tzabanis, and the aforesaid George wishes to go and find and buy back his wife; but unable to afford this enterprise he has come to you, Ioannis Papadopoulos, of Nikolas, from the village of Malia, requesting that you give him sufficient money for him to go and recover his wife from the hands of the infidel; and you, Ioannis, wishing to help as much as you can, but not having enough ready money, gave him two gold rings, which you sold to Dimiris Diplaras for the sum of eleven gold ducats ... With this sum George, the brother of the aforementioned Konstantis Tzabanis went and bought back his wife, but on his return to Crete, both he and his wife were captured by Turk corsairs, and we no longer know where they are to be found ...

From the same source comes an inscription built into the church walls in the village of Skepasti, near Mylopotamos:

1592, the fifth indiction, March 3rd: the holy church of the All-holy Virgin was founded by commission of the priest Nikodimos of Tamaros whose wife was lost to him as a slave twenty-eight years old and came in 1600, the Christian Easter, March 23rd.

It is noteworthy that in neither case does the lost wife have a name, make of it what we will. The price of a beautiful woman in the slave market (and presumably to buy back by the family) was 80–100 ducats (a strong man was only 60); that of an old woman, 30–40 ducats. (It should be said, though, that Ottomans were by no means the only traders in Greek slaves: Christians in other parts of the Mediterranean were involved in the same trade.)

By 1644, Crete was seen as something of a Christian bastion against Ottoman incursion and the Ottomans sought war and conquest of the island. They used a pirate raid as a pretext. They accused the Venetians of attacking a Turkish ship on which one of the passengers was the Sultana. In fact, that was probably the name of the ship and not the status of the passenger, but the ploy worked.

The siege of Canea (Chania) by Ottoman forces began the following year. Women were fully involved in its defence, not only feeding the defenders, carting soil and digging graves, but fighting on the battlements of the fort beside the men. After two months, the town was forced to surrender; the remaining inhabitants were sold into slavery.

In 1646, Ottoman forces came ashore at Souda Bay – then in their hands – and plundered and burnt villages along the way to Rethymnon, in spite of orders to the contrary from their leadership hoping to win over the local population, some of whom had, over the years, shown signs of welcome. As the enemy approached Rethymnon, the authorities decided to evacuate women and children and old men, many of whom were already suffering from an epidemic of plague. Rosemary Bancroft-Marcus, using a literary source of the time, describes the departure:

Cowering under the whistling bullets, the women embraced their menfolk for the last time, and turned finally to the boats with their children and their pathetically small bundles of clothes. Terrified and weeping, their faces yellow and sickly, they pleaded with the boatmen to approach and let them embark, offering money for a place on board. They faced the sea knowing that they had left everything of their past lives behind — their homes, their possessions, their menfolk and their whole way of life. Many of them had probably never been in a boat before. Some were so wretchedly ill that they begged to be landed at Fraskia; there ... they died of a surfeit of water. The rest were taken to Irakleio and herded into arsenals as a temporary refuge.

When the refugees reached Candia (Herakleion), they were refused help – both because they were contagious and because the town was already full of refugees. They managed as best they could in the countryside, many of them dying. Those remaining in Rethymnon when it fell in 1647 were taken prisoner, without their babies, and those for whom there was no ransom were sold as slaves.

Ten of the most beautiful women and girls who were taken to Istanbul were presented to the Sultan for his harem at Topkapi. Among them was three-year-old **Evmenia Vergitzi** (or **Vorias**) (1843–1715), daughter of the village priest of the village of Kamariotis (south-west of Candia). At the age of four or five, she was married to Mehmet IV who had then just come to the throne, and was much the same age. She was his first, and favourite, wife, known as HH Mah-para Ummatallah Rabia Gul-Nuz (Spring Rose-water) and mother of two future Sultans (Mustapha II and Ahmet II ). She is buried in the Imperial Ottoman mausoleum in Istanbul. (Finding Evmenia's village in Crete was one of my best moment's of research in Crete; see itinerary p. 233.)

The Ottoman forces now controlled strategic parts of Crete and set about taking Candia. That siege was to last 20 years – the invaders resisted by strong walls, built with forced labour and still standing today, and the help of European mercenaries and international pressure. **Catherine of Braganza**, Queen of England, for example, involved herself, though failing to stir her husband, Charles II, to action. Meanwhile, much of the countryside, with many of its villages destroyed, came under Ottoman rule. There are accounts of men selling their wives and children and converting to Islam in the hopes of improving their lot.

In 1669, Candia finally capitulated; its citizens were given eight days to leave. The Venetian authorities did so taking their archives with them to Venice. Some upper class women had to be dragged to the boats by their menfolk because their sheltered lives had ill-prepared them for the unknown. Crete was to be under Ottoman rule until 1898.

# 12
## The Ottomans

### AD 1669–1898

The city of Candia became a very different place following the siege and the absorption of Crete into the Ottoman empire. The Ottomans now called it Kandye, the Cretans dubbed it Megalo Kastro, 'Great Fortress', in honour of its bravery. However, the American traveller Bayard Taylor, visiting it in 1857/58, suggests that educated Greeks in Crete and elsewhere restored the ancient name 'Heracleion'. Since different travellers use different names – foreigners' quotations well into the twentieth century persevere with Candia – for ease of recognition I shall now use, where appropriate, one of the current spellings, Herakleion.

Many of Herakleion's buildings had been destroyed and, although the city centre was soon patched up, the southern outskirts, particularly round the Fortetsa Hill near Knossos, remained strewn with rubble and human remains for some years. Most of Herakleion's inhabitants, Cretan and Venetian, had fled. They were replaced by Ottomans practising Islam. Churches, including San Marco, were turned into mosques. It became common, too, for Cretans to become, at least superficially, Muslim, mainly because it avoided the new poll tax and restrictions on property which affected male non-Muslims. Sometimes whole villages converted which meant that, in time, fewer Christians were shouldering a heavier tax load.

Crete (Ottoman name Kirit) was divided into three pashaliks – Kandye, Rethymnon and Khania – governed by pashas. Because Ottomans tended to be urban, they took over the main towns; Cretans now tended to live in the countryside. Those who refused to accept the new conditions increasingly took to the mountains.

Land which had belonged to Venetian nobles or leading Byzantine families was confiscated: it now belonged to the Sultan and was given to his military leaders; indeed, a strong military presence was a feature of the next 200 years. These large landowners were known as beys and they might also command a military garrison. The smaller landholdings, Venetian fiefs or lands of the Latin Church, were taken over by agas. Crete was run by agas and by janissaries who were former Christians from throughout the Ottoman Empire recruited by way of tribute into the Sultan's army. They had an unsavoury reputation. Cretans who converted to Islam found the military career thus open to them attractive. Cretan Christians were not only liable for tax but were attached to largely unsympathetic Ottoman landowners and harassed by janissaries; this harassment included sexual assaults on women.

The subjects of the Sultans who, from 1453, ruled their Empire from Constantinople and took over in Crete, are sometimes called Turks. Contemporaries loosely called the invaders Turks because the original marauders from the direction of Mongolia were Turkic people. But since the Empire extended by this time over the Middle East and what we loosely call the Balkans, including Greece, and by 1683 its forces were to reach the gates of Vienna, Ottomans seems more accurate. And, to them, Constantinople was Istanbul (Istanbul), though it retained its old name among Christians, and what the Ottomans called Khania retained its Venetian name Canea (I shall use, where appropriate, the more modern name and spelling Chania). By 1898, the Ottoman Empire was the 'sick man of Europe', much reduced, and Turkey and Turks become more appropriate names.

The change in the religious culture of the island affected many women. Ottoman men had often come without families. Mixed marriages were not officially allowed; in practice the incomers married Cretan Christians who were thus required to become Muslims. Often the husbands allowed their wives to continue practising Christianity.

Women could also approach the court on their own and convert, according to **Molly Greene** in *A Shared World: Christians and Moslems* *in the Early Mediterranean* (2000), thus gaining some personal liberty. Under Islamic law a Christian man could not be married to a Muslim woman, so a Christian woman, by converting to Islam, could dissolve her marriage. **Ayse Hanim**, for example, having divorced Michael by this means, married Ali b. Abdullah, probably also a convert and already a prospective partner. If such a convert woman did not remarry, she could gain control over her children. (Of course, a husband could obstruct any such plan by converting himself!)

On the whole, ties between converts to Islam and their relatives or members of their community who were still Christian remained strong; although there could be animosity, it was not automatic. And often the Greek culture of a Cretan wife predominated through wider family ties in a supposedly Muslim household. As Molly Greene concludes, harking back to Venetian times, it is possible

that Cretans were already accustomed to thinking in terms of a 'public' religion (Latin Christianity, Islam), traced through the male line, which brought certain concrete benefits, and a 'private' religion (Orthodox Christianity), which was maintained by the women of the family.

According to a French traveller, 60,000 Cretans had converted by 1699. Although when a whole village converted it was not uncommon for the Orthodox priest to be included, the Orthodox Church – which had regained its pre-eminence over the Latin with the change of regime – was, not surprisingly, unable to support the pragmatism of its flock. A woman marrying a Muslim and converting was not, according to the English traveller Dr Richard Pococke in 1739, 'admitted to the sacrament, till she is at the point of death, and must then renounce her husband'.

Some women found that it was not marriage they were offered by Muslim men. Post-war pressures and change of regime led to an upsurge of prostitution in the towns. Prostitutes were often women who had been raped by the invading troops and became, therefore, unmarriageable. There was another exploitative system which could also lead to prostitution. In spite of the strictures of the Koran, as the Pasha of Candia wrote in 1763,

... the Muslims take into their homes and maintain *kapatma* — or *pesleme* — women without the sanction of a lawful marriage who are selected from among the young girls of the Christians and, being exposed to adultery, leave their illegitimate infants in the doorways of the mosques and hamams [bath-houses] or abandon them in remote places, where they are either devoured by dogs or taken up by the reviled infidel and, having been transported to their churches, are then exposed to the eternal darkness of their faithless Christian religion ...

The Pasha's complaint was directed towards local imams (priests) who were accused of being responsible for such a state of affairs and were instructed to

Search and discover the houses of those who are unlawfully living with an adopted non-Muslim partner within the town, and all those who show a willingness to enter into marriage let them proceed to wed with proper sanctity, whether the partner is a second, third or fourth wife; for those women whom the man refuses to marry and who are in an interesting situation (ie pregnant), you must designate a sum for maintenance and return them to their guardians or relatives. Whichever women do not wish to marry, yet do not wish to stop their relations with the man, or have nowhere else to go and are wholly helpless, you must hand over to their priests ...

The Pasha's concern did not produce much result: the system continued causing social problems, particularly in Herakleion. The authorities did arrange some elementary form of social welfare, when it was established that a Muslim was the father of a child. The Christian girl **Margia**, for example, was awarded four paras daily in 1754 for every one of her children, of whom Kemfili Mehmet, an Islamised Cretan, was the father.

By 1739, when Pococke described Turkish women, perhaps he meant the daughters of a union between a Cretan woman and an Ottoman man: 'It is said the Turkish women, who veil, are more beautiful than the Christians.' The mystery of the veil no doubt added allure. He wrote of those who were still overtly Christian:

The Greek women do not cover their faces, but wear a muslin veil upon their heads, and bind up the hair in ribbands, and roll it round their heads, so as to make it a high dress; they tye their petticoats and aprons near as high as their armpits; and when in high dress, they wear a sort of short stays, adorned before with gold lace. The women never sit down to eat with the men that are not of the house, and though they are not so strict as the Turks, yet they rarely come into the room where any strangers are.

The observation about eating still holds true in some households.

The Oxford scholar Robert Pashley, travelling a century later, contradicts Pococke concerning appearance; he wrote in 1834:

There is scarcely any perceptible difference, to an eye neither practised nor skilful in observing articles of female apparel, between the dresses of Greek and Turkish ladies in this city. The Christian fair one conceals her charms from every eye, when she once leaves the interior of her husband's house, as completely as any of her Mohammedan neighbours. Before I was aware of this *Greek* concealment of the face, I was not a little surprised to find myself graciously regarded by a pair of eyes belonging, as I supposed, to some unknown Turkish lady, but which, as I afterwards found out, were those of my hostess. Her husband says that he thinks the custom even still more proper for a Greek's wife than for a Turk's; for if she did not observe it, she might attract the gaze of some true believer.

How a woman dressed may well have depended on class, where she was and what she was doing. Where the women who were involved in economic activity in Venetian times disappeared to can only be surmised.

Whatever damage had been inflicted on Crete's economy by 20 years of Venetian resistance to an Ottoman takeover and the emigration of richer inhabitants was partially repaired by both trade with the rest of the Empire and with Europe, in particular with France. A trade agreement was signed which led to an increase in demand for Cretan olive oil to be made into soap; this led, in turn, to an increase in the planting of olive trees and then to the setting up of workshops and eventually factories.

There is no evidence of women in workshops or factories, but olives were very much a part of women's lives, as were the silk and embroideries which were also sought after by the French. One traveller describes how, following a marriage ceremony, the bride visited the groom's mother to be told which piece of land or house was now hers, and how many olive trees. Olive groves were passed on through the generations and could be given as the dowry of an olive farmer's daughter.

The olive harvest was traditionally undertaken by women and children. Another English traveller (Captain Spratt, 1853) talks of meeting on the road a woman who parted with the words, 'and I am now going to some acquaintances and friends to beg for [from?] them a little bread till the time of the olive picking'.

A French consul (Hitier) based in Chania in the 1840s recounted how, at the busiest time of the harvest, women day-workers would be hired in large numbers under the strict surveillance of a man from the farm concerned. The harvester would be paid in kind, two-sevenths of the oil produced by the olives she gathered. She had to feed not only herself during that time but also the man who crushed her olives at the press; he in turn would carry her oil to the nearest town.

In the village of Kakotikhi in Sphakia, Pashley describes being surrounded by women when he started to make enquiries. 'I learnt', he wrote, 'that they come down here during the winter to gather olives, and that they have been so employed for five or six months.'

There is still a Cretan dialect word meaning women who gather the olives from the ground once the men have knocked them down (*masochtres*). Another word means, in general, to gather, but, used alone, to gather olives (*masono*). When in England you might strike up a conversation by saying 'Nice day, isn't it?', in Crete you would ask, 'Have you finished gathering your olives' (*epomasochsete*)? I am reliably informed that this ploy may be used by a young man wishing to get to know a young woman.

While women were largely responsible for the work of the olive harvest, at least one other woman greatly benefited, and

9. Cretan peasant woman, mid-19th century, from Pashley,
*Travels in Crete*

spread her largesse. Pashley, travelling to Perghe, a village east of
Rethymnon, noted:

There are about 1000 olive trees, which are the property of the Sultana ... the biennial
revenue obtained by the Sultana from this and three other villages, had reached
36,000 piastres at the outbreak of the Greek revolution [1821] ... the villagers
in each of these places used to cultivate all the Sultana's lands, and had half the
produce as their share. They enjoyed so many privileges and immunities, that their
condition could not be compared with that of any other rayas ... in return for all

these prerogatives, the consequence of there being some of the Sultana's property situated in the villages, their only obligation was to keep in repair the aqueduct of one of her mosques.

Most of the prosperity generated by trade benefited the mercantile community and towns, which were Ottoman dominated, and even so the ports were not maintained. Venetian roads had fallen into disrepair. Some sources suggest that because Cretans suffered so much under the Venetians there was some encouragement given to the Ottoman invaders in the seventeenth century. But that optimism was misplaced. Christian Cretans, particularly in the countryside where they predominated, also endured extortion, hardship and discrimination from the Ottomans. As under previous yokes, they began to fret at the chafing and react, nowhere more than in Sphakia where the first major revolt erupted in 1770.

The leader was Yannis Vlachos, otherwise known as Daskaloyannis (John the Teacher), a well-travelled shipowner and merchant with Russian connections. He was convinced by Catherine the Great's favourite Count Orlov that if the Cretans rose against the Ottomans they would receive help from Russia as part of its continuing conflict with the Ottoman Empire.

The Russians failed to appear; the Cretan rebels retreated and, before they could send their wives and children abroad, the Ottoman forces set upon them, massacring them or taking prisoners. Vlachos' wife was wounded and his two eldest daughters were captured.

Vlachos eventually gave himself up and, betrayed by the Ottomans with whom he had negotiated a truce, was flayed alive. His movement was crushed and Sphakia was devastated. Sources long disputed what happened to his daughters. A plausible outcome suggests that **Maria** was given in marriage to a Turkish bey, allowed to keep her religion and, after her husband's death, became a nun on the island of Tenos. **Anthusa's** fate only came to light, apparently, in 1939. Already married when she was captured, she was allowed to return to her husband, the cobbler Pakhynakis, as long as she stayed in Herakleion and never returned to Sphakia.

A more widespread and violent revolt coincided with the 1821 uprising in Greece which led eventually to freedom there. In Crete it took three years to crush the rebels and, during that time, many women were to die.

Once again the revolution broke out first in Sphakia; officially it was declared near Chania on 14 June 1821. Reprisals were immediate: a group of Muslims entered a convent at Korakies, near Akrotiri, on 19 June, raped and slaughtered the nuns, and left the convent burning, never to be re-established.

Churches, convents and monasteries and their inhabitants were a common target. Soon it was the turn of the Paliani Convent, the oldest in Crete, renowned at the time for its beautiful embroideries and its sacred myrtle tree. All but one of the nuns were murdered and the convent razed. The elderly **Parthenia** somehow escaped and afterwards raised funds to rebuild (see also pp. 133 and 139).

Whole areas of Crete and its villages were laid to waste and the people killed or sold into slavery. Later travellers often met women who had been made slaves at this time and somehow returned. The woman near Anogia who told Spratt that she was waiting for the olive harvest also told him that 'My husband was killed by the Turks; my four sons were taken from me to Alexandria, whither also I and my only daughter were taken and sold as slaves.' Her sons were still there but she had been bought by the Austrian consul at Candia and lived with him as a servant for seven years thereafter 'as recompense for the purchase money.' (See also itinerary p. 239.)

Her later fate was quite common: European travellers or consuls regarded it as a matter of good form to buy slave girls in order to release them. The best-documented story is of **Kalitza**, daughter of Alexandhros **Psarakis**, chief magistrate of Apodhulo in the Amari Valley.

In 1821, there was a plague in the village, so Kalitza's father placed her and her brother in the care of a woman living some way away.

Knowing that marauding Ottoman soldiers were nearing his village, he was reassured about his daughter's safety as the villagers took to the mountains. Unfortunately, an Ottoman straggler turned off the main route to gather herbs, saw the isolated cottage and forced entry. He carried off the woman and five children, including Kalitza and her brother.

At first Kalitza was purchased, with several other Cretan girls, for Mustapha Bey's harem in Cairo. But on the way there, the ship was captured by Greeks and taken to the island of Caso where the captives were released. Mustapha Bey sent a force against the island which retook the captives and transported them to Egypt. By 1924, Kalitza was in the slave market in Alexandria. There she was bought by the Scottish traveller and Egyptologist Robert Hay who married her in 1828 and, in 1829, returned with her to her village to the amazement and joy of all concerned. The house that Hay built for Kalitza's family in Apodhulo is described by later travellers; thereafter, the couple lived in Scotland.

Whenever possible, the inhabitants of an area would flee in advance of Ottoman troops and reprisals; they took to the mountains or to large caves, sometimes going deep into hillsides, which had traditionally served as refuges. This was all right if the caves remained undiscovered, but several ugly incidents took place when Ottoman forces learnt of hideouts.

In February 1823, Hassan Pasha, with a force of 16,000, trapped 2,700 Cretans, mainly women and children, in the Milatos cave near Neapoli. Fifteen days later, after being guaranteed safe passage, the refugees emerged; the men, mostly old, were massacred, the women and children sold into slavery (see itinerary p. 308).

In October 1823, 370 villagers, together with 30 or so armed men, cattle, and as many of their possessions and supplies as they could save, took refuge in the Melidoni cave (half-way between Rethymnon and Herakleion) where Minoans probably worshipped Eileithyia. Hussein Bey and his forces learnt of their sanctuary. The siege lasted three months during which the cave was constantly bombarded. At a certain stage a Cretan woman was sent in to negotiate but she was shot and her body thrown out. In frustration the Ottomans attempted to seal the entrance but their attacks continued to be repelled. So they filled the apertures with combustible material and set fire to it. All inside were asphyxiated (see itinerary p. 242).

Histories and guide books give the bare bones of the brutal events of Ottoman times but for a re-creation of what took place between 1821 and the next major uprising of 1866, you cannot do better than *The Life of Ismail Ferik Pasha* (1996) by the Crete-born writer Rhea Galanaki. It is a historical novel about a boy, Emmanuel Papadakis, who, in 1821, was kidnapped by Ottoman forces under Hassan Pasha during a raid on a cave, probably the Diktaian, up on the Lasithi Plateau (see itinerary p. 294).

Ismail was a real character about whom only the odd fact can be found mixed in with legend, but his fictionalised life story, from kidnap to bondage in Egypt, to general in the Egyptian army, and Minister of War returning to Crete in 1866, provides a most accessible insight into Crete and the Ottoman Empire of the time. Following the boy's kidnap, the fate of his beloved mother can only be imagined as he grows up in Egypt; he has three versions, of which these are two:

Unable to shut out his mother's image, he visualized her ... not as he had last seen her, but dressed in her Sunday best and wearing the double crown of her long tresses. In this guise, he was told, she had been taken to Constantinople as a slave and there ascended to heaven at the very moment she lifted the hem of her skirt to step across the landing-board to the marble quay that would lead her to some Turkish harem. In the same guise, it was said that on the first night of the attack she murdered the Albanian who abducted her from the cave; he attempted to rape her, never pausing to think that his newfound slave still loved her husband and children. The Albanian's blood dyed her silk dress black, and this explains how she was able to escape unnoticed from the enemy camp, from the frenzy of the blood-crazed soldiery.

In real life, most women who suffered between 1821 and 1824 were victims who were unable to do anything to help themselves. There was at least one known woman, however, who took the initiative. Rodanthe's story will be told, in as much detail as I have scavenged, in an itinerary devoted to her (see pp. 310–15). But she was a young woman from the village of Kritsa, just below the Lasithi Plateau, who, aged 23, was abducted by an Ottoman commander, not so much as a slave during conflict but because he saw the beautiful and educated daughter of the high priest of Mirabello and took a fancy to her. He carried her off to his headquarters from where she escaped and joined the partisans. Another woman, **Marigo Spiridopoula**, was still remembered in 1904 in the same area as having fought throughout 'the war' associated with 'the Revolution'; I am assuming this refers to 1821–24.

In 1824, after Cretans had suffered enormously from defeat and Ottoman reprisals, and about 60,000 had fled the island, the rebels of Sphakia surrendered. Some 1,500 inhabitants of their region had been killed. By late May the revolution was over and Crete became a supply base for Ottoman forces as the Sultan tried to stamp out revolution on the Greek mainland.

Trouble flared up again in 1825 and the rebels were for a while successful – 400 Muslim Cretans were besieged and then killed in a mosque at Neapoli (showing that barbarity was not one way (see also p. 147)), and an Ottoman force was defeated. But success was not to last.

In 1828 another revolt erupted but it came to an arbitrary end in January 1830 with the Protocol of London, negotiated by the British, which set up an independent Greek state but left Crete outside it. Ships belonging to the European Powers – who had no intention of allowing Crete to be part of Greece – arrived off Herakleion to impose order under a ceasefire that was supposed to benefit Christians and Muslims. Following further massacres and imprisonments, a group of citizens wrote, 'In the streets of the towns of Crete the daughters, sisters, women and beloved children of the Greek Cretans are sold like pieces of meat.'

The Protocol of London granted Crete to the Albanian-born viceroy of Egypt, Mehmet Ali, as payment for his services to the Sultan. The island was to remain under Egyptian domination, with a strong Albanian component, for ten years. Revolts were followed by reprisals and repression. It was during this period that Pashley visited Crete and he wrote of the village of Vithias, 'The only male inhabitant ... is a young Mohammedan ... The rest are all widows. In many places in Crete, the number of widows is large; and in one village of Lassithi they actually form the entire population.'

In 1841, Mehmet Ali turned against the Sultan, and the European Powers negotiated the Treaty of London under which Crete returned to the suzerainty of the Sultan. 1841–66 was a period of relative calm during which various Cretans and committees explored political strategies for the future, which was usually seen as union with independent Greece. The most interesting of these discussions for us was an unusual 'anti-revolutionary' movement which wished to promote an autonomous island state, independent of mainland Greece and under the protection of the British.

The force behind this idea, which was widely supported among the upper echelons, clergy and laity, was the teacher **Elizabeth Kontaxaki** (or **Vasilakopoula**). The British consuls in Chania who presumably gave Elizabeth encouragement in the 1860s were Frank Drummond Hay, there with his Spanish wife between 1863 and 1865, and Thomas Sandwith (1865–69).

It is thanks to the American traveller and writer Bayard Taylor who visited Crete in the late 1850s that we are able to get an interesting and informative view of this woman, unique in the Crete or Greece of her day. Taylor wrote in *Travels in Greece and Russia: With an Excursion to Crete* (1959) of his arrival in Chania:

In the evening, we paid a visit to Mademoiselle Kontaxaky, better known throughout the East as 'Elizabeth of Crete'. I have a letter to her from Mr Hill, in whose family she was educated. Her profound scholarship, wit, enthusiasm and energy are characteristics of the rarest kind among the Greek women of the present day, and have therefore given her a wide celebrity. Of course, her position is not entirely a pleasant one. While some of the Greeks are justly proud of her, others dislike and some fear her. Her will, talent and a certain diplomatic aptness give her considerable power and influence, the possession of which always excites jealousy and enmity in a Greek community. Consequently, she has many enemies, and is assailed at times by the meanest slanders and intrigues. She is about thirty years of age [in 1857], of a medium stature, and, with the exception of her lambent black eyes, there is nothing very striking in her appearance. She speaks English, Greek and French with almost equal fluency, and has the ancient Greek authors at her fingers' ends. She talks with great rapidity, ease, and with a rare clearness and sequence of ideas, in narration. I was interested at finding in her the same quickness and acuteness of mental perception for which the old Greeks were famous.

The Reverend Richard Hill and his wife Frances Mulligan had been sent to Athens by the American Episcopal Church in 1831. There they founded the American School for Girls, a charitable institution which trained generations of Greek schoolteachers. It is not clear where and when Elizabeth taught but she moved in many circles (see itinerary p. 264).

Education in Crete, most of which was under church auspices, had suffered since the revolt of 1821 but was given some impetus by the Egyptians and further developed under two Greek brothers who had returned home from exile in 1837. A school set up in Chania, with American money and with George Psaroudakis as headmaster, had 400 boys and 150 girls, with four men and two women teachers. It was shut down by the Ottoman authorities in 1843, though Psaroudakis taught elsewhere until 1851 and there were other girls' schools to be found in other towns. Wherever Elizabeth taught, nothing seems to have come of the movement whose main spurs were the hope of avoiding further violent confrontations with the Ottomans and the recognition that the European Powers would not countenance union with Greece. The next rebellion was to start in 1866.

There is something dispiriting about recounting another cycle of violence – a recurrence of Crete's fate over so many centuries. What long-term damage did it do to people, to women? The Paliani Convent which the nun Parthenia had raised the money to rebuild and reopen in 1826 with herself as abbess was once more destroyed. In charge at the time was **Agathangeli**, a shrewd and bold woman who had ensured that the convent provided a haven for resistance fighters – though that was not necessarily why it was destroyed (see pp. 127 and 139).

In September, the Ottoman army entered the nearby village of Hagios Mironas. Its women and children had taken refuge in the Sarchos cave (see itinerary p. 246). They were slaughtered. By 8 November, Ottoman forces had surrounded the great monastery of Arkadi further north. Inside were 300 armed rebels and 600 women and children. The besiegers managed to smash down the fortified entrance with cannon and prepared to rush the inner courts. At that, the defenders detonated the powder magazine and a huge explosion ripped the building apart, killing most of those inside and hundreds of attackers (see itinerary p. 242). The world outside Crete at last began to take notice of what was happening there: committees of support and letters of outrage from prominent people were to start a slow process leading up to 1913.

One of the next targets for Ottoman forces was the Lasithi Plateau, and this is where Rhea Galanaki's novel picks up the story again because Ismail Ferik Pasha, Lasithi-born and now Egypt's Minister of War, had arrived in Crete to take command of the Egyptian contingent of the Ottoman army. He reads the military reports and muses on his reactions:

There were loud complaints about the fighters' families wandering homeless and destitute, seeking refuge in mountain caves ... about the burning of villages, the loss of family property ... it was rumoured that the men often straggled off on their own in search of bread to feed their families up in the caves. Winter was closing in, and they would have a hard time of it in the mountains. ... I had no intention to harm them, but then they had no way of knowing what I had in mind; but they knew very well that one man alone, no matter how powerful, no matter if he commanded a whole army, could not exercise total control over his men.

Then he arrives up on the plateau with his forces: 'I took the same road I had walked along as a prisoner; only this time I was on horseback, riding with a mighty army ... among the raped women, the slaughtered men, the shackled, abducted children of this war, I would re-enact my family history.'

He has to watch the progress of his troops through his binoculars: 'The women and children were evacuating the plateau, and their loud lament mingled with the lowing of the animals plodding ahead with their loads.' When the fighting is over, he visits his home village of Psychro, and finds the house where he was born (see itinerary p. 294).

As a result of the adverse publicity that had reached the outside world after the destruction of the Arkadi Monastery, the Sultan was now persuaded by the Powers to adopt a policy of concession and conciliation.

What has gone unremarked in the reconstructions of Crete's history and, particularly as regards the intercession of the Powers, is the part probably played by Baroness von Schwartz. The only remnant of her existence is her abandoned house in the Chalepa district of Chania (see itinerary p. 267) and her account of her part tucked into her publication of the letters written to her by the Italian revolutionary Giuseppe Garibaldi. She became his mistress, probably in 1857, and, for 20 years thereafter, remained his friend, spy, translator, literary agent, publicist and foster mother to his illegitimate daughter.

**Mary Espérance Kalm Brandt** was born in London in 1818, the daughter of a Hamburg banker resident there. (Her mother was Susanne Stephanie Sylvestre.) Although Espérance spent little time in England over the next 81 years – living in Italy, Germany, Greece, Crete and Switzerland – she retained British nationality. Her first husband was a banker cousin who made her unhappy and committed suicide, her second (1842) was the banker Baron Ferdinand von Schwartz. They travelled widely and adventurously, using her eight languages, and she became a writer, adopting the penname Elpis Melena – the Greek for Hope (Espérance) Black (Schwartz). All her books, some of which are in my bibliography, use that name.

Her marriage was dissolved in 1854 and she met Garibaldi three years later. In 1866 (five years after Italian Unification), the affair over, she left for Crete – her reason for choosing the island unclear. She arrived just before the uprising began. In her publication of her letters from Garibaldi, she adds linking passages, often to explain a remark of his; thus, she writes: 'Shortly after my settlement in Crete, there broke out in that island the great war of independence, which lasted three years. Ignorant of the Cretan character as a whole, I interested myself strongly on behalf of the insurgents, risking my life for them on different occasions.'

Garibaldi replied on 5 August: 'Speranza Amatissima, You have devoted your life to the freeing of nations. Such work well becomes you, noble soul.' A little later, she detailed the part she played:

As long as possible, accompanied by the Abbot of a monastery, I attended secret meetings of the insurgents in the mountains, and, with another object, I made long excursions about the island. But after having been made prisoner at Cape Grabusa, whence I was fortunate enough to escape from the hands of Turkish soldiers, and having received at Candia an official letter from Ismail Pasha, Governor General of the island, forbidding me to take a step out of the capital or to return to Canea by land, I thought myself lucky in obtaining a small sailing boat wherewith to pass the eighty miles of coastline as far as Khalepa. Almost a prisoner in my little house, I confided to my pen the task of publishing throughout Europe the sufferings of the Cretans, and the injustices of which they were victims. I printed my little work, *The Isle of Crete Under Ottoman Rule* [in German], and wrote several articles for the German newspapers; and the Russian and American consuls, prevented by their official position from overtly supporting the insurrection, were very glad to find in me a medium for the diffusion of their own ideas by the press of different countries.

What she was doing at barren and unpopulated Cape Grabusa (Gramvousa), to the far west, she leaves the reader to imagine. This was long before the days of women travellers to Crete. Back in Chalepa, she became ill and barely noticed the bullets whistling through her vineyard and past her windows. She would not have roused herself

... had not the Cretan leaders themselves begged me to be their interceder with Mr Gladstone. This confidential mission made me leave my bed, and set out by boat for Syria at the end of December in order to reach Rome in time to meet the great English statesman there before he returned to give parliament the benefit of his powerful voice.

William Ewart Gladstone had, until earlier that year and the fall of the government, been Chancellor of the Exchequer and Leader of the House of Commons – a man of great influence and a renowned orator always on the side of the Eastern Christians. His speech on behalf of the Greeks of 30 July 1867 is well-known, and in 1897 he was to produce a spirited pamphlet on the freedom of Crete. Although some of Elpis Melena's writing about Garibaldi has been questioned, and she was obviously something of a romantic, her efforts for Crete were more widely recognised in correspondence of the day, as the itinerary will show.

Following intercession by the Powers, a general amnesty was granted in 1867 and a form of limited autonomy; a General Assembly was established. However, while 250,000 or so Christians had 38 members in it, 70,000 Muslims had 36. Conditions did not markedly improve for Cretans.

Not all Ottoman pashas were obstructive, though, and Reuf Pasha made some obvious improvements. This is of particular interest to us because they were remarked upon by the only woman traveller to Crete in the nineteenth century whose account I have been able to find.

The English artist **Mary Walker** gives a positive impression of the Crete she visited twice in the 1870s and 1880s – one visit for as long as six weeks. (I have had to guess when she was there from one or two hints she drops.) She had lived in Constantinople since 1855; by the time she published her book – *Eastern Life and Scenery*, in 1886, she had been there 30 years and gained some acclaim as the portraitist of high-class Turkish women, including the Sultan's favourites, and the illustrator of friends' accounts of their travels. She also taught at the Turkish girls' school established in 1870 near the Yerebatan cistern.

She was obviously familiar with, and apparently sympathetic towards, Turkish culture and, of course, it was not her country that was under Ottoman domination. She wrote, 'Canea owes much of its present day comfort and prosperity to Raouf Pasha who has been three times Vali, or Governor, of the island, where his gentle, conciliatory rule gained him universal goodwill.' But Mary's two chapters on Crete are much more than a whitewash of Ottoman occupation.

There were no hotels, so she stayed in a convent in Chania, and she gives us a marvellously evocative view of the multicultural city as she looks out of her window into the street below; she starts first thing in the morning:

On the opposite side of the street stands a well-built house. The ground floor is divided into three shops – a chemist's, a grocer's and a small cafe. The first floor stands back in the shadow of a broad balcony, but towards seven o'clock a glass door opens, and the lady of the house, a Greek, comes out and leans upon the balustrade. She wears a French dressing-gown, and her splendid hair falls in thick braids upon her shoulders, whilst she slowly sips her black coffee, indifferent to the early studies of little hands that are playing, somewhere in the background, an air from 'Norma' followed by 'La Mère Angot', quite out of time and with numerous false notes.

A little later, the city wakes up:

The population of Canea is by this time in movement. The Arab women flit by enveloped in white winding-sheets; the negresses display their gay colouring amid their floating draperies; the Turk wears the turban or the fez, according to his preference for ancient or modern customs; coaches roll noisily over the stones; there are equipages and even street carriages at Canea.

A chant which reaches us from the neighbouring mosque announces the passage of a Mussulman funeral. This procession differs in many respects from those at Constantinople; they seem to have preserved here some customs of the Christian rite – the coffin is preceded by two boys carrying incense, and followed by a great crowd of Greeks and of Mussulman Cretans. The bier is covered with red silk veils and gauze, above the usual shawls, and a garland of artificial flowers, mixed with gold, surrounds the pointed end which marks the head and is carried forwards. It is a woman's funeral, and while it passes a monotonous chant is kept up by the funeral train.

Even two centuries after the first Christian women had converted to Islam, the two religions and communities could obviously still exist side by side in one person's life, and death.

Mary Walker also notes that other women's traditions continue strongly – traditions that probably date back to Minoan times:

The women, both Mussulman and Christian, spin and weave a strong cloth, as well as very handsome many-coloured striped coverlets of woollen or cotton. In the districts removed from European innovations, some of the old costumes may still be found: women's garments, richly embroidered in colours, the designs bearing evident traces of Venetian taste and style; but these curious relics of high-art needlework are not much in favour with the Cretan dames, who prefer any modern tinsel to the heavy splendours of their grandmothers. Mr Sandwith, lately H.B.M Consul in Crete, made, during his long residence in the island, a very large and beautiful collection of these ancient embroideries, bought at a very high price, for the Cretan peasant woman knows how to make a large profit on her 'antiquities' if she sets small store by them as wearing apparel.

Those embroideries are even more sought after today and, unfortunately, way beyond the normal purse to buy, as you can find in a backstreet of Chania.

I have quoted at some length from Mary Walker (and quote from her again in two itineraries, see pp. 265, 270 and 273), not only because she gives us an unparalleled view of late nineteenth century Crete in the only woman traveller's account available but also because her book is miserably rare. Another disappointment is that I can find no evidence of her having drawn or painted during her visits to Crete. But she did exhibit, including at the Paris Salon in 1867 and the Imperial School of Fine Arts in the Istanbul suburb of Tarabaya in 1880.

Did Mary Walker visit Crete before or after the rebellion of 1878? The violence was followed by the Chalepa Agreement. By this, not only were Greeks to outnumber Muslims in the Assembly, but a Christian governor was appointed. The most striking feature for women was the setting up of Educational Associations and, in 1881, the passing of an Education Bill by the Assembly. Under it education was made compulsory for both sexes.

That was a real advance: in 1870, in the region of Lasithi, 1,456 boys and 68 girls attended school. So the census figures on literacy in 1881 are hardly surprising; they show that 97 per cent of Christian women were illiterate (82 per cent of men); for Muslims it was 88 per cent for women (81 per cent for men). This discrepancy between religious groups was probably because Muslims lived mostly in towns.

Yet another rebellion broke out in 1895 – the last violent (as opposed to political) confrontation. In 1897, a village to the south of Herakleion came under attack. It's Turkish name, Kanli Kastelli ('Bloody Castle'), dated from a previous Ottoman attack in 1647 when many had died on both sides. This hillside town, probably inhabited in Early Minoan times, and which the Venetians had hoped to turn into a new capital, was dominated by a Venetian fortress. From there, 100 men and 200 women with forty rifles between them held out against an Ottoman army of 4,000. Today the town is known as Prophitis Ilias (see itinerary p. 227). Not far to the west is the Paliani Convent of which, in 1898, the abbess was **Dionysia**. It was she who experienced the Ottoman raid on the convent that followed those of 1821 and 1866 (see pp. 127 and 133).

But that same year, the Great Powers took the opportunity of negotiations between mainland Greece and the remains of the

Ottoman Empire – which they had contrived, successfully, to weaken – to impose a settlement on Crete. It was granted autonomy under Ottoman suzerainty, with a Greek High Commissioner, the King's son, Prince George. From this settlement, Crete's unification with Greece was only a matter of time (15 years).

# 13
## Modern Times

### AD 1898–1947

The last Ottoman troops left Crete on 2 November 1898. By then the island was already under the military control of the four Great Powers: eastern Crete under the French, Herakleion under the British, Rethymnon under the Russians, western Crete under the Italians, and Chania under the joint control of all four. Prince George arrived as High Commissioner on 9 December.

Britain's part in these arrangements may well have been influenced by information received by **Queen Victoria** from her eldest daughter, **Victoria, Empress of Germany**. Following the marriage of her daughter Sophie to the future King of Greece in 1889, the Empress visited Athens and also kept in close touch with developments. Her published letters show that she passed on strong opinions. Sailing back from Athens in June 1896, for example, she wrote of reactions to the uprising that started in Crete the previous year:

When I left the thought of Crete was uppermost in everyone's mind. The situation is a very sad and painful one. Of course I heard most from foreigners and not from Greeks who are very cautious and reticent about it. Public opinion was much divided as to the course the Greek Government had taken. Many thought that Greece had lost her opportunity for *ever*, as she sent *no* ships to protect *her* subjects at such a terrible moment while other Powers did! The Cretans themselves are furious with the Greeks and say they have abandoned them in the hour of need and changed and left them at the mercy of the enemy!! This is really very hard. There were three Greek iron-clads lying in Phalesan Harbour quite ready to go with their steam up – provisions on board for a fortnight, ammunition and all, and waiting for orders. In order to please the Great Powers and to show how little the Greek Government wishes to encourage a rising in the Island the ships were not sent!! Of course the newspapers abused the Government, while it was really a sacrifice on their part which is very hard to take ... Bulgaria was freed the other day – the rest of Greece was freed 60 years ago. Italy has been liberated from a far less cruel monster. Why should not a movement be favoured of saving these wretched people from a dominion which is really quite dreadful.

And, in August that year: 'I am glad to see that most other European Powers are coming round to Lord Salisbury's view with regard to Crete ...' By September she was able to note: 'Crete thank God is in a better state. The Greeks will never forget England's kindness and I hear their gratitude is great. What they feel towards the other Powers I had rather not say; after all it is but too natural.' There were still hurdles to be jumped, and the Empress comments on them and quotes passages from Sophie's letters to her in 1897 and 1898.

From the period of the Great Powers emerge two women in Crete with names, and another without. The little we know of them gives an impression of life in that strange half-light period. The British administration in Herakleion introduced English law; which M.N. Elliadi suggests resulted in the following case:

A person having discovered that his servant was stealing from him, he discharged her without giving notice to the police, with the result that, to the great astonishment of all, he was fined, the reason being that though he rid himself of her, she was thus allowed to continue her bad practice elsewhere, whereas a good citizen should not only be a guardian of his own property, but also that of others.

A beneficent principle, no doubt, but not part of English law, then or since.

The British suffragette **Jane Esdon Brailsford** (née Malloch, 1874–1937) went immediately from her marriage to Henry Bailsford in September 1898 to Crete where he was serving as foreign correspondent for the *Manchester Guardian*. She had studied Greek and philosophy at Glasgow University and had aspirations as a writer but there is, unfortunately, no evidence that she wrote anything about her time in Crete. The novel she is known to have been writing there was never published. It may well be that she helped her husband, as relief agent for the Grosvenor House Committee, to distribute barley to Christian inhabitants; certainly, when the couple were later sent to Macedonia she was formally involved in relief work there. I mention her because she is so early a British woman in Crete and it may well be that a diary or letters exist, waiting to be uncovered. Of her life in Chania, a letter from her husband of 29 October gives an idea:

We drink every day 'Vins des Balkans' at lunch and dinner, we dine with the Russian admiral whenever we get a chance, and as a last resort we sit on our balcony ... we are making our first essay in house-keeping under quaint conditions – a little thin house of five rooms – two storeys – very commodious for rats & mice – no carpets no fires, the minimum of chairs and tables, but what compensates for everything a view from all our many windows which would busy a landscape painter for a year. There are snow capped mountains from one window, a valley clad with olive groves from a second, the distant town with Venetian ramparts & Turkish minarets from a third, & then above all the sea, sometimes like glass & sky blue, sometimes storm-tossed, white & green – throw in an island, five distinct ranges of hills, two old castles, & still it is short of our view.

**Mme Hortense** (Adeline Guitar? c. 1863–1938) was a Frenchwoman from Provence whom more than one writer has written about (with conflicting details). At the age of 16 she was lured to the brothels of Marseilles. In 1897, in her thirties, she travelled to Crete where the ships of the Great Powers lay off Souda Bay. There she was taken up first by the Russian Admiral Andreyev. But so irresistible were her charms that she was soon entertaining the other admirals too. She is said to have distinguished them by the scents which clung to her in the morning – a rather nice, role-reversal conceit: 'Cologne for the Englishman, violet for the Frenchman, musk for the Russian and patchouli for the Italian.' They drank champagne from her slipper, from between her breasts, and from her navel. As she was rowed ashore from an admiral's ship in the morning, a salute would be fired (see itinerary p. 291). But when the admirals and their fleet left,

Mme Hortense went to ground, probably in the brothels of Chania. We shall meet her again (see pp. 149, 244 and 264).

With the departure of the admirals and the rolling up of the red carpet, reality set in for Prince George. (Marie Bonaparte, his wife from 1907 and a later visitor to Crete, might have smoothed his path.) Initially the island was full of hope as the first government was set up with 138 Christian and 50 Muslims elected to the Assembly. The first Cretan constitution of April 1899 made free education for girls and boys compulsory. In the year 1899–90, there were 35,844 pupils at elementary school. High schools with three classes were set up for girls in Chania, Rethymnon and Neapoli, and a girls' school with five classes in Herakleion.

Important from our point of view, too, was the introduction, in 1900, of archaeological surveys of Minoan sites and civilisation, the giving of permission to foreigners to start excavating, and the setting up of an archaeological museum which ensured that their finds would remain in Crete. Before that formalisation, there was already scope for foreigners to take advantage of the changing situation. Arthur Evans was very early on the scene, not just assessing sites but also gathering the beginnings of his collection that now graces the Ashmolean Museum in Oxford. The inspiration for his great work, epitomised by Knossos, was the garnering of stone seals. In 1895, he wrote that 'women called them "milk stones" and wore them round their necks as charms of great virtue'. With whetted appetite, he

therefore made a house-to-house visitation in the villages, and by one means or another prevailed on many of the women to display their talismans. I soon discovered that ladies of a certain age were not altogether averse to parting with their 'milk-stones' for a consideration, but with the younger women it was a more delicate business. In some cases I succeeded in swapping stones of smaller archaeological value, the lactiferous qualities of which, however, I could safely guarantee. But not unfrequently all permission was useless, and the only reply was, 'I would not sell it for ten pounds! Don't you see my baby?'

On the broader political front, there was soon upset; after all, Crete's political status had been imposed by the Great Powers on Turkey,

Greece and Crete. In 1905, Eleftherios Venizelos, who had resigned as Minister of Justice in 1901, started a revolt at Theriso (the home town of his mother; see p. 275). The rebels declared union with Greece and set up a government there in the White Mountains. Prince George resigned in 1906 and left Crete. By 1913 Venizelos who had, meanwhile, become Prime Minister of Greece in 1910, had won the day. On 14 February 1914, the flags of the Great Powers and Turkey were lowered from the walls of the fort at Souda Bay. The island was now part of Greece – a status for which many had given their blood.

In some ways, Crete was to change quickly, in others to remain surprisingly the same. It became possible for foreign women to visit almost as a matter of course, as will be emphasised in the chapter that follows. Others not travelling for their work also began to arrive. We have already met Ellen Bosanquet: her husband, Director of the British School at Athens, wrote to her from Palaikastro where he excavated the Hymn to Zeus while she remained with her children on the mainland (see pp. 79, 165 and 368). But Ellen did make brief forays to Crete, starting in 1904, and included glimpses of them in *Days in Attica* (1914). It was still not easy to travel internally, however; indeed, not much had changed since Mary Walker was there 20 or so years earlier. Ellen describes how

Travel in Crete needs little preparation. Although it is real travel (not a mere committing of yourself to the charge of railway and hotel officials) it brings small hardship and much delight. Except at the coast towns, Canea, Retimo, Candia, Sitia, there is no regular inn. In a village of any size hospitality is offered by some well-to-do peasant, who is probably pleased at the novelty of the visit and prides himself on making lavish entertainment.

... In one week we were the guests of a bishop, an abbot, an officer of gendarmerie, and a cheesemonger. In each case we were treated so hospitably that it disturbed us to reflect on the expense and trouble to which our hosts had put themselves and for which we could offer no immediate recompense.

And the towns were little changed physically:

The Candia of to-day still looks like a Turkish town, though a few modern 'European' buildings are rising. One notes with sadness that new houses imitate those of modern Athens and forsake the pleasant courtyard style so appropriate to a hot climate. A European house has its best face to the street; a Moslem's house turns its back to the public. A passer-by would hardly guess at the jars of growing flowers, the fountains, fruit trees, and courts of inlaid pebbles that wait behind the closed doors in those blank, high walls.

... In spring a pervasive smell of orange blossom tells of the gardens hidden behind the walls. Occasionally, a Moslem woman in a black veil flits along, like a black bundle, from one door to another. The sombre effect of the street is heightened by her featureless humanity. It is remarkable how seldom one sees women in the main streets of Candia. The Christian women seem even more home-keeping than the Moslems who have the protection of the veil. 'Walking across the market-place in Candia feels like going into the Union without your brother,' so I once heard an English girl describe her impression of the Moslem atmosphere in the town.

One has to assume that the English girl was one of our scholars – if only one knew who!

Emilia De Sanctis Rosmini (see p. 166) expressed herself more strongly at the first sight of Crete's women, this time in Chania in 1910. Her husband, the archaeologist Gaetano De Sanctis, had been invited to join the Italian dig at Phaistos and she was along for the ride. She exploded in *Dalla Canea a Tripoli* (*From Chania to Tripoli*, 1912):

The Turkish women of Crete are enclosed in a circle of slavery much tighter than that which reduces their sisters of the Bosphoros, slavery of which the outer manifestation is the robe, nearly always black, which clumsily hides their shape like a sack of the brotherhood, the black mantle which hugs the head like a nun's wimple, descending to their thighs, and then the thickest veil which completely covers the face. But that veil is not enough for the jealous obscurantism of Turkish husbands. Why, to better hide the features of these wretched women, they are armed with a little black umbrella that is always open.

We will meet Emilia again in the itinerary that includes Phaistos (see p. 249).

Arthur Evans' 21-year-old half-sister Joan (see p. 166) visited Crete just before going up to Oxford and just before the First World War. She noted the same phenomenon more phlegmatically in her memoirs, *Prelude and Fugue* (1964):

Candia in the spring of 1914 was my first experience of a Mohammedan city, unvisited by tourists. My mother busied herself making notes in the Museum, and Nannie and I explored the town. We were conscious at first of being more looked at than usual, and realized, about the second day, that we were to all intents and purposes the only unveiled women about the streets. Christian ladies stayed at home, or came out discreetly at dusk to pay calls on their neighbours; we did not see them. The rest were Mohammedans, and veiled. Everyone was courteous to us; the Imams showed us their mosques, and we had a strange shock in seeing that one of them was of medieval Gothic and had once been a Christian church.

Not much appeared to have altered since the political upheaval of 1898, but in the countryside change was less subtle: Arthur Evans talked to his muleteer while prospecting archaeological sites in 1898 and learnt how he had helped rescue some Muslim women and children from Christians. Leaving Arthur Evans and Knossos two years later, Harriet Boyd noted:

Our first day's ride took us over a Veneto-Turkish high road that serves several villages, many of which we found utterly ruined, about an equal number of Mohammedan villages burned by Christians, and of Christian villages burned by Mohammedans in the insurrections that had ended only two years before our visit.

There are more details of what took place at Etia, near Siteia; Charles Currelly, later excavating at Palaikastro, told how

The Mohammedans were unsuspecting, and had no watch; when they heard the first volley fired they sprang up in total darkness, of course, as their little lamps are difficult things to light. Parents grabbed their children and what weapons they could find, and all ran to the mosque.

Once assembled there, they found themselves very badly armed, and therefore called for a parley: they offered, in return for the sparing of their lives, to march away leaving behind them everything they possessed — their fields, their animals, their implements and their household gear — everything but what they had on their backs. These terms were accepted, and our villagers swore on the Gospels that they would be truly carried out; but they demanded that all arms should be passed through the mosque windows so that the Mohammedans, when they came out would be completely unarmed. The weapons were handed over, and the Mohammedans were told to come out and form a line to march away. They came out and drew up in line, the mothers with their babies, the old people helping with the children, and the men carrying some of the smaller ones. As soon as they were well in line, our people let loose with their new guns and killed them all except one little girl, who ran out from the line towards the Christians. A small boy, who had followed his relatives to the Mohammedan village, tripped her and threw his dark cloak over her, and the little girl was wise enough to lie hidden till all was over.

Not surprisingly, Muslims from the countryside began to flee in ever larger numbers; meanwhile Christians were returning from exile. This movement of populations was to gather further momentum.

Conflict had often flared between Greece and Turkey following Greek independence in 1832. Between 1920 and 1922, Greece sought to reconstitute the Byzantine Empire with its capital at Constantinople by encroachments onto the Turkish mainland. It ended in disaster – the sacking of Smyrna, the Greek City on the coast of Asia Minor. The conflict was brought to an end by the Treaty of Lausanne of 1923. Under this there was to be a compulsory exchange of populations. Greeks fleeing Asia Minor needed a home and, for many of them that was to be Crete. But it also meant those Greeks settled in Turkey having to leave and the forced repatriation of Muslims from Crete, many of them originally wholly or partly of Cretan stock.

This population exchange may have been joyful for some, but was full of incomprehension, heartbreak, and bitterness for others as they fled, watching incomers taking over their homes, property and businesses. The writer **Elli Alexiou** was born in Herakleion in

1898 (d.1988). One of her short stories, 'The Fountain of Brahim-Baba', has been translated into English for the anthology *Greece: A Traveller's Literary Companion* (1997). It is set in Thrace, on the mainland, at this time of forced population exchange, but it is written in the first person and it is hard to believe that she did not have her birthplace in the back of her mind (see also p. 194). The narrator introduces the historic moment:

Not much time went by after that, when the order was issued for all the Turks in our area to move to Turkey and the Greeks from there to move here. At first no one could believe it. Such a thing was unimaginable. The newspapers wrote all about it, over and over again, in large striking headlines, and the Turks and Greeks read it together, gathered here and there, on the street corners and in coffee-houses. But the newspapers just write whatever they want ...! Things like that can't happen. Can you just lift up a whole people, push them out of their homes, uproot them from their own land? Are they a kind of bundle you just pick up and dump somewhere else? You can draw off oil when it's mixed with water, they said; but you can't separate milk from water. Because after so many years of living with one another they'd grown together through all kinds of bonds, businesses, buying and selling, friendship. They were like two different plants that you raise in the same flower box, and for all that each feels foreign to the other, under the soil their roots have become intertwined and likewise their branches above ground.

But it was true, and Elli Alexiou shows the effect on the women of both communities, those Muslims leaving, and those Christians left behind, with great skill and compassion.

One of the strangest revelations during the population exchange came in Rethymnon where Fatma, an attendant in the Turkish baths, escaped extradition. It was not surprising for it was the Provençale, Mme Hortense, now aged 60. Perhaps, after years in the brothels of Chania, age had forced another change on her; long gone were the days when she had entranced four admirals (see p. 143). On her deathbed (in 1938, perhaps in Ierapetra), Mme Hortense was attended by a priest who is said to have later pronounced: 'She was a saint ... I tell you. I do not know whether she sinned in her youth

... But I swear on the cross of my office that she lived a saintly life during her last years and died a saint, having done so much good to other people.' The priest was obviously Greek Orthodox because he was married; his wife, **Amalia Tzovalakis**, considered Mme Hortense her bosom friend.

Some 30,000 Muslims left Crete; around 3,352 Muslim-owned houses were made over to the new arrivals. And such largesse contained the seeds of dissension because 200 or so years earlier Muslims had taken the best property, and now newcomers, Greek Christians though they were, benefited, rather than those families who had stuck it out. But in 1930 the sequestrated properties on both sides were transferred to the two national governments under the Ankara Convention.

To travel in Crete, as a group of French yachtswomen sailing through the Aegean did in 1929, was to have no conception of all this upheaval. We shall meet two of them, Marthe Oulié and Hermine de Saussure, excavating at Mallia in the mid-1920s (see p. 167 and itinerary p. 304), but, of their rambles on the island, Marthe wrote in the *National Geographic Magazine*:

Whenever we arrived in a village young girls in white fichus came to take us by the hand and escort us to their homes. Outside the houses we often saw picturesquely clad tailors at work.

Let us enter one of these houses.

Through a door cut into a high wall of stone, we enter a small courtyard, where we find a sheep whose wool is later to be woven by the women of the household. A second and lower door opens into a large room with an arch separating it into two. This is the *kamaros-piti*, where the family eats, sleeps, and works.

In a corner is a hearth where, upon a few large stones, a fire of boughs is burning. A bed, usually covered with embroidery, and weaving paraphernalia may be observed.

All around the room are photographs of young couples, with the man always seated and the woman standing ...

During the pleasant months of the year the family sleeps on the flat roof of the house. Here, too, the cotton crop and the nuts and almonds are dried.

By the 1930s, the old lace and embroideries for which Crete was famous were said to have been bought up by speculators. Those wishing to buy modern examples then of work executed by 'young Cretan girls' were directed towards the 'Patriotic Institute' in Herakleion, or an 'establishment under the management of **Mrs Damberghi**, an English lady'. Both of these were close to the museum. And those designs came from Knossos and represented a revival of Minoan art and a flourishing of Cretan nationalism. By then, too, **Mme Calucci** had an establishment selling Cretan embroideries in Athens. She was originally from Crete, had studied art in London, and was responsible for a resurgence of the craft in Crete. The arts of weaving, lace making and embroidery are still passed on from mother to daughter (see pp. 247 and 285).

By the start of the Second World War, Greece had a fascist government, though it also had ties to the Allies. Life for its people was to be very difficult for many years to come, including long after the end of the war. Crete was to share much of that grief but also to experience some differences.

In March 1941, the Germans invaded Greece as part of their campaign to occupy the Balkans. In Athens were two Englishwomen who were to find themselves in Crete during the war. **Mary Wynn Thomas** had been an undergraduate at St Hilda's College, Oxford, 1929–32. Her studies included classics and archaeology and a scholarship took her to Athens where, at the British School (of archaeology), she became friendly with Mercy Money-Coutts and Edith Eccles who were to be part of both Crete's war and whom we continually meet in its archaeological history. Mary worked with Aurel Stein at the British Museum, 1934–35, and then at the Victoria and Albert, 1936–38. Her marriage to Robin Burn in 1938 took her to Athens in 1940 when he was appointed first British Council representative to Greece. They arrived in Athens as the Germans invaded the Netherlands, and Mary began cipher work first for the British Embassy and then for the Royal Air Force. In April, the British community started to evacuate Athens. Mary and Robin gave up their allotted places to their Greek teacher and his Jewish wife, and a little later left on a Polish cargo ship which was saved from being bombed because it carried, too, some German prisoners.

Churchill having announced that 'Crete will be held', the couple jumped ship at Souda Bay so that Robin could keep the British Institute open in Herakleion. As Mary was to write for St Hilda's *Report and Chronicle* (1996–7):

We made our way to Chania (Canea) and found the British Brigade HQ. A major, whom we saw, did not think much of two civilians who had slept in coal dust, but he brightened when we said that we could cipher. His own cipher staff had not had their boots off for forty eight hours. We were welcomed into the office, a windowless cellar with a sand floor, a trestle table and deck chairs. The electric light was poor and, in any case, went out in air raids so we came to depend on a hurricane lamp. We were given tin helmets and ate in the army mess. A soldier told me he had never seen a woman so far up the line. Greek women clearly did not count. For two days we manned the Brigade cipher office while the army staff had a well earned rest. On one occasion we were given time off for a swim, as we had had no baths for some time; a German plane flew over us at a cliff-top height and for a split second I saw the pilot's face. His bombs fell in the sea.

In her report for 1973–74, giving a slightly different slant to her life, Mary remarked that 'I felt very conspicuous in a cotton frock and a tin helmet amongst all the soldiers'. The couple stayed in Chania for three weeks, but when the Allies knew that there was to be a German paratroop invasion, they were ordered to leave, and to be at Souda Bay to join a Sunderland flying boat to Alexandria, and so to Cairo and the British General HQ Middle East. They were to return briefly to Crete in 1945, as we shall see.

The German parachute drop into Crete of May 1941 was to have even more significance for **Joanna Stavridi** (1903–1976). She was the daughter of Sir John Stavridi, Chairman of the Ionian Bank in London, and his wife Anina Olga Valieri. Dilys Powell describes Joanna in 1939 as 'a tall, dark, deep-voiced girl in her early thirties who had not yet found her path in life'. But she did hope to be an artist. At the outbreak of war, she volunteered as a nurse and two months later was on her way to Athens to train at the Red Cross hospital. She had found her vocation.

When the Allies evacuated the mainland, she left with the British Embassy staff on a yacht that was bombed and sank. The survivors reached a deserted island in the Cyclades and Joanna tended the injured. The party eventually made their way to Crete where boatloads of troops, Greek and Commonwealth, were retreating from the mainland. Joanna was assigned, as matron, to the Seventh General Hospital between Chania and Maleme – a Red Cross hospital in a tent (see itinerary p. 281).

There were no other women nurses and she was not allowed to eat with the other hospital staff. Eating on a tray in her room was not to last because the hospital was in the track of the enemy bombers which started to soften up Crete ready for invasion on 14 May. The wounded had to be moved to caves on the beach, and they multiplied: soon there were 500 stretcher cases, British, New Zealand, Australian and Cypriot, and German parachutists. Joanna would work 24 hours on, 24 hours off. Then she was instructed to move inland with two sick doctors and important medical equipment. By this time, the retreat of the Allies within Crete had started.

Joanna was expected to be evacuated with them from Sphakia to Alexandria when Crete fell on 30 May, but the transport for her little party failed to show up. She went back to nursing in the caves. The Germans, whose first purpose in Crete had been to take Maleme airfield in order to move in reinforcements and supplies, had arrived there. They started flushing out the caves of the last vestiges of Allied resistance. Joanna lay face down on a stretcher waiting, having changed hastily from battle-dress into a Greek nurse's uniform. The Germans who found her, once they had got over their surprise, behaved correctly, repatriating her at her request to Athens where, helped by the United States Embassy, she continued nursing and then teaching English and helping British officers to escape. Her story, when it reached England, turned her into something of a heroine and it is nicely told in *The Villa Ariadne* by Dilys Powell, who was a friend and had the details from her first hand. The new *Dictionary of National Biography* entry for Joanna's father says that she was awarded 'the distinguished war certificate'.

**Georgina Anyfantis**, aged 22, fled from the mainland to Crete when her family was killed by the Nazi invaders. According to the American journalist **Betty Watson**, who had arrived in Athens just before Italy invaded Greece in 1940 and described Greek resistance in *Miracle in Hellas: The Greeks Fight On* (1943), Georgina 'asked for an opportunity to fight with the army defending Crete'. Betty, who seems to have visited Crete briefly before the Germans allowed her to leave Athens via Berlin in June 1941, continued Georgina's story:

She was given a uniform and assigned to a machine-gun post on the edge of a landing field. The post was attacked by Nazi bombers, and only Georgina survived. Later in the day German troop carriers approached, flying low. She manned the gun, waited until the aircraft were close, then fired point-blank. Two planes, each carrying twenty men, crashed. Georgina escaped from the field before it was captured by the Nazis and evacuated with the main British forces to Egypt. She is now serving as a volunteer in the South African Women's Air Force.

With the invasion of Crete by German paratroopers and bombers on 20 May 1941, came the chance for Cretan women to show their mettle. The island's government refused to sign the armistice and its people continued fighting, turning, over the coming years, to the guerrilla tactics in which they were so practised. Betty Watson writes:

Among the first prisoners brought to Athens by the Germans, during the battle of Crete in May, 1941, was a woman wearing a cartridge belt. She was Maria Georgibalaki, the wife of a mayor, a university graduate, who put on one of her husband's uniforms when she learned that the main body of the army was being evacuated from the mainland. Like a modern Joan of Arc, she led her fellow-townsmen in battle, shooting at the German parachutists who landed on the island by the thousands. She claimed seventeen German soldiers killed by her own hand. It was said that she was.brought before General von List in Athens, and that when he saw her he asked why a woman should so disgrace her sex as to take up arms and kill. She is supposed to have replied, 'The women of Crete do not consider it a disgrace to fight against the destroyers of civilisation.'

Further glimpses of Cretan women are to be found in an anthology – *Greek Women in Resistance* (1986) (available from bookshops in Crete) – edited by Eleni Fourtouni. Argiro Kokovli tells the story of **Levendokaterini** – 'Noble and Brave Katerini' – from the village of Fourne near Chania ('Levendis' is a word applied to men). **Katerini** is the 21-year-old war widow of **Theodoros**. Her two children are hiding in a cave in the ravine with the rest of the children, women

10.  Cretan women 1941–1944, from Matton, *La Crète*

and old men. When she takes food up to the cave, she notices a gun slung over the shoulder of an old man; the rest of the story is told in the itinerary that includes Fourne (see p. 277). The writer **Victoria Theodorou** joined the Cretan resistance at the age of 15 in 1941 and served as a messenger, helping to keep supplies and information flowing between Chania and the mountains. **Evangelia Fotaki** was a journalist and writer from Herakleion. Her role in the resistance was to write for the Free Press.

Before the Germans were driven out of Crete, an Allied military mission arrived back in Crete; indeed, some of the officers, such as Tom Dunbabin, had never left but stayed with the partisans in the mountains. Once the Germans had retreated from their military headquarters at the Villa Ariadne, the house Arthur Evans had built beside the excavations at Knossos (see itinerary p. 203), it became the Allied headquarters; from there the new occupants liaised with the National Organisation of Cretan Liberation.

One of the activities requiring urgent implementation in 1944 was the distribution of relief supplies, especially to those areas where the Germans had conducted reprisals. This was to be a skeleton organisation that would eventually be handed over to UNRRA (United Nations Relief and Rehabilitation Administration), but now people were needed who knew the villages and those there who could be responsible for the supplies reaching the right hands. Two obvious choices were Mercy Money-Coutts and Edith Eccles who, based at the Villa Ariadne, had worked as archaeologists before the war with Hilda Pendlebury under the direction of her husband John (killed resisting the German advance in May 1941). The two had worked in Crete for some years, knew the language, the villages and the people.

Opposition to two women in this war-zone was marked. But Mercy, who had worked for British Intelligence and the Red Cross, who knew people and had money, managed to get herself to Cairo. There she was momentarily balked but she was liaising with Dunbabin in Crete and he knew a caique captain who had been putting people on Crete for years without the permission of the local authority, as long as the money was right. Mercy was landed on the south coast, 30 miles or so from the Villa Ariadne, and hiked there. Once she was established, Edith Eccles was allowed to join her by a more orthodox route from Athens. They set up house in the Taverna, an annexe in the villa grounds, sharing it, initially, with men in uniform.

In March 1945, Mary and Robin Burn were due special leave from the Embassy in Athens and were encouraged to go to Crete to bring back information – such as whether or not supplies were being properly distributed. At the Villa Ariadne, Mary found her friends; Mercy greeted her arrival with the pronouncement, 'Well, if you want to see some relief going on, we have got three 3-tonne lorries going to the Amari valley tomorrow. You'd better come along.'

This particular consignment was nine tonnes of woollen goods knitted by the women of Australia, each one marked with the name and age of the knitter, to thank the islanders for looking after their menfolk as they were forced to leave in May 1941. In his unpublished account of his wife Mary's life, written for their family in 1989, Robin Burn describes their adventures. Sometimes the thanks were the most difficult part to deal with:

At almost every other house, a door would open and a daughter of the house or a young wife, in her best clothes, would say 'Will you not come in and rest yourselves?' – after walking, except at the first house, probably from the next door one, as she knew perfectly well. Then, after general talk with Papa, which we grew good at diverting to ... the fortunes of the village under the occupation, before long there would be what Mary came to call 'the ominous chink of little glasses'. It was home-distilled brandy. If kept under observation, Mary would take a token sip; she would in any case whisper to me 'Drink yours quickly!' Then (just like a girl) under cover, with luck, of the passing of other refreshments, she would switch glasses.

After about four of these entertainments, we were unanimous that we had got to be firm, or we should get nowhere – certainly not up the hill.

Many of the villages in the valley had been razed to the ground; most were full of widows and orphans but, as they noted,

Cheeringly, we were shown some of what was being done locally towards rehabilitation; largely by women, often headed by the primary school mistress. Such were often the unsung heroes (nothing specially feminine about it) of Greek rural survival under the occupation; and in this case, whereas the sight of a burnt-out school building might reduce a man to despair, it was often a woman, not ashamed of little things who, if she found one book in the ashes not irretrievably ruined, would fish it out and look for another. A barn, out in a field, which had escaped the notice of the deprecators, had become thirty small boys' dormitory. With one blanket among three, beds of bracken and their body heat, they had survived the winter. Blankets were high on Mercy's list of priorities, but the competition was formidable.

The driver of Mercy and Edith's truck was Michael Seiradakis, a native of Sougia in the south, with a small business in Chania selling produce from his home village. During the German occupation, using this as an excuse, he had carried messages about German convoys from the resistance committee in town to its allies in the mountains. Now, he and Mercy had an understanding and were to marry in 1947. The Burns worried about the headlines: 'English Hon. marries her Cretan driver.'

Ursula Brock was to visit Mercy in Chania in 1950 when Ursula's husband was preparing his book on the Fortetsa cemetery (see p. 70). In her unpublished record she wrote, 'Rumour had it that she had married her muleteer.' Rather, she found a charming war hero, active in the business that Mercy had funded. The English aristocrat and archaeologist contentedly lived a Cretan family life, in a typical Chalepa house (see itinerary p. 271), with two children who were to grow up to have distinguished international careers. (Mercy, as her great niece Harriet discovered when she visited Sougia in 2002, is something of a heroine in her husband's home town where she founded a school and where there is a street named after her; see itinerary p. 279.)

But post-war Crete was not a happy place. Civil war raged in Greece and its effects were fully felt on the island. Women who had fought in the resistance were particularly vulnerable; they, and any left-wing sympathisers, were rounded up by order of the government in Athens. Levendokaterini was tried for 'anti-national' activities and executed; Victoria Theodorou and Evangelia Fotaki were sent to exile on the island of Trikeri. Evangelia died as a result of that hardship in 1972 (before the Greek dictators fell in 1974). She had written a piece, 'White Terror', in memory of women who were killed during the civil war; part of it concerns Crete:

Outside Heraklion, Crete, in the labyrinthine cellar of a large house surrounded by acres of orange groves and barbed-wire fences, were located the infamous stables of Boutava. No one ever came out of there alive without the humiliation of signing the Declaration of Repentance.

In Boutava the folklorist Maria Liadaki and her friend Maria Dranaki were tortured in the fall of 1947. They had both just been released from a concentration camp on a special furlough and were returning to Crete. They disappeared as soon as they disembarked at Heraklion. All efforts to locate them by relatives were fruitless.

Two years later the skeletons of the two women were found inside a cave. Every bone in their bodies had been broken, and their severed heads were placed in the crooks of their arms.

In the preface to *Greek Women in Resistance*, Victoria Theodorou writes words which cannot be bettered for ending this historical view of Crete's women from neolithic to modern times: 'For the first time in the history of Greece, in the ranks of the Resistance movement women and young people were treated as the equals of adult men at home, at work, in strategic planning and in danger and sacrifice.'

# 14

## Archaeologists and Other Scholars

### AD 1900–1970

It was in Crete in 1901 that the first woman archaeologist, the American Harriet Boyd, directed her own excavation. That find, Gournia, brought her to the attention of the archaeological world not just because she was a novelty but for its own sake – it was the first Bronze Age Minoan town excavated. Her reputation has grown in recent years with the interest in women and archaeology and the history of the discipline more generally.

Harriet made her way to Crete, aged 29, at a time when acceptance of women as professional archaeologists was virtually unthinkable. As late as 1915 the archaeologist J.P. Droop put on paper hostile thoughts which today raise a wry smile but which he meant seriously; and they may well have been typical. He had a long association with the British School at Athens where women had been admitted since the 1890s, but they were not allowed to live in, nor to excavate. This is only a few lines of his diatribe:

My reasons are two-fold and chiefly personal. In the first place there are the proprieties ... it is not everywhere sufficiently realised that the proprieties that have to be considered are not only those that rule in England or America, but those of the lands where it is proposed to dig; the view to be considered is the view of the inhabitants, Greek, Turk, or Egyptian ... My chief objection lies in this, that the work of an excavation on the dig and off it lays on those who share in it a bond of closer daily intercourse than is conceivable, except perhaps in the Navy ... that is one of the charms of the life, but between men and women, except in chance cases, I do not believe that such close and unavoidable companionship can ever be other than a source of irritation; at any rate I believe that, however it may affect women, the ordinary male at least cannot stand it.

A few women, such as **Sophia Schliemann**, wife of the excavator of Troy from 1871, were allowed near digs because they were wives; indeed, Sophia took an active part in excavations at Mycenae, including the 'Tomb of Clytemnestra'. Margaret Murray found a progressive archaeologist prepared to let her assist in Egypt in the 1890s. But as late as 1913, women were still excluded from anthropology, to which archaeology was connected, partly because of the need to protect them from knowledge of the sexual practices of 'primitive' societies. This same thinking extended to university degrees: a noticeable number of the women in this chapter were, with reluctance, allowed to study at Oxford and Cambridge just before and just after the turn of the century – leading to the establishment of women's colleges – but they were not awarded the degrees they had earned until 1920 (Oxford) and 1948 (Cambridge).

It was not until the late 1960s that women archaeologists began to teach in universities in any numbers. Even so, between 1976 and 1985 in the United States, while 36 per cent of the doctorates were gained by women, only 15 per cent of faculty members were women. Women now direct excavations but it has been a long road.

Following the end of Ottoman rule in Crete in 1898, and as knowledge of Arthur Evans' excavation at Knossos spread from 1900, Crete became increasingly attractive to archaeologists and other scholars. Women, too, against the odds, began to arrive through the breach in the wall created by Harriet Boyd. Many of those who worked on the island over the subsequent 60 years or so concentrated on a particular site and more details of their lives and work will appear in the relevant itinerary, building on the references that have already appeared in this historical section. Here, I set out a chronology of the earlier women archaeologists and other scholar/travellers – 1900–70 – and such bare biographical bones as will provide easy reference.

**Harriet Ann Boyd** (1871–1945) was a graduate in classics of Smith College, Massachusetts, who, in 1896, began postgraduate work at the American School of Classical Studies at Athens. While there she became involved in local politics and, during the Greco-Turkish war of 1897, served as a voluntary nurse in the Greek army. In the last of her four years in Athens, she was awarded one of the Agnes Hoppin Memorial Fellowships, set up to 'lift the restrictions on women in the study of archaeology'. Having decided that she was 'not cut out for a library student', she was ready to get her hands dirty. Here she faced her first apparently insurmountable barrier: as she also wrote, 'The regular School excavations gave occupation to the men students but did not afford enough material for the women also.' Nothing daunted, and encouraged by her nursing friend, Schliemann's widow Sophia Engastromenos (whose mother was Cretan), she set off in April **1900** for Crete where Arthur Evans had just started excavating at Knossos. Having watched him for a day or two and taken his advice, she continued towards the Bay of Mirabello, accompanied by her friend Jean Patten (see below), a mainland Greek 'servant', Aristides, who was to become her foreman, and his mother, whom they called Manna, as chaperone and cook.

She started digging first at Kavousi and that work provided material for her Master's thesis at Smith College where, between 1900 and 1906, she was to teach Greek archaeology, epigraphy and modern Greek. In 1901, she started excavating the site at Gournia and continued to do so in 1902 and 1904, meanwhile also directing colleagues at the nearby sites of Sphoungaras, Vasiliki and Pacheia Ammos.

Her major work was *Gournia, Vasiliki and Other Prehistoric Sites etc 1901, 1903, 1904* (1908) under her married name Harriet Boyd Hawes. It was the first published monograph on a Minoan site. This very large and gorgeous book is, unfortunately, only available in specialist libraries.

Marriage in 1906 to the English anthropologist Henry Hawes, whom she had met in Crete, put paid to her archaeological career, though not to her political and humanitarian activities nor her involvement in Greece. Around her husband's career and motherhood, she lectured at Wellesley College 1920–36, and, with him, wrote *Crete: The Forerunner of Greece* (1909). The quotations I have ascribed to her in the Minoan sections come from this little book which has hardly dated and is easy enough to come by on the internet. Her article 'Memoirs of a Pioneer Excavator in Crete', published posthumously (1965) under her married name, also makes easy reading if your library keeps *Archaeology*. Her daughter Mary Allsebrook has written a lively and easily obtainable biography, *Born to Rebel: The Life of Harriet Boyd Hawes* (1992; 2002) and there is an entry by Vasso Fotou and Ann Brown in *Breaking Ground: Pioneering Women Archaeologists* (2004) G. Cohen (ed.).

**Jean P. Patten**, the botanist who accompanied Harriet Boyd to Crete in **1900**, had been a classmate at Smith College and was a friend of long standing. Building on four years of botanical research at the Polytechnicum at Dresden, her contribution to *Gournia* was a description of the spring flora on the Isthmus of Hierapetra, together with a list of the 240 plants she had collected. The following year, her research took her back to Germany.

**Blanche E. Wheeler** (later Mrs E.F. Williams) was another college classmate of Harriet Boyd. She shared the discovery of Gournia in **1901** and worked there that season. She also contributed an appendix on Minoan religion to *Gournia*, based on a shrine found near the top of the hill.

**Adeline Moffat** (1862–1956) was a social worker who joined the Gournia team in **1903** as its artist. Her exquisite work provides some of the illustrations in *Gournia*.

**Edith Hayward Hall** (1877–1943) joined Harriet Boyd's team at Gournia in **1904**. She was also a graduate of Smith College (1899) and from there undertook graduate studies in archaeology and Greek at Bryn Mawr College, teaching in a girls' school to support herself. She was awarded the May E. Garrett European Fellowship to study at the American School of Classical Studies at Athens and she, too, was later awarded an Agnes Hoppin Memorial Fellowship. From her work at Gournia – excavating the north trench – she gathered material for her doctoral dissertation, 'The Decorative Art of Crete in the Bronze Age' (1907). This led to her position as a lecturer in classical archaeology at Mount Holyoake College. She excavated at Sphoungaras in 1910 and in 1910 and 1912 at Vrokastro where she was in full charge. *Excavations in Eastern Crete: Vrokastro* (1914) has been republished in facsmile, not difficult to get on the internet, but less technical are her articles in various journals (see bibliography). In 1915, she married lawyer and gentleman farmer Joseph M. Dohan. She spent many years in charge of the University of Pennsylvania Museum and as review editor of the *American Journal of Archaeology*. There is also a chapter about her in *Breaking Ground: Pioneering Women Archaeologists* (2004) G. Cohen (ed.).

(For all the above women, see the itinerary 'Harriet Boyd and the Americans', pp. 333–58.)

**Jane Ellen Harrison** (1850–1928), who won a scholarship to Newnham College, Cambridge in 1874 and was later (1898) its first Research Fellow, furthered a new movement in classical studies (with Gilbert Murray, whom she met in 1900, and Francis Cornford) turning from textual criticism to studies informed by anthropology, archaeology and philosophy. They have become known as 'the Cambridge Ritualists'. In her 'Reminiscences of a Student's Life' (1925), she described how her visits to Crete, starting in **1901**, and particularly the finds at Knossos and Palaikastro, had been the inspiration for *Prolegomena to the Study of Greek Religion* (1903) and *Themis* (1912) (see pp. 11, 80, 197 and 368). These two books were central to her work, and her influence, particularly on future Newnham students and on the exploration of women's role in Minoan Society, has been considerable though some of her views are now rejected. Jane was active in 1912, as the Hellenic Society representative to the British School at Athens, in facilitating access for women students. There are several biographies, the most recent and comprehensive Annabel Robinson's *The Life and Work of Jane*

*Ellen Harrison* (2002). Virginia Woolf's lecture at Newnham – which became *A Room of One's Own* – was delivered as a tribute to Jane Ellen just after her death.

**Dorothea Minola Alice Bate** (1878–1951) was only 17 when, with neither qualifications nor encouragement, she started work in the Bird Room of the British Museum as a volunteer; she became an eminent palaeontologist, associated with the Natural History Department of the Museum for 50 years. In March **1904**, she arrived in Crete to follow up sightings in early Roman times, and by later travellers, of giant mammal remains dating from the Pleistocene era (see pp. 287, 308 and 372). She spent nearly five months exploring caves, particularly in the environs of Chania, but also in the east where she met members of the Gournia team. She published two learned descriptions of her work on Crete – an appendix to Aubyn Trevor Battye's *Camping on Crete* (1913), and 'Four and a Half Months in Crete in Search of Pleistocene Mammalian Remains' (1905). Her more lively diary is unpublished. In the front of it are her ground rules for palaeontological exploration:

1. Blessed are those who expect nothing for they won't be disappointed
2. The Lord helps those who help themselves
3. Never refuse a letter of introduction
4. If you want anything done well – do it yourself

Her legacy is broad: from three hides she bought in Chania, Greek and Italian researchers were alerted 88 years later to the existence of a special Cretan wild cat (*Felix Sylvestris Cretensis*), a live specimen of which they were able to trap. Her study of animal refuse in Palestine laid the foundation of the ecological-economic approach developed by Dorothy Garrod. She is described as a pioneer of the science of archaeology. A biography by Karolyn Schindler is forthcoming.

**Ellen Bosanquet** (1875–1965) followed in the footsteps of her father, the historian Thomas Hodgkin, by studying history at Somerville College, Oxford (1896–1900). Following her marriage in 1902 to Robert Carr Bosanquet, Director of the British School at Athens, she provided support to him, as well as a better atmosphere there for women students, still unable to live in. **Gisela Richter** (b.1882), a student there in **1904**, remembers babysitting the Bosanquets' first child. (Gisela was friendly with Edith Hall, then at the American School, and a lifelong friend of Harriet Boyd whom she also met through that School and with whom she travelled briefly to Crete and Knossos.) Ellen did not accompany her husband to his excavation at Palaikastro over several seasons, but did travel within Greece and occasionally to Crete. In **1904**, for example, she visited Gournia and met Harriet Boyd and Edith Hall, and they accompanied Ellen's group to Palaikastro. The result of her travels was *Days in Attica* (1914) (see pp. 187 and 257); she also edited her husband's letters to her from Palaikastro (and other papers), *Letters and Light Verse* (1938) (see pp. 79 and 369). *Late Harvest: Memories, Letters and Poems* (n.d.) is a slim volume of her own verse and memories (see p. 367).

**Emilia De Sanctis Rosmini**   Frederico Halbherr set up the Italian Archaeological Mission to Crete – based at Gortyn and Phaistos – in 1899. In **1910**, Gaetano De Sanctis joined the mission at Phaistos, bringing with him his wife Emilia (see p. 248). She had been his student at the University of Turin where he had 'above all appreciated her courageous graduation thesis on the necessity of religious teaching in an Italy not so much secular as masonically-inclined and anticlerical'. As a result of her three and a half months' stay in Crete, largely near Phaistos, and her subsequent stay at an archaeological dig in Libya, she wrote *Dalla Canea a Tripoli: Note di Viaggio* (1912). She later produced several publications on religious themes.

**Joan Evans** (1893–1977) was Arthur Evans' much younger half-sister. She visited Knossos for the first time in **1914** (see p. 200). Following those travels, she went up to St Hugh's College, Oxford, to read for a diploma in classical archaeology, palaeography and medieval history. She later became a Fellow of St Hugh's and donated a house to the college. She is best known for her writing about medieval France. Her importance to the scholarship based at Knossos started with the 1936 index she prepared for her brother's four volume *The Palace of Minos* (1921–35). He died in 1941 and she published the first biography of him in 1943. In 1964 she published her autobiography, *Prelude and Fugue*. In 1960 she visited Crete, almost as her brother's reincarnation, for a ceremony to thank the staff of the Villa Ariadne. In 1962, she contributed generously to the building of the Stratigraphical Museum attached to the Villa Ariadne, and in 1966 opened it. She was appointed DBE in 1976 and was a Chevalier of the Légion d'Honneur. (Additional details supplied by Nicola Coldstream.)

**Marthe Oulié** (1901–1941) and **Hermine de Saussure** (later Seyrig) are better remembered in the literature as intrepid women sailors. Marthe (seaman boatswain-cook) was known to her women sailing companions, such as the Swiss traveller Ella Maillart, as Patchoum, and Hermine (captain), as Miette. In their book *La Croisière de la Perlette* (1926) they hardly mention Crete, let alone the fact that they excavated at Mallia in both the 1924 and 1925 seasons. Marthe was already a scholar – a graduate of the Sorbonne – and working under the French School at Athens; she was to produce a doctoral thesis on Minoan animals for the Louvre School of Archaeology, Paris, published as *Les Animaux dans la Peinture de la Crète Préhellénique* (n.d.). Since they did not write about their archaeological work, details are best found in their successor Henri van Effenterre's *Le Palais de Mallia et la Cité Minoenne* (1980) (see pp. 304–6). Marthe published 'To Crete: Four French Girls Sail in a Breton Yawl for the Island of the Legendary Minotaur' in the *National Geographic Magazine* in 1929, but it is disappointing, being largely full of sailing and earlier photographs of Crete taken by an unrelated man (see p. 150). She later wrote at least two biographies one, with some help, in English; she had spent 'a few terms' at Oxford. Hermine married the archaeologist Henri Seyrig and gave birth to Delphine who became a famous film star.

**Gina Reggiani**   The Italian School at Athens was not established until 1915; in **1923** she went briefly to Crete to study animals and plants in Minoan iconography but her stay was interrupted by the political situation – presumably the exchange of populations. It may well be, too, that Marthe Oulié had pre-empted her in her choice of subject.

**Margherita Guarducci** (1902–1999) was a graduate in Greek language and literature of the University of Bologna. She entered the Italian School at Athens in 1927, as the third year of her graduate studies at the National School of Archaeology in Rome, and visited Crete for the first time that year. In **1928** she joined Halbherr at Gortyn and returned for at least ten seasons thereafter, working on the inscriptions that he had started collecting in 1884. She travelled throughout Crete adding to the collection and, following Halbherr's death in 1930, she took over his monumental work, publishing it in four volumes of Latin as *Inscriptiones Creticae* (1935–50) (see pp. 73 and 252). Between 1931 and 1942, she was professor of epigraphy and ancient Greek at the University of Rome; she is best known for her work on the evidence for the tomb of St Peter under the high altar of San Pietro.

**Luisa Banti** (1894–1978) graduated in ancient history from the University of Florence in 1927, having struggled against parental opposition until 1923, when she was nearly 30. Her first interest was the Etruscans, and it was to that subject that she later returned during a distinguished career in Italian universities. But she was first to be diverted by Luigi Pernier's invitation to Crete in 1930 to assist his excavations at Phaistos. She joined him formally in **1932** and took part in annual excavations there and at Hagia Triada until 1939, at the same time working on Greek manuscripts in the Vatican Library. Pernier died in 1937 and she was left, therefore, to complete *Il Palazzo Minoico di Festos* (1951). She returned to Crete after the war and produced a guide to the Italian sites – *Guida agli Scavi Italiani in Creta* (1949), almost a diary of her travels round on horseback (see pp. 254–5). Both Margherita Guarducci and Luisa Banti, whose paths hardly crossed though they were contemporaries in Crete, are said to have been married to archaeology. Their work is discussed in *Lettere dell'Egeo: Archeologhe Italiane fra 1900 e 1950* (2003) by **Giovanna Bandini**.

**(Elizabeth) Dilys Powell** (1901–1995) is best known in Britain as a distinguished film critic, particularly for the *Sunday Times*, and broadcaster, but she had a parallel, and equally important, life as a reservoir of first hand knowledge about the British archaeologists and other adventurers in Crete from the time of her first visit in **1931**. She met her first husband, Humfry Payne, when they were both at Oxford; she at Somerville College reading modern languages (1921–24). By the time they married, in 1926, he was an archaeologist, established in Athens where he was to become Director of the British School; he died young in 1936. She wrote a biography of him – *The Traveller's Journey is Done* (1943) – and *An Affair of the Heart* (1957) and other books about her love affair with Greece. But her lasting memorial is *The Villa Ariadne* (1973) which tells the story of those who lived there, or passed through there, from 1906, when it was built overlooking Knossos by Arthur Evans, whom she knew, to her last visit to Crete in 1971 (see pp. 203 and 210). If you take only two books to read in Crete, this should be one of them; you can also buy it there in paperback.

**Hilda Pendlebury** (née White) (b. c.1891) *The Villa Ariadne* tells us something of the story of the wife and husband team, Hilda and John Pendlebury, though rather more about John who is a legend in Crete following his brave and awful death resisting the German invaders of Crete in 1941. Hilda White and John Pendlebury were students together at the British School at Athens; she was there in 1927–29 following her time at Newnham College, Cambridge, and a spell as senior classics mistress at Bridlington High School. They married in 1928 when she was 37 and he was 24. They arrived, in 1930, to live at the Taverna, the annex of the Villa Ariadne, when he was appointed Curator at Knossos (until 1935), but they had already travelled together in Crete in **1928** (see pp. 232, 240, 288 and

361). She was to subsume her career in his, though she worked as an archaeologist at the sites he directed in Egypt and Crete, and she tramped Crete with him for his chef d'oeuvre *The Archaeology of Crete* (1939), and doubtless contributed her share to its contents. Her name is on several scholarly papers with his and those of Edith Eccles and Mercy Money-Coutts about pottery contained in the Stratigraphical Museum at Knossos and their excavations on the Lasithi Plateau (see pp. 203, 298 and 300). One of her own travel accounts was published as 'A Journey in Crete' (1964) in *Archaeology*. There is an unpublished diary of her travels in the archives of the British School at Athens, which I have not been able to see, together with some letters home from that first 1928 trip which I have. They had two children (1932 and 1934). A biography of Pendlebury, which will presumably include material about Hilda, is apparently in preparation.

**Mercy Money-Coutts** (later Seiradaki) (1910–1993) was also a member of the Pendlebury team (see Hilda Pendlebury above) at Knossos. She read modern history at Oxford, Lady Margaret Hall (1929–32), and it was probably there that she heard that Arthur Evans was looking for student helpers for new excavations at Knossos under John Pendlebury. It is assumed that she helped there in **1930–31**. She was part of the 1933–34 intake to the British School at Athens which included Edith Eccles (see below), and the two were to remain firm friends and colleagues. They went to Crete together during their first year in Athens, helped the Pendleburys to complete their cataloguing of the Stratigraphical Collection at Knossos and were later involved in the publications (see p. 205). The four of them also travelled widely in Crete in 1934 for his book. Mercy did half of the text drawings. She returned to Crete in 1935, continuing with the Pendleburys who still worked there, though John was no longer curator at Knossos. Their excavations on the Lasithi Plateau, starting in 1936, continued until 1939 (see pp. 298–300). Much of the site publication for the Trapeza cave was Mercy's work. Until the Second World War, she and Edith travelled widely in the Aegean, exploring archaeological sites. She was asked by Athur Evans to organise the Knossos section of the

London exhibition to celebrate the 50th anniversary of the British School at Athens, and her illustration of a hoard of double gold axes is in volume IV of his *The Palace of Minos*. Details of her wartime work, her return to Crete in 1944, and her life there afterwards can be found on pp. 156–8. In 1962, the family moved to Athens where she later became a part-time library assistant at the British School. There is no non-scholarly writing about Crete by her, but there is an entry by **Elizabeth Schofield** in 'Breaking Ground: Women in Old World Archaeology' M. Joukowsky (ed.) <www.brown.edu/research>.

**Edith Eccles** (1910–1977) was part of the Pendlebury team (see Hilda Pendlebury and Mercy Money-Coutts above) at Knossos. Following a degree in classics from the Royal Holloway College, London (1928–1931), she obtained a certificate in archaeology from Liverpool where she was taught by John Droop, author of the hostile views on women in archaeology quoted at the beginning of this chapter. While studying, she also worked as librarian and assistant secretary to the Institute of Archaeology (1932–3). She was a student at the British School at Athens, 1933–34. She arrived in Crete, probably in the spring of **1934**, at the suggestion of Humfry Payne, the Director, to further her research on 'a general history of gems and seal-stones of the Late Minoan period, their antecendents and survival'. She was involved in the Pendlebury team's reorganisation of the Stratigraphical Collection at Knossos, and in the publications that followed (p. 205). She also joined them on many of the expeditions through the island for his book. Under Pendlebury's successor at Knossos, R.W. Hutchinson, she was involved, from 1935, in the excavation of the Villa Dionysos, and work at Palaikastro and Praisos and with Spyridon Marinatos at the cave sanctuary at Arkalochori. She was awarded the Mary Paul Collins Scholarship in Archaeology at Bryn Mawr College, 1936–37, to study Greek archaeology, continuing her work on Minoan gems and seal-stones. Thereafter, she travelled and worked in the Aegean, particularly Chios. In 1944, she joined Mercy Money-Coutts in Crete, based at the Taverna, Knossos, in the delivery of supplies for what became UNRRA (see pp. 156–8).

11. Vronwy Fisher (later Hankey) and Edith Eccles, 1939,
courtesy of the British School at Athens

Multiple sclerosis brought an end to her archaeological career, but in 1946 she joined the research department of the Foreign Office (Greek and Turkish section). The above information (and the quotation from Droop) comes from the entry by Nicoletta Momigliano in M. Joukowsky, as above.

**Vronwy Fisher** (later **Hankey**) (1916–1998) is the last of the pre-Second World War women archaeologists at Knossos, though she is perhaps better known for her post-war work at, for example, Myrtos Pyrgos; indeed, she was a leader of the later generation. Having been taught Latin and Greek by her father, she read classics at Cambridge (Girton College); her studies included Aegean prehistory and she visited Crete briefly during a university tour. In **1938** she became a student at the British School at Athens and, in December, the curator at Knossos asked for volunteers to excavate a tomb there. She returned for a week in the spring of 1939, joining John Pendlebury and Mercy Money-Coutts at the excavations on the Lasithi Plateau. Until the war, she also excavated at Mycenae and, even in 1940, was able to help Hutchinson excavate a chamber tomb at Knossos. In 1941, she married the diplomat Henry Hankey, starting life as a diplomatic wife in Madrid in 1942. Later, in Rome, she worked on Latin transcriptions and, in most of her husband's subsequent postings, in spite of having four children, she kept up her scholarly involvement, particularly in Beirut. In 1970 and in subsequent seasons, she joined the dig at Myrtos Pyrgos directed by Gerald Cadogan who was accompanied by his wife Lucy Cadogan, author of the novel *Digging* (1987) (see pp. 328–30). Vronwy shared a room there with Cressida Ridley (see p. 326). She studied finds at the Stratigraphical Museum, Knossos. She continued working on 'Pyrgos Pottery of the Late Minoan period, on Chronological Problems and on the Distribution of Aegean Pottery in the Near East'. She was also a guest lecturer on cruises in the Mediterranean and on the Nile. She visited Knossos nearly every year between 1972 and 1992, often accompanied by her husband who drew for her. 'A Personal Reminiscence' appeared in *Aegaeum* (1998). She was joint author (with Peter Warren) of *Aegean Bronze Age Chronology* (1989). She has an entry by Gerald Cadogan in M. Joukowsky, as above.

**Micheline van Effenterre** (née Cochard) (b.1915) was born in Montreux, Switzerland. Having decided to become an archaeologist at the age of ten, she learnt German. After her baccalaureat in Lausanne she studied classics and archaeology in Paris under Charles Picard, and history of art and Greek archaeology at the Ecole du Louvre under J. Charbonneaux. To earn a living she worked as assistant to the lawyer Leopold Dor who needed help in reading German books on Mycenaean archaeology. She travelled to Athens with him in 1937 to work on the Mycenaean room of the National Museum. When he was asked to support the publication of a prehistoric excavation by the French School at Kirrha, near Delphi, in 1938, she was able to take part in her first excavation, and met there the French archaeologist

Henri van Effenterre. They married in 1939. On the outbreak of war, he was called up, while she worked for the Ministry of Foreign Affairs. They were reunited after he had lost an arm, been imprisoned by the Germans and then released. She helped him with his doctorate, and then with his future researches, while bringing up their six children. He had excavated in Crete, at Mallia, as a student in 1932; in 1954, he returned there with his family to plan new excavations. She took part in the following seasons of excavation, until the publication of his *Le Palais de Mallia et la Cité Minoenne* (1980) (see pp. 306–8). In Paris she specialised in Minoan Mycenaean seals, published the seals of the 'Cabinet des Medailles de Paris' (MS IX, 1972) and worked with the Marburg team at several congresses in that field. In 1991 she published *Les Minoens* (with an architect) (see p. 22). She has published several articles, sometimes with Henri, the most recent being 'Le Travail Professionnel des Femmes dans la Crète Antique' (1999) (see p. 16). (Information comes from an intitial interview with Micheline van Effentserre in 2003 and subsequent conversations.)

**Mary Renault** (pseudonym of Mary Challans) (1905–1983) was an undergraduate at St Hugh's College, Oxford, where she read English (1925–28) and planned to teach. But she also knew that she wanted to write so, to gain experience of life, she returned to Oxford to train as a nurse (1933–37). There she met her lifelong companion Julie Mullard. At Oxford she had attended lectures by Gilbert Murray, Professor of Greek, and had regularly visited the Ashmolean Museum where she was entranced by the replica of the bull-leaper – a figure excavated at Knossos by the museum's curator, Arthur Evans. Although her first novels had nothing to do with Greece, it was a subject waiting its time. After the Second World War, during which she returned to nursing, she and Julie emigrated to South Africa (1948); there she wrote the first draft of her best known novel – *The King Must Die* (1958). But on a visit to Greece and then, briefly, to Crete and Knossos in **1954**, she saw the settings for her novel and, in particular, the fresco of the bull-leaper (see p. 46). She rewrote what she had written, with Theseus as a bull-leaper. Her interpretation of what happened at Knossos, based on detailed research, was not dismissed by archaeologists; indeed she was invited to the British School at Athens. There is also a sequel – *The Bull from the Sea* (1962) – both are kept in print and available in paperback in Crete. *The King Must Die* is my second recommendation if you take only two books to Crete (see also Dilys Powell above). Mary published other novels set in ancient Greece, and *Mary Renault: A Biography* by David Sweetman was published in 1993.

**Enrica Fiandra** (b.1926): After graduating from the Polytechnic of Turin, she won a competition to study architecture at the Italian School at Athens, 1955–56. From 1955, she worked for the archaeological service of Turin but was seconded to the School at Athens between 1956 and 1961. She has had a long and varied career in various centres in Italy, but her major contribution to scholarship is her works on the stratigraphy and chronology of the Minoan palace at Phaistos, where she started work in **1955**, and on the administrative systems employed in the Eastern Mediterranean (fourth to first millennia BC), with special reference to the use of clay sealings. Unlike her predecessors, Margherita Guarducci and Luisa Banti, who followed in the footsteps of their masters, she was independent-minded, and it is her interpretation of aspects of Phaistos, rather than that of Doro Levi, director of the School and the site, which many find more convincing (see pp. 255–7). She was responsible for the construction of a specialist stratigraphical museum at Phaistos (not open to the public). Her correspondence and cartoons comprise half of Giovanna Bandini's *Lettere dal'Egeo*. Her most influential article is 'I Periodi Struttivi del Primo Palazzo di Festos' (1962).

**(Jessie) Jacquetta Hawkes** (1910–1996) stated at the age of nine that she wished to be an archaeologist. Daughter of the Nobel Prize-winning biochemist Sir Frederick Hopkins and Jessie Ann Hopkins, she was the first woman, starting in 1929, to study archaeology and anthropology at degree level at Cambridge (Newnham College). She then embarked on her career of excavation in Britain. She married the archaeologist Christopher Hawkes in 1933 and worked and published with him until their divorce in 1953 and her marriage to the writer J.B. Priestley, with whom she also wrote. In 1959, she was sent, as archaeological correspondent for the *Observer,* to Crete, and visited Knossos where her student son, Nicolas, was excavating nearby. *Dawn of the Gods: Minoan and Mycenaean Origins of Greece* (1968) is a generously illustrated and readable scholarly book – not difficult to come by on the internet. In 1972, during a second, more recreational trip to Crete based at Agios Nikolaos, she visited Gournia, Palaikastro and Zakros. Her highly personal novel *A Quest of Love,* of which one chapter is set in Crete, at Knossos and Vathypetro, was published in 1980 (see pp. 32, 55 and 225). Her numerous books on archaeology did much to popularise the subject. She was also a founder member of the Campaign for Nuclear Disarmament. A biography is in preparation. Additional information has been supplied by Nicolas Hawkes.

(**Anastasia**) **Sosso Logiadou-Platonos** was born and brought up in Herakleion and studied history and archaeology at Athens University. Following her marriage to the archaeologist Nicholas Platon in 1952, she found herself involved in archaeology, especially in the years of the excavation of the palace at Kato Zakros, 1962–90. She was his chief collaborator, sharing with him many aspects of the fieldwork. She has described this in two articles in an Athens magazine (*Techydromos*); it is best captured in English for the general reader in a long article about the excavations at Zakros by Joseph Alsop in the *New Yorker* (August 1966) (see pp. 376–7). She helped in the production of her husband's book, *Zakros: Discovery of a Lost Palace of Ancient Crete* (1971), including the photography. She was also involved in excavations in the Siteia area. At the same time, she was for many years curator at the Historical Museum of Crete and the National Historical Museum in Athens, and later worked at the Ministry of Culture in Athens in the department dealing with relations between foreign archaeological schools and the Greek government. Following her husband's death, she was unable to bring herself to return to Zakros for some time. Their son Lefteris has continued his father's work there and their archaeologist daughter,

Maria, is also involved. In 1998, Sosso returned to Zakros and, since then, has assisted in the preparation of the final publication, as well as helping her children with other aspects of their archaeological work. She has published articles, translations and encyclopaedia entries in Greek. At least two illustrated guidebooks can be found in English: *Knossos* and, with Nanno Marinatos, *Crete* (information from Sosso Platonos, 2003 and 2005).

**Elisabeth Ayrton** (née Walshe, 1910–1991) read English and archaeology at Newnham College, Cambridge (1939). Her first husband (m.1933) was the novelist Nigel Balchin. With her second husband, the painter and sculptor Michael Ayrton (m.1952), she started travelling in Greece, particularly Crete, in 1957. With his support she had started writing. She published a study of Greek architecture, *The Doric Temple* (1961), the novel about illicit digging for Minoan artefacts in southern Crete, *The Cretan* (1963), also published as *Silence in Crete* (1964) (see pp. 323–5), and, with her husband, *Minotaur!* (1984), though she is probably better known for her original writing on the history of cookery. She also wrote other novels. She has an entry in the new *Dictionary of National Biography*. (Additional information from her daughter **Frejä Gregory**, 2004.)

**(Efthymia) Efi Sapouna-Sakellaraki** (b.1937) has, from her marriage in 1963, worked as an archaeologist on equal terms with her husband Yannis Sakellarakis. Born in Piraeus, she studied in Athens, Heidelberg and London. By 1961, while still a student, she was in charge of excavations on Corfu. She also worked at Myrsini, eastern Crete, with Nicholas Platon (1961). In 1963, newly married, she and Yannis joined the Platons at Zakros where they excavated a Minoan villa just outside Epano Zakros, while the major excavation of the palace continued at Kato Zakros (see pp. 377–9). The greatest achievement of the Sakellarakis team has been their finds at Archanes: the palace at Tourkoyeitonia in the centre of the town (1964–); the cemetery at Phourni, just outside (1965); and the sanctuary of Anemospilia on Mount Juctas (1979); (see p. 29 and itinerary pp. 61–2). They published a two-volume scholarly account of their finds *Archanes: Minoan Crete in a New Light* (1997) and a shorter version *Crete: Archanes* (1991) which is for sale in Archanes. The illustrations, several of them reconstructions by her, bring the Minoans to life. She has also published *Minoan Crete: An Illustrated Guide* (1994) which ingeniously shows both the archaeological site and, superimposed, how it may have looked in Minoan times. (Information supplied by Efi Sapouna-Sakellaraki, 2002–4.)

**Elizabeth Warren** (née Halliday) is a graduate in classics of Newnham College, Cambridge who, during a gap year in 1964, was attached to the British School at Athens. On a visit to Crete, she met at Knossos the research student Peter Warren, whom she later married. He directed the excavation at Myrtos Phournou Koryphi from 1967 (see p. 15, and itinerary p. 331) and she was part of the team, responsible for cooking, commissariat and *apotheke* (stores). She participated, too, in the study sessions 1967–70, cataloguing and drawing finds. She worked with him on the finds from Lebena (near Gortyn), 1971 and 1999–2001, cataloguing and drawing pots; at the Royal Road, Knossos, in charge of a*potheke* and cataloguing in 1971, and as trench supervisor in 1972. She performed similar functions at the Stratigraphical Museum excavations, 1978–99. Her publications include 'A Late Minoan Figurine from Kritsa' (1970) in which she probes, in words and drawings, a headless, armless clay female figurine until she almost brings it to life (see itinerary pp. 316–17). (Information supplied by Elizabeth Warren 2003–4.)

Elizabeth is representative of an archaeological phenomenon, perhaps best described by Rachel Hood in her chapter 'Artists and Craftsmen' in Davina Huxley's *Cretan Quests: British Explorers, Excavators and Historians* (2000):

In turning over the publications of important British work in Crete during the latter quarter of this century, a certain family element creeps into the acknowledgements. Elizabeth Warren did all the drawing, and typing of the manuscript, for Myrtos (Phournou Koryfi) excavated in the south of Crete by her husband. Elizabeth Catling played a major role, drawing as well as sorting pottery, for the work on the Knossos

North Cemetery Tombs edited by her husband Hector, and Nicolas Coldstream. Much other drawing was done by Nicola Coldstream and Diana Wardle, both scholars in their own right, as well as being the wives of archaeologists.

**Rachel Hood** (née Simmons), too, is the wife of an archaeologist – Sinclair Hood. Before they married, having read classics, she worked as part of the archaeological team on the island of Chios, where she was in charge of a trench and, when the colleague in charge of the commissariat was called home, took that over. Married, in 1957, and with a family to look after when her husband excavated in Crete, she was much less involved in the archaeological work. As well as the chapter quoted from above, her interest in the subject has resulted in *Faces of Archaeology* (1998) in which she wrote texts for the caricatures by Piet de Jong (artist and later curator at Knossos). Unfortunately for us, although de Jong and his wife Effie lived at Knossos for some years, it concentrates on mainland Greece and Turkey, rather than Crete.

**Nicola Coldstream**, while providing drawings for her husband and other archaeologists, has also successfully pursued her own career as a historian of medieval architecture (not of Crete). But some married women have obviously subsumed their professional career into that of their husband – at least one making a conscious decision to be a wife and mother in Crete. How far a link can be made with the position of women in archaeology more generally is suggested by Lucia Nixon's observation in 'Gender and Bias in Archaeology' (1994):

A look at the footnotes naming project staff in final and preliminary reports will usually show that as many women as men will be listed and thanked. But most of the men will usually be out in the trenches, or climbing every mountain in their survey area, while the women will usually be working 'at home' – in charge of the field lab, or storerooms (commonly known as *apotheke*), cataloguing, drawing, getting supplies – in short, doing the archaeological housework.

It should be said that these jobs are not being disparaged – they are essential – merely that they do not prepare the woman, often a trained archaeologist, to direct fieldwork. **Lucia Nixon** herself, an archaeologist married to an archaeologist, does direct, and one can only go so far in ascribing frustration to earlier generations of women, as response to my probing has shown me. But **Nicoletta Momigliano** has been able to write, 'In 1986 I worked on a "mixed" excavation in Crete … where the (male) Director made no secret of his preference for all-male teams'.

For those interested in the position of women in archaeology, *Women in Ancient Societies* (1994), in which Lucia Nixon's chapter appears, is one of seven books reviewed together by Tracey Cullen in 'Contributions to Feminism in Archaeology' (*American Journal of Archaeology*, 1996). She sums up her review with a validation of the exploration undertaken: 'At the very least, adopting the concept of gender as an analytical category ignites the imagination, reinserts people into our study of historical process, and challenges the alleged neutrality of scientific discourse.'

**Tracy Cullen**, of the American School of Classics, is also the editor of *Aegean Prehistory: A Review* (2001) which details a synthesis of recent research. These books are for the initiated, as is *Crete 2000: A Centennial Celebration of American Archaeological Work on Crete 1900–2000* (2000), in which the work of Harriet Boyd and Edith Hall finds its place with that of the American women who have followed them.

Many of the women in this chapter were pioneers; they have laid the trail for the women who follow them. Whatever their continuing setbacks, women archaeologists who have started their career in Crete since 1970 are numerous, too numerous to have entries here (though several have been mentioned in recreating the earlier years, and others will emerge later).

I shall now further explore, through the itineraries, how you can best enjoy the interaction between women, history, books and places.

# Women's Places
# (Itineraries)

## Introduction

This is not a comprehensive guide to all the places in Crete that have a connection with women – for one thing, women have made up half the population from time immemorial; the whole island has always been their domain. With a few exceptions, therefore, the itineraries contain places I have managed to visit during the course of three trips to Crete, totalling seven weeks, over three years – 2001–03. I fitted in as much as I could within the constraints of ill-health, well-being, and imposing on my husband as driver on often demanding terrain. You need not only stamina but a head for heights, and Crete is rather larger, particularly longer, than you might think.

The itineraries here are not necessarily as we followed them – more as I have refined them for you. And they are map-driven or thematic suggestions that you may well need to break up into manageable day trips. Unless you live in Crete, you are unlikely to be able to visit them all, so I will give some priority hints, which can only be personal. After our first trip, I thought we had seen everything I needed to cover, but one – Vrokastro. How wrong I was I discovered as my research continued.

The itineraries should be followed in conjunction with the history section of this book, including the biographical details in the last chapter. I do not attempt to go into all the details of a place, some of which are given in the history section, but merely to try and get you there, locate our women and give you a flavour of the place through them and books by and about them. The historical details are, however, cross-referenced. A good map is essential, and a good general guidebook would be a bonus. I usually travel with several but, if I was taking only one, it would probably be Pat Cameron's *Blue Guide: Crete* – she is a woman (though she doesn't make any concessions to that); a new edition came out just before our third trip; and she seems to be the most culturally comprehensive.

# 15
## Herakleion

No matter where you decide to stay, if you only have time and inclination to visit one place, it must be Knossos. It does not lift the spirits like many other sites because it is so restored and so full of tourists – but it is one of those places in the world, like the Taj Mahal, Petra, the pyramids, Angkor Wat, that have to be ticked off the list. If you only go there, don't think all the archaeological sites are like that; if you are lucky elsewhere, you will be the only visitor.

If you visit Knossos, you should also go the same day to the Archaeological Museum in Herakleion where the finds from Knossos and from all over Crete are housed. You then have to decide which to do first. On our first visit to Crete, we did Knossos, followed by the museum. On our third, we visited the museum again and, having seen so many more sites, we appreciated it that much more. There is more to see than the museum in Herakleion but, if you are driving from a distance, Knossos and the museum are probably enough for one day.

We saw nothing of the city on our first visit, when we had driven from Chania in the west and were spending the night beyond Agios Nikolaos in the east, so, when we were staying at nearby Archanes the third year, we attached to the museum a leisurely few hours of enjoyment of the city. Much depends on where you stay. Since there is so much to see in the environs of Herakleion, it makes sense to roost within striking distance.

In the past, the first view of Crete was usually Herakleion or Chania from the water, so I will start with how the artist Mary Walker, steaming in from Istanbul in the 1870s, and barely stopping, first saw Herakleion from 'between the massive battlemented walls of the Venetian fortifications that formerly protected the entrance of the port':

What a picturesque scene! What a singular mingling of East and West does this port of Candia offer to the spectator! The immense vaulted ruins of the arsenal recall the vanished glories of Venetian galleys that once found shelter there; while the Lion of St Mark – boldly sculptured on the wall of the great bastion – seems still to defy the dreamy East, with its golden sunlight, its palm-trees, seen here and there above the battlements; the turbans, the veils, the languor, the neglect, the decay of all surrounding objects.

Ellen Bosanquet, seeing Herakleion for the first time in 1904 on a visit from Athens where her husband was Director of the British School, wrote in *Days in Attica*:

The Venetian town of Candia is now deeply embedded in the later Turkish houses, but here and there a corner of Venice comes to the surface. If one begins to look out for her it is astonishing how often the West smiles out through the Eastern veil. The mosques cover churches. The Turkish houses are set on Venetian foundations. A narrow Turkish street may hold a cloister wall or a text from the Koran adorn an Italian fountain. One notable instance of Venetian work is the doorway, with a design of grapes and acanthus, hidden in a narrow street below the Eastern Telegraph office. Arches and plinths that must have belonged to the same Italian building can be traced far down the side lanes.

Marthe Oulié visited Herakleion for the first time in 1924, on her way to dig at Mallia (see p. 304). By then, not only was Turkey no longer in control of Crete, but Muslims were beginning to leave in droves – and yet the Ottoman Empire's influence lingered: 'We were sorry to leave noisy and dusty Candia,' she wrote in *La Croisière de la Perlette*, 'with its facades and minarets stretching into the distance where violet mountains lay veiled in sun.'

How far can you still see and feel Venice and Istanbul in Herakleion today?

On the whole, the capital of Crete is to be avoided, particularly in a car, because it is hell to get in and out of and the sprawling suburbs contain no history and little atmosphere, but the centre is rather unspoiled, easily walkable and delightful, and would be worth visiting even if the Archaeological Museum were not there. Since it is, and you are planning to visit it, bear eastwards as you enter the city and park in the museum car park. Finding the museum under your own steam by car will require you to keep your head and be lucky – neither I nor a map can help you more than that since Herakleion is in a permanent state of roadworks, diversions and look-alike one-way streets. The car park is round a bend below the museum.

## Wandering Aimlessly

Once on foot, walk westwards the short distance to the **Plateia Kornarou**. In the far corner of the square (sort of north-west), from where you will walk up Odas 1866, is a pavement cafe. You will know when you have arrived because you will see the Bembo fountain (Venetian) and, a few tables to your right, a Turkish fountain house known as a *shadirvan*. In Ottoman times, water was distributed free to passers-by from the grilled window set into its facade; today it is from that small octagonal building set about with red hibiscus trees (not bushes) that you will be served your coffee as you settle down under the autumn sun to soak up the atmosphere.

The *shadirvan* was probably built soon after the Ottoman conquest of Candia in 1669 when the Venetian church, San Salvador, was turned into a mosque, the Valide Djami. *Valide* was the title of the sultan's mother, so it is supposed that the mosque and *shadirvan* were part of a pious foundation established by Turhan Hadice, mother of Mehmet IV in whose reign the conquest took place.

Turhan Hadice was of Russian extraction, therefore presumably a slave, and first wife, from 1641, of Ibrahim I. When he was deposed and murdered in favour of his six-year-old son Mehmet IV in 1648, she became *Valide*. Mehmet IV's grandmother was the regent, but she too was murdered in 1651. Turhan Hadice then became regent until her son reached his majority. There is another link with Crete: Mehmet IV had been married as a child to a slave girl, hardly more than a toddler, from the village of Kamariotis on the north of the island (see p. 117 history, and itinerary p. 233).

12. Plateia Kornarou, *shadirvan*, and Valide Djami, mid-19th century, from Pashley, *Travels in Crete*

Two centuries later, Pashley included this picture in his account of his travels; here you can see the *shadirvan* not much different from today, give or take a cafe table or two, though the Valide Djami, the minaret of which is seen here in the background, has gone. The veiled figures in the foreground give us some idea of the appearance of nineteenth century Muslim women. There is much to ponder as we set off up Odas 1866 which celebrates the last great uprising against the Ottoman Empire (see p. 33).

Today **Odas 1866** is a street market – what **Jan Morris** describes as 'Herb-scented, carcass-hung, brass-shining, hammer-ringing'. It is a good place to buy presents, such as sachets of herbs. We bought 'DICTAMOUS for breakfast and medicine for stomach and colds spesial tea from mountains Crete', which Cretans have used since mythological times, so who is to say that it isn't effective? (See pp. 59 and 235.)

Continue north across an intersection until you come to Plateia Venizelou, the Morosini fountain on your left and the columns of **Basilica San Marco** on your right – it, too, was converted into a mosque. The reason for visiting the basilica, or at least its steps, is Ellen Bosanquet's visit and description of 1904:

The mosque on the site of that which was once the Church of San Marco is worth visiting for the sake of the odd column bases in the interior. They are shaped like inverted Corinthian capitals. On the steps of this mosque a number of old Turkish ladies sit cross-legged beside piles of home-woven goods: carpets, aprons, and gay stockings, which they offer for sale. They are very friendly and very merry, and they seem to enjoy themselves in their shady corner where they can gossip and watch the life of the square.

Today, it is the Hall of Hagios Markos, an exhibition centre housing replicas of frescoes such as those from the Panagia Kera at Kritsa (see p. 315). There is a bookshop with foreign-language books and newspapers across the road.

A few yards further on, on your right, is the Loggia and, behind that, the **City Hall** (formerly the armoury). Walk in front of the **Loggia** or, more intriguing, round the back of the City Hall to the far side. There is a pleasant-looking cafe in its lee and the rather splendid Hagios Titos to your right, but you are searching the northern facade, towards the road, of the City Hall. There you will find the remains of a Venetian fountain (dating from 1602) decorated with the figure of a woman, rather ravaged by time – she is thought to be the personification of Crete. (This statue was originally set into the Loggia and probably dislodged during an earthquake.)

Walk now towards the waterfront. Don't hesitate to look in jewellery shops; you might want to reconnoitre prices of a reproduction 18 carat gold Mallia bee pendant, the irresistible original of which you will see in the museum after lunch (see pp. 23 and 306). (You can also buy one at 'It's All Greek' in London.) Then, it is time for sustenance and, overlooking Candia's seaward fortifications, you can tuck into some fish and good Cretan wine, trying not to remember the boatloads of distraught and disorientated women fleeing when Candia fell to the Ottomans in 1669, after a 20-year siege (see pp. 117–18).

Now, gather up your reserves of energy – you will need them – and head back east the short distance to the Archaeological Museum.

## Archaeological Museum

Remember that many museums and sites are closed on Mondays. This one is not, but it does open late – midday. Another tip: if you are individuals, rather than part of a tour group, once you have bought your tickets, ignore the off-putting queue; you can go straight in. The museum may well be overcrowded in the summer but, in the autumn when we went, it is fine. Now, room by room, I am simply going to note what womanly things there are to see – many of them have been mentioned in the historical text (with their room number), so you can marry information. I shall not give glass case numbers, because they are often not marked. You may have limited time or energy, so I am highlighting the unmissables.

### Room I – Neolithic and Prepalatial (7000–1900 BC)

You would expect to see here the terracotta goddess figurine with legs like French loaves from Kato Chorio (see p. 12) but she is, instead, in the Giamalakis Collection – room XVIII. Terracotta, incised female figurine from Phaistos. 'Beak-spouted' jug which shows Vasiliki pottery style. Clay libation vase in the shape of a female figure with arms folded across the breast (mother goddess). Cycladic female figurines in ivory and white marble. Ornaments of gold sheet. **Finds from Tholos tomb C from Phourni, Archanes** (see pp. 17 and 223).

### Room II – First Palace (Old Palace) (1900–1700 BC)

Jug with incised representation of the fertility goddess from Mallia. Female figurines from Tylissos (see p. 231). Eggshell cups from Poros, near Herakleion. **Fashionable female terracotta figurines** from **Petsophas** (see p. 24–6 and 371). Seals from the seal-engraving workshops at Mallia.

## Room III – Old Palace (continued)

Vessels in Kamares style. Eggshell cups. **Phaistos disc** (see pp. 21–2 and 254). **Fruit stand and bowl with dancing women from Phaistos** (see pp. 28–9 and 254). Tablet with Linear A script.

## Room IV – New Palace (1700–1450 BC)

**Faience figurines of snake goddesses/priestesses from Knossos** (see pp. 39–41). **Faience models of garments** (see p. 39). **Ivory figurine of a bull-leaper** (see p. 45).

## Room V – final phases of the Palace at Knossos (1450–1300 BC)

Terracotta figurine of a goddess. Linear B tablets (see p. 57). Clay model of a house from Archanes. Small gold pendant of a seated female from Poros near Herakleion. Ivory mirror handle, silver pins and earrings; other jewellery. Vessels in painted floral style.

## Room VI – cemeteries at Knossos, Phaistos and Archanes

Terracotta figurine of a kourotrophos (mother and child) goddess. **Finds from Tholos Tomb A Archanes**. Bronze mirrors, tweezers and pins. Spindle whorl. Gold signet ring with a scene of the 'reception' of the goddess. Gold ring with the goddess and a winged griffin from Archanes. Gold ring with women performing a sacred dance. **Finds from the cemetery at Phourni Archanes** (see pp. 221–5).

## Room VII

Large Terracotta figurine of a female figure with multiple breast-like protrusions on her body. **Gold bee pendant from Mallia** (see pp. 23 and 306). Gold pin with head in the shape of a flower. Gold signet ring with goddess, ship and tree. **Gold double axes from the cave at Arkalochori** (see p. 205).

## Room VIII – Palace at Zakros

Big cross-armed woman with topknot from Piskokephalo. Headless, bell-skirted woman.

## Room IX – New Palace period, East Crete (Gournia, Palaikastro, etc) and Myrtos

Vase in the shape of a basket decorated in double axes. Seal-stone of goddess between two griffins.

## Room X – Post Palatial – 1400–1100 BC

**Circle of female figures dancing from Palaikastro** (see pp. 54 and 369). **Minoan goddesses with upraised arms (MGUAs), for example from Gazi near Herakleion** (see p. 62). **Terracotta figurine of warrior goddess on a horse from Archanes** (see p. 62); rhyton in the form of a pregnant woman; headless girl on a swing.

## Room XI – Sub-Minoan, Proto-geometric and Early Geometric (1100–800 BC)

Clay plaque with a relief figure of a goddess raising her arms from Kavousi. Large MGUA from Karphi (see pp. 68–9). Models of couples making love, pregnant women, women feeding their babies, and a child in a cradle – votive cave offerings. Candelabrum in the form of a bowl with a model of a goddess. Bone figurine of a naked goddess.

## Room XII – Geometric and Orientalising (800–650 BC)

Funerary urn with MGUA with snake coiled round her from Fortetsa. Figurine of a naked goddess. **Funerary urn depicting dead man and mourning woman. Wine jug with scene of lovers, possibly Ariadne and Theseus from Arkades. Funerary urn with scene of woman and male figure in helmet, possibly Ariadne and Theseus from Fortetsa. Decoration on bronze tripod cauldron of man in boat abducting woman – perhaps Ariadne and Theseus from Idaian cave** (see p. 71). Two-handled vase of goddess of vegetation, holding tree, with birds. **Gold ornament with a cross and birds in crescent ending in women's heads** (see p. 71). Piece of sheet gold with goddess and two male attendants from Idaian cave.

## Room XIII – Minoan sarcophagi

## Room XIV – Minoan wall paintings

**Hagia Triada sarcophagos** (see pp. 61 and 258). **So-called 'Lily Prince'** (see p. 43). **Ladies in Blue** (see p. 35). Dolphins from so-called Queen's megaron. **Bull-leapers** (see p. 45). Kneeling woman. Procession of women and men. **Procession of women**.

## Room XV – Minoan wall paintings

Women dancing in sacred grove. Women in tripartite shrine. **La Parisienne** (see p. 36).

## Room XVI – Minoan wall paintings

Dancing girl from Queen's megaron. **Woman bull-leaper wearing gold jewellery.**

## Room XVII – Giamalakis collection

**Neolithic terracotta seated fertility goddess with fat legs from Kato Chorio** (see p. 12). Parts of MGUAs. **Painted Protogeometric terracotta model of shrine with MGUA inside from Archanes** (see p. 63). Bronze figurine of goddess riding on lion. Diadem depicting Mistress of the Animals taming two wild goats from Zakros.

## Room XVIII – minor arts of Archaic, Classical, Hellenistic and Roman times (seventh century BC to fourth century AD)

Archaic terracotta figurines depicting Athena from Gortyn, and one of Athena in helmet. Figurines from sacred shrine of Demeter at Gortyn and of Demeter mourning Persephone's death (see p. 253). Bronze sheet with depiction of Athena from Dreros. Terracotta figurines of a naked goddess of love and fertility. Gold diadems of scene of Artemis amongst animals.

## Room XIX – monumental art of the Archaic Period

(Above the entrance) **Lintel to the temple at Prinias (Rizenia), two goddesses seated** (see p. 75). Goddess and naked goddesses from temple on acropolis at Gortyn (see p. 253). **Grave stele of woman with distaff from Prinias** (see p. 75). **Stele of black stone with hymn to Zeus from Palaikastro** (see pp. 79 and 368–71). **Statues of Artemis, Leto and Apollo from Dreros** (see p. 76). **Athena with wig-like hair from Eleutherna** (see p. 75).

## Room XX – Classical, Hellenistic and Greco-Roman sculpture

**Statue of Aphrodite behind bowl on stand from Nymphaeum at Gortyn** (see pp. 88 and 253). And many statues of Athena, Artemis and Aphrodite.

Watch out for a special exhibition for which objects may have been moved from their designated room. The bookshop at the museum is good value and its own catalogue *Herakleion Archaeological Museum* (Andonis Vasilakis) most useful and beautifully produced – an excellent guide and memento, but heavy!

The American novelist and traveller **Edith Wharton** (1862–1937) visited Crete in the spring of 1926, during a cruise of the Aegean, and just before a damaging earthquake hit the island. The only public record (one paragraph) she left comes at the end of her autobiography *A Backward Glance* (1987), when she writes of her stay in Herakleion, that her party

Beheld in all their plastic perfection the glorious Minoan jars garlanded with seaweed and sea-monsters, the slim Prince Charming of the lilies, and the frivolous young ladies leaning from their box above the arena to watch the young acrobats leap from bull to bull, where, a few weeks after our visit, the Museum floor was strewn with their shattered fragments.

She never wrote 'The Sapphire Way' that would have told the full story of her trip – and provided a companion volume to the *The Vandis Cruise* (2004) – the record of an 1888 trip to the Aegean which excluded Crete.

A visit to the museum can be intriguingly brought to a close by **Rhea Galanaki**'s short story 'Black and White' in *Greece: A Traveller's Literary Companion*. It is not as accessible as her novel about Ismail Ferik Pasha; indeed, it is rather opaque. I suspect it may be about the civil war in Greece that grew out of the Second World War. Galanaki has been described as a member of the 'Polytechnic generation' who confronted the Colonels in the 1960s and 1970s, and who were formed 'in the conviction that literature had a conscience'. Ideally, the story should be read in the museum garden. This passage, at least, is comparatively straightforward, though the woman is on a horse:

Suddenly she understood why they had talked about love in the museum garden. There all the lovers of Knossos were long dead, but they stood by the girls like angels with whatever little things they had salvaged or that had preserved them. There the words of love remained indecipherable on the Phaistos disc, something that made love a mystery or a game but never a self-evident truth. There, too, the

13.   Rhea Galanaki, from Galanaki, *The Life of Ismail Ferik Pasha*

decision of some friends from the group to take the university entrance exam for archaeological studies signified an erotic approach to death, typical of their romantic adolescence, she thought, except that at that time they had not yet been able to understand. She guided the horse out the door to avoid the modern scene.

Rhea Galanaki and her writing suggest modern women and Crete; the passage that ends this itinerary harks back to an older Herakleion and one of our characters seen through the eyes of Crete's best-known (male) writer, Nikos Kazantzakis. David MacNeil Doren and his partner, Inga, stayed in a hotel in the city in about 1962, during their six-year sojourn in Crete. He wrote of that night in *Winds of Crete*:

The proprietress looks like a reincarnation of Madame Hortense, the aging 'Bouboulina' of *Zorba the Greek*. A very demure, petite, dark-eyed chambermaid shows us to our room and makes it ready, moving swiftly and silently. During the night I go out to the toilet, which is on the next floor, and meet the chambermaid who is coming up the stairs with a man. They go into the room above us, and unmistakable activities occur ... and recur ... until the small hours. Next morning the maid comes into our room with hot water for coffee, as demure, as chaste as ever, with downcast eyes. She is probably earning her dowry thus, so we tip her as well as we can.

**Kazantzakis**, his wife **Galateia**, her sister, Elli Alexiou (see p. 148), both also Cretan born, and Lilika Nakou (see p. 244), were members of a group of writers in Athens known as 'Generation of the Thirties'.

# 16
## Knossos

We arrived by car at Knossos from the west. To get to it from the highway, you have to follow the signs that take you off that road and through the outskirts of Herakleion. Once again, keep your head. As you approach Knossos, there are several car parks all touting for business; they are probably much of a muchness and the attached taverna where we had lunch afterwards was surprisingly adequate for an attraction so obviously catering for tourists.

We had been advised to see Knossos with a guide so, when solicited, we agreed. We assumed it would be just us and that we would set off immediately. But, no: Pavlos waited until he had 20 or so clients and that took nearly an hour while we kicked our heels. Meanwhile, we had told him that I was particularly interested in women, and Derek in arbitration. Eventually, we set off under hot October sun, fearing the worst. We were pleasantly surprised: Pavlos appeared well-informed and, somehow, we had chosen the right subjects to be interested in: there even came a point when he told us that the high priestess, because of her wisdom, was called upon to resolve disputes. The only reference he could give us was that he had recently been on a refresher course.

But I am not going to describe Knossos in detail. Its Minoan past, and that of some centuries thereafter, is sketched in chapters of my historical survey and each aspect of the site needs the specialist and intricate handling of a good guidebook. My purpose here is to call up the spirit of the place through the women who have visited it since the beginning of the twentieth century. A happy by-product is some, often unorthodox, interpretations you will not find in a guidebook.

Most of the women will be travellers or scholars. By way of introduction, and to illustrate how the dream of Knossos long predated the formal excavations there, **Lady Mary Wortley Montagu**, returning from her husband's posting to Constantinople in July 1718, saw Crete on the horizon and strained her eyes towards Knossos, 'The scene of Monstrous Passions'.

But the first modern woman to leave her mark on Knossos was not a visitor: she and her family owned the site and what I rather like is her readiness to take Arthur Evans on. **Fatoume Tsalikopoula** was married to Sami Bey Liatifzade, the wealthy owner of a soap factory as well as a house and its land on the Kephala at Knossos. They had three sons and a daughter and, when he died in 1885, the children inherited the land and Fatoume's brother Said Bey Tsalikas became their guardian.

Evans negotiated with the guardian to buy the land which comprised three quarters of the site he wanted; a quarter was already in his hands, purchased in 1894 from **Zehra Ulfet Hanim**, daughter of Nalband Hasanaki Hadji Mehmet Aga. In 1895, Fatoume herself bought from her children the land Evans was after. And, unfortunately for him, the quarter he had bought from Zehra had unspecified boundaries with the land that was now Fatoume's.

Various court cases took place which are described by **Anne Brown** in *Arthur Evans' Travels in Crete 1894–1899* (2001) and, although they are rather convoluted and, therefore, difficult to follow, I like to think that Fatoume was satisfied when, on 2 March 1900, some years after negotiations had opened, a contract of sale was eventually signed with Evans. Fatoume had, of course, to keep out of sight during the signing.

The story illustrates some aspects of Crete's history: Fatoume Tsalikopoula's name seems both Muslim and Greek, in the tradition of the mingling of the cultures since the seventeenth century and 'Turkish' women, though keeping out of sight, did own land and involve themselves in hard-headed business transactions. You have to wonder what happened to Fatoume and her family in 1923, when so-called 'Turkish' Cretans were compelled to leave (see p. 148).

The excavations at Knossos started three weeks after the signing of the contract.

Harriet Boyd was the first woman visitor, in mid-April **1900**. Evans had not even been excavating a month the day she arrived at the site but Harriet saw what he initially called the 'Throne of Ariadne' being uncovered against the north wall. She recalled 'Our intense excitement as, in the presence of Dr Evans, a workman removed the last earth from "the oldest throne in Europe" and the stone chair stood forth intact' (see also p. 41). Within a day or two, she set off to find her own sites (see p. 334).

Jane Ellen Harrison, the Cambridge classicist, arrived for the first time in **1901**. Her imagination had been caught not by Minos' daughter Ariadne but the sister who eventually married Theseus (see pp. 51–3). She wrote to her colleague Gilbert Murray on 21 April:

I simply must write to you from Phaedra's home address ... you will want to know the last great find — Mr Evans showed it to me an hour ago — the Minotaur himself, *seated on a throne* (a seal impression), with a worshipper before him. Zeus is nowhere. I always knew he was a tiresome parvenu, and I have been doing my best to discredit him for years — he is so showy and omnipotent — and now at last I can chant a true Magnificat to the old bull-headed god. He has a beautiful curly tail in the seal, which would pervert the most orthodox. What a dear delight it is to 'put down the mighty from their seat!'

That visit, that find even, was to inspire Jane Ellen's first major work *Prolegomena to the Study of Greek Religion* (1903). But all was not intellectual on that trip: she continued with a message for Murray's wife:

Please tell Lady Mary that I have taken rooms for her next year in a beautiful little Turkish harem, with a well and a loggia and a lemon tree, and a few rugs — not much else, except, thank heaven! an excellent cook. I think of her with mixed emotion, every time I drink too much wonderful Cretan wine, which is daily. It is such an amazing red-gold — it would be the undoing of old Achelous [god of a river in Epirus, Greece] himself. Everything is beautiful here. I know now why Phaedra was homesick for her great sea palace; it makes Athens seem cramped and chilly and meagre.

14    Jane Ellen Harrison, aged 33, from Harrison,
*Reminiscences of a Student's Life*

Ellen Bosanquet's view of Minoan women was probably influenced by those of Evans, and perhaps those of her husband, already excavating at Palaikastro (see p. 367), when she wrote in *Days in Attica* (1914) of her visit to Knossos in **1904**:

The women's quarters in the Palace ... are carefully planned, beautifully painted and elaborately secluded. The pleasant eastern terrace, where the queen and her ladies could walk, is screened from observation from the other parts of the palace.

  And yet, looking at the sprightly profiles on these frescoes, one realizes that the seclusion was not due to jealous Orientalism, but rather to a form of Minoan chivalry that sheltered a fine bloom of its civilization. These Minoan ladies are well educated. They have heard talk of men and affairs, and their delicate little noses have grown a slight upward tilt to mark their conscious superiority. The fresco with the massed tiers of women's faces shows that they were allowed to visit public amusements – bull-fights perhaps. They often laughed. And they often, Ariadne-like, took the law into their own hands and interfered successfully in affairs of state. There is something awe-inspiring in the wonderful porcelain figures, in big busby hats and furbelow petticoats, who brandished snakes and stare with fierce black eyes. Here is feminism run riot. Are they votaries of some ancient mother-goddess, or of the goddess Fashion only?

If ever there was an example of interpretation filtered through its time and perception, that must be it. She was to return in 1930 and write more personally (see p. 202).

On 7 April **1904**, the palaeontologist Dorothea Bate, having taken a boat from Chania to Herakleion, rode from her hotel to Knossos to see Arthur Evans. Her later comments neatly linked her hunt for fossil remains with his finds:

The extinction of the deer, which doubtless provided the sport beloved of Artemis and her votaries is, geologically speaking, of quite recent date. This is shown by the discovery of some of the horns in the shrine of the 'snake Goddess' in the Palace of Knossos, dating back to about 2,000 BC.

The meeting was obviously useful for he also told her of his animal finds in the Diktaian cave, one of the places where Rhea is believed to have given birth to Zeus, on the Lasithi Plateau (see itinerary pp. 287 and 298).

So far, the women visitors had fitted in well with the continuing work at Knossos, but some were just plain tourists, and then there was the American dancer **Isadora Duncan**. In **1904**, she and her family spent a year near Athens where she built a modern arts commune in the Mycenaean style. Unfortunately, she recorded nothing of her visit to Crete in her autobiography; we have to depend on the account of Arthur Evans' ward, James Candy; he wrote:

In the early days of the excavations at Knossos, Sir Arthur did not have the time to show visitors around the Minoan Palace, so when the famous dancer, Isadora Duncan, arrived one day, Sir Arthur asked Dr Mackenzie to escort her around the site. She was very impressed with what she saw and on arriving at the Grand stairway of the Palace, she could not contain herself and threw herself into one of her impromptu dances for which she was so well known. Up and down the steps she danced, her dress flowing around her. Dr Mackenzie was very shocked and told Sir Arthur that he did not approve as it was quite out of keeping with her surroundings. Sir Arthur was very amused and from time to time would tease him about this episode.

The restored grand staircase did not find universal favour. Emilia De Sanctis Rosmini let slip the **1910** opinion of the Italians – then working at Gortyn and Phaistos (see itinerary p. 248) – when she wrote in *Dalla Canea a Tripoli: Note di Viaggio* (1912):

The English continue their work of excavation and restoration. But my untutored eye cannot distinguish between the old truth and the new truth that wishes to seem old. With staircases partly rebuilt, columns heightened, outer walls propped up, inner ones repainted, not even the good Minoans would recognise their home, and imagine how enraged archaeologists of the future will be when, in addition to discussions of antiquity, they have to decide if this or that restoration should be done in one or the other way.

Her words are given an added poignancy – in terms of restoration and crowds – by the account of the next woman to describe the site. Joan Evans, Arthur Evans' half-sister, arrived at Knossos in **1914** during his absence, but 'as soon as we landed,' she wrote in her autobiography, 'his two servants arrived from the Villa Ariadne to look after their master's female relations; our first task was to have it explained to them that it was unnecessary that they should sleep lying across the thresholds of our bedrooms'.

They settled in Herakleion and explored the town; then:

On fine afternoons we would drive out to Knossos, less restored than it is now, and in April a wilderness of wild flowers. We had it to ourselves except for the guardian [Manolaki?], an elderly Cretan who was a party to a blood-feud and was hung all over with antique weapons. He used to pipe to his goats and pick us great bunches of frail pink roses. We would stay there until it was nearly dark, watching the long shadows creep over the flawed alabaster facings of the walls, and hearing no sound but the guardian's piping and the sigh of the wind down the long corridors.

The servants Joan mentions are undoubtedly **Maria Chronaki** and her husband Kostis who had been there since 1907. Nearly half a century later, Maria was to remember Joan when she came again. Dilys Powell writes in *The Villa Ariadne* of 1960:

Presently Maria, engulfed in black skirts and shawls, emerged from some inner darkness. She appeared to be chuckling; she remembered, apparently, an earlier meeting with Joan Evans. But when? For in 1935, after all, the visitor had not reached Crete. Ah, much earlier than that; and amid general applause it was disclosed that she recalled seeing Joan as a girl when with her mother – Arthur Evan's step-mother – she had come out to the island before the First War.

**Winifred Lamb** (1894–1963) was part of that first generation of British women archaeologists to make their mark, hers on mainland Greece (see also p. 41). But in the spring of **1921** she and two friends at the British School at Athens, **May Herford** and **Lilian Chandler**, went over to Crete. Knossos had been neglected during the First World War; indeed excavations did not restart until 1922. But Winifred was impressed enough; she wrote home:

Yesterday (Sunday) we went to Knossos. The palace is more wonderful than that of Phaistos but less perfect and the situation is disappointing. But what pleases my childish soul in these Minoan palaces are the staircases and steps – think of running up and down a prehistoric staircase of 4 flights as at Knossos!

**Hazel Ffennell** was not so impressed a year later. She had been brought up in South Africa in a rich and cultured family. In 1920, her father had bought Wytham Abbey near Oxford. By the time she visited Knossos, aged 17, in **1922**, she was well-travelled, a linguist, a sculptor and a poet. The party, which included a seasick Arthur Evans, had proceeded through the Mediterranean on a yacht. Hazel wrote in her diary of driving from Herakleion to Knossos:

Sir Arthur was very much annoyed at finding a whole heap of building stones piled up against an old and beautifully carved Venetian fountain, but we soon all climbed into landaus, and set out for Knossos. Along the road which wound between green fields, vineyards, hills, and orchards, we passed many of the Cretans riding astride on their donkeys. Sometimes with a couple of fowls slung over the saddle, sometimes with a rifle laid across their knees and a belt of cartridges at their waist, but oftener the animals were loaded with wobbly sheepskins full of wine. At length we drew up amid dark and damp palm trees before Sir Arthur's house.

Knossos, not quite a heap of stones as usual, but on the verge thereof, lies on the slopes of a hill, overlooking the slopes of another, and a winding road. There are many stone staircases leading into different chambers, none of which can really be called palatial, and a great many large earthenware vases for holding treasure, and the small throne of King Minos, were about the best things there. The Royal Villa, lately found through excavating where 2 stones appeared at the foot of a mule track, was fairly well preserved, and after we had eaten our lunch in the throne room we came back.

Hazel was not to fulfil her potential: by 1939 she was dead. In *Hazel: The Happy Journey* (n.d.) her family published some of her writing, including parts of her diary but there is very little more about Crete.

Cruising through the Aegean in **1930**, Ellen Bosanquet wrote to one of her children on Easter day (recorded in *Late Harvest: Memories, Letters and Poems* (n.d.):

The morning at the ruins (Knossos) was also made glorious to me by the riot of yellow marguerites flooding over everything. They are a bigger plague than dandelions and have been more legislated against than any crime but they flaunt on unabashed and there were other darlings too — anchusa and poppy and vetch and spurge and convolvulus. It was just *the* moment for flowers. Then Sir Arthur Evans came out and fetched us up to his house for lunch and it was just a dream of old times, with the country bread and wine and goats' cheese and salad and finger-bowls with orange blossom floating in — And the butler fell on our necks and said he had saved Daddy from drowning years ago, and another blue coated old guard came up and said did

I remember 'caressing' his baby son 25 years ago and would I now come and see his daughter who was ill. It was all too poignant and heartwarming.

Dilys Powell, who arrived in **1931** for her first visit to Knossos with her husband Humfry Payne, Director of the British School at Athens, tells the story of what happened when the news of the engagement of two archaeologists, Hilda White and John Pendlebury, was announced in 1928, not long after they had first visited Crete together. 'Never a week passes', said Duncan Mackenzie who had so disapproved of Isadora Duncan, 'without some fresh scandal at the British School.' It may have been that any relationship between fellow students was shocking, or it may have been because Hilda was 13 years older than John; certainly his father was against the marriage.

That same year, as you will see in several other itineraries, Hilda, John and fellow students from Athens had travelled through Crete and ended up visiting Knossos. John was invited by Evans to stay at the Villa Ariadne, but not Hilda, for 'No womenfolk are invited to stay in that Bachelor haunt.'

In **1930**, the Pendleburys arrived at Knossos, John to be curator there in Mackenzie's stead, and moved into the Villa Ariadne's annexe, the Taverna. Dilys was somewhat nervous of the Pendleburys and the Villa set-up but, after a wet and muddy visit to her husband's site at Eleutherna (see p. 241), she was welcomed with hot water by Hilda, and records: 'Suddenly in Hilda's attentions, I recognised the face of genuine friendship.'

That warmth was the beginning of a nest of women working at Knossos – Hilda (see p. 169), Mercy Money-Coutts (see p. 170), Edith Eccles (see p. 171) and, later, briefly, Vronwy Hankey (see p. 172) – none of them to be known except to archaeologists, though Hilda emerges from Dilys' book. Dilys reports, for example, Hilda's mischievous remark about the much-restored Knossos, and Evans' grand manner, that 'Sir Arthur ought to live there in the end.'

But the best picture of Hilda's work comes from Mary Chubb's *Nefertiti Lived Here* (1998) about the Pendleburys' 1930 dig in Egypt

15. Hilda Pendlebury, courtesy of the British School at Athens

at Amarna where the head of Nerfertiti was found. Mary Chubb, who worked with them, described Hilda as 'Small and blue eyed and cheerful ... Hilda was the right wife for an archaeologist, for as well as running the domestic side of the dig, she was a classical scholar in her own right, and after marrying John had gone on to extend her work to Cretan and Egyptian archaeology.'

Mary records how Hilda and John registered 78 discoveries together and gives an intimation of one of Hilda's archaeological roles when she writes: 'When something fragile was found, needing infinite care (and therefore time) and a light touch in handling, an appeal usually came up to the house, and either Hilda or I, or both of us if we could, went down to the dig.' Hilda was a patient tutor to the less experienced woman and was involved in elucidating many links between ancient Egypt and Minoan Crete.

If only there were a description as detailed as Mary's about Hilda's work at Knossos or, indeed, an account by her of her life there. Mostly she is remembered in the annals of Knossos for helping to reconstitute the stratigraphical collection which was to prove invaluable to later scholars.

Much the same can be said about the time and work of Mercy Money-Coutts and Edith Eccles from when they arrived at Knossos in **1934**. Neither of them left any writing but learned articles, mostly in collaboration with each other and the Pendleburys on the stratigraphical collection; Mercy was later to go with Hilda and John to excavate on the Lasithi Plateau (see itinerary pp. 298 and 300), and both were often to accompany the Pendleburys in their tramp through Crete for John's chef d'oeuvre. Strangely, the two are almost absent from *The Villa Ariadne*. I have, however, found one useful letter from Mercy among Arthur Evans' papers at the Ashmolean. Dated 29 May 1934, at the end of Mercy and Edith's first formal season at Knossos from the British School at Athens, it gives a delightful glimpse of the two women's character and their status then at Knossos – as well as how archaeology worked in those days, at least under the shadow of Arthur Evans. A large part of the letter reads:

Dear Sir Arthur,

I don't know whether you remember me coming to see you last winter, but I have been at Knossos as a student during most of this season, in company with Miss Eccles, also of the B.S.A. and am writing about some events which occurred there soon after Mr Pendlebury's departure.

The day before we ourselves were leaving the island a man came to us with seven gold votive double-axes, the stem of another, and some fragments, possibly from gold knives. These he wished to sell and suggested that you might be willing to make an offer for them. The axes, of which I enclose photographs taken from both sides of the blade and a detailed description, are reputed to come from a cave near Kalochorio, which was accidentally discovered by some children about a fortnight ago. Plato (Marinatos' understudy at the Museum) heard of this cave on Sat May 19th and went to see it on the following Monday. He told Miss Eccles, who was in the Museum on Tuesday, that it was a magnificent site, with a number of bronze double-axes as at Arkalokhori, or some gold ones, of which he had obtained one specimen. That same morning, while I was up at the Villa, Manolaki came and told me that a 'friend' of his had in his possession some gold double-axes, found in a cave, which he would like us to see. At that time I knew nothing of Plato's investigations and I agreed to view the objects the next day, May 23rd. It was not until we saw each other later in the morning that Miss Eccles and I realised that the caves in question must be one and the same.

We saw the axes as arranged, and said that we would write to you about them. The man who brought them was a very shady looking individual ... but as you may judge his stuff was amazing.

Owing to his furtiveness and appearance of dishonesty we were at first sceptical about the genuineness of his goods. The circumstances of their finding are not too convincing ...

The main objection to the objects themselves is that they are much more solid than any Minoan gold yet discovered ... Some of the axes appeared to us at the time to be more genuine than others, but they must probably be judged as a whole. Manolaki appeared to have no doubt that they were Minoan and after discussing the matter from every angle we are ourselves convinced of their genuineness. If the thing is a fraud it is one which has been arranged with much care, and there is considerable capital behind it. But probably a chemical analysis is the only means of proof.

We ourselves left Crete the day after they were shown to us, and now that the photographs are printed we are writing to ask you what you would like done ...

The main objection to your buying them is of course that for the benefit of Archaeology they should if possible not be separated from the other finds from the same site, which will presumably go to the Candia Museum ...

We are however quite prepared to return to Crete to act as your agents in their purchase, provided that the Museum has not already got them. We could, we believe, do this unsuspected because Miss Eccles has some work to finish there, and even said that she might be back ...

We have throughout acted on our own initiative because we did not want to implicate anyone else at the B.S.A but the one responsibility which we cannot take is as to the genuineness of the objects. ...

The axes were in the end found to be genuine and they feature in volume IV of Evans' *The Palace of Minos* (pp. 346–7), and the photographs and drawings by Mercy and Edith are acknowledged. The treasure can be seen in room VI of the Herakleion Museum.

We were keen to visit Arkalochori on our drive from Archanes to the far east of the island because of that letter, because the double axe is assumed to be a symbol of the goddess, and there were other votive offerings there to her, and because the cave is claimed as yet another site where Rhea gave birth to Zeus. But we gave it a miss: there is no public access to the cave because, following landfalls, it is unsafe; we were also advised that the road that way is several hours slower than the direct highway to the north.

Mercy's letter stands as an example of the careful scholarship of the two young women so early in their careers, and of the excitement of the archaeological chase; all was not sorting and cataloguing thousands of sherds at Knossos. Edith later worked at Arkalochori.

The last of the pre-Second World War women archaeologists was Vronwy Fisher (later Hankey), in **1938** a student at the British School at Athens. When the curator at Knossos then, Richard Hutchinson, called for volunteers to help excavate a tomb, she and a friend volunteered and set off for Herakleion; 'and so to Knossos by rickety taxi', she wrote in *A Personal Reminiscence* (1998). She continued:

The Villa Ariadne, Evans' home in Crete, was maintained in his absence as though he were about to return .... Kosta the cook, a mild man with a fierce expression and extravagant moustaches, had ruled the kitchen wing for many years ... It was rumoured that he regularly saved the leaves of the tea-pot after Sir Arthur had enjoyed his cuppa, dried them on the roof, and re-packeted the product for sale in the market – genuine English tea, as drunk by *Kyrios* Evans. ...

During the dig at the Tholos Tomb I learned the form and significance of the *matinades*, and picked up Cretan dance steps at the wedding of the daughter of the foreman Manolaki Akoumianos (the wolf), whose archaeology had begun as Evans' barrow boy.

None of them could begin to imagine in 1938 what lay ahead. Dilys Powell wrote of her visit to Knossos in 1935:

Meanwhile in the pale crumbling soil beyond the sultana vines the cluster of tombs was being methodically opened and cleared. Sometimes a south wind brought dust and mosquitoes and lassitude; but at the noon-time break in the work, or at night when we dined on the terrace, the archaeologists still wrangled with happy obstinacy. I began to take life in the Villa for granted. We should pick it up again next summer; that seemed as natural as midday.

But next summer Humfry was dead ... three years later the War broke my remaining ties with Crete.

In fact, Dilys was to see Knossos again, but not until 1958. Mercy and Edith's war work in Crete from 1944, based at Knossos, is described on pp. 156–8. As for Hilda, she returned only to try and discover how John had died in May 1941, not far from Knossos, resisting the advance of the Germans.

War came to Knossos – the Villa Ariadne was used as German headquarters – but Knossos had seen many people come and go over several millennia. It simply waited for its next visitors.

The first for us was Mary Renault. The historical novelist was in South Africa when she started writing *The King Must Die* (1958) set, to a large extent, at Knossos in Minoan times. She had already written a rough draft when she visited Greece in **1954**; from Athens she took a tour through the islands, stopping briefly at Crete, with a rushed visit by taxi to Knossos. What she saw through her imagination, she incorporated into her novel:

Picture to yourself all the king's palaces you ever saw, set side by side and piled on one another. That will be a little house, beside the House of the Axe. It was a palace within whose bounds you could have set a town. It crowned the ridge and clung to its downward slopes, terrace after terrace, tier after tier of painted columns, deep glowing red, tapering in towards the base and ringed at head and foot with that dark brilliant blue the Cretans love. Behind them in the noonday shadow were porticoes and balconies gay with pictured walls, which glowed in the shade like beds of flowers. The tops of tall cypresses hardly showed above the roofs of the courts they grew in. Over the highest roof-edge, sharp-cut against the deep blue Cretan sky, a mighty pair of horns reared towards heaven.

The sight winded me like a blow in the belly. I had heard travellers' tales third-hand, but pictured them in the likeness of what I knew. I felt like a goat-herd who comes in from the back hills and sees his first city.

It was not just the setting that was suddenly alive: that day, a group of workmen happened to be putting in place a newly restored mural. It was the original of the bull-leaper whose acquaintance Mary had first made as a copy in the Ashmolean Museum when she was a student at Oxford. She rewrote her novel, therefore, with Theseus as a bull-leaper and, indeed, all the young women and men who came to Knossos as victims to be fed to the dread minotaur in the labyrinth. The quotation above was Theseus' view of Knossos, as well as Mary's.

If you have any difficulty, as you tramp round Knossos in the sun with a gaggle of tourists, in picturing it as it was (in spite of the restorations), and the Minoans as they might have been (or as we would have liked them to be), the best remedy is to curl up with *The King Must Die*.

Jacquetta Hawkes visited Knossos, too, in **1959**, and later remembered it for the Minoan chapter in her novel *A Quest of Love* (1981). This is her heroine's first view from a hilltop on the way from her home at Vathypetro, after two years' absence:

The grey bulk of the Palace climbing block by block over its hill, was like an island lapped by its gardens and the sacred olive grove. Here and there the red columns stood out against the stone, and at the centre the straight-ruled gap among the roofs was the Holycourt, the very bosom of Our Lady and of our land. I could just pick out my aunt's among the mansions round the Palace, while covering the gentle slopes on all sides except where the ravine was dark with trees, were the tight-ranked houses of the town. At this distance their neat, clustered shapes made me think of my honeycombs.

Dilys Powell's return to Knossos in 1958 was followed by several thereafter; on each one she built up images, recollections and research for her book. In 1971, she was there for the last time before publication and what she wrote reeks of nostalgia and farewell, but also an appreciation of continuing endeavour:

Thirteen years since I had first seen Crete after the war. It was with the feeling that I was retracing my own life that I went down the road and into the Palace of Minos.

   The site looked more disciplined than before. More of the restored buildings and stairways, it seemed to me, had been roofed in with plastic. The fresco copies were all under glass and the swallows no longer nested behind them. Signboards in English and Greek made the labyrinth more manageable. All the same I still pulled up short on the edge of high walls. The summer flowers, mocking the schemes of the scholars, flaunted over the evidence so carefully left for future generations. Summer chrysanthemums, sprawling across the great central court, softened its severe rectangle. Plumbago trailed candid blue blossoms. Stonecrop rooted in the interstices of crumbling cement, and purple mallow and dusty white umbelliferous flowers crowded in forgotten pits. A sweet musky scent drifted from slopes dotted with spires of acanthus, spiny as a hedgehog.

From the archaeological site, Dilys made her way up the road, arriving at the Stratigraphical Museum, opened by Joan Evans in 1962, and wrote:

I had not expected to find anybody working. Memories rushed back from the distant past — the chance, inquisitive, uninstructed visitor, the exasperation of the archaeologist interrupted on the job. Apologetically I introduced myself. And again the memories: three people at work, Dr Warren [assistant director, British School], his wife [Elizabeth], another girl; a table covered with sherds; stacked shelves; the sense of concentration on identifying, piecing together, tabulating, noting. The functional building with its storage space and its workrooms enclosing a central courtyard — the amenities were beyond the dreams of the generation I had known. But the dedication was the same.

Dilys writes often of life at the Villa Ariadne and the Taverna before and just after the war, but modern reality is better suggested by Lucy Cadogan's novel *Digging* (1987). Her heroine, Laura, arrives from England and takes a taxi from Herakleion to Knossos; her friend Jenny is married to the director of a dig in the south of the island, but Knossos is their base:

A stone building faced her after she paid the taxi and was left in peace. She started to lug her case up the stone steps which crossed a moat. How strange that this should have been Sir Arthur Evan's home in Crete, which surely should have been a pretty white villa with a blue door into a courtyard shaded by lemon trees and trellises of vines. The dark green wooden shutters and low ochre walls exuded the atmosphere of a wet day in Middlesex.

'Laura!'

Slowly Laura turned around. Jenny looked worried.

'What's wrong?'

'You've made it. Well done.' Jenny grabbed Laura's suitcase and led her away from the gloomy building. 'This isn't where we stay, except in emergencies.' She walked ahead, back the way the taxi had brought Laura, down the gravel drive, to another, smaller, white building called the taverna.

'Come down and I'll make you a cup of tea.'

Later, Jenny shows Laura to where she will be sleeping: 'A square room with a blue linoleum floor, and [she] indicated the fourth bed against the far wall. "You're in the girls' dorm," Jenny ordered. "I hope you've brought earplugs, because the nightclub goes on all night full blast."'

The Villa Ariadne, up the road towards Herakleion from the archaeological site and on the opposite side of the road, is not open to the public. It is up to you whether or not that discourages you from venturing up the secluded drive.

Lucy Cadogan has brought the Villa Ariadne and the Taverna up to date in prose; **Ruth Padel** does the same for Knossos itself, but poetically. Though now best known as a poet, she did a PhD on Greek tragedy at Oxford, has taught Greek at Oxford and Cambridge, lived in Greece and excavated Minoan tombs at Myrtos Pyrgos (see itinerary p. 325). In her collection *Summer Snow* (1990), 'South Wind' includes these lines summing up certain aspects of Knossos:

> A plundered faked-up palace rests
> above us — house of ponderous myth
> for a million foreigners each year,
> shattered on a day in spring
> when the wind blew from the south.

But behind the scenes, the work of scholars continues, building enthusiastically on the work of those who have gone before. One of my favourite examples is an experiment carried out by Lucy Goodison which she describes in 'From Tholos Tomb to Throne Room: Perceptions of the Sun in Minoan Ritual' (2001) – a learned article which cannot completely conceal the scholar and her feelings.

Picture Lucy creeping into Knossos before dawn, with permission, of course, with one of the guards and a photographer beside her. She is headed towards the 'Throne Room' to see where and when the first light, rising over the ridge of the Prophitis Ilias hill to the east, will fall, as it must have done thousands of years before. Lucy explains how 'Traditional archaeology favoured a view of prehistoric religion as centred on fertility, associated with the earth and an earth goddess.' But she is interested in the sun. She describes one of the clues she followed: 'A conversation with a local farmer who pointed out the different points of sunrise as it moves along the ridge, correlated with different times of year, drew attention to the way in which the contours of a familiar hill can serve as a sort of calendar, a "calendar hill". And she describes how, 'At the Palace of Knossos, observations made by the photographer Carlos Guarita [her companion] drew attention to an interaction of landscape, building and sun creating specific dramatic lighting effects from sunrise shining in through the doorways of the "Throne Room" complex at certain times of year, which the people in control of the palace may have deliberately utilized in ritual.'

This phenomenon only became apparent when the photographs were developed; at a certain moment, as the published photographs show, the sun, entering the doorway, illuminates the throne and whoever is seated there, while the rest of the room remains in shadow. Lucy is building on the work of Helga Reusch which took account of the wall paintings of griffins around the throne, and concludes that 'this seat may have been the site where epiphany of the goddess was enacted'. Not content with this conclusion, she adds that 'modern and classical symbolism assigning a male gender to the sun could be inappropriate in the context of rituals which may have involved female figures'.

All very fascinating. Yet, somehow, it is not so much the archaeology, the Minoans, Knossos – or even the ingenious theory of how a priestess impersonated the goddess to best effect – that interest me most, but the late twentieth century scholar as detective, talking to farmers, infiltrating Knossos at dawn, sitting on the throne as the sun hits it, driven by a bee in her bonnet. And what Lucy does, as we stumble wearily away from Knossos, is to allow us to link all aspects together.

# 17

## From Archanes to the Paliani Convent

*Archanes (Anemospilia, Tourkoyeitonia Palace and Phourni),*
*Vathypetro, Prophitis Ilias, Paliani Convent*

### Archanes

Just down the road from Knossos, on the main road from Herakleion to the south, is a wide bend turn off to the right. It leads first to Kato (lower) Archanes and, from there, further south-west, to Epano (upper) Archanes – the bigger of the two and usually just called Archanes. We found it a useful place to stay for best seeing this central part of Crete, and we did so for a week at the Villa Archanes, a conversion into a few flats (of which the bigger are the more comfortable) built round a small swimming pool, with a delightful staff and the possibility of eating well in-house in the evening.

Archanes is of particular interest to us: not only is there a woman archaeologist involved, but the woman finds are perhaps the best in Crete. In addition, several sites between them cover all stages of Crete's early civilisation, from Neolithic to 1200 BC.

To concentrate on Efi Sapouna-Sakellaraki is by no means to minimise the importance of the team created in 1963 when she not only married Yannis (John) Sakellarakis but they also began their joint excavations in Crete, work that continues. They were not the first husband and wife to work together: Hilda and John Pendlebury (Knossos and Lasithi) and Micheline and Henri van Effenterre (Mallia) had done so before them, and they were contemporaries of Sosso and Nicholas Platon with whom they worked at Zakros. But Efi has, perhaps, become better known in her own right.

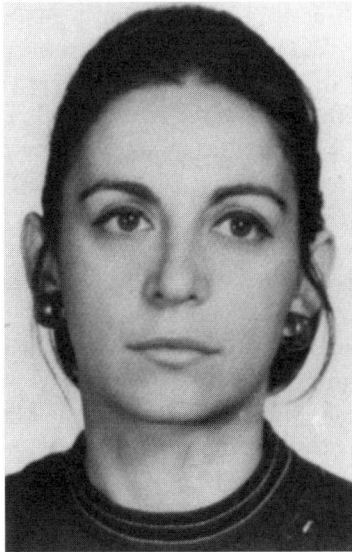

16. Efi Sapouna-Sakellaraki, courtesy of the subject

The most accessible book describing the couple's work is *Crete: Archanes*, written by them and published in English in Athens in 1991; it was followed by their more comprehensive scholarly two volumes in 1997. The slim book is still fairly detailed about the excavations, but there is enough of interest to the general reader, and the minutiae of the contents of each room and tomb unearthed become compulsive. The illustrations are marvellous, particularly of the gold jewellery, and several of them are reconstructions by Efi. *Crete: Archanes* can be bought on the internet direct from the publisher (as I did) or more easily in Archanes itself. Yannis Sakellarakis' *Digging the Past* (1996) includes a chapter, including fine illustrations, about work at Archanes (I discuss his book in more detail on pp. 237–8). And, although the couple usually wrote together about Archanes, and the excavations have been teamwork, it will make easier reading if I describe their work as if from Efi's pen.

Modern Archanes, a prosperous small country town in the prefecture of Herakleion, is in a fertile, vine-growing valley, probably little different from its earlier times. Overlooking it is Mount Juctas (said to be where Zeus – son of Rhea – was buried). The 1912 excavations in the centre of the town began to reveal what Arthur Evans suggested was the summer palace of Knossos. The Sakellarakis team concluded 50 years later that what they were unearthing was one of the most important sites in Crete in its own right – a city surrounding a palace with villas (and towns) such as Vathypetro dotting the countryside beyond.

The uncovering, in 1965, of the cemetery at Phourni on a nearby hill to the north-west extended the possibilities of research. This continued in 1966 with the discovery of the Minoan shrine of Anemospilia on the northern slope of Mount Juctas to the north-west of both Archanes and Phourni. The Sakellarakis suggest that, even so close to Knossos, Archanes was the home of members of the 'royal family' and an administrative and ritual centre. While there is evidence of women's lives in the palace, it is in the cemetery and shrine that women's skeletons – queens or princesses or priestesses – have been found.

You may only have limited time in Archanes, in which case you should concentrate on Phourni. But if you have a day or two, consider visiting the sites chronologically, starting with the little **Archaeological Museum** to be found on your right just before the main road (Kapetanaki) leading to the town centre reaches the narrow one-way system. Although most of the valuable finds are now in Herakleion, some remain and there are replicas, photographs and explanations that set the scene. It is closed on Tuesdays.

## Anemospilia

This is where, at the end of the First Palaces period, it seems that a human sacrifice took place to try and avert the catastrophe of an earthquake – where the skeleton of a priestess was found sprawled on her face (see also p. 30). The site is not easy to find. There is always hope that signs will be improved. Starting behind the main square at the bottom of the town, and taking account of one-way streets, follow the sign for Mount Juctas. The road is longer, more winding and less good than guide books suggest and we got lost and had to persevere. Go past the rubbish dump falling down the hill on your right, and continue round bends climbing steadily upwards. On a bend on your left is a small white house with a veranda facing the road; soon after, as you round the bend taking you behind the hill, on your left, is a fence, a few steps up from the road, and the sign for Anemospilia, which you are likely to miss as you drive past.

The gate may well be closed. Never mind! Walk round the fence and you can see enough – and its position says much of what the shrine is about. It overlooks a wide plain splashed with dark green far below. Standing there, you will understand the name, Anemospilia – 'Cave of Winds'. Mount Dikte is to the east, Mount Ida to the west; below are Knossos, Herakleion, and the Cretan Sea stretching northwards.

This shrine was unearthed in 1979 and brought the Sakellarakis team to the attention of the wider world because of the grisly finds. After the event that destroyed the shrine, Anemospilia, which is dated to the first half of the seventeenth century BC, was never reused.

The sprawling position in which three of the skeletons were found and the rocks strewn around immediately signalled the cause of their death – a cause confirmed by further forensic examination. It is worth noting that these are some of the very few human remains discovered in Crete outside cemeteries, which leads Efi to suggest that 'It has often been maintained that at the first signs of the first pre-seismic tremors people took their most valuable possessions and left their houses promptly.'

The skeletons of three people were found in one of the chambers of the shrine (and one who had probably just left it carrying a jar full of sacrificial blood), as well as the paraphernalia of sacrifice (usually animal). Those inside are deemed to have been a priest, a priestess and the male sacrifice. Efi describes the priestess:

... found in the south-west corner of the room was the skeleton of a woman who had fallen on her stomach with her right hand to her head and her legs apart. The woman was 1.54m [4 ft 9 in] high, about 28 years of age and, as anthropological examination indicated, was a carrier of sickle-cell anemia ... The woman was handsome with a round, smooth forehead and a small delicate nose.

This last judgement was determined by the reconstruction in clay of the woman's head by the Medical School of Manchester University showing, too, full lips and deep set eyes.

Evidence suggests the fate of the male skeleton found on a raised slab and the conclusion that 'the earthquake must have occurred after

17. Reconstruction of Minoan priestess, c.1700 BC, Anemospilia, courtesy of the University of Manchester

the sacrifice had been performed and prior to any attempt to remove the victim from the altar'. The whole of this scene is reconstructed not just in words but in a graphic illustration by Efi.

The final irony is the probable reason for the human sacrifice:

Animal sacrifices are known in Crete, with the bull being the most common offering. This seems also to have been the main sacrifice at Anemospilia judging by the special vases with the bull decoration used to gather sacrificial blood. Even here, however, a resort to the ultimate sacrifice was made for the general good, namely to save the area from seismic catastrophe. When the inhabitants left their houses to flee the earthquake, the priesthood remained at the shrine at Anemospilia to perform a human sacrifice, the ultimate offering; but in vain.

Looking through the fence at this quite skimpy archaeological site, you need Efi to help you visualise what went on. But looking downwards, buffeted by the wind, across the plain to the sea, anything can be imagined.

## Tourkoyeitonia Palace

Finding this site was not much easier than Anemospilia, even though it is in the centre of Archanes. It was not signposted when we were there but that might be because there were nearby building works. You are looking for Tourkoyeitonia (Turkish Quarter) between the parallel streets Ierolochiton and Makri Solaki. Your best bet is to start at the Archaeological Museum (see p. 216) and, walking 100 yards or so away from the centre, take a turning north on your right; you come to a narrow road (Ierolochiton) running parallel to the main road and there it is. If all else fails, ask at the bakery. This site, too, was closed when we found it. But, again, you can see to some extent from different parts of the fence. It is striking how much the site is part of the town itself, houses rising all round. If the site is open, *Archanes* will help you make something of this palace, first built around 1900 BC, at the same time as the other great Minoan palaces.

In Antechamber 2, on the east wall, there is evidence of a wall painting depicting a woman, possibly a priestess, holding a branch. Efi writes that 'She wears a dress with frills and has her hair elaborately gathered and with long curls.'

Area 17a, which has not yet been fully excavated, has a description in the book which takes my fancy:

The upper stories seem to have been residential quarters, unlike Areas 18 and 19 which were industrial, since only fragmentary finds were made of loom weights and conical cups. Perhaps a loom existed on one of the upper floors, or possibly some of the upper floors were allocated as women's quarters given that one ivory and two bronze pins and a silver earring had fallen thence, to be found in a lower level to the south.

It is that one silver earring that strikes home. How often in your life have you lost one earring and searched unsuccessfully, because it has fallen down somewhere or rolled under something? Did a woman do that all those years ago?

But that silver earring may have another significance. Efi also writes: 'Beads, another personal item, were found scattered around the palace, evidently a sign of a sudden departure.' Given that earthquakes and rebuilding are so much a feature of Minoan civilisation over centuries, what if that earring fell through time?

And was the woman who lost her earring one of the weavers to whom I have devoted space in the historical section? On page 38 of my history section there is Efi's description, from *Archanes*, of the process she has deduced from the women's quarters of this palace.

Following the earthquake of 1450 BC, which seems to have been so devastating to much of Crete, Archanes, having lived through the various stages of Minoan civilisation, was rebuilt and entered a new and splendid existence under the Mycenaeans. It is in this period that the royal cemetery at Phourni came into its most interesting phase for us. It was was probably in use between 2400 BC and 1200 BC when the last great earthquake occurred, ending the glory of Archanes. Until 1964 and the excavations of the Sakellarakis, it was unknown.

## Phourni (cemetery)

It is possible to walk to Phourni from Archanes: you take a left turn just past the Town Hall as you leave town. Beset by heavy colds, we were conserving our strength, and so went by car. Driving from Herakleion/Knossos, the signpost in Kato Archanes is quite clear, in the middle of the village on the right. But from Archanes to its smaller sister, the signpost is facing the wrong way and you may miss the sharp turn left up the hill where two cafes face each other across the square.

The road is at first signposted but, as it becomes an agricultural track, signs peter out and you have to keep your head, bearing left, for a few kilometres. You are almost there when you pass through a pine wood. The car park is at the top of the slope and the cemetery then falls away downwards.

Almost immediately on your left, down a secondary slope, is the best preserved and, I think, the most physically satisfactory of the Tholos Tombs – A. We 'did' A last and it provided a fitting climax. But Efi's finds in D, which is at the bottom of the slope and physically unprepossessing, are perhaps more emotionally satisfying.

Tholos Tomb A is an almost perfect beehive, with a passage leading into a wide vaulted chamber; this is the first of the undisturbed royal burial places discovered (many have been got at by robbers). And there in the side chamber, into which you can just squeeze but see little, the team came upon the remains of a woman. Efi describes her:

Fortunately, a few remains of the skeleton helped preserve the burial position, with the head facing west and the pose in the foetus position. Thus the exact location on the body of the mostly gold small objects, mostly belonging to necklaces, could be established. The groups of gold bead were also discovered, one in the shape of rosettes and the other in the form of small palmette shaped papyri. These had without doubt been sewn onto a garment since the first group was found at the waist along the length of the body, and the second along the length of the legs. The person buried here would have worn a long ankle-length, gold-trimmed ritual gown similar to that known from figures depicted on wall-paintings where the vertical and horizontal fringes of similar garments are adorned with like motifs.

Apart from the two groups of small finds mentioned above, nearly all the others were found around the breast. These included, together with the necklaces: three gold signet-rings, a gold clasp, a gold ring and two small gold caskets ...

And in the pages following are photographs of the stunning jewellery which can be seen in the Herakleion Museum (room VI). If the jewellery (and several domestic utensils) had not been found, the poor state of the skeleton would have made it difficult to decide that it was probably a woman. The jewellery and other finds throw general light on Crete and the life of its people during the Mycenaean period. Efi continues:

The finds suggest the social rank of this woman since it is generally accepted that the amount of funerary offerings reflects the position enjoyed by the deceased during his or her life. This woman's burial, adorned as she was with a long gold-trimmed garment, is without parallel in Crete. The amount of gold and other jewellery found is almost as much as that found in all the contemporary chamber tombs at Knossos, and, of course, is richer than other similar burials in the Knossos cemetery.

There is no doubt that this woman was of 'royal blood'; but she was not simply a consort. Efi also deduces that she held priestly office, first suggested by the depictions on the rings but it is then reinforced: 'The deceased's identity as a queen-priestess is most powerfully attested by the sacrifices made in her honour, in particular that of the bull.' Then, referring back to the first find, of a man, in the main tomb, she adds: 'Moreover, this double religious and civil nature is also attested in the shaft burial within the very same Tholos Tomb A.' The woman's seals and rings also emphasise that she was connected with administration.

Tholos Tomb B (2100 BC) is said to be the most important architecturally, and there were some women buried there, but not identifiable or individual in the same way. A find of particular interest is that of a gold ring depicting a goddess and a griffin.

Tomb C was found to be the best preserved with some special figurines, ivory and marble, of women from the Cyclades (the island group to the north with its own prehistoric civilisation) with whom Cretans then traded. They are unique because usually such figurines were probably broken on purpose as offerings during tomb cult rituals. Without these finds, those relations between the Cyclades and Archanes in the Prepalatial period would remain undetected. There are replicas in the Archanes Museum.

Standing apart from that complex is the Funerary Building (4). This, it was decided, was where the carers for the dead lived. There was evidence there of both wine-making and weaving.

Tholos Tomb D, like Tholos Tomb A, stands separate from the others – the southernmost 'building', towards the right. It is hewn from hard rock and quite a bit smaller than A; it is also in a poor state because the roof collapsed. Here the team found a woman – the only occupant – lying on a wooden bier with her head placed against the south-east wall and her feet facing south-west. Efi describes the scene and the interpretation in the sort of intricate detail which illustrates the depth of experience and care needed by an archaeologist:

Despite the disturbance to the burial occasioned by the collapse of the roof, the skeleton's position and even the use of various offerings and the position of jewellery worn by the deceased were determined with certainty. The dead woman held a bronze mirror with her left hand just in front of her face. On her head she wore a single gold diadem of 37 rectangular beads depicting double argonaut motifs, while three necklaces adorned her breast. The first of these consisted of 50 beads: 20 granular and globular beads made of gold, 29 of glass paste and one of sard [yellow or orange red cornelian]. The second was made up of 32 faience beads and the third of 15 drop-like beads, also of faience. 13 drop-shaped beads of electrum [amber] found in a very fragmentary form should perhaps be attributed to the third necklace. It is noteworthy that this material is very rare in Minoan Crete. Another eight glass-paste papyrus-shaped beads must have belonged to the second or third necklace.

The adornment undertaken on the dead woman, did not, of course, neglect her hair (two locks of which would undoubtedly have been gathered by two gold rings found *in situ*), or her gown held at the shoulder by two glass-paste pins, or the gold-trimmed material that covered her head and shoulders. 67 gold beads with twelve-petal rosettes on one side should be attributed to the latter garment. That these beads originated from a piece of fabric – and not from a necklace – is confirmed not only by the fact that only one visible side was decorated, but also by the holes at the edges from which they could be sewn on. A similar gold bead which did belong to the necklace in the pyxis [vessel] has only one hole, this time clearly for suspension and decorated on both sides.

These words are supplemented by this painting by Efi of the woman as she must have looked lying there covered in jewels, a container of other jewellery, denoting wealth, at her head. Below this in *Archanes* is a photograph of the scene as it was found, the jewellery in place, the remains of the woman herself barely discernible but remnants of the mirror quite clear beside her face. These illustrations are followed by photographs of the remarkable jewellery restrung as you can see it in the Herakleion Museum. Again, because of the wealth displayed, the woman must have been of 'royal blood'.

18.   Painting reconstruction of woman, 1450–1050 BC, found in tholos tomb D, Phourni cemetery, by Efi Sapouna-Sakellaraki, courtesy of the artist

Efi suggests that the roof probably collapsed at the end of the Mycenaean period in Crete; on top of it were three other, later, burials, allowing the archaeologists to determine that the cemetery at Phourni continued in use up to the end of the eleventh century BC – bringing to an end 1,400 years.

As you leave the site, even in the book, you are overwhelmed by what your imagination tells you about the life of those women. And you ask, did the priestess or princess live in the palace in the Turkish Quarter? Did her predecessor function at Anemospilia? And then you wonder about the excitement that Efi and her husband must have felt when they discovered her and then interpreted each minute aspect of what they found. When I asked Efi what she felt, she replied: 'One of the most exciting moments was when I touched the scattered beads and recreated the necklaces, a subject which many times during my work was a problem, and of course when I saw the woman looking into the mirror at eternity.'

## Vathypetro

To get to Vathypetro from Archanes, you take the road out of town to your right just past the post office. The drive is a few miles (5 km) on a good road. You come to it on your right, clearly marked and visible.

Vathypetro is one of the best known and accessible country houses from the Second or New Palace Late Minoan period and I have already introduced it in some detail on pages 32–4 of the history section. I have, too, introduced Jacquetta Hawkes' heroine, Ianissa, from her novel *A Quest of Love* (1989). That chapter and a good guidebook such as Pat Cameron's *Crete: Blue Guide* seem to be all there is, apart from scholarly articles, to make the site accessible.

Once again location is everything, and this may not only have had some religious significance in relation to terrain but was probably on the main route south from Knossos to the Mesara Plain. The excavation of the manor house of some 20 rooms downstairs and some up eventually revealed itself more as a complex in two parts, possibly built at different times.

The site is, in some ways, disappointing because, to conserve it, and to house some finds, the archaeologist of the 1940s and 1950s constructed what look like two cement bunkers – in which are evidence of wine and oil production. They were intended as a museum but you now look through rusting bars. But, as you stand on the edge of the site and look out over the broad and beautiful plain towards the twin peaks of Prophitis Ilias in the distance, you can certainly imagine Ianissa's life.

There may well have been a town or village nearby – no substantial evidence has yet been found probably because of modern vine cultivation. But, in any case, the many people attached to the manor, serving someone like Ianissa's father, the 'squire' or 'lord', were self-sufficient. Jacquetta sums it up:

All our servants, indoors and out, were free and easy; it was part of my father's old fashioned management. He still believed in clan ties and tried to keep them alive. Most of our household were our kin through the clan, and I believe that the older ones really did regard my father as the head of their family. That was one reason why he had always refused to have a town house or claim his place at court. Instead he lived out here on the estate and gave all his mind to running it. He had set up the pottery and the weaving shop and saw to it that the fields were all cultivated. Our yields of wheat and barley were the heaviest in the whole region and our flocks of sheep the largest.

Many clay loom weights have also been found which suggest weaving, perhaps even textile production.

Ianissa loved the gardens and took pleasure in watering the plants and watching the birds. But her real love is given credibility when you walk away from the beauty in front to the side, to what looks like a quarry falling down the side of the hill, and the link is made between the clay remains there and her work as a potter – a subject I have explored on pp. 33–4. Potters' wheels and a kiln were found, and Jacquetta Hawkes brings it all alive when she writes:

The pottery was as delightful to me as ever, though the wheels were at rest on their pivots and I could not hope to feel the perpetual wonder of the gleaming vessel rising from the lump of clay. The whole place smelt of clay, however, the most refined of all good earthy smells. It lay in heaps beside the great stone kneading troughs.

The kitchens were in the northern area of the eastern complex and it is assumed that a staircase led to a main room. From the base of a column there fell a single golden earring. To read this in a learned article about Vathypetro is to have the same frisson as I felt at Archanes. The earring is apparently on display in the Herakleion Museum (showcase 101). Did it fall with the rest of the building when Vathypetro was finally destroyed, probably by an earthquake in 1470 BC, or did someone lose it earlier?

## Prophitis Ilias

We found that plain stretching westwards from Vathypetro irresistible. Happily, we had already planned to cross it to get to Prophitis Ilias and, from there, to the Paliani Convent. The convent has a history of interest to us but the best way to visit it may not be from Vathypetro. You may prefer to do it starting from Herakleion on the main road down to Gortyn, Phaistos and Hagia Triada (see p. 247).

However, we did it from Vathypetro, Derek full of cold and fever – not our best move. It started easily enough. Go back to the main road towards Archanes and, before the town, take a little road off to the left signposted Mount Juctas. Don't turn almost immediately right for that climb, but left, for Prophitis Ilias. It looks good – miles of vineyards stretching ahead and those alluring twin peaks beckoning.

But then you come across bifurcations with no signs. You have to guess. Occasionally a farmstead allows you to ask, '*Prophitis Ilias, parakalo*?' A kind person points. That is how they would have gone from there, knowing the way – not the way back to a direct route, if there is one (the map says there is). We forded the occasional stream. My guilt at having planned this route grew heavier. Eventually, we made it. Feeling well, it would surely have seemed a pleasant adventure.

Prophitis Ilias can be visited much more directly from Herakleion (19 km to the north). Indeed, Nipharus Phocus wanted to move Khandakas (Herakleion) to Prophitis Ilias, then called Temenos, when he took it back from the Saracens in 961 (see p. 95). He built a fortress on a rocky outcrop there. Later, the Ottomans called it Kanli Kastelli ('Bloody Castle') after a battle in 1647 when they were repulsed by the Venetians. They besieged it again in 1897 when a local force of 100 men and 200 women held out for five hours with only 40 rifles against an army of 4,000 (see p. 139). Those 200 women are the reason to go. But driving with difficulty, and a feeling of intrusion, through the narrow-streeted town which climbs up one of the peaks, trying to find something to latch onto was frustrating. It would have been better to persevere on foot, apparently you can see Vathypetro from the top. But there was nowhere to park. Driving towards the town on the hill, and away from it (having bypassed it) is best; you can see vestiges of the fortress, allowing you to imagine bloody sieges and brave women. Again, location is all.

## Paliani Convent

An interesting outing from Herakleion could also consist of a drive directly from the capital to Prophitis Ilias, and then across country west to Venerato on the main road south – Paliani is on the town's eastern outskirts. We also approached it from Prophitis Ilias, and that means you don't have to go into Venerato. Keeping our eyes skinned, we spotted a sign indicating sharply downwards to the left. Paliani is reasonably well signposted, though a bit further than you expect.

The convent, which enters the records in Byzantine times, in AD 668 (see p. 93) has a brave history, particularly during the Ottoman period – in 1821, 1866 and 1897 (see pp. 127, 133 and 139). Then the nuns – Parthenia who rebuilt the convent, became its abbess in

1826 until her death in 1866, reputedly aged 133; shrewd Agathangeli and the progressive abbess Dionysia – were steadfast in the face of depredations.

It is also very much a feature of the Goddess Movement Pilgrimages (tap into the internet) 'with its sacred tree and wonder-working icons of the Panagia (Mary)'. **Carol P. Christ** in her personal account *Odyssey with the Goddess: A spiritual Quest in Crete* (1995) describes what it means to her, and she returns annually to Crete leading a group. The sacred myrtle tree, celebrated on 24 September and said to be over 1,000 years old, holds in the crook of its branches the icon of Mary (celebrated on 15 August), the finding of which led to the convent's foundation. It is said, too, either in addition or instead of, that following the sacking of the convent and massacre of the nuns in 1821, the icon was found under the myrtle tree. The worship of a holy tree is said to link back to Minoan times. There are, for example, trees, sometimes olive, on several gold rings, and on the Hagia Triada sarcophagus (see pp. 61 and 258).

Paliani has also been famous, since 1821, for the handicrafts of the nuns – knitting, embroidery, lace-making, sewing and weaving.

I think we must have visited the convent on an off-day. Guidebooks suggest that the nuns are 'hospitable', which is not unusual for such establishments. We saw three nuns of so venerable an age (and with black habits apparently worn uncleaned since they entered the convent) that they did not notice us. We saw the sacred myrtle tree hung about a bit like a Christmas tree, but we did not cut a dry twig from the lower branches as pilgrims are wont to do. The convent is self-sufficient, partly through sales of its lace and embroidery, but we pressed our noses against the locked door of the little shop. Wishing to be supportive, and gather more information, we did get it opened by an unsmiling middle-aged nun but had to leave empty-handed as far as handicrafts were concerned. Perhaps it had been visited by a coach-load that morning. Another explanation is the suggestion (found on the internet) that the convent is not communal but that each nun earns her living by her handiwork. I find that hard to believe, having seen the age of some of them.

The most interesting time to visit the convent may well be between 1 and 15 August when each afternoon the nuns seek the Virgin's blessing under the tree. I suspect the glory days are past; but the fact that it has survived is itself an achievement, and when we were there it was as tranquil as many of the lesser-known archaeological sites.

# 18
## From Tylissos to Rethymnon

*Tylissos, Kamariotis, Mount Ida – Idaian cave, Anogia, Eleutherna,*
*Arkadi Monastery, Melidoni cave, Rethymnon*

The inspiration for this itinerary came from the enslavement in 1645 of Evmenia Vergitzi (or Vorias) of the village of Kamariotis. My hopes were raised when I found the village on a map and on a geographical line with other places that had some woman connection. It would surely be worth the effort of trying to find it.

Our base for the itinerary was Archanes, at the end of September 2003, and, because it was when we both had feverish colds, we divided it into two; indeed, we only got as far as Tylissos on our first outing, and did not complete the itinerary as set out here on the second – we only got as far as Anogia. Thereafter, with what paper guidance I can give you, you are on your own.

### Tylissos
open 8.30 a.m. to 3.00 p.m.

The prosperous village, 14 km from Herakleion, lies in the shadow of Mount Ida (also known as Psiloritis). The archaeological site is within the village bounds – turn left as you enter the village, and left again; it should be marked.

Tylissos flourished throughout Minoan times but the main excavation is of three large Neopalatial houses which are seen today as part of a town which had its heyday at the height of Minoan civilisation. When we arrived we were, first, accosted by the wife of the guardian who, filling our hands with currants, was anxious to show us her stock of embroideries in their nearby house. Released, we discovered that the site, surrounded by pine trees and a wild purple convolvulus hedge, is quite charming; indeed, Derek pronounced it his favourite. And I liked the fact that the chief road engineer directing operations near the site was a young and lively woman. But my reason for going in the first place was a letter home from Hilda White (see pp. 289, 349 and 360) dated 3 March 1928. She wrote:

On the Monday afternoon before we left [Herakleion] we had a lovely expedition. It had been a grey wettish morning but it cleared about noon & we and the proprietor of the Minos got a car to Tylissos which is about two hours drive to the west of Knossos. It is fairly high up in the foothills of the Ida range so we ran into snow towards the end of our drive. The roads on the flat were very muddy in places & once we had to get out & walk. It was lovely when we got to the snow as it was brilliantly sunny & Mt Ida pure white & with a shimmering robe of snow haze. The village was a perfect mess of melting snow & I was glad I had on my rubber boots. One old hag was much amused at them as she thought I must be pretending to be a man — all the Cretan natives wear top boots with native dress — & thought she had detected me in my pretence. When we got out of the village the snow was crisp & unmelted & the country looked lovely. It was about the most interesting site we saw, so much of the houses remained standing & they are big & elaborate, palaces or at any rate buildings of great importance.

On our way back our chauffeur tried to charge the spot where he'd stuck coming, with the result that we stuck seriously & something smashed, so that we walked the last three miles home. It was a most lovely evening so it was quite a good thing from our point of view though bad for the owner of the car.

The journey today should be less gruelling, and the road is, at least, sealed, but then Hilda, as you will increasingly see, took everything in her stride.

## Kamariotis

We made a meal of finding Kamariotis, turning off to the right miles too early – the penalty of following old maps on which no direct road to the village was marked – and, indeed, nearly giving up after we had been round (and back and forth along) a large circle of almost deserted, hilly and barren, almost hostile countryside, with no one from whom to ask advice but goats. Only as we tried to get back to 'civilisation' – deciding that Kamariotis was inaccessible by that route – did we happen upon our goal.

When we finally left the village and regained the east–west road from which we turned off, we discovered that there was a new, wide, and well-signposted turning off towards the village. You may well wish to do it the easy way, so just hold your horses until, 6 km before Anogia, you see a signpost. I'm glad, though, that we went astray because it allowed us to see the landscape in which Evmania and her women family members lived – one probably little changed since

19.  Sultana Mah-para Ummatallah Rabia Gul-Nuz (Spring Rose-water), from Detorakis, *History of Crete*

1645. Though how the family came to seek refuge in Rethymnon, instead of staying put in this isolated corner away from the direction in which the Ottoman troops were moving is not easy to understand. Pages 116–18 will not only give you the historical context of the little girl's fate, but also tell you of how she became Spring Rose-water, the first and favourite wife of the Ottoman Sultan Mehmet IV.

Once you have found Kamariotis, you are taken back in time to the seventeenth century. You pass a charming little church on a rocky outcrop overlooking the village and a valley. Park and climb, first to the church – surely the one of which Evmenia's father was the priest – and then explore behind it where there are some ruins; it is not too hard to imagine they were once the priest's family home.

Drive on further into the village and there are many houses which look centuries old. Finally you come to a square in which you have to turn round. Ahead are two monuments to the fallen and what looks like a modern community hall but, to the right, is an old fountain built into an old wall which was surely there in Evmenia's day.

Without wishing to inflict coach loads of intruders on an unspoilt and probably unsuspecting village, overlooked by guidebooks, I do recommend this visit as something unusual and highly satisfying.

## Mount Ida – Idaian cave

### open 9.30 a.m. to 4.00 p.m., except Mondays

The draw of Mount Ida is that it is the other main location where Rhea is said to have given birth to the god Zeus. I tell the story in the itinerary that includes the Diktaian cave because you probably have to plump, at least in your imagination, for one or the other, and we visited Mount Dikte – rising above the Lasithi Plateau first (see p. 295). But, if Zeus was born elsewhere, he was raised on Mount Ida, and the rivalry between the two sites for the visitor trade is unobtrusive. Both are confident that they are the place, and pilgrims in the past treated both places as sacred – Zeus, of course, being a Johnny-come-lately, as far as the Minoans were concerned. As for the physical experience for the visitor, Mount Ida is the easier. The setting of both is stunning.

After turning left off the main road just before Anogia, you climb for 22 km – a narrow, winding but good road. During the first third of the climb you are on the edge looking down to the coast; the second third is barren rock landscape without edges; the last, you are on the edge of a strange escarpment overlooking the flat, dry, bleached Nida Plain.

Your first stop may be a rather utilitarian taverna, also looking across the mountain plain, where local people go in large parties for Sunday lunch, all dolled up, high heels and all (not really high-heels terrain). There was no free table but we ate rather delectable cheese and honey pies standing.

On the floor of the plain, the German artist **Karina Raeck** has laid out flat the 'Partisan of Peace', her contribution to healing the wounds made by German reprisals inflicted on Anogia for wartime resistance (see pp. 238–40). The installation is made up of 5,000 stones taken from opposite the Idaian cave with help from shepherds of the Nida Plain in which it rests. A photograph of Karina and her co-workers is contained in the well-meaning *Where Zeus Became a Man: With Cretan Shepherds* (n.d.) by another German, **Sabine Ivanova**. There is also a photograph of the 'Partisan of Peace', and other fine illustrations of the whole area and its people.

Shepherds are very much a feature of Mount Ida, and Sabine, who is settled in Crete, based at Milatos (see p. 308), spent some time getting to know and understand them in the mountains and in the village of Anogia. Her book, in German, Greek and English, has some useful insights. My favourite anecdotes have at their core a delightful pun which can lead the unwary astray but is useful for those women who, Sabine suggests, come to Crete for its more sensual pleasures.

Crete's best-known herb is dictamos (dittany), a plant of the marjoram family which has healing properties recognised since time immemorial. I drink the brew myself when I'm feeling a bit under the weather (see pp. 59 and 186). In Cretan dialect it is called *erodas*.

The Greek for sexual love is *erotas* which Cretans pronounce *erodas*. So Sabine tells how

A female tourist climbs up on Mount Psiloritis [Ida], going higher and higher because there the air is clean and the view spectacular. On the steep rocks she meets a shepherd who invites her with traditional Cretan hospitality to sit down with him which the woman accepts with pleasure. He asks her gesturing if she's hungry, she answers 'ja, ja', and eats with him olives and cheese. He asks gesturing if she's thirsty, she answers 'ja, ja', and drinks wine with him. At that other hungers of the body awaken inside her and knowing her host a little better by now she voices them (in the northern, uninhibited way) directly with one of the few Greek words she knows: 'Erotas, erotas!'

The shepherd, at a loss, repeats: 'But I told you, as high up as we are you don't find Erodas! Only further down!' and points downhill.

The woman gives up disappointedly and walks back down towards the sea. The shepherd still perplex [sic], follows her with his eyes shaking his head and says realistically: 'You don't need Erodas, you need a man to take you to bed properly!'

That story is doubtless apocryphal, but 36-year-old Sabine experienced her own version during her research in the mountains aided by a 20-year-old shepherd:

After some minutes of silence he offers me a deep, sensual, meaningful look, smiles encouragingly and asks: 'Do you want Erodas?'

I'm as much taken aback as I'm flattered and at a total loss for words right now. I remember the well-known words from Alexis Sorbas that it would be a sin for a man not to make love to a willing woman (because that's what God made her for, isn't it!)

So to make sure there are no doubts I say a little more irritatedly than I feel: 'But listen, X, how can you even ask that?'

He realizes at once that I'm not one of those willing women and corrects himself cleverly. 'No, no, you don't understand what I mean. I wanted to know if maybe you want Erodas' (without the sensual gaze I know that he means the herb now), 'the herb, you know', he adds unnecessarily.

Even more at a loss than before because I don't want to offend him I think for an answer. Fortunately I have an idea and turn the tables on him: 'No, No, no, I did understand you. It's only that I don't want Erodas because I already have it in my garden!'

Many early visitors to Crete note the abundance of medicinal herbs, particularly on Mount Ida.

You may well be sensible to park at the taverna and walk the rest of the way to the cave. We drove 2 km further on, a narrow, rocky, almost impossible track – how would anyone pass going the other way? But the walk would have been half an hour, mountain goat stuff (and we met plenty of those, and sheep). We were lucky to find a parking space where we could turn, but there were anxious moments. Then it was a 50-yard walk to the cave. Where the Diktaian cave goes down, down, down, the wide-mouthed Idaian cave extends sideways and inwards.

I became more interested in the cave when I was looking into the work of Efi and Yannis Sakellarakis (see pp. 214–25). I came across the English version of his beautiful book *Digging for the Past* (1996). In this thoughtful, even poetic, exploration of his life as an archaeologist, is a chapter on the Idaian cave with outstanding illustrations, including an unposed one of him and Efi in the cave. As it happens, Efi was not part of the archaeological team that Yannis directed here from 1982, but she visited him.

Featured, too, are some special finds which you should bear in mind as you venture into the cave. From the Archaic period there is a miniature ivory plaque in the Daedalic style (see pp. 75–6) of the Mistress of the Animals. She is dressed in an ornate chiton (see p. 38) and has the hairstyle of the seventh century BC. From the beginning of that century comes the head of an ivory pin used to gather a woman's garment, depicting two back-to-back women's heads wearing polos. Perhaps the most enviable objects are two pieces of jewellery stolen from the cave in 1884 and reassembled by the goldsmith J.G. Mitsotakis. On his death, his widow, **Terpsichore**, sold the gold neck-plate from the end of the eighth century BC depicting three female figures – it is now in the Archaeological Museum of Athens.

I bought my copy of the book in the Herakleion Archaeologic Museum. It's rather heavy but worth having, not only for the inscription, 'For Efi, for the realization of what Homer taught: "Our moving together".'

## Anogia

This is a village born of destruction that has spent its life since being destroyed and rebuilt. In Venetian times, Axos, the next village along, was a centre of rebellion, so the Venetians destroyed it. A new village emerged – the first mention of Anogia is 1583 – imbued with the spirit of rebels, bandits and fugitives. Such attitudes lasted until at least 1944, when the Germans destroyed Anogia in reprisal against the partisans working with British agents in the mountains – the kidnapped German General Kreipe was brought this way.

When you get to know the village and its people as Sabine Ivanova did and as the French anthropologist **Françoise Saulnier** did for her published 1980 doctoral thesis *Anoyia: un Village de, Montagne Crétois*, you obviously become very conscious of that past. As visitors who have been up to the Idaian cave and are only too ready for lunch, it becomes a place to seek a pleasant taverna. But we found it so full of foreign visitors who eyed us without friendliness from the security of their taverna tables, and so full of little places where women were too keen to sell their woven wares, that we left hungry.

I suspect that was a false impression and that hunger made us hypercritical. However, Sabine Ivanova does pick up on a theme explored by Sonia Greger on the Lasithi Plateau concerning weaving (see p. 299). Sabine explains that the handmade wares in Crete are often too expensive for tourists, so many shops stock goods made in China instead. She concludes, 'So the art of weaving, once supposed to be a gift of the ancient Greek Goddess Athena will probably here also ... be forgotten soon. Let's hope that together with it Cretan women's pride and independence doesn't get lost too.'

In *Where Zeus Became a Man*, Sabine introduces us verbally and pictorially to several Anogia women with whom she made friends and from whom she learnt. Elderly widows still remember their loved ones shot, and their village burnt down, in 1944, and Sabine quotes from a poem by **Katerina** (Katika) **Parasyris**, whose husband was shot when she was pregnant with their second child, which starts:

> Four *Palikaria* the Germans caught and tied their hands
> Young men, just married or betrothed.

But as you read what Sabine writes, you should remind yourself that she is German, and Katika, who had remained unmarried in memory of her husband, obviously accepted her for what she is. Memories have not faded, but bitterness is not passed on.

1944 was by no means the first time that Anogia, like Axos before it, was caught up in resistance to an invader. Françoise Saulnier tells how, in the 1822 revolt against the Ottomans, Stavros Niotis, a rebel leader up in the mountains, gave his sister in the village a sheep's bell and told her to ring it should an enemy troop approach. 'The sister rang the bell 8 times and Niotis and Balmetis, waiting in ambush by the roadside, killed them one after the other.' In due course the village was destroyed.

In 1866, when rebels from the area were victorious over Omar Pasha and Rashid Pasha, the Ottomans destroyed the village again. When villages were laid to waste in Ottoman times, the inhabitants who weren't killed, mostly women and children, were taken captive and sold as slaves. In the Ottoman chapter, on p. 127, I tell the story of an Anogia woman to whom this had happened some years before the English traveller Spratt met her.

Françoise Saulnier quotes a long poem, written by **Irini Anagnostaki** following the 1944 reprisals, which she has translated from the Greek into French, so that my English translation from hers

must lose most of the poetry; I quote just a few couplets to convey
the sentiments if not the music:

> Flowers do not open, birds do not sing
> They have burnt our Anogia, hold it to you in pity.
> One Sunday morning at the hour of Mass,
> The Germans came to Anogia looking for men of the Resistance ...
> The mountains dressed in black and the old Psiloritis
> Cry for the village of Anogia, for the heroes of Crete. ...
> They lit the fire and turned you to cinders.
> They destroyed your beautiful houses, pillaged your possessions:
> Your trousseaux, your riches, and your flocks of sheep so numerous. ...
> The birds came from Egypt to spend the summer
> But at Anogia they found no walls to shelter their nests.

And she ends:

> Those who write of Anogia's suffering
> Should have studied at University.
> But I am just an unlettered woman, with children.
> And if I've made mistakes, my brothers, forgive me.

Unfortunately, Françoise Saulnier's ethnographic thesis, the result
of several stays lasting months in the 1970s, is rather inaccessible (I
found a copy only in the Bodleian Library, Oxford) and useful only
for determined scholars. But if you see a bent old woman in black
in Anogia, imagine her past.

The next three places may well be too far too add to a day's journey;
perhaps they would be best visited coming from Rethymnon, or even
the direction of Chania, but they fit geographically and you will know
your circumstances.

## Eleutherna

By 1929, Hilda White, who visited Tylissos in March 1928 with John
Pendlebury, was married to him. Following the visit they made to

Crete in 1929, he was to be offered and to accept the curatorship of Knossos. At the same time, another young man, Humfry Payne, had just been appointed Director of the British School at Athens, and he was married to Dylis Powell (see p. 169), whose *The Villa Ariadne* is such a mine of information about Knossos, the Pendleburys, their contemporaries and their times. Humfry Payne's Cretan archaeological site was to be Eleutherna, and in 1929 he went on a recce there with the Pendleburys. Dylis was not with them, but was to meet Hilda at Knossos in 1931 (see p. 203).

Little of Hilda's writing of her experiences in Crete has been published; everything else I quote in this book is from unpublished letters, but in 1964 *Archaeology* published 'A Journey in Crete' which includes the visit to Eleutherna and Arkadi. The party approached it from a foray to the Archaeological Museum in Rethymnon and Hilda wrote, in a way which makes for regret that more was not published, given that, over the years, she tramped and clambered the length and breadth of Crete with John (see p. 375):

The acropolis of Eleutherna stands like an island amidst encircling valleys and is approached by a causeway. We pitched our camp on a terrace of olive trees at the northwest end; on a lower terrace there was a crop still green, and amongst the tall shoots grew wild gladiolus. As I lay on my camp bed in the open, I saw at dawn the pale wheat, the brilliant magenta of the gladiolus, grey-green olives against a clear blue sky and, far off, the snow-covered peak of Ida. So still was the weather that at night a candle set on a rock beneath the olives burned unwinking.

There was no water on the acropolis; a small zig-zag path led down on the northwest side near a Byzantine fortification tower to a spring, and going down it recalled to me the rock-cut pathway to Enneakrounos down the Acropolis at Athens.

Almost two days we spent in this enchanted spot while Humfry Payne investigated the site with a view to its future excavation. When these excavations took place, proof was found of the occupation of the site from Geometric until Byzantine times.

Eleutherna was one of the main towns of the Archaic/Classical period (700–330 BC), and it was here that the large stone figure of Athena in the Daedalic style (Herakleion Museum, room XIX) was found (see pp. 75 and 192).

## Arkadi Monastery

The Pendlebury/Payne party went on to the Arkadi Monastery – whose terrible 1866 destruction (including the death of 600 women and children) I put in context in the Ottoman chapter (see p. 133). Hilda Pendlebury sketches in those events but shows in the rest of her account of their visit how the destruction of the past had led to ultimate rejuvenation:

The monastery stands in a lovely upland plain dotted with vast ilex trees and is one of the largest and most prosperous in the island. The abbot entertained us most hospitably, giving us clean airy bedrooms, inviting us to his own table and plying us with food and drinks; breakfast was extremely varied, including coffee, a mug of milk and cognac.

Owing to this hospitality and some interesting conversation, as the less remote Cretan monasteries are much interested in the outside world and like to keep abreast with its politics, it was nearly 8:30 a.m. that we got under way.

## Melidoni cave

open all day, every day

To reach Melidoni from the Arkadi Monastery, you will have to wiggle north-east onto a bigger east–west road, and then turn off that – the village and cave are signposted.

The cave was a traditional sanctuary – Eileithyia was worshipped there (see p. 11) – but it is better known and revered today because of what happened there in 1866, when women and children refugees from Melidoni and nearby villages were deliberately suffocated by smoke (see p. 128).

Robert Pashley travelled through this area 15 years later and talked to the men who had taken to the mountains and come down to find the remains of their loved ones. 'Who could describe the anguish of these unhappy men', he wrote, 'when they saw lying dead on the ground, and despoiled even of their clothes, those whose safety they had vainly imagined to have been secured when they were once within the grotto?'

He was taken to the cave and noted: 'at the entrance is a group of skulls: in the first cavern also are two heaps of skulls and human bones'. Going deeper and deeper into the intricate complex of caves he adds: 'Near the great central mass [of stalagmites] the bones and skulls of the poor Christians are so thickly scattered, that it is almost impossible to avoid crushing them as we pick our steps along.' Back in the village he identifies some of the dead:

The Proestos of Melidhoni, Konstantinos Konstantudhakes, my host, had two sisters, one sister-in-law, and twelve other relations in the cave: his wife lost a sister with all her children, and two uncles. The other surviving villagers of Melidhoni lost their relations in a similar way. Melidhoni, before the Greek revolution, contained 140 Christian and ten Mohammedan families; about four times its present population.

## Rethymnon

This introduction to one of Crete's larger towns is sadly incomplete and concentrates on the Venetian fortress which still dominates the town; my researches have not allowed me to do better. Perhaps you can help.

The artist Mary Walker, in Crete from Istanbul in the 1870s (see p. 136), tells us in *Sketches of Eastern Life and Scenery* what Rethymnon looked like from the sea as her ship paused in the roads on the way to Chania:

At the foot of the Fortress that crowns a high rocky eminence on the west; two or three palm-trees, and some minarets, varied by glittering church crosses, show the position of the town. Around the bay a few swelling hills pleasantly wooded, country houses, olives and vineyards, a small fort upon the shore, and — far off amongst the clouds — the vague outline of Mount Ida, compose all the impression that can be formed of Rethymo, before yielding once more to the agitated character of these Cretan waters.

This passage from Michael Herzfeld's *A Place in History: Social and Monumental Time in a Cretan Town* (1991) brings the scene more up to date:

The Fortezza is an ambivalent presence for Rethemniots. On the one hand, it is an impressive remnant of their links with the West European awakening ... But it is also a reminder of past tyrannies, Nazi as well as Venetian and Turkish, in its last real inhabitants the destitute and the formerly enslaved, and its physical proximity to the brothels an unsavory memory. A local town-planning official has suggested that only full restoration and recontextualization — with a 'green-zone' replacing the brothel district — can dispel its darker shadows.

Photographs in the book are mostly by Herzfeld's wife, Cornelia Mayer Herzfeld.

Michael Herzfeld mentions **Lilika Nakou** (1899–1989), a 'Paris-polished' teacher who, in 1956, published an autobiographical novel which 'still excites lively controversy'. Unfortunately, this novel, first written in French as *Madame Do-Re-Mi* (1947), is not readily available and it, too, reinforces the Fortezza's image: 'The hapless young teacher', Herzfeld recounts ' accidentally led the adolescent girls in her charge to the Fortezza for an educational stroll, not realizing it was a brothel zone!' At the time of Herzfeld's study, Lilika's novel, by then a television series, still rankled. A biography by Deborah Tannen came to hand too late to elaborate on the young Athenian writer who spent 1933 teaching in a boys' and then a girls' school in Rethymnon.

As if that were not enough about Rethymnon's prostitutes, I have to remind you of the discovery there in 1923 of Fatma, once the enchanting Mme Hortense who earlier entertained all four Great Power admirals in Chania (see pp. 143 and 149). Did she work in the shadow of the Venetian fortress?

Though the fortress is not only associated with prostitution, it's historical connection with women is largely unhappy. It was the fall of the Fortezza in 1645 that led to the taking of Rethymnon by Ottoman forces. I describe the scene on p. 116. And one of those taking refuge within its walls then was the little Evmenia Vergitzi from Kamariotis (see p. 147)

Near the Fortezza is the archaeological museum. Of contemporary art, Pat Cameron describes the private collection of the late **Eleni Frantzeskaki** which was bequeathed to the municipality and, until 2000, was on show in a gallery opposite the nearby Kanakakis Centre for Contemporary Art. 'The work of this self-taught Cretan artist', Pat writes, 'was inspired by the traditional folk motifs that she collected all over Greece. Her beliefs in the role of women in society and the importance of the ecological movement were ahead of her time in Crete.' Because Pat's *Blue Guide* was not available to me in time, I did not pursue this lead; if you are a determined traveller, perhaps you could, and let me know – and, indeed about any other relevant women and places in Rethymnon.

# 19
## South to the Mesara Plain

*Mironas and Kato Asites, Matala and Kommos, the Italians, Vori, Gortyn,
Phaistos, Hagia Triada*

There are two main routes from the north to that central south area
dominated by the archaeological sites of Gortyn and Phaistos: one
is bearing south-east from Rethymnon; the other, south-west from
Herakleion. If you leave from Herakleion you can consider visiting
one or two places on the way.

## Mironas and Kato Asites

If, instead of taking the main road south, you peel off at the junction
of the east–west, north–south routes, onto the network of minor
roads going via Mironas and Asites, you could remember the women
and children slaughtered in the nearby Sarchos cave by Ottoman
forces in 1866 (see p. 133). This cave, and that incident, though
mentioned in historical records, does not appear to be a place of
pilgrimage like the Melidoni (see p. 242) and Milatos (see p. 308).
A British wife and husband team who live in the area and, under
the team name Scott Davies (Paula Scott and Mike Davies) have
published *Riding the Minotaur* (1999), describe a nearby cave system,
a lake and an underground stream which 'comes out in a cave in
Sarhos'. They continue: 'Some of the inner chambers of this cave
contain hundreds of bats hanging from the roof. We have explored
this cave system but found no evidence of human occupation except
for the entrance chamber which is still used as a shelter for the
shepherd and his flock.' They do not appear to be aware of 1866

(see p. 133), and 1944 wartime reprisals are much closer to home for people round here.

This does, however, give me the chance to introduce to you their interesting book (available in Crete) about buying a property in Kato Asites, doing it up, experiencing Cretan bureaucracy, and participating in non-tourist village life. As I've discussed more than once, women's weaving and embroidery done for sale to visitors is in competition with cheap imported wares (see pp. 238 and 299), so it is refreshing to read of such work done on their own account:

From an early age girls are taught needlework and start to replicate the ancient patterns used to make the table cloths, antimacassars, doilies and pillow cases that will form the basis of their 'bottom drawer'. Women spend all their spare time, particularly during the winter, on this craft. On warm days they sit outside in small groups, facing the wall, chatting while they prepare these items for their daughter's wedding.

You can also nip through to **Kroussonas**, famous for weaving, and the nearby **Hagia Irini Convent**, whose nuns sell their needlework for a living. Further on the Mironas road is the ancient site of **Rizenia (Prinias)** (see pp. 75 and 253). Between Rizenia and Hagia Varvara, there are some strange rocky excrescences known as *Tis Grias ta Tiria* ('Cheeses of the Old Woman') – don't ask me why, and I haven't seen them but they are said to cause sudden and inexplicable rainstorms. If you stick to the main north–south road from Herakleion, you can turn off to the Paliani Convent and Prophitis Ilias (see pp. 27–8).

We were staying near Chania so took the Rethymnon route and, as we decided that it was not an itinerary to do in a day there and back, we decided to stay at the seaside resort of Matala.

## Matala and Kommos

Matala is now very much a tourist centre, but in the mists of time things were different. This book starts on its beach, sheltered by a long cliff honeycombed with caves (Roman tombs), once so fashionable with hippies (now an archaeological site); here Europa came ashore on the back of a bull, the god Zeus in disguise (see p. 3).

In early Minoan times Matala was the chief port for Phaistos. After the Gortynians captured Phaistos in c.220 BC, it became their port. Just north of Matala is the ancient site of Kommos, since 1965 excavated by a wife and husband team – **Maria Shaw** (née Coutroubaki) and Joseph W. Shaw – of the American School of Classical Studies. The second temple there, dating from the eighth century BC, has a shrine with Phoenician attributes, and Phoenician pottery has also been found. Trade between this area and Phoenicia is deduced but I have come across no scholar suggesting a link between that trade and the myth of the Phoenician princess Europa.

Matala is perfectly nice if you like popular seaside resorts, and local people were certainly very kind to me when I broke a bone in my foot that evening strolling along the prom. The chef at the restaurant at which we then dined came with a bag of ice, while the manager hovered sympathetically; and the landlady at our clean, spare pension bathed my foot in warm water. The clinic in Mires the following morning did not have an X-ray machine but bound me in a tight bandage sprayed with painkiller. On our return to Chania that second evening, I was advised that accident and emergency was best visited in the evening, and we could not fault the efficient, speedy and kindly treatment I received. Though, be alerted, some airlines will not allow you to travel in a plaster cast (because of undue swelling and, presumably, potential legal action); it must be slit.

## The Italians

Four modern women fuel our interest in this area, all Italian scholars; indeed, this is another of the four spheres of foreign influence that dominated early twentieth century archaeology in Crete. Frederico Halbherr set up the Italian Archaeological Mission to Crete – based at Gortyn and Phaistos – in 1899. In 1910, Gaetano De Sanctis joined the mission at Phaistos, bringing with him his wife Emilia Rosmini (see p. 166).

## Vori

The couple stayed in the village of Vori, today just off the main east to west road, the other side of it from Phaistos. (Before you get to Vori you pass the **Kalyviani Convent**, on the right, where the nuns run an orphanage and a school; they also support themselves by weaving, embroidery and other handicrafts.) Vori is a pleasant, quiet village where you might prefer to stay.

Emilia De Sanctis Rosmini passed most of her three and a half months in Crete there, and it was rather more off the beaten track than it is today. Emilia, as you may have noticed in her descriptions of women under Turkish rule (see p. 146) and the work at Knossos (see p. 200), tended towards the negative and the literary. Although she was university educated (she had been her husband's student), she was not included, or chose not to be included, in the Mission's work; instead, she was left on her own most of the time in Vori while the men went off exploring likely terrain and supervising work at the archaeological sites. At first she communicated by sign language; gradually she picked up some Greek words 'in common use' from the domestic servants. She passed her days in a cocoon of implicit loneliness; as she put it herself, 'I went to study at the school of solitude.' There she tended to see the darker side of Crete; as a result, she wrote of the people of Vori in *Dalla Canea a Tripoli* (1912):

The women, sitting at their loom, or in the doorway, nearly all dressed in mourning, for death has abundantly harvested in each house, carry out their work like automatons, without a flicker of joy ever enlivening their apathetic faces, closed as if by a numb sadness. The young ones, not at all ugly, live mainly inside because there is always the danger of abduction. Then, the men, too, nearly all brown and handsome in a masculine way, spend their time silently smoking, sitting or lounging in the cafe like statues. The sentiment of love, when it is not polluted by the murky fantasies that civilised men attach to it, when it is simply, naturally displayed, goes straight to its goal and, when it is not poisoned by malaria, prepares physically healthy and strong generations. But here at Vori the wing of death wanders over everything and the sign of fever past or that which is to come is the pallid tinge of the sad and emaciated faces.

Don't worry about malaria today, but there are mosquitoes in Crete and you will want to take the usual precautions. Emilia's book is not easy to come by; indeed, I have only had access to it through Giovanna Bandini's *Lettere dell'Egeo: Archeologhe Italiane fra 1900 e 1950* (2003), and the same mostly applies to the Italian archaeologists who follow – their scholarly works are available in specialist libraries such as the Sackler in Oxford. The acclaimed Vori **Museum of Cretan Ethnology** (open 10.00 a.m. to 6.00 p.m.), with its wide range of cultural artefacts of the eighteenth and nineteenth centuries, gives a different impression from Emilia's – a good antidote.

## Gortyn

If you come from Herakleion, you will arrive first at Gortyn; from Rethymnon, the order is Hagia Triada, Phaistos, Gortyn. I am going to start you at Gortyn; it was the place where the foreign women who started to arrive in Crete in 1900 headed for. Harriet Boyd, on her way to learn from Frederico Halbherr before looking for her own site, left Knossos and wrote of the journey towards Gortyn:

To the south a magnificent panorama, far below us the great Messara plain and beyond this, through gaps in the coast-mountains, the brilliant Libyan Sea. Our guide told us there were once fifty Mohammedan villages in this plain 'Now it is a desert', he said, but ... a richer lovelier tract of land cannot be imagined.

Ellen Bosanquet, who visited Crete for the first time in 1904, wrote in *Days in Attica*,

Even if there be time for nothing else, ride across the hills to the great Messara Plain, put up at Gortyna — where you can wash in a Greek sarcophagus, and sleep in a guest-chamber approached by a staircase of ancient Doric capitals — and then ride on next day to Phaistos and Hagia Triada, where Italian scholars have unearthed the homes of the Minoan princes of Southern Crete.

And Gortyn is where Zeus brought Europa from Matala in those mists of time. Images of the goddess at Gortyn, or Gortyna, are pervasive throughout history and the festival there was called Hellotis, the Cretan name for Europa. I had assumed that Zeus transformed himself from a bull to seduce her, but that does not appear to be so. A series of coins from the Archaic/Classical period depicting the marriage of Europa and Zeus was found at Gortyn, and another coin has Europa on one side sitting under a willow tree and the bull Zeus on the other licking his flank. Traditionally it was a plane tree that Europa and Zeus lay under to conceive Minos. And there was, according to the Greek philosopher and botanist Theophrastus, still such a tree there in the fourth century BC, evergreen to celebrate the mystical and mythical union. Indeed, according to Pat Cameron, there is still a *Platanos Orientalis* at Gortyn, near the watermill beyond the fenced area behind the Odeon.

The British traveller Thomas Spratt talks of fragments of a rearing sculptured bull found at Gortyn in the 'large theatre', nearly life-size and with them the torso of a sitting female figure. The bull has part of a female hand on its shoulder and scholars had deduced by Spratt's day (1865) that 'It was a group representing Europa upon the Bull which characterises some of the coins of Gortyna.' These finds are now in the British Museum. I assume the 'large theatre' is that across the River Mitropolianos from the Odeon.

Most people go to Gortyn to see the Hellenistic-Roman Odeon, not so much for that building but for the remains discovered from an earlier structure on the site: the extraordinary slabs of limestone on which were inscribed in the fifth century BC what is known as the Gortyn Code – the laws of the people living in the area in the seventh century BC. I give details of the contents of the code and its historical context on pp. 72–5 – a clear picture emerges of laws affecting women then. If you see nothing else at Gortyn, see this. I have to say that it is all I saw: it was our second day and I somehow hobbled from the nearby car park to the Odeon and back.

A great deal of scholarly work has been done on the code and other inscriptions, particularly for the four volumes (in Latin) *Inscriptiones Creticae* (1935–50) under the editorship of the epigraphist Margherita Guarducci (see p. 168). She joined Halbherr at Gortyn in 1928 and returned there for ten subsequent seasons, working on the inscriptions he had started collecting in 1884. She travelled widely, adding to the collection and, following his death in 1930, saw their ambitious project through to fruition. As for Halbherr's early opinion of Margherita, when she was 26, a letter he wrote in 1928 to the director of the Italian School at Athens is instructive:

As you will know, we have with us Miss Guarducci who researches at all levels and works to her and my satisfaction. It seems to me that of all your women students this one is without any argument the best. Fortunately in Crete this year there is no typhus. This allows me to expose her to a few short but demanding journeys without anxiety.

In a conference paper of 1996 – 'For Love of the Truth' – delivered only three years before her death at aged 97, Margherita described those little journeys; here is a taste:

In the Crete of those days there were no roads fit for a vehicle, and there was just one which joined Canea to Heraklion, and one from Heraklion to the Messara Plain as far as Gortyn, not going as far as the Libyan Sea, that was all. ... When I went about on the back of a mule, [the foreman] Zacharis, in Cretan costume with its trousers and waistcoat, followed me faithfully. We travelled with two little camp beds and a tent if we couldn't find lodgings, but other times we were offered hospitality by kind families.

Sites other than the Odeon are not as accessible or as obvious and cover a wide area. If you are keen to explore, consider getting **Athanasia Kanta**'s *Phaistos, Hagia Triadha, Gortyn* (1998) which has a good separate map of all three sites and some lovely, and useful, illustrations, all in colour, which will help with identification.

Opposite the Odeon, too, a little north-west of the theatre (on the southern brow of the hill), is the fenced Temple of Athena also dating from the Archaic period (seventh century BC) and, below that, Athena's altar of sacrifice; also found there was the relief carving of a triad of feminine deities with hair like judges' wigs (Daedalic), naked except for polos (see p. 192). This and the seated cult statue of Athena are in the Herakleion Museum (room XIX).

Another of Gortyn's prosperous times was after the Roman conquest in 68 BC when the city state co-operated with Rome (see p. 86). Other remains date from that period, lasting until AD 330. The Temple of the Egyptian Divinities or the Sanctuary of the Egyptian Gods is south-east of the Odeon. This temple was dedicated to Isis, the principal goddess of Ancient Egypt, and her husband Osiris. It can be dated to the first to second century AD from the inscription that tells of its rebuilding by Flavia Philyra and her two sons (see p. 89).

Not far to the south-west is one of two nymphaeums (second century AD), an enclosed fountain built as a shrine to the nymphs, young semi-divine girls who personified the countryside, particularly rivers and streams. A statue of Aphrodite, with a bowl protecting her modesty, now in room XX of the Herakleion Museum, comes from one of the nymphaeums (see pp. 88 and 192). And far to the east is a Temple of Demeter and Kore. Excavation by the Italian School continues.

## Phaistos

Phaistos is, after Knossos, the second most important archaeological site in Crete. For that reason it tends to be well-visited, though there should be nothing like the crowds at Knossos. Having only ever gone to Crete in the relative cool of the autumn, I have no idea what the crowds and heat might be like in the high season.

Most of what you see excavated is of the Second Palace, though people settled there from the earliest times: neolithic female figurines have been found (see p. 10); there are bits of the First Palace, and a great deal of Kamares ware from that period – including the eggshell fine cups. I discuss on pp. 28–9 the significance of two Kamares pieces, a bowl and an offering stand depicting women dancing (both in room III of the Herakleion Museum). And there are remains dating from Hellenistic times. Athanasia Kanta's map colour-codes the different periods, as does the smaller site leaflet you get with your tickets.

The most famous artefact found at Phaistos is the disc, now also in room III of the Herakleion Museum. The pictorial script covering both sides has still not been decoded; I discuss on p. 21 efforts by Melian Stawell to do so in the 1920s. The disc was found in 1903 in a series of clay chests in what is called the archive room, not far from what is assumed were the quarters of the ruling family. At the opposite extreme of the entrance to the site is a temple of the Classical period thought to have been dedicated to Rhea (Zeus' mother). Melian Stawell thought the Phaistos disc was dedicated to Rhea, but the temple and the disc are by no means contemporary and her interpretation was not accepted.

The disc was found under the direction of Frederico Halbherr, and it is noteworthy that the methods of excavation and preservation at Phaistos owe nothing to those of Arthur Evans at Knossos. This undoubtedly explains Emilia De Sanctis Rosmini's disapproving comments about Knossos (see p. 200).

The third of our Italian women in this area – Luisa Banti – arrived initially in 1930 and then regularly from 1932 (see p. 168). Although eight years older than her colleague Margherita Guarducci at Gortyn, Luisa came to Crete after her, having had to fight parental opposition for some years before becoming a scholar. But then Halbherr's colleague Luigi Perniers invited her to join him at Phaistos. She took part in excavations there and at Hagia Triada until 1939. When Perniers died, she completed *Il Palazzo Minoico di Festos* (1935) – chronicling the Italian Mission's finds of 1900–34. She also returned to Crete after the Second World War and, travelling round on horseback, produced a scholarly guidebook to the Italian sites, *Guida agli Scavi Italiani in Creta* (1949).

In a heading 'Excursion from Candia to the Messara', she advises visitors to spend their first morning at Gortyn and the afternoon at Hagia Triada in order to arrive at Phaistos that evening and spend the night in the Hellenic Tours Hotel there, for

Few spectacles are so splendid and picturesque as the sunset and the dawn; there are few memories so unforgettable as the absolute and overwhelming calm of the night hours, interrupted only by the trilling of crickets and the croaking of frogs.

The setting of Phaistos, even by day, is fine though the extensive site itself is a little confusing. It suited me best to appreciate its sweep, rather than to try and follow its particulars.

Although their years at the Italian excavations overlapped, Luisa and Margherita were not apparently close friends, but Giovanna Bandini, in summing up their lives and work in Crete, finds common threads:

Like Margherita Guarducci, Luisa Banti had crossed Crete from one end to the other, climbing along hills on horseback, fording rivers, and propelling herself down the side of mountains; she had studied and excavated in the torrid heat of summer and in the freezing cold of late autumn. She, too, like Guarducci, had done it in the name of a mission more spiritual than that of the Italian Archaeological Mission to Crete, a vocation in which the push towards doing research was also the expression of profound religious faith. Both Banti and Guarducci 'married' archaeology and turned their profession into a sort of apostolate, in a renunciation – probably conscious – of their private life, a choice for which they have been dubbed by fellow scholars 'women without lipstick'.

Elsewhere, Giovanna Bandini reports that Margherita Guarducci would have liked to be a mother: 'But I had to be continually on the move – how could I have children?'

Enrica Fiandra (see p. 175), who arrived at Phaistos as an architect in 1955, was rather different from her colleagues of the earlier generation. Doro Levi, Director of the Italian School at Athens, had taken over from Perniers, and Enrica's relationship with him was not that of an amanuensis. Her views on Phaistos were not the same as his and many scholars have found hers the more convincing: they proposed two different interpretations of the stratigraphy and history of the site.

Enrica's letters from Crete take up half of Giovanna Bandini's *Lettere del Egeo* and are sprinkled with cartoons like the one here. It depicts the stratigraphical museum which she set up behind the cafe at Phaistos (not open to the public) and a portrait of her friend Clelia Laviosa. The caption reads, 'Fire protection system set up by Enrica who believes blindly in the luck of the Professor.' The seated figure to the left is marked 'the large hunchback of Vori', suggesting that Emilia Rosmini's comments about the health of the people of Vori 40 years earlier may have had some validity.

*sistemazione antincendio fatta dall'Enrica che crede ciecamente nella fortuna del Prof.*

20. Cartoon by Enrica Fiandra of Stratigraphical Museum, Phaistos, courtesy of the artist

Conditions at Phaistos in 1955 were pretty primitive, even though Enrica travelled by Vespa instead of on horseback or by mule. There was no electricity until 1959; there was no running water and the accommodation was still torrid in summer and freezing in the autumn. In 1957, she spent several months at Phaistos by herself and was to do so in subsequent years. She was camping and only later built the mission house. She felt completely safe, however. Her Greek was good enough to understand and be understood and she gained respect from the workmen – about whom she wrote little character sketches – not because she was a foreigner, or educated, or a woman – even though from time to time she experienced gallantry – but because she was as capable as them.

In 1960, because of the unhygienic conditions in which she lived, Enrica became ill; then she was looked after 'like a Prussian colonel' by **Maria Nidavriadaki**, a sort of housekeeper. This Maria had replaced **Maria Fasoulakis** (1892–1970) whom Halbherr had adopted and sent to study in Italy; she later married Zacharis Iliakis, the Mission foreman (presumably the same Zacharis who accompanied Margherita Guarducci, see p. 252).

The following year, Levi tried to stop Enrica giving her views at a conference, nor could she publish; only he, as director, could do that. But on the breakup of their relationship, she thanked him for all he had taught her.

It is a pity that reading matter by or about these Italian women is not, apparently, available in English, but I hope I have given you enough of a flavour of their lives and work to imagine them at Phaistos and elsewhere.

## Hagia Triada

open 8.30 a.m. to 3.00 p.m.

This site is much more intimate than Phaistos and is assumed to have been the summer residence of the rulers of Phaistos, situated as it is just 3 km away. Though the villa dates from the New, or Second, Palace period (about 1600 BC), there is evidence of settlement, as at Phaistos, from before the Minoan palaces to the Ottomans.

Ellen Bosanquet visited the site in the early days of excavation and explains, in *Days in Attica*, how

The Messara Plain becomes an oven during the summer months, and it seems to have been for the sake of escaping the excessive heat that they built another settlement an hour's ride from Phaistos in a cooler spot. On the southern end of the same rocky ridge, with a wide outlook towards the sea on one side and the snows of Ida on the other, the Italians are now excavating a series of villas of the same period as the palace.

The rulers' quarters are in the north-west of the complex, in the corner of the L-shape. Here were found fine frescoes showing two women; one seated at an altar or shrine, another picking crocuses. A nearby stalking cat particularly took Ellen's fancy, allowing her imagination full rein:

The well-known fresco of the wild cat stalking a pheasant comes from a set of rooms that may well have belonged to the princess of the reigning house. Her apartments are set to the north, and from the cool terrace outside there is a view of the sea, and snow mountains that sets one thinking of Etna's white slopes against the blue sea and coast of Sicily. The rooms here are small and must have been as exquisite as they were tiny. The little light-well set round with three columns each of a different marble and the diminutive doors and passage suggest the toy-home of a petted little Minoan lady, dainty as Japan and gay as Paris.

But the best-known artefact comes from a Postpalatial tomb in the burial ground to the north-east of the villa. The painted stone sarcophagus is given pride of place in room XIV of the Herakleion Museum. It is apparently from the Mycenaean period but suggests the continuing practice of Minoan funeral rites (see also p. 61). Not surprisingly, this exceptional relic has provoked more than one interpretation.

I cannot help but be taken by that of Henri van Effenterre, as propounded by his wife Micheline in *Les Minoens*, which uses on its cover the image I reproduce here. This woman, Micheline suggests, is the reigning queen Pasiphae, wife of Minos and daughter-in-law of Europa. The corpse inside the sarcophagus is Phoenix, father of Europa and founder of the Phoenicians. In front of Pasiphae is the

21.   Queen Pasiphae on Hagia Triada sarcophagus,
      from van Effenterre, *Les Minoens*

bull, Zeus and, in front of him, Europa. Needless to say, not everyone agrees. But I would be less than human if I did not relish a theory from serious scholars that allows this itinerary neatly to join the two ends of a circle.

# 20
## Chania

*Archaeological Museum, Wandering Aimlessly*

Chania is, perhaps, the most accessible of Crete's big towns but, for our purposes, identifiable places within its bounds are a bit limited, and its quaint harbour, strung as it is with tavernas, inevitably confirms to you that you are a tourist. In the environs of the town, however, there are some unusual villages, fewer archaeological sites than further to the east of the island, more places suggesting modern women's history and concerns. Chania is, therefore, the hub from which the next itinerary radiates, first south and west, then eastwards.

On our first visit to Crete we spent three weeks at Megala Chorafia, on a hill overlooking Souda Bay, 20 minutes' drive east of Chania, but we were so busy going round and about that we visited it infrequently. It would obviously repay more attention than we gave it. I suspect one should, ideally, stay in the town for a few days and roam almost aimlessly in the cool of the evening. While doing this, remember women who have wandered the streets of the old town before you; I will remind you here of those mentioned in the historical section. And I made one intriguing discovery while writing this chapter.

If you have limited time in Chania, the place to head for is the particularly pleasing archaeological museum, once a church and a mosque; to go there first will allow me to sketch the story of Chania's earliest years through its women.

### Archaeological Museum

seaward end of Chalidon Street;
open Tuesday–Sunday 8.30 a.m. to 3.00 p.m.

Since 1960, excavations taking place on the south-east of Kastelli hill have suggested an important Bronze Age settlement dating back to at least Prepalatial times. This site has only recently opened to the public. The problems of excavating in the middle of a modern town, one which also flourished in Venetian and Ottoman times, are obvious, and some finds have been made in the process of recent building. But it is believed that another, later, Minoan palace existed there, one which had been rebuilt more grandly following the destruction of c.1450 BC. And in Mycenaean times – particularly following the later destruction of Knossos c.1380 BC – what then existed became the centre of power on the island. When Mycenaean power came to an end in its turn Chania, or Cydonia (a much larger area), flourished in the Dorian period under King Cydon (see p. 78).

To establish the pedigree of King Cydon (sometimes Kydon), we are back to legendary times, though there is mention of the place name 'ku-do-ni-ja' on Linear B tablets found at Knossos. Cydon was said to be the grandson of Pasiphae and Minos, and the son of their daughter Acacallis (sister of Ariadne and Phaedra from a union with the gods Apollo or Hermes (see p. 78). The women at that time probably lived under the Gortyn Code (see pp. 72–3) and managed the family's property while the men were away fighting. Unfortunately, as a result of building activity, remains within modern Chania still elude archaeologists.

It is from Hellenistic times, 330–67 BC, when Cydonia was one of the most powerful city-states, that finds exhibited in the museum, and connected with women, begin to bring Chania's history alive. One of the most alluring finds, partly because the family concerned is identifiable, came from the Mathioulakis house rock-cut family tomb found just to the south-west of today's law courts in the Hagios Ioannis district (south east Chania; open only to specialists). Maria Andreadaki-Vlasaki, archaeologist and director of the museum, tells us in *The County of Khania Through its Monuments*, that it is 'an outstanding example of funerary architecture'. This subterranean tomb was approached by a staircase and had nine burial chambers opening off from a narrow vaulted corridor. The graceful late fourth century BC Tanagra terracotta figurine of a woman's head and one shoulder now in the museum were found there (see also p. 83).

In a simple cist grave in the same area, archaeologists found an exquisite gold necklace and elaborate gold earrings from the third century BC – also in the museum (see also p. 85). These jewels are as striking as any you will see.

And from another family tomb came a now complete figurine of a woman in flowing robes, with a dark, v-necked bodice and an upturned brim of a head-dress. A charming marble statue of Aphrodite, from the late Hellenistic period, is rather less clothed; her robe has slipped down to her thighs. I cannot help noticing that these three women have slightly inclined heads, suggesting expected modesty, even though Aphrodite is naked and the stance of the robed woman is determined.

From this same period, but from Lissos on the south coast (see pp. 84 and 279), came a broken statue of Hygeia found in the remains of the Asclepeion (ancient health centre), and a delightful little girl who is quite happy to look directly at someone who has thrown her a ball.

Just before the Roman conquest of Crete of 67 BC, Cydonia showed itself somewhat intransigent towards Rome – an attitude which led to the pre-eminence of Gortyn in the Roman colony (see p. 86). But there are some attractive remains from the Greco-Roman period of Cydonia. A statue of Artemis was found in the sanctuary of Diktynna at Kisamos (in the far west) (see p. 87). Although she is missing both arms and a leg, her fashionably short tunic with its saltire and her direct gaze distract from these losses.

From this period, too, come some fine mosaic floors found during the building of modern Chania. One, from the Singer plot, shows Poseidon and **Amymone**, one of the Danaides, daughter of Europa and Danaus. I'm not sure Amymone wants to go with Poseidon, there are signs of resistance, though he has rescued her from a satyr (p. 87). Whatever the truth, she had a son by her rescuer. From the nearby Vardinoyannis plot – known as the Dionysus House – came the mosaic of Dionysus and Ariadne on the island of Naxos. She looks in a bit of a swoon, or a drunken stupour. To pinpoint the area from where these floors were excavated, look at a modern map of Chania and find the Municipal Market. The plots, now built on, are in the area just south of that, bounded today by Zymvrakakidon, Chatzmichaligiannari and Tzanakaki streets.

The museum has several grave stelae, often depicting women, but my favourite – partly because I came upon it so unexpectedly and it was found at Aptera, a few steps from where we were staying – dates from the third century AD (see p. 89). I will describe the life of Sumpherousa in more detail when we reach that archaeological site (see p. 283) but, should you go to the museum first, please don't miss her; there is a legible version of the inscription beside the stele mentioning our hamlet of Megala Chorafia, the previous name used for Aptera.

After a good session at the museum, you may decide to have lunch at one of the tavernas round the harbour. Just before you settle down, there is an inviting bookshop on your left. Books are in many ways the best mementoes of any trip, but if you are determined to have more than a kitsch reproduction of a Minoan artefact, one of your best bets is the museum shop to your right as you come out of the museum – hardly more than a shop window. There Derek bought me a silver ring, approved by the Ministry of Culture Archaeological Receipts Fund, made from a seal in the Herakleion museum, showing 'a priestess holding a hammer or an axe over her right shoulder' from Vathia, fifteenth century BC; the original of haematite. I bought Derek a more-convincing-than-usual copy of the Phaistos disc. The **Cretan House Folklore Museum**, run by two women, is just beyond (south), down an alley.

## Wandering Aimlessly

We had lunch at the Mesostrata Taverna in the courtyard of an old Venetian villa in Zabeliou Street (turn left off Chalidon before you reach the harbour). From here westwards is the oldest and most picturesque part of Chania that remains. In the quiet of the evening, or first thing in the morning, when all the establishments catering to tourists are shut, it must be very pleasant.

To the east of the Chalidon, (Admiral) Kanevaro and (Admiral) Potier Streets abut. The author of the novel *Madame Hortense* (Campanis, 1982), claims that the woman adored by those Great Power admirals (see p. 143) lived, appropriately between them, in Catré Alley (bombed in 1940). (I found a French translation of this book in the Greek Librairie Epsilon in Paris.)

Nearby, the Kastelli hill overlooking the harbour is a constant in Chania's history. Standing there, it is not easy to return to Venetian times (AD 1204–1669). The main Venetian corso, now the Kanevaro, ran east to west through the walled city and was lined with palazzos, including that of the governor. They are no more, though you can still see remains, bits of walls, arches, doorways. In 1665, all this fell to the Ottoman invaders after a two-month siege in which women played their part (see p. 116). The Venetian records of Chania were all lost, unlike those of Herakleion on which much of the Venetian chapter in my history section is based. We can assume that a similar way of life for women existed in Chania.

The Ottomans, too, governed from Kastelli hill but most of what was left from the 1665 siege and Ottoman reconstruction over three centuries of rule was destroyed by German bombing; there is little but modern buildings to see now. But imagine here, in its Ottoman heyday, Elizabeth Kontaxaki, also known as Elizabeth of Crete (see p. 131). The British artist and comic poet Edward Lear visited Crete in the spring of 1864, staying in the Chalepa district with the British consul Frank Drummond Hay and his Spanish wife. He wrote in *The Cretan Journal* (1984) of going to dine one evening at Ismail Pasha's residence, and added: 'Elizabeth of Crete, in a brown gown and velvet bonnet, passed us as we went in.'

I have told you as much as I know about Elizabeth, but more remains to be dug out about the movement she instigated; there are, apparently, papers in the **Historical Museum and Archives** of Crete (Sphakianaki 20, south of the Municipal Gardens). The museum also has displays depicting Crete's history from Byzantine times onwards.

In the 1870s and 1880s the English artist based in Istanbul, Mary Walker, visited Crete twice. I have quoted extensively about Chania from *Eastern Life and Scenery* (1886) in the historical section (see p. 136). Mary gives a real feeling of the cosmopolitan nature of society then and conveys a lively impression of Chaniot women, one quite different from Emilia De Sanctis Rosmini's unhappy description of 1910 (see p. 146). Unfortunately Mary is too discreet about specific locations so, although she minutely described the occupants and diversions of the street where she stayed (see p. 137), I have been unable to place it. Giving a more overall impression, she writes:

It is in the harbour of Canea that the finest remains of those high vaults, built by the Venetians for use of their galleys, may still be seen. Nine of these, in good preservation, form two sides of the interior basin, and serve as an admirable foreground to the picturesque masses of the ancient city — its houses of old stone, bronzed by the burning sun of this southern climate; its wooden dwellings, blue or rose-coloured; its terraced roofs or spreading eaves; all this warmth and brilliancy repeated in the still waters, and backed by the majestic range of the snowy mountains of Sphakia.

There were once twenty three of the barrel-vaulted *arsenali* (dockyards) which housed the venetian galleys, of which nine remain (east of Kastelli hill), some used commercially, others for exhibitions. The White Mountains, which impress all our informants, have the same effect today. Leaving Chania one day, Mary passes the **Public Gardens** (Tzanakaki Street) just north of today's Historical Museum, and writes even more fulsomely:

I had left the town, passing at first through a rough street, and by the sombre vaulted passage under the Venetian fortifications, which is at all times encumbered by horses and mules, by Cretans, Levantines, Arabs, negroes, and negresses: on the outer side is a small market-place for fruits and vegetables. The road follows for a few minutes the line of the moat, then by a sudden turn to the right brings you to the public garden. But one can have no thought for this garden, however pretty it may be: the open country spreads before us its illimitable beauties, dazzling, majestic, or tender, as the eye may fall on the beautifully wooded plain, with its villages and 'tchiftliks' [farms] half buried in the rich masses of foliage; or rise to the high uplands of the Riza [plain], clothed with a verdure tenderly veiled by distance. Above these heights again the eye follows with delight the gigantic outline of the White Mountains of Sphakia, every gold crag and peak rising from the azure and violet haze of its deep gorges, and reposes at length upon the highest summits, scarcely traced upon the blue heavens by lines of eternal snow.

In 1898, just as Ottoman rule came to an end, Jane Brailsford arrived in Chania (see p. 142). She and her husband were similarly beguiled: from one window, they saw the snow-capped mountains; from another, 'a valley clad with olive groves', and from a third, 'the distant town with Venetian ramparts and Turkish minarets'. Harriet Boyd, stopping briefly on her way to Herakleion two years later, wrote home:

The port of Canea is very picturesque. In the background rise the White Mountains. The town lying along the edge of the sea looks Italian rather than Greek — the houses are gaily painted and have projecting balconies. To the right and left of the port are Venetian forts. The one at the right is well preserved and is garrisoned by the Four Powers ... The four flags were run up while our boat was in harbour ... Mosques and minarets add to the quaintness of the town.

The flags were raised on the **Firkas Tower** (seafront, far west) in February 1898 when Crete was proclaimed a republic (see p. 141), and the Greek flag in 1913 when Crete was united with the mainland.

Mary Burn and her husband Robin, who spent three weeks in Chania at the beginning of the Second World War, were based at British headquarters there – where that was, she does not say; but what she does write (see pp. 151–2) conveys the fevered and exhausting atmosphere of the time.

Daphne Thynne, Marchioness of Bath (1904–1997), arrived in Chania in 1950 to take photographs for a book being written by Xan Fielding who was part of that team of British servicemen remaining in, or sent to, Crete during the war, after Allied forces had been forced to evacuate (see p. 153). He published *The Stronghold: An Account of Four Seasons in the White Mountains* in 1953 and **Daphne**, having divorced the same year, became Mrs **Fielding**. She wrote of their stay in Chania in *Mercury Presides* (1954): 'We stayed with a family in part of a ruined Venetian palace over-looking the old harbour, a seamen's quarter completely distinct from the rest of the town, which takes its character from the modern market-place.' The **Municipal Market**, built in 1919 in the centre of town on the site of an earlier one, is a lively and colourful attraction.

In the nineteenth and early twentieth century, the smartest place to live was **Chalepa**, to the north-east of the gardens. Mary Walker wrote: 'The consuls, as also some families of wealthy merchants, have their private dwellings at Khalepa, a village covering a rising ground at half-an-hour's distance to the south-east [north-east?] of the city.'

Maps of Chania showing Chalepa are rare but the *Europcar* one not only includes it but has marked the intriguing '**Baroness Schwartz's House**' (on the corner of Katsanevaki and Devoga Streets). Unfortunately, I failed to spot this when I could have done something about it – let alone came across the house wandering aimlessly; but, as you will have seen in the Ottoman chapter (see p. 134), from reading nothing about her in the normal run of books about Crete, further research has produced details of quite a girl.

Baroness (Espérance) von Schwartz, the Anglo-German writer under the pseudonym Elpis Melena, moved into the house in Chalepa in 1866. The Greek Ministry of Culture website says that it was built in 1860 and describes it, beside a photograph, as 'an exquisite example of Neo-classical architecture' and 'one of the most important buildings of Chania.' It is 'protected by a preservation order' but 'abandoned'. We are also told that from 1865 the house became 'the centre of social and philanthropical activity in Crete'. It was that remark that set me off.

And it is to the collected correspondence of the pianist and composer Franz Liszt that we owe more about Espérance's involvement in Crete and elsewhere than she wrote about herself. They had become friends following the end of her second marriage in 1854 when she held a salon in Rome. On March 15 1870, Liszt wrote to Espérance in Crete, 'When will your Crete volume ... be finished? Shall you return this summer for publication?' This obviously did not refer to the book about Ottoman rule in Crete that she had published in 1867 (see p. 135). She did publish another book in German in 1874 which translates: *Crete-Bee, or Cretan Folksongs, Sayings and Maxims of Love, Thought and Morality*. It remains apparently untranslated and looks a funny little book. She may have been referring to the collection of this material when she wrote of travelling round Crete in 1866 not only to help the insurgents, but 'with another object'. *Von Rom nach Creta* (From Rome to Crete) (1870) is more about the journey, in a yacht – only a few rather inconsequential pages at the end about Crete. Your German needs to be good and your enthusiasm boundless to penetrate these books, available in the British Library or the Bodleian, Oxford, for example.

On 22 March 1883, Liszt wrote to her again, from Budapest, when she had sent him money to distribute following some local disaster:

Chère Excellentissime,

It is really extraordinary that after so many years of constant practice in works of mercy you are not ruined. Your life seems to me one vast symphony of generosity, munificence, charities, gifts and attentions as delicate as they are costly. To begin with there are Garibaldi and his people, and to continue indefinitely there are those poor German fellows, ill in Rome, and buried there at your expense; and then the fighting Cretans, the infirm people in your hospital at Jena, the societies for the protection of animals, etc. etc.

I admire you and bow before your perpetual kindness and goodness – all the more because you exercise them unobtrusively as it were in the shade, without any flourish of trumpets and drums. ...

I preferred to send your gift in the name of Madame E de Schwartz, and not to mix up your nom de plume of Elpis Melena with it. ...

As well as her revolutionary and charitable work at various stages of her sojourn in Crete – which was broken sometimes by long stays abroad – Espérance looked after, and had educated in Chania, Garibaldi's daughter Anita (born c.1858) – a difficult young woman who tended not to appreciate her benefactor's ministrations.

In 1875, for reasons which no one, least of all Espérance, explains, her long friendship with Garibaldi came to an end. Anita left her

22.   Baroness Schwartz, from Elpis Melena, *Garibaldi's Memoirs*

house and, within a year, was dead, aged about 17. Espérance, feeling betrayed, continued to live in Chalepa until 1896. She had published her version of Garibaldi's autobiography – the manuscript of which he had entrusted to her – in 1861; in 1884, two years after his death, she published his letters to her. Their authenticity has been questioned, but they ring true to the uninitiated, and are fascinating, given Garibaldi's place in history. They are available in English.

In 1896, she left for Ermatingen on Lake Constance in Switzerland. There, in 1899, she died, and was buried, forgotten in Crete, save for her house and a note of it on a tourist map. By the time you read this, probably while it is being printed, I hope to be in Chania on the trail of Espérance and her house.

The physical Chalepa of Esperance's day is best described by Mary Walker:

In the environs of Canea the finest and most salubrious air is found at Khalepa, a hill-side rather stony, rather wanting in trees, compared to the luxuriant vegetation of the plain and of the lower slopes of the Rhiza; but this bareness is forgotten before the magnificent panorama of the bay of Canea and of the point of Suda. From a healthy eminence, scented by a multitude of aromatic plants, that rises behind the English Consulate, the view is magnificent; and those who have once gazed on it, and who may have enjoyed the frank and cordial hospitality of that stone house in the midst of the heather, will carry with them from Canea, and above all, from Khalepa, a happy and imperishable remembrance.

By the twentieth century, Chalepa was described as 'leafy'.

Another Chalepa inhabitant at the end of the nineteenth century was **Eleftherios Venizelos**, the Cretan revolutionary who brought about unification with Greece and was twice Greek Prime Minister; his house is now a **museum**. (I shall be concentrating more on his mother and wives in the next itinerary; see p. 272). The **mansion of Prince George**, High Commissioner of Crete from 1898 and against whom Venizelos struggled, is also here. Across the street from it is the Russian-style Greek Orthodox church of **St Mary Magdalene** (between Skra and Dagkli Street), endowed by Prince George's sister,

**Grand Duchess Maria of Greece** (1876–1940; she married first Grand Duke Georgii Mikhailovich of Russia). I can find no evidence of her physical presence in Crete but suspect she visited her brother.

Mercy Money-Coutts Seiradaki and her family lived in Chalpa after the Second World War (see p. 158). It was a delight to read of yet another move by David MacNeil Doren and his partner Inga (see p. 194) and discover that he wrote of Mercy's house Bella Vista:

We had found a vast ten-room villa that towered high above a rocky cove of the sea like one of those wave-girt monasteries of Mount Athos, a place with so many terraces, stairs, store-rooms, hidden alcoves and outbuildings that we could hardly keep track of it all. It had once belonged to the Swedish Consul; the present owner, an English lady who had married a Cretan, was now in Athens.

From Chania, Daphne Thynne and Xan Fielding set out for the White Mountains, which we shall now do. Daphne describes that journey over half a century ago from where some local buses still go:

Most of our journeys into the White Mountains started and ended in the market-place. We would set out in a crowded bus of incredible antiquity, hemmed in by fellow passengers weighed down by overflowing baskets and bulging coloured knapsacks and carrying clusters of live chickens upside-down in each fist. Like the Cornish, these Cretans sounded in normal conversation as though they were shouting in anger; and there was always one voice shriller than the rest, rising on a higher note of hysteria, that dominated the whole journey.

These buses had no fixed time-table. They would start as soon as they were full, when the last passenger had squeezed into the overcrowded gangway and the last goat or sheep had been strapped on to the roof; and they would reach their destination hours later than we expected, our progress depending on the driver's thirst or temper, both of which had to be relieved in every village we passed; on the state of the roads, which sometimes had to be cleared of boulders by a man running in front of us, and on the condition of the vehicle's engine, which had to be allowed to cool at the top of every hill.

# 21
## Environs of Chania

*Mournies, Perivolia, Theriso, Meskla and Alikianos, Fourne, Sougia and Lissos, Maleme, Aptera and Megala Chorafia, Armenoi, Samonas, Kalyves, Kokkino Chorio, Gavalochori, Kalamitsi Amigdali*

### Mournies

The revolt that broke out in 1895 (see p. 139) led to the resolution of 1898 – Crete became an autonomous republic under Ottoman suzerainty. The Great Powers administered this change until Prince George of Greece arrived as High Commissioner (see p. 141). His Minister of Justice was the revolutionary and lawyer Eleftherios Venizelos.

However enthusiastically Cretans welcomed Prince George, many still hankered after union with Greece – a move towards which the High Commissioner took no steps. Agitation grew, stoked by Venizelos who resigned in protest in 1901.

Venizelos was born in Mournies, just south of Chania in August 1864 at a difficult time for Cretans under Ottoman rule. It is his mother, giving birth a century and a half ago, that draws us to Mournies – then the favourite summer resort in the hills for the rich of Chania.

**Steliani Despina Plumidaki** (1820–1898) of Theriso, further south into the White Mountains, was from the family of Field Marshal Chali and married the rich merchant Kiriakos Venizelos Krivatas. Aged 44, she gave birth to Eleftherios – the fourth of six children, of whom three died in infancy.

Two years after Venizelos' birth, as a result of his father's participation in the uprising of 1866 (see p. 133), the family went into exile on the island of Syros. We have to imagine every detail of Steliani's life, for biographies in English of the Greek leader, her son, take no account of her; indeed, I am not even totally confident about her name. But the family house in Mournies where she gave birth is still there, on your right, in the main street coming from Chania. It is now apparently a museum – not open when we went looking.

Mournies is not a particularly picturesque village, but the people are pleasant. To get a feeling of the place at the time Steliani and her family spent their summers there, we are rescued by Mary Walker's impression; she leaves Chania and writes:

The road crosses a little bridge turning in the direction of the Rhiza – the green and smiling spurs of the high Sphakiote mountains. The air is fragrant with the scent of thousands of aromatic plants that carpet the rough ground; then you reach vast fields of olives – tall, full, and leafy as forest trees – that throw the shadow of their spreading branches across the bright red earth. So red, indeed, is it, that the tuft of grass or the shoot of young corn appears by contrast tinged with a fine sky-blue. I have nowhere remarked earth so deeply red as that of Crete: may it be for this reason that the olive here attains a height and strength far superior to the olive growth in southern France or Italy? Many of the stately trees date from the Venetian times; they may be recognised by their enormous trunks, bent and twisted into a thousand strange and picturesque coils.

The road soon afterwards sinks between orange plantations, protected by hedges where the aloe and cactus are mingled with high bushes of myrtle in full flower; and as we gradually draw near the hills, the deep ravines (at present dry) blush with the rich colouring of the oleander; on the edge of the gully the waving plumes of tall ferns and of the dwarf palm complete the graceful picture.

We reach the village of Murnies, and the carriage stops under the vine trellis that serves as entrance to a rustic 'cafe'. The 'cavedji' comes out in haste; he wears the Cretan dress; sleeveless waist-coat, large red waistband, the soft fez, and the high yellow boots. He offers the glass of water that precedes the coffee; it is perfumed with orange flower, and the coffee itself partakes of this national essence, which harmonises badly with its natural aroma.

To get to Mournies today, you have to be careful how you leave Chania, and how you turn off the highway that runs almost the length of the island. The landscape, too, has changed a bit, though further inland the difference is less marked.

## Perivolia

To continue the itinerary, you take the turning to the right marked 'Perivolia' off Mournies high street before you reach the Venizelos house. This is much the route Mary Walker must have taken during two visits to the area in the 1870s and 1880s; she wrote:

Much honey is made in the environs of Murnies and of Perivoglia, a charming village on the mountain side, embosomed in orange groves, plane-trees, and olives. The hives are baskets, reversed, and thatched with heather. The quality of the honey is most excellent, for the peasants, not satisfied with the great abundance of aromatic plants that cover the ground, send their bees in their hives, for change of air and nourishment, to the perfumed slopes of Akrotiri.

In this part of the country the myrtle hedges are very luxuriant, and (in the season) covered with the delicate perfumed blossom; but the shrub which principally scents the air, and which is found here in profusion, is the 'lavdanum' ...

... The terrace of Perivoglia is a favourite rendez-vous for holiday-makers from Canea. It is delightful to rest in the shadow of its spreading plane-trees, soothed by the cool ripple of the spring, and to gaze down on the heaving billows of foliage that cover the slopes and spread out at the foot of the mountain until they melt in the broad stretch of yellow sand that marks the shore and completes the exquisite colouring of the picture by its contrast with the deep ultramarine of the wide expanse of the Mediterranean[Cretan Sea]. Against this azure background the red ramparts and snowy minarets of Canea stand out in clear relief ...

## Theriso

From Perivolia, you drive towards Theriso through the Theriso Gorge, the only Cretan gorge through which you can drive. Of course, you can also walk it but, not being a gorge-walking traveller (unless they have something specific to do with women), this was my only Cretan gorge, and I loved it. It was a rain-threatening afternoon and we were the only car on the road – real partisan and goat country.

When Venizelos began to plan serious revolt against Prince George in 1905 (see p. 145), he hesitated to make his mother's home village his base – failure might mean its destruction. He was by then a widower: his wife, **Maria Katelouzou**, had died in 1894, aged 24, giving birth to the second of their two sons. He was not to meet his second wife, the Anglo-Greek **Eleni** (or Helena) **Schilizzi** (1873–1959) until 1912, in the Greek Cathedral in London, when he was Prime Minister of Greece; and they were not to marry until 1921. Although she visited Crete in 1927, her renowned charitable activities took place on the mainland (and there is now a Schilizzi Foundation, based in London, to fund the studies of Greek students in Britain).

In 1905, therefore, the focus of Venizelos' life was politics and the struggle to unite Crete with Greece. He approached the Theriso village President the evening of his arrival and explained his plans. During the night the President visited every house to ask his flock's opinion; by morning, all had agreed that Theriso should be revolutionary headquarters. When Venizelos warned that the village might be razed, the President replied: 'If the Prince burns the village, the remaining land will be holy ground.' Revolution was declared from Theriso on 10 March 1905. Prince George left Crete in 1906, and the republic moved inexorably towards union with Greece at the end of 1913.

Today there is a museum in Theriso, up a path to your left. It does not appear to have been Steliani's family home, and she had been dead since 1898, but it is worth a visit and must be typical of the surroundings in which she was brought up. Among the photographs on the walls of the museum is one of an English woman journalist in Edwardian dress, dating from September 1905; her identity intrigues me.

The journey so far has been easy. To continue this way by car, you really do have to keep your head, particularly if you are a lily-livered passenger, for you are now up in the White Mountains and it is pretty precipitous. Some young neighbours who copied our drive the following day thought I had much exaggerated the frisson-potential, but I can still recall the lurching of my heart. The views are, of course, stunning! Drive, or walk, round the curve of this ridge, through Zourva, hardly more than a cafe, to Meskla.

## Meskla and Alikianos

In Meskla is a fourteenth century chapel dedicated to the Virgin (next to a modern church) on the site of which, in Roman times, was a temple to Aphrodite. But I have brought you to Meskla because it was the headquarters of the Kandanoleon uprising against the Venetians nearly four centuries before Venizelos raised the flag of revolt at Theriso. I have told the story in some detail in the history section (see p. 113). Often I have had to decide unilaterally where to elaborate, in history or the relevant itinerary, and it seemed that those events must go chronologically among the other revolts against Crete's colonial masters.

As you drive on to Alikianos, so you come to where the fatal wedding breakfast occurred after the marriage of Kandanoleon's son Petros and the Venetian Molino's daughter Sophia. The remains of the Molino country house (also called the da Molino Castle) still exist near the fourteenth century church of Hagios Giorgios (in the village follow the signed Koufos road). If you ask, you will be directed to an orange grove behind some houses opposite the church. The overgrown ruin still has a lintel on which are carved the words *Omnia Mundi Fumus et Umbra* ('All Worldly Things Are Smoke and Shadow').

This whole area is steeped not only in the blood of the Kandanoleon revolt and the reprisals against it, but that of the Second World War. It hardly seems possible, for the beauty and tranquillity of the miles of orange groves are marked. Don't hesitate to stop and buy fresh produce, oranges in season, from a stall.

**Fourne**

In between Meskla and Alikianos is the village of Fourne. It is here that the story of Levendokaterini – 'Brave and Noble Katerini' – took place as the Germans overran the west of Crete in May 1941 (see p. 155). Argiro Kokovli, who introduces her in *Greek Women in Resistance*, describes how

Fourne lies at the end of a fertile valley among gently sloping hills. The earth there is rich, watered by many springs, wells, and brooks. The people are hard-working and have made their land a bountiful garden in all seasons. Fourne is always beautiful, but in the spring it is splendid, glowing. The hills are green then, dotted with flowering shrubs of many colors. The fields are lush with clover, and the orange groves hum with honeybees harvesting nectar from fragrant blossoms.

The women, children and old men of the village take to the caves for safety in 1941. Katerini goes to bring them food and notices an old man with an ancient gun over his shoulder:

'Grandfather, give me your gun,' she whispers timidly. A wild look from the old man nails her. His grip on the gun tightens. This thing he has heard is beyond imagining; give up his gun? His comrade for over seventy-five years? This living extension of his arm? 'Give it to me, I will honor it,' she says again, louder.

The old man stares at her.

'Give it to her, grandfather; give it where it's needed,' the women urge him. 'It's a sin to waste it. Katerini is worthy of it.'

The old man lowers his arm and slowly lets the gun slip off. A tear falls from his half-blind eyes.

'Take it, Levendokaterini, take it, for freedom, for our island. Use it well.'

Levendokaterini stands next to the men on the bridge, tucks her skirt up over her knees, chooses a hole in the wall, and takes aim.

The eventual fate of Levendokaterini, together with that of other Cretan women who had been active during the war, is told on p. 159.

## Sougia and Lissos

From Alikianos, you can join the main east–west highway along the north coast, and I shall bring you back here to go further westwards. But first I am going to take you south on a diversion.

During the war, there were partisan and evacuation routes south, through the White Mountains, and today there is a road system that allows you to make the journey from Alikianos (and you can go by bus from Chania). The unspoilt fishing village of Sougia was the family place of Mercy Money-Coutts' husband, Michael Seiradakis, and I have written of how they met and married (see p. 158). Before they settled in Chania, they lived for a while in Sougia, and Mercy

23. Mercy Money-Coutts, courtesy of the British School at Athens

founded a school there. In 2002, therefore, her great-niece, **Harriet Pottinger**, visiting Crete for the first time, resolved to visit Sougia.

Harriet found not only that memory of Mercy is still strong there, and that a street is named after her, but was also told that Mercy had excavated at nearby Lissos. I have asked around among archaeologists about this, but no one can confirm Mercy's work there. Formal excavation of the Hellenistic and Roman site, including the Asclepeion (see p. 83) was by Nicholas Platon. But since there are women artefacts such as a statue of Hygeia from Lissos in the Chania Museum (see p. 262), and since Harriet walked there in Mercy's footsteps, I am including here Harriet's account of that walk. What is more, since many people go to Crete to walk and, since I always had too much ground to cover to do so, I hope that Harriet's experience will be particularly enjoyed by walkers who are tempted to walk from Sougia to Lissos (little more than an hour) – more original than doing the much-visited Samaria Gorge to the east:

The walk itself was lovely, and not particularly arduous. You go west along the seafront to the little harbour at Soughia, through a metal gate, and follow the dry river bed through the gorge. I expect it's not quite so dry in the winter though. After a while you start to climb a zigzag path up the south side of the gorge to the top (about 1,000 ft above sea level? no more, I shouldn't think) where you cross a flat-ish area not unlike the moors [in England], with low scrub, a few stunted trees and lots of rocks and rocky outcrops (limestone). The biggest difference was that the bushes are MUCH thornier than British gorse — they'd rip you to shreds in no time at all! The far side descends steeply into the valley of Lissos, so after the flat bit on top you reach the edge of the cliff and look down to see a lush green valley of open grassy fields and olive trees with lots of building remains clearly visible on the lower slopes, surrounded by mountains on 3 sides and a very pretty little bay/beach on the 4th ...

The west side of the island has risen fairly recently (and the eastern end has sunk correspondingly) and the 'tide' mark on the cliffs is clearly visible about 5 metres above current sea level. There are remains of a biggish building at about the old sea level on the cliffs by the western end of the beach. Whether this was an old harbour building or what I have no idea, but it appeared to be of the same era as everything else.

I'm not a botanist, so I can't tell you the names of the plants along the walk, but the gorge was pretty green and there were several small flowers (especially higher up) as well as the bushes, shrubs and trees — lots of pink cyclamen and little yellow and white star shaped flowers and heather. There was that typical greenhouse smell of foliage and earth that you get when it's hot but has been raining and the ground is still a bit damp — lovely. Higher up the shrubs gave way more to pine trees, as is normal for deciduous to give way to coniferous with altitude. The walls of the gorge were quite narrow in places, curving up and overhanging the path by several hundreds of feet of red and orange rock. The path was fairly rough, and we had to scramble over rocks in places, but it was easy to follow by the occasional painted markers.

There were goats roaming around some with bells, a few in the gorge, but mostly in the Lissos valley, picking their way in and around the remains. Apart from the few walkers we saw, Lissos seemed remarkably untouched by time or people. Obviously after 3,000+ years there was considerable decay of the buildings, but not nearly as much as we're used to seeing. Many of the buildings still had rooves, in that they appeared to be built as arches. They were all very small with very small windows and doorways and thick walls ... There were lots of bits of old tile and clay lying around but the most extraordinary 'debris' were the two large pieces of carved marble that we saw ... and all the lintels and columns etc and the stairway by the temple. The temple itself was amazing —to think that the floor, which was incredibly intact for something so old, is still there, and that so much of the building remains still. This was the only area which was (half-heartedly) fenced off from the goats, but it was freely open to visitors through an unlocked gate ...

I suppose the fact that Lissos is only accessible by boat or by a good walk over rough ground serves well enough to keep it fairly undisturbed ...

Pat Cameron recommends that you travel to Lissos by boat and walk back; but Harriet makes the reverse walk sound attractive.

## Maleme

Come back from the south to Alikianos and retrieve the main west to east highway in the north. The rest of our exploration west of Chania was devoted to Joanna Stavridi who nursed between Maleme and Chania in May 1941; I tell almost all that I know of her story on p. 152. Her father's papers, as chairman of the Ionian Bank in London, merely show that his staff were proud to read of her heroism in the *Daily Telegraph* of 19 August 1941. Attempting to follow in her footsteps added nothing; Joanna's brave weeks seem to have been obliterated. Of course, there is the German Military Cemetery at Maleme where so many of the parachutists who invaded Crete are buried. But the coastline between Maleme and Chania where she nursed in caves is now a ribbon development. I have tried by other means to establish where exactly she nursed along that shore, without success. At Hagia Marina, a Minoan cave sanctuary was discovered some years ago, but all that area is now holiday beaches and all that goes with that.

Beyond Maleme, Crete is much less developed and would undoubtedly repay loitering – p. 93 gives you some leads; it is also an area where the palaeontologist Dorothea Bate explored in 1904 (see p. 165), and if fossils and caves are your particular interest you will, no doubt, get hold of her article and appendix.

## Aptera and Megala Chorafia

Come back now to Chania, but we won't stop; instead, drive along the edge of Souda Bay, past the Allied War Cemetery where Hilda Pendlebury's husband John is buried (see pp. 156 and 208). In 1898, you may remember, the ships of the Great Powers were hove to here and the admirals were visited by Mme Hortense (see p. 143). The bay is now a Greek and NATO naval base – in October 2001 we watched the England v. Greece soccer match in a cafe surrounded by American sailors on the alert for Afghanistan. Today's use makes an ironic juxtaposition with legendary times.

Turn right up the hill, just before the Turkish fort on your left, to Megala Chorafia and just after the houses come to an end, you are at the archaeological site of Aptera. From here you get the best view of the islets in Souda Bay. Aptera means 'wingless', and one of the explanations is that here the Muses and the Sirens, half-woman, half-bird, engaged in a musical contest. When the Sirens lost, they threw themselves from these heights into the bay, plucking off their wings as they did so, and became that little cluster of islets.

This was our view in 2001 when we spent three weeks in a converted traditional house with a shared swimming pool. We would stand by the pool and see not only the whole of Souda Bay but the Akrotiri Peninsula the other side, and behind us the White Mountains. So Aptera, five minutes' walk away, was our local and, even when, for our last week, I had one leg encased in a plaster cast, I tramped contentedly around it. Indeed, in Megala Chorafia, people digging in their garden regularly find remains of the past, so that the whole area exudes history as well as being wonderfully scenic. The hamlet had no shops but at least two tavernas, one, Taverna Aptera, run since 1986 by an English woman, Elizabeth, married to a Cretan, and makes a good base for the area. We went through Pure Crete (not to be confused with Simply Crete with whom we have also travelled), the Cretan end of which Elizabeth has been responsible for.

In the Greco-Roman period, the city state of Aptera controlled Souda Bay. Excavation of the site (open 8.30 a.m. to 2.30 p.m.) is continuing and it is becoming more accessible. Maria Andreadaki-Vlasaki, Director of the Chania Archaeological Museum, dug there for five years and her colleague **Nana Niniou** is the current director of the site. The city was destroyed by an earthquake in the seventh century BC and what was left was overrun by the Saracens in the ninth century AD. The modern-seeming buildings are the former monastery of St John founded in the second Byzantine period, but avoid being sidetracked by it; I know of no nuns.

Just inside the gate of the fenced bit are the remains of a double (bipartite) temple to Demeter (see p. 59) from Hellenistic times, excavated in 1942 by a German archaeologist. This quirky little temple is one of my favourites but the real lure of Aptera is prompted by the stele in the Chania Museum (see p. 263). Although tombs on the site range from Geometric to Roman times, this may be one of the stelae called 'chance finds' from what used to be the granary of the farm attached to the monastery.

The inscription, dating from the third century AD (Roman period) celebrates the life of **Sumpherousa**, a 30-year-old 'foreigner of the Libyan race'. All the citizens in her adopted place of Aptera were saddened by her sudden death, but it is her husband, Neikon, who proclaims his broken heart. He speaks to her of his love but she doesn't hear. It is so rare to know of a real woman dating back so far that the whole of Aptera still seems to be Sumpherousa's place and she looks for ever over the bay beneath.

## Armenoi

Further inland from Aptera are older archaeological sites – Minoan tombs at Stylos, for example, which you come across as you drive along deserted roads through olive groves. But we also enjoyed the modern charms of the area. Twice we drove for Sunday lunch to the Drosostalia Taverna at Armenoi. Not only is the food excellent – perhaps the most varied and enticing local dishes we ate in all our visits to Crete – but this open-air restaurant is full of large extended families interacting and making hospitable gestures towards you. You also get other glimpses of village life: a shepherd woman driving her flock, a young man pinning anti-war posters to the trees that shaded us. For a few hours we did not feel so much like tourists.

## Samonas

But perhaps the least touristy afternoon was the drive up the hill to the village of Samonas in search of local honey – not only nice on your breakfast yoghurt but so much a part of Crete's history (see p. 243). It was another of those uphill, hairpin-bend drives that I never get used to, and when we arrived at the top, we mistook where honey was to be bought, and landed up in a private garden where the family – Pangona, Despina, Aspasia and Roussa from several generations – entertained us for an hour or so under the grape vines that covered their terrace. We were plied with grapes and walnuts, were shown embroidery done by the women of the house, and took photographs to send to them; eventually someone turned up with honey. Most people visiting Samonas probably go for the acclaimed Byzantine church of Hagios Nikolaos in a valley beyond the hamlet. I believe that our friends may be the guardians of the key.

## Kalyves

You will only do these things if you are staying in the area. You might not, for example, if just passing by, drive down the hill into Kalyves in the lee of the Itzedin Fort (Turkish name) – built as a Venetian defence overlooking Souda Bay – in which political prisoners were held in the time of the Greek Colonels. Before you reach the beach chalets of Kalyves, the Kiliaris flows into the sea and the land is flat and reedy. It is here that I imagined Odysseus coming ashore naked after being shipwrecked and being woken by the laughter of **Nausicaa**, the daughter of Queen Arete (see p. 64), and her handmaidens come to do the washing. Did they then take Odysseus to Chania to meet the Queen and King? I know it is more fanciful than I should allow myself, but I never could avoid it as we drove down nearly every day to do our shopping. Kalyves is a pleasant village but the swimming at the beach did not attract us more than once. Further along the coast, there are fish restaurants at Almiridha; perfectly nice, but I would recommend swimming there even less – dangerous currents, as we found out.

## Kokkino Chorio

This whole horn of land between Chania and Rethymnon, the point of which encloses Souda Bay, is known as the Apokoronas and suffered considerably during Ottoman times (see p. 101). We much enjoyed driving its byways. In Kokkino Chorio we visited a workshop where glass is recycled by Balkan glassblowers to make new glass objects, and bought two mottled pink and green tumblers which remind us of happy days – no women, though! We were on our way to Gavalochori where there is a feast of women things.

## Gavalochori

Head first for the Folklore Museum (open daily 9.00 a.m. to 8.00 p.m.) – a fine house partly built in Venetian times and added to under the Ottomans. It was inhabited until the end of the twentieth century by Maria and George Stilianakis whose heirs gave it to the Gavalochori community. Now, as a museum, it is beautifully laid out and full of fascinating household and craft objects and costumes. Silk has been woven locally since the Ottomans planted mulberry trees round the village – silkworms imported from China and Japan (see also p. 38).

Nearby is the Women's Co-operative. Anastasia was on duty when we visited it. She not only held strong political views which she hoped to put into practice as a local councillor, but she was demonstrating Kapaneli work which the women of Gavalochori have done since Venetian times. A small bolster is stuffed with straw and covered, then silk thread is woven round pins stuck into the bolster, creating silk lace.

In 2001, the co-operative was in its fourth year and there were 40 women involved, mostly older, though Anastasia seemed in her late twenties. She had learned kopaneli from her mother who had learned it from hers. We bought two sets of cotton pillow cases and two sets of napkins from the shop.

## Kalamitsi Amigdali

Driving further along that eastern flank of Apokoronas, we reached Kalamitsi Amigdali. There by the roadside is another women's co-operative. From there we bought an example of their speciality, a rug woven out of silk waste. We were also given several silkworm cocoons as a memento.

If you were driving from Chania directly eastwards, you would probably miss out all this area, which would be a pity. The women's silk and cotton handcrafts here seem less affected by cheap competing imports and hardsell than in the better-known centres (see pp. 238 and 299).

# 22
## Lasithi Plateau

*Katharo Plateau, Kroustallenia Monastery, Magoulas and Psychro, Diktaian cave, Trapeza cave, Tzermiado, Karphi, Kardiotissa Convent, Mallia, Milatos cave*

Crete is very much a place for enthusiastic walkers and lovers of wild flowers, and some itineraries show that several of the women who visited it before us walked great distances, not always from choice, though they seem, mostly, to have enjoyed it. So I start this itinerary with you walkers in mind. By the time you close this book you will know that I am pretty weedy and suspect that I did not walk from Kritsa to Lasithi.

### Katharo Plateau

One of the traditional walking routes is via the sister Katharo Plateau which lies between Kritsa (see itinerary pp. 309–17) and the Lasithi Plateau. A compelling introduction to Katharo comes from the palaeontologist Dorothea Bate in her 1905 article 'Four and a Half Months in Crete in Search of Pleistocene Mammalian Remains'. She wrote of May 1904:

Kritsa was visited at the earliest opportunity, and here a small number of isolated hippopotamus teeth were brought in by the villagers, and at length an old man appeared who professed to know the locality from which they came. The following day he took us to the upland basin of Katharo, which is about three hours from Kritsa and nearly 4,000 feet above the sea. Although already past the middle of May, at this height it was bitterly cold, a keen wind bringing with it a damp and all enveloping fog. This spot is not permanently inhabited, only a few shepherds staying here with their flocks during the summer months when they and their beasts obtain shelter in rudely built and indescribably filthy hovels; the only other buildings being one or two small dedicatory chapels. A few crops of corn and vetche struggle for existence, while a number of fruit-trees grow in shelter of the northern hills ...

My guide first took me to the top of a rounded hillock in the eastern half of the valley, where a few fragmentary remains were found lying on the surface, where some debris evidently of volcanic origin, such as lava, etc., was also observed. During the next few days trial trenches were dug in a number of places in this vicinity, teeth and bones of a pigmy hippopotamus being found in varying quantities and at different depths ...

The presence of these hippopotamus remains shows that the deposit in which they occur is almost certainly of fresh-water origin, and this is easy to believe when it is remembered that before a channel was worn through the barrier of surrounding hills there was probably no outlet for the accumulated waters, which in that case would transform the valley into a lake or swamp, according to the season of the year.

Considering the ordinary habitat of the hippopotamus, it is curious to find numerous remains of a small species at the unusual height of nearly 4,000 feet above sea-level, and that amongst rugged and barren mountains.

In the far west of the island, Dorothea found remains of pigmy elephants and, commenting on those finds in her appendix 'The Caves of Crete' (1913), she opens more doors when she writes, 'It was not surprising to find remains of these two dwarf species, for parallel cases existed in other of the Mediterranean islands – Malta, Sicily and Cyprus.' Our astonishment at these finds is somewhat assuaged by those of very small human remains on Flores Island, Indonesia. Laypeople have learned the term 'island dwarfing', whereby, on islands, with limited resources and lack of predators, large mammals get smaller and little ones get bigger over succeeding generations. It still seems extraordinary that there should once have been hippos and elephants on Crete, however small.

In 1928, the archaeology students from Athens, Hilda White, Margaret Rodger and John Pendlebury, walked to the Lasithi Plateau from Pacheia Ammos (see also pp. 349 and 360), and Hilda wrote in a letter home on 24 February:

Next morning we left at 7 for a very long walk to Psychro right up in the Lasithi mountains. We thought it would take eight hours without a pause for lunch but as a matter of fact it took nine. I had made up my mind to walk the whole way but I was jolly tired for the last mile or so.

The first part of the walk was simply lovely, winding in & out above coves of the Gulf of Mirabello & it was sunny & the water very blue. Then we began to climb up & at about 12 we came to the mountain village of Tapis where we had lunch. We have been seeing the most wonderful anemones everywhere & this day saw some bright crimson ones – lovely things. After lunch we began a very long & steep ascent & it began to get cold. We reached 4000 ft & then went along a path skirting the mountain side (very grim) & with mountain streams bubbling across it every now & then. It began to snow but we were walking fast & did not feel the cold very much. Then came the long descent of course. The mountain paths are incredibly stony, sharp jags & ridges of rock so that you have to pick your way from jag to jag as there is no foot space between. At last we got down to the plain & saw various villages. John & I were behind & kept hoping that each village would be the one but it was a long way & about the farthest village.

I'm sure they still make women like that. And Hilda, by then married to John, was, as you will see, to return to the plateau to excavate under hardly less demanding conditions.

### Introduction to Lasithi Plateau

You need to make decisions about visiting the Lasithi Plateau, assuming that you are going by car. Visitors' main objective tends to be the Diktaian cave, where Rhea gave birth to Zeus. If that is yours, there are several ways to get to the plateau for a day trip: from the west, the north and the east. We went from the east via Neapoli, entering near the Kroustallenia Monastery, and left from the north via Karphi and the Kardiotissa Convent, reaching the coast at Mallia. If you only visited the Diktaian cave, the site at Mallia would fit well into the end of your jaunt, and perhaps even the Milatos cave – for that reason, I am placing them in this itinerary (and because they don't fit neatly anywhere else!).

But if you want to visit all the places mentioned in this itinerary, I suggest you consider spending a night on the plateau (make sure you take a jersey/jacket). We tried to do too much in a day, arriving back at Istron overtired. If you climb (by car) to the plateau via Neapoli, and are spending the night there or nearby, you could also visit Houmeriakos just down the road (see the Rodanthe itinerary, p. 313). It's all a question of having a good map, keeping your head and knowing your energy levels.

The tourist centre of the plateau these days, and a good base for walkers, is Hagios Giorgios (which we did not visit); it is, therefore, probably the best place to stay; or my informant, whose paternal family comes from Tzermiado, suggests the Kourites hostelry there, which has a good taverna (perhaps a bit full of tour groups at lunchtime in the season).

I recommend two books by women to read in your room on the Lasithi Plateau. *The Life of Ismail Ferik Pasha*, the novel by Crete-born Rhea Galanaki from which I have already quoted (see p. 129) is ideal for its history; *Village on the Plateau* (1985) by the anthropologist **Sonia Greger** gives unique contemporary insights.

Rhea Galanaki, while setting her story in Ottoman times, goes back to the Venetians (see also p. 99):

Scarcity of corn had forced the Venetian rulers to let the villagers resume cultivation of the plateau, that *spina nel cuore di Venezia* ['thorn in the heart of Venice'], as the conquerors called it. Long before that, in the thirteenth century, wishing to pluck that thorn from her heart, Venice had inflicted harsh reprisals on the plateau; banishing the inhabitants, uprooting the fruit-trees, forbidding farming and cattle-grazing on pain of death or amputation of the culprits' legs. Venice was fully aware that the plateau was a place where rebels sprouted as thick as weeds among the corn and hid under sheep's bellies, while the non-combatants were only too willing to supply their armed countrymen with corn. This punitive policy lasted two hundred years;

the plateau, forsaken by humans, turned into a wilderness, until the time that the Most Serene Republic lifted the ban on settlement, cultivation and cattle-breeding. In the next century, when the Peloponnese [mainland Greece] fell into Turkish hands, Venice decided to send a few loyal families from Nauplia and Monemvasia to settle on the plateau.

## Kroustallenia Monastery

Among the refugees from the Peloponnese were, as I have related (see pp. 114–15), the d'Anassi sisters, Pallantia and Theokliti, who were given land on which to establish monasteries or convents – religious houses in Crete tended to be for both nuns and monks. Pallantia retrieved the remains of the Kroustallenia Monastery which had been originally founded at least as early as 1241 but fallen into abeyance when the Venetians ordered the plateau abandoned.

The Kroustallenia has had an eventful history, always being a rebel stronghold against foreign invaders. It was destroyed in 1821 and then rebuilt. Revolution broke out again in 1866. Rhea Gallanaki tells how Ferik Pasha, who had been kidnapped from the plateau years before, returned at the head of an Ottoman army (see also p. 129). Once again, the rebels and refugees retreated within the Kroustallenia. On the third day of fighting, Ferik Pasha tells how:

We gained hold of the entire south side of the plateau and set fire to four villages and the monastery of Kroustallenia, which housed an ammunition depot and a workshop manufacturing cartridges, no longer of any use to the rebels, since their weapons were a disparate assortment of models from different periods and of different calibres.

Resistance to German occupation nearly a century later was also centred in the monastery. But today it is tranquillity itself, housing a mere handful of monks. I suggest, if you are entering the plateau via Neapoli, or come by foot from the Katharo Plateau, you make the monastery your first stop. You are likely to be hospitably received by at least one monk, perhaps even given generous sustenance, though you may learn little from him about the Abbess Pallantia – for that you have to rely on my limited knowledge!

You will have seen the basin of Lasithi stretching before you as you come down into it but, from the top of the monastery's perch, you gain another perspective on this extraordinary agricultural bowl, with its ring of villages round the edge, and imagine Kroustallenia as a stronghold, more than once full of refugees and rebels.

## Magoulas and Psychro

Driving clockwise from the Kroustallenia Monastery, and passing by Hagios Giorgios (which has a well-regarded folklore museum), you come to the turning for Magoulas, just before Psychro. Setting the scene for her ten-year study in the 1980s, Sonia Greger suggests how Magoulas fared in Ottoman times:

The story is told of a Turkish *Pasha* who lived in a Magoulas house which stood just opposite the one where I live and who, like me, had a good view of the central village spring. The story goes that the young Magoulas maidens would dance in the space before the spring every month. The *Pasha* would watch from his window and select a virgin to be brought to him. This practice continued until he selected the daughter of the head man in the village who was brave enough to wound the Turk very seriously. (This was told me with a piercing stare, but I could not ask what form of wound since I did not know the Greek for castration and did not want to use sign language. Nor did it seem appropriate to ask why their fathers permitted the girls to dance so provocatively.) The *Pasha* was posted to Iraklion ...

These villages have become immortalised by Sonia Greger and I am running the two together because, having reached Psychro before we realised we had passed Magoulas, we met there one of the women whom Sonia had known. We stopped at Antulla's taverna – the Souvlaki O Stavros, right-hand side going towards the Diktaian cave – to ask how we might find the house of Ferik Pasha and, what with one thing and another, returned there for lunch.

Hospitality was unconfined: we were plied with Lasithi 'samosa', tomatoes and olives, *horta* and Lasithi potatoes with tomatoes, flavoured with fennel, and honeyed 'chapathi' (*Dikanopita*).

Antulla, it turned out, was one of Sonia's knitting school members. Sonia writes:

By about 1981, that is before I went to live in Magoulas, I was collecting embroidery motifs and, realising that feature of their 'logic' which enables almost all of them to be set out in grid form, and being myself no embroiderer or weaver, I began to reinterpret the motifs for use on my knitting machine ...

A woman friend in Psychro ... shared this interest, and she learned to use the machine. We collected designs. I punched cards, and between us we produced several experimental garments with Cretan motifs. Like Magoulas women, she had work to do on the *kampos* and with animals, and could only work with the machine intermittently. It was through this that I was first introduced to the women's life in Lasithi.

The knitting school Sonia eventually established was located through Psychro on the left, 100 yards past the ceramic shop on the right. But the building is now locked and abandoned; the school is no more. Sonia tells, as well as the life of the Lasithiots through an anthropologist's eyes, how she and her project fared, and the problems introduced by tourism. It is a salutary, as well as an informative and sympathetic book.

Relations between women and men are, naturally, constantly shifting in most modern societies, but of her time and place Sonia recounts a telling Lasithiot anecdote:

The smallest incidents exhibit [the] responsibility, incumbent upon the male, to lay down the law. I am driving some friends to visit the husband's sister one hour's journey away. Three minutes from home his wife remembers we have left behind three dozen eggs, meant as a gift. Her voice is raised in immediate panic and I prepare to turn and go back to fetch them, for the sister has no chickens and no eggs. Husband who is normally a very quiet personality and converses little, says three quiet words from the back seat: 'Oshi, leo ego' (No, I say); so we continue without question and without eggs to the sister's house.

Sonia's women's co-operative, formed in 1989, had to try and operate within this culture and, indeed, within Greek political and religious culture more generally. She tells the story as it unfolded in the slimmer volume *Letters from Lasithi 1984–1993: A Decade of 'Development' in Cretan Mountains* (1993). Unfortunately, her poor health in more recent years has hobbled her activities and study. You should find Sonia's books in Crete; failing that the Hellenic Bookservice in London is a good place for books about the island; Oxbow Books in Oxford stocks archaeological and historical books.

After our lunch at Antulla's taverna, we returned to our mission of finding the family house of Ferik Pasha, born Emmanuel Kambanis Papadakis, and were rather surprised when Antulla seemed to know its whereabouts. Following her directions, turning left a few yards from the taverna, and leaving Derek with the car parked intrusively, I discovered something of an unspoilt Lasithi village – only the main street is lined with tourist shops and tavernas. I was taken in hand by a woman who gave me a handful of shelled walnuts from those spread out to dry on her veranda, and her friend, who was picking apples, gave me an armful of those.

As for the Papadakis house to which my guide led me, it was a mere overgrown plot with some old building stones, almost an archaeological site. I was momentarily jubilant but, returning to Antulla, realised that it had probably belonged to a later Psychro Papadakis hero; indeed, his statue is a few yards before the taverna. But was it also the house, earlier, of Ferik Pasha's family? Rhea Galanaki tells, through his eyes, how he found the house at the end of the fighting, when most of the village was destroyed:

The door creaked open. I stepped inside, closing it behind me. Then I leaned back against its thick boards, trying to feel the grain of the wood, the knots, the nails that delineated the door's skeleton. Sudden tears forced me to shut my eyes. Blindly I began to suck in the familiar air ...

I had no way of knowing whether anybody had lived in this house after my mother, since I had accepted the version according to which she had lived and died here alone. I was unable to find any evidence of a stranger's presence, for the house was completely bare. I remember every single object that had been in it with an extraordinary clarity: the simple appurtenances of a rural household, the few things needed to bring comfort to toil-worn bodies.

Seventy years later, those toil-worn bodies at least had access to medical care. Hilda White and her companions arrived in the village, after their gruelling walk from Pacheia Ammos, and Hilda wrote:

We got there in the end after splashing through endless muddy lanes. We had an introduction to a German doctor and his wife at Psychro & they gave us the most wonderful welcome. We were told to make ourselves absolutely at home: given a wonderful tea, slippers, stockings, beautifully comfortable beds & every imaginable kindness. They had two beautiful Alsatians & an overgrown fox-terrier — their only family except for a spotless tabby called Mitsi. They were so sweet to us & we were so tired & cold that kindness was never more welcome.

That letter says nothing about visiting the Diktaian cave: the party left the following morning to follow the path out of the plateau to the west.

## Diktaian cave

open 8.00 a.m. to 7.00 p.m.

The Diktaian cave is one of Crete's most significant archaeological sites, mainly because it is where the goddess Rhea gave birth to Zeus who was to become the most important god in the Hellenic pantheon (see p. 51). And, because of that, different places vie to be known as his birthplace (see pp. 207, 234 and 371). As far as modern tourism is concerned, it is probably as well to allow both Mount Dikte and Mount Ida to be birthplaces or, if that stretches it a bit, one the birthplace, the other where he was reared.

Poor Rhea had to seek refuge in one or other of these dank, dark caves because her jealous husband, Kronos, believing a son would usurp him, consumed each one as he was born. When Zeus was born,

Kronos was given a swaddled stone instead, which he swallowed, and the Kouretes danced around the living child clanking their shields to drown his cries. What Rhea suffered thus giving birth is not commented upon in any of these tales. The baby was looked after by the nymph Melissa (bee) who, it is assumed, fed him honey and milk from the goat Amaltheia.

Another, less common, story has Zeus returning to the Diktaian cave as an adult, bringing Europa whom he, in the form of a bull, had inveigled from Phoenicia. It is here that he seduced her, not under a plane tree at Gortyn (see pp. 3 and 251). If I'd been Europa, I would have given in at Gortyn.

Following earlier exploratory expeditions, David Hogarth started digging at the Diktaian cave in 1900. Harriet Boyd (see p. 160), having packed off her Kavousi treasures to Herakleion by boat in July that year (see pp. 333–7), left for that city herself via the Lasithi Plateau in order to visit Hogarth's excavation. She sets the scene for us in the 1965 article 'Memoirs of a Pioneer Excavator in Crete':

We arrived just as his workmen were taking a break after what were probably the three most astonishing days of their lives. They had expected to find curious things up there, for, in collecting cave-mould for top-dressing of their fields they had scratched up bronze and stone objects ...

No one was prepared for this energetic Englishman, who with dynamite and crow-bar cleared the upper cave of fallen debris, and penetrated to the damp depths of the lower cavern where scarcely a villager had ever ventured.

After an examination of the upper cave, we were asked if we cared to slip and slide down the ooze-covered rock into the depths below, where we could discern the twinkling lights of the workers. The air was stifling but laughter and cries announcing good luck reassured us. Down we went to the very edge of a subterranean pool. Then Mr Hogarth ordered a magnesium wire to be lit and we beheld a scene as strange as mind can imagine.

We stood in a grotto fantastically framed by stalactites. Silhouetted against this background were the figures of men and girls bending over the pool dredging its depths, and of others searching the mud-filled hollows of the rock, or, stranger still, taking from crevices in the stalactites themselves bronze objects of every description. Our host told us that in the first three hours after the discovery of these naturally formed niches, offerings had been found at the rate of one a minute! It was indeed a notable deposit, including bronze blades, pins, tweezers, brooches, rings, needles, many small simulacra of the double-axe — sacred symbol of the Great God, whose birthplace the grotto was believed to be — bronze statuettes, sealstones etc.

Hogarth himself, in his autobiography *Accidents of an Antiquary's Life* (1910), describes how local women became involved, and their contribution:

As a master of labour, I have met with least reluctance from women in Moslem lands ... But Eastern Christians are usually more prudish or more fearful, and I expected that no Lasithi woman would work. Sure enough they proved coy, and at first would only watch from afar two trained girls brought up from Cnossus as lures; but on the third morning a cosmopolitan villager, who had fought — or looted — in France in 1870, sent up his wife and a daughter to help his son and the ice was broken. A laughing mob ran up the hill tossing sieves and clamouring to be listed, and with their sisters, cousins and aunts, who brought up the midday meals, made the terrace before our cave the gayest spot in Lasithi ...

Once the women were involved, the work expanded:

Unwilling and not hopeful, the men clambered down into the abyss, and the women especially, who had been working hitherto in sunshine at the Cave's mouth, moaned at the sight of the clammy mud in which they must now stand and search by the smoky light of petroleum flares. But complaints soon ceased, as first one and then another picked a bronze out of the soil which had lodged on the upper rock slopes.

The small treasures left in the cave millennia before as gifts to the god, often by women pilgrims, were, as Hogarth says, 'Picked out easily enough by the slim fingers of girls.' And he noted that

Washing the blackened potsherds [the soil] contained was set a gang of women, who are always more patient in minute search than men, and less apt to steal. It is always well to have a few women among your diggers. The men labour better in their company, and with a vivacity which is of no small value where boredom spells failure.

Dorothea Bate visited the cave in May 1904, only because the Ascension feast day meant that she couldn't get anyone to work in her hippo trenches. She was particularly taken by the 'large pool of deliciously cold water at the bottom'.

To visit the cave today and picture Harriet and Dorothea then, presumably in the clothes of the day, without all the facilities set in place for the milliard trippers who file down every year, is to wonder. You may have gathered that I am not a cave person, and not one who copes well with sites full of other people. You clamber down an almost sheer slope, clutching a rope handrail, avoiding a stream of people going both ways, sure you will miss your footing and land in Rhea's birthing pool (not a recognised description); the air is freezing (don't forget your jacket) and there's not much to see but the pool, stalactites and stalagmites. Of course, you should go but, frankly, I only did it for you!

Some people climb to the cave from the tourist area by donkey, and there is much pressure on you to do so; if you are frail, it may be an idea. Coming down is less hot and tiring – there is a proper sealed path. Lunch at Antulla's came as a real consolation. Read what Sonia Greger says about tourism and the local culture either before or after your visit.

### Trapeza cave

Retrace your steps anti-clockwise from Psychro to Tzermiado, the administrative centre of the plateau. The way to the Trapeza cave should be clearly marked in the town but those signs give out and one marked Kronia leading to the cave is misleading. As we to'd and fro'd along a road trying to find the site, we were much helped by an old woman leading a tightly held very small donkey and a goat. She offered me a handful of shelled walnuts and wanted her photograph taken. Her information merited crossing her extended palm with silver as well.

The reason for visiting yet another cave that day was not so much because people had lived there since neolithic times (see p. 13) but because, in the 1930s, a team of British archaeologists under John Pendlebury and including his wife Hilda (formerly White) and Mercy Money-Coutts (see p. 170) excavated there. Unfortunately, the women seem to have left nothing to convey what they experienced, just their contributions to a learned report. You have to use your imagination.

## Tzermiado

Back in Tzermiado, we felt we ought to contribute more to the local economy and take back a memento of Lasithi women's handiwork. The man in the shop couldn't understand my insistence on something made in Lasithi – Crete or Greece must be good enough. It wasn't. But his wife (?) **Dimitria** appeared, swore to God (crossing herself) that she had embroidered the blouse she persuaded me to buy – it took her three weeks, and her daughters also embroidered garments; her mother had made a little rug on display. And when we were already back in the car, she handed us in two apples.

Back in England, I compared the blouse with one almost identical (apart from the colour) that I had bought in Macau (labelled 'Made in India'). Would Dimitria really have crossed herself? Sonia was somewhat non-committal when I asked her opinion. And in *Village on the Plateau* she writes:

Attempts to produce apparently ethnic crafts by mass production methods have brought onto the market a great bulk of cheap tourist goods which, though sometimes attractive, are definitely not ethnic. These goods are produced primarily on the Greek mainland, though there are a few small weaving factories in Crete. Some goods are imported from, for example, Tai Wan. One shopkeeper I know tells foreign women how his mother spent her whole winter making a certain article by hand. When the customers have left, and knowing I have been listening, he apologises to me for the lie but says that an essential part of business is telling customers what they want to hear.

Anyway, I like the blouse and want to believe that Dimitria bought the basic garment wholesale, perhaps with the design already pricked out, and then embroidered it; certainly it appears to have been done by hand.

## Karphi

By this time we were tired, but we still had two places to visit. We took the road out of Tzermiado towards the pass down to Mallia. Almost immediately on our right was the track towards the peak and archaeological site of Karphi ('nail' or 'spike'). We went a few yards up, decided that neither we nor the car were up to it, and retreated. (Apparently you can drive half-way up, then walk for half an hour.)

Karphi is another site excavated by the Pendlebury team, and another settlement where the last Minoans took refuge (see pp. 66–9). At one time in the 130 years before the eleventh century BC, the settlement probably numbered as many as 3,500 inhabitants. Dilys Powell rather colourfully interprets Karphi from her knowledge of the Pendleburys and their work: 'On its rocky perch it disclosed what there was every reason to identify as one of the castles of the "robber barons" thought to have taken over Crete when the great Minoan civilisation was disintegrating.'

The women may have been more peaceable: spinning and weaving implements (spindle whorls, spools, loom weights and bobbins) were found in at least half the rooms. I cannot help wondering, though, how they worked at that height when their fingers must have been numb with cold.

Karphi also had several bench sanctuaries, both private and public, and the typical Minoan goddesses with upraised arms. I particularly like the one found here which, instead of a solid drum base, usual with these MGUAs (see pp. 62–3), has slender ankles and feet peeping out of a front opening. As Pendlebury commented, 'The goddess must have needed them to reach her lofty shrine.' (See Herakleion Museum, room XI).

Mercy Money-Coutts published 'Pottery from Karphi' in 1960, by then under her married name of Seiradaki (see p. 158). But Mercy's greater claim to Karphi fame, as far as I am concerned, was her determination to beat the super-athletic John Pendlebury in daily races up to the Karphi site, described by Vronwy Hankey who watched it – a competition that has entered archaeological and family folklore. Mercy's great-niece, Harriet, hopes one day to follow in her footsteps up Karphi, having done so in Sougia and Lissos, on the south-west coast (see p. 279).

Karphi has a special place, too, as the last excavation before the Second World War changed much in Crete (see pp. 151–9). Dilys Powell, though, ends the Karphi excavation on a high note when she writes of how the Pendlebury team related to their neighbours:

In 1938 when [John] and Hilda arrived at Tzermiadha they were greeted by 'five village elders – who had suitably liquored up for the occasion – with a gallon of wine and a set speech on the benefits we had conferred on the district'. At the end of the season there was a civic banquet in a garden in the plain, and the following afternoon they were accompanied by the Mayor and town council as far as the next village, where more refreshment was offered, while on their further journey towards Knossos they met two policemen who, refusing to let them eat their own food or drink their own wine, gave them yet another party.

## Kardiotissa Convent (Kera)

Drive now towards the northern pass leading down to Mallia and passing on the way the village of Kera. Karphi rises up like a spike on your right. Wending your way down, you will come to the Panagia Kardiotissa ('Virgin of Tenderness' or 'Virgin of the Heart') Convent which celebrates the Virgin's birth on 8 September.

This religious establishment was probably founded in the second Byzantine period (961–1204) though it is also dated 1333, and, following the abandonment of the plateau under the Venetians, and its resettlement in the mid-sixteenth century, was, like the Kroustallenia Monastery, resurrected by a refugee family from the Peloponnese – this time the Magganaris. It, and the extensive lands the family acquired, were to remain under their leadership for several centuries.

The monastery was destroyed by the Ottomans in 1822, in 1841 and in 1866–67 and was never completely to recover, though building work was carried out in the 1950s and 1960s. Not much remains, therefore, of any of the old structures, though restoration in the 1970s has revealed Byzantine frescoes in the *katholikon*.

Today the Kardiotissa is a convent where nuns tend the gardens and run a shop selling their handiwork. But its main claim to renown is the extraordinary history of its icon of the Virgin. Tradition say that the Ottomans took the icon to Istanbul (Constantinople) but that it returned to Kera the same night. That happened three times. The icon is said now to be in the church of San Stefano in Rome; but a copy was made in 1735 and it may be that which is on display in the Kardiotissa chapel. None of those details is completely clear, for Sonia Greger reconstructs in fictional form the true event she attended in 1982, when the icon came home to Kera.

In 'Rea and Theo Come to the Plateau' one of three parts of her slim volume *Ariadne: A Cretan Myth* (1992) (see also p. 52), she has Rea, a young graduate from Chersonissos at the western base of the plateau, joining the procession bearing the icon on its return as it passes through her town. In the crowd climbing up to Kera, Rea meets Theo. Through them, their extended conversation, and intense relationship lasting just for that day, Sonia tries to understand the importance of the icon to Cretans. This attempt is well-summarised in a remark Rea (presumably named after the mother of Zeus) makes to Theo following a discussion about feminism and the position of women and about patriarchy and power more generally; Rea is a modern woman but she explains:

'When I found myself in the channel of people moving towards the ikon today, down at Chersonissos, I thought I was dying. I was so penned-in. I blamed it then on the Church and the black-robed priests who seemed to stop my breathing. Yet at the last possible minute I came to the Panaghia; and as I kissed her a great draught of air, or cool water, poured into me. I was reborn; and felt stronger than ever before.'

Not only is it unclear if the icon returned in 1982 is the original or the copy, but there are so many icons of the Virgin in the chapel that I did not know which I should particularly be admiring. Being quizzed, Sonia says it doesn't matter if the icon is a copy – the issue is its effect.

When you have 'done' the Kardiotissa, you can wind down to the coast feeling that you know just a little more about women and the Lasithi Plateau.

## Mallia

The northern pass from the Lasithi Plateau hits the coast just to the west of Mallia. The village, or town, straddling as it does the main highway from Herakleion to Agios Nikolaos and the east, creates something of a bottleneck, and is very much a tourist centre. Three kilometres east of the busy main street, in the middle of the flat coastal plain, you will see a signposted turning to your left, leading you down towards the sea. There is a proper car park and other facilities.

There was a settlement at Mallia as early as Prepalatial times, but the Minoan town and palace date from the First Palace period, and habitation and rebuilding continued through until the Postpalatial period. Excavation started there in 1915. By 1922, it had come within the sphere of the French School at Athens, where it has remained.

The Quartier Mu whose family workshops I have described (see p. 22) are from the earlier period, as is the most outstanding Minoan jewellery find, the Mallia bee pendant (see p. 23). Pat Cameron will expertly lead you through the site, including the cemetery at Chrysolakkos down by the sea where the bee pendant was found. But the guide books will not tell you about Marthe Oulié and Hermine de Saussure (see p. 167) or Micheline van Effenterre (see p. 173).

Marthe and Hermine were to join the French team at Mallia in the 1920s. I have already introduced them to you briefly when, in 1929, they were sailing around the Aegean (see p. 150). Sailing was their passion, and their passport to freedom, as it was for a group of their friends, and it was not their first Aegean trip.

The best known of the group was the traveller and Olympic yachtswoman (1924) **Ella Maillart** (1904–1997) a friend of Hermine, whom she called Miette, since girlhood. Ella wrote of her:

Bobbed chestnut hair with a fairer lock in front, clear grey eyes, and a frank and delicate smile – there was a light in her face. Later, reading Homer, I felt that Pallas Athene must have looked like Miette. She had been baptized Hermine because her absent-minded father, when he came to make the entry in the town hall register, had forgotten which name had been chosen, and could think of nothing else!

They sailed together regularly, and Ella also describes Marthe's arrival in the group:

Miette was sailing *Perlette* around the Greek islands, training a girl, nicknamed Pa-tchoum, who might later come to the South Pacific with us. Pa-tchoum was a student of archaeology who had written something on Minoan art and who was going to dig in Crete.

Ella disdains dates in her autobiographical miscellany *Cruises and Caravans* (1942), but she tells of how later 'We wound up that summer with six weeks near a primitive Cretan village, excavating under Pa-tchoum's order.' I have not found another source that includes Ella in the dig at Mallia, but we do know that the 'something on Minoan art' was Marthe's published thesis *Les Animaux dans la Peinture de la Crète Préhellénique* (n.d.). All Marthe and Hermine write of their excavation in Crete in *La Croisière de la Perlette* (1926) is:

In two months, interrupted by frequent excursions to the Minoan sites of Mesara plain to the east, and the high plains in the centre, we had unearthed a corner of

24. Martha Oulié and Hermine de Saussure on board *La Perlette* from Oulié, 'Four French Girls Sail ...'

the prehellenic town of Mallia, spending our days digging under a torrid sun, and our nights in a shelter made of branches by the sea.

It is from Henri van Effenterre that we glean more details about those he called 'two astonishing figures' who came to be known 'rather irreverently' as '*les petites filles*'. Over 50 years after their time there, he published his major work *Le Palais de Malia et la Cité Minoenne* (1980). In it he continued:

The two friends came to the Bay of Mallia in 1924 and 1925. On land they exchanged the ship's log for the dig log. They explored a new area of habitation between the Mill beach and the palace. These were the *Gamma* houses, crammed between little streets of complicated chronology. They revealed many interesting architectural features of the period. On the island of Christ, Marthe Oulié and Hermine de Saussure also went to excavate a series of tombs which gave us for a long time the most beautiful vases found in the Mallia area. Certainly it would be easy to make fun of this amateur kind of archaeology, a bit romantic, a kind obviously unthinkable today. But if you compare the publication of the *Gamma* houses that Demargne was able to write up from the notes of the petites filles with any scholarly volume devoted to the soundings in the other houses, to the south west of the palace, if you were to compare the publication of the graves of the little island of Christ that we were able to produce ourselves based on the notes of Marthe Oulié with the results of an impeccable expedition led to the same place in 1969, you have to ask yourself who contributed more to archaeological knowledge. 'Ah, I wish they'd left it for us to do,' sigh the virtuosos of the square dig and the anthropological analysis. Are we absolutely sure that without all the work of that heroic time, the Mallia site would be still largely available to the scalpel and the brush of the archaeologists of today, more methodical and precise than their ancestors? It would no doubt have been given over to the bulldozers which are converting the north coast of Crete into a tourist riviera.

The *Gamma* houses were found between the palace and Mill beach on the coast to the north west. The islands in the bay are omitted from any map I have found.

After the Second World War, in 1954, Henri van Effenterre returned to Mallia, this time with his archaeologist wife Micheline and their growing family. Micheline's chef d'oeuvre was to be *Les Minoens: l'Age d'Or de la Crète* (1991); in it she describes with suitable lyricism the finding of the Mallia bee pendant:

In the summer of 1930, on the rocky coast of the Bay of Mallia, battered by waves and at that time still fairly hostile, in an excavation which had seemed, until then, a rather deceptively turned-over burial ground, Pierre Demargne made the discovery of the bee pendant — the most beautiful of all Minoan jewels. There was not a true accurate archaeological context for these few grams of gold, escaped from the smelting which, as the peasants said, should have been the sad fate of the other treasures from Chrysolakkos (the name signifying gold pit) pillaged in former times to pay taxes to the Turkish pasha.

To see this pendant in the Herakleion Museum (see p. 189), or to own a true replica as I shall on the day this book is published, is to begin to appreciate the significance of its find and its escape from the fate of other treasures buried with their owners millennia before. It is also

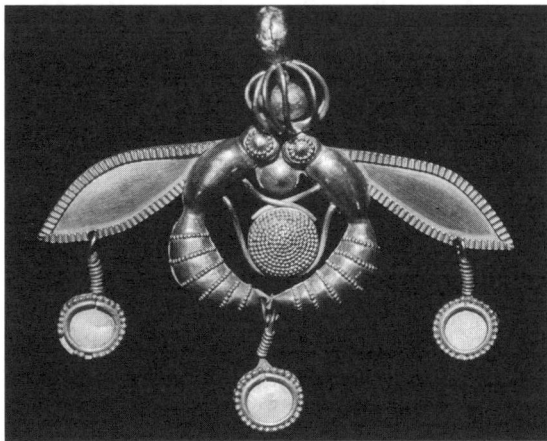

25.  Mallia Bee Pendants, 1900–1700 BC, Archaeological Museum, Herakleion

to realise that the plunderers were acting not merely from gold lust but because the value of the gold was an economic necessity.

Micheline van Effenterre's life at Mallia was hardly more comfortable than it had been for the '*petites filles*' 30 years earlier. I asked her to describe her work there and she replied:

You have asked me if, at Mallia, we women had really excavated! Of course we did but not with a spade or any other implement. We had workers from the neighbouring villages and even a foreman to direct them. Our work consisted of sitting at the top or the bottom of a hole, following the progress of the workman in order to measure the depth at which an object was found, to draw or, at least, to describe it, to indicate everything possible to class it in its context and in its state, etc. etc. It was often tiring, sometimes exciting. But that lasted the whole day and each one as tiring as the last. That description is adequate, but it doesn't include everything.

Whatever Mallia township is like today, the site itself may, if you are lucky, only have a few other visitors, and it is possible to imagine Marthe, Hermine and Micheline and, even, the woman who once wore the Mallia bee, if woman it was. As Micheline writes, 'The jewel guards its secret.' Neither should we forget the woman who was taken as a slave from Mallia in 1560 (see p. 115).

## Milatos cave

If you were returning to Herakleion after visiting the Lasithi Plateau, you may or may not divert a short distance eastwards to Mallia. But only if you were going further eastwards would you now want to go on to the Milatos Cave.

Just before you turn, on the main highway, south-eastwards towards Agios Nikolaos, take a minor road north-eastwards. The large cave – or series of caverns – is in the hills behind the village and is a place of pilgrimage for Cretans because of the massacre or enslavement of women and children refugees there by Ottoman forces in 1823 (see p. 128). At the main entrance is a modern chapel. This is a different sort of cave from the Diktaian or Trapeza but typical of other caves in Crete that symbolise its more recent history (see also pp. 128 and 133).

The fate of the refugees is central to the novel by Rhea Galanaki which featured elsewhere in this itinerary. And Dorothea Bate was aware of its unhappy history when she visited the area in 1904; but her history and discoveries were of very much earlier times:

Along the coastline east of Candia no cave deposit was found until Melato ... Here one was discovered on the bare hillside to the north-west of the village, between it and the sea. No part of the former cave was to be seen except a few fragmentary portions of the stalagmitic flooring showing above the ground, and containing remains of a pigmy hippopotamus.

The next itinerary, Rodanthe, will continue the theme of Cretan women's fate in Ottoman times, and take us further east and south from the Lasithi Plateau.

# 23
## Rodanthe of Kritsa

*Kritsa, Faneromeni Monastery, Kritsa (continued), Houmeriakos, Kontaratos field, Panagia Kera, Kritsa (continued)*

So intriguing is the story of Rodanthe, and a bit legendary, that she merits an itinerary of her own (see also p. 130). I shall describe the events of her life chronologically, which is not the way you would follow them on the map.

We visited the places in two journeys on separate days, based at the Istron Bay Hotel where we stayed one night in 2001 and for two weeks in 2002 as a package with Simply Crete. It is an upmarket hotel – you can wear a nice frock in the evening and not feel out of place – with appropriate rooms, view and facilities. From it, we also visited the Lasithi Plateau (see pp. 287–308), the American sites (see pp. 333–58) and the south-east coast (see pp. 318–32).

This, briefly, is the chronology of Rodanthe's life, linked to place: She was born in Kritsa, educated in the Faneromeni Monastery, abducted from Kritsa by the Ottoman commander of the district and taken to his headquarters at Houmeriakos, escaped, joined the partisans against the Ottomans, and died at Kontaratos, a field just outside Kritsa. On the map, travelling from the north towards south east, you would move from Houmeriakos, to Kontaratos, to Kritsa, to Faneromeni. In theory, you could do it in one day, in one sweep. I don't advise it because Kritsa has other things to offer, and the site of Lato is nearby (see p. 318), as are Agios Nikolaos and its museum (see pp. 319–22).

We had, on our earlier visit, been lucky enough to interest Maria K., head receptionist at the Istron Bay Hotel, in our project. On our return, she introduced us to a friend (Michalis M.) who was to take us to Vrokastro (see pp. 351), and another, Michalis G., a teacher in Kritsa who was au fait with the life of Rodanthe.

## Kritsa

We drove what we thought was a clever back way from Istron to Kritsa to meet Michalis G. – clever, not only because it looked like a shortcut but because it must be the way that Rodanthe was taken – on foot or by donkey – to the Faneromeni Monastery. It had been raining heavily; the road was much churned up, full of bifurcations, and unsignposted. We arrived late for our appointment. We should have taken the main road; why don't you look at the map and decide what fits in with your plans? The road is probably sealed by now, as so many are becoming so thanks to European Union money.

Rodanthe was born in Kritsa – a village then of some 1,000 souls – in 1800, the daughter of the high priest of Mirabello. We were taken by Michalis to the house but it is in no way marked, so I will give you here the notes I scrawled as we walked along. Find the new Hagios Giorgios Church (1955), turn right and up at the Olive Press (perfectly decent for a light lunch), follow a narrow path bearing right and up; then left and up; turn left into a little playground. The house abuts this. It has a rusty metal door, with inset broken glass, and a small cross above a stone-framed, glassless window. In case my instructions don't work, it may be worth asking for 169 Rodanthe Street.

The house was uninhabited (though it had been occupied until ten years previously) and in complete disrepair. We had hoped to get in but the woman with the key was not there. Everyone in the street – many of them women in black – offered us their facts and opinions. The whole length of the block up to the next little passage had belonged to Rodanthe's extended family and was similarly unoccupied.

## Faneromeni Monastery

Rodanthe not only grew up in Kritsa but it was from there that she was abducted when she was 18. But now we must move to when she was five. This entails a visit to the Faneromeni Monastery, founded in 1204 or 1293 high on a hill above the bay to the east of Istron. Its location and structure, later revised and added to, were intended as protection against the Venetians.

Driving toward Gournia, you turn left at the sign to Panagia Faneromeni and over the main highway to get you away from the seaward side and climbing up the precipitous hillside. The road quickly becomes narrow, serpentine, unsealed, rocky and fairly high on the nerve-wracking scale if you are on the passenger side towards the edge looking down. But par for the course for Crete.

None too soon, you find yourself in the lee of the high, whitewashed walls of the monastery, and park – undoubtedly best out of season; ours was the only car there. From here you can see across the bay and across the countryside – the Vrokastro peak rises up in the middle of a wide plain. You can even discern the route that Rodanthe would have taken from Kritsa.

You are quite likely to find the monastery completely deserted apart from a few cats. Wend your way upwards to the little chapel (*katholikon*), which is the reason the uninitiated come; here again, an icon of the Virgin Mary was found in a cave, subsequently built into the chapel. Panagia Faneromeni means 'The Virgin Revealed'.

A monk may finally turn up, and is likely to be hospitality itself. In 2002, there were only five monks in residence; once there were nuns and monks but the last nun died some five years previously. Brother Paisios, with his adequate English, was pleased, as we sat round the kitchen table, by our interest in Rodanthe, and happy to show us where the secret school was held, just on your right as you enter the monastery. There is little information about its origins, hidden from the Ottoman authorities, but the monastery did gain a reputation as the religious and intellectual centre of Eastern Crete and was a meeting place for rebels against the Venetians in 1293 and thereafter. We know about the school, and indeed Rodanthe, only because the poet M. Dialynas mentions it in his epic poem *I Kritsotopoula* ('The Maid from Kritsa'), about our heroine. As far as I can determine, this has not been translated. There is also a novel in Greek, *Rodanthe of Kritsa* (by Kostas Dandoulakis), to which I have not had access.

Rodanthe came to the monastery in 1805. The monks taught not only young people who sought refuge but children from the surrounding countryside as well. In a hidden chamber, little Rodanthe studied, under the dim light of oil lamp or candle, the ecclesiastic epistles, the life of Alexander the Great, and the ancient glory of Hellenism.

Part of the secret school, which was originally blocked off, is now a store-room, and the other part is inaccessible down some steps, as was intended at the time, but it is not at all hard to use your imagination.

### Kritsa (continued)

The years passed and the educated and patriotic girl grew into a beautiful young woman. We move back to the house in Kritsa. When she was 18, the story goes, she was spotted by Hurshit Aga, the local Ottoman commander. I suspect, because of the date of her death, and the events leading up to it, that she was more likely 23, or that she was born later than 1800. At all events, in spite of the commander serenading her at her window, she refused to give in to his blandishments. One night, therefore, when three days before her mother had broken her leg and the family was most vulnerable – perhaps father away from home – Hurshit Aga and some cronies rode along this little street and abducted Rodanthe, melting into the darkness across the plains northwards to Houmeriakos, where he had his headquarters.

The drive there is fascinating, particularly if you are picturing Rodanthe flung across a saddle or held tightly round the waist in front of her captor. You will pass the field of Kontaratos where Rodanthe was killed, but we will come back to that; and you will go past the drive to the archaeological site of Lato, which features in the next itinerary (see p. 318).

## Houmeriakos

We went to Houmeriakos from Kritsa via Neapoli, but you can also get to it from the main highway from Herakleion to Agios Nikolaos – just look out for a sign taking you southwards. Neapoli, a pleasant town in the lee of the Lasithi Plateau, is where, in 1825, 400 Muslim Cretans were besieged in a mosque and then killed (see p. 130).

We had been given probably misleading information about the house to which the Ottoman commander took Rodanthe. This meant, as we drove uphill through the narrow streets of the village, getting wedged across a junction between higgledy-piggledy houses, much endangering flower pots, residents' tempers and our nerves. There was a strong smell of burning rubber. Always be wary of narrow Cretan streets in cars; if you want to get to the top of a village, it is often better to go round than through.

Eventually, we limped back to the main square and debriefed the cafe proprietor who assured us that what had been the Ottoman headquarters was a few yards from the cafe. Leaving the car in the parking area of the square, we walked along the main road that runs through the village and there, on the left, found the Romana Portella – a restored Roman arch leading to an abandoned and dilapidated Venetian house. But the big bunches of grapes covering a trellis through the archway and an orange grove through a locked gate allowed the imagination full rein.

Here, during that first night of captivity, Rodanthe slit Hurshit Aga's throat – presumably with his own knife – dressed in his clothes and escaped through the window.

Now disguised as a youth, she joined the local Cretan rebel group under Captain Kasanis. She was known as Sponomanolis ('beardless Manolis').

## Kontaratos field

It is three days later. We come back to Kritsa and drive northwards for a mile or two, on the way to Lato. On the right of the road you will see a little, white model of a church; a bit further on, on your left, there is a concrete water tank by the roadside, apparently covered in red graffiti. It records how, in 1823, on Kontaratos field, on the other side of the road, the Cretan freedom fighters, and villagers from Kritsa, totalling 1000, engaged with 30,000 Ottoman troops.

During the course of this engagement, Rodanthe was hit by a bullet in the chest – only then did they discover that she was a woman. She died 20 minutes later and entered Cretan legend. Her father died of grief soon afterwards.

The field is still there, wide and flat, fringed by olive trees and low hills. There is unlikely to be anyone else about. If you are lucky, no cars will pass. Walk out into the field, across the stony red earth. The silence is palpable but, if you listen hard, you will hear the cries and cracks of battle, then the small thud as Rodanthe falls.

## Kritsa (continued)

Back in Kritsa, in the middle of Melina Mercouri Square, you will find a pleasing bust of Rodanthe, erected in 1978. The plaque reads 'Rodanthe (Kritsopoula), daughter of the high priest of Kritsa, fought heroically against Ottoman forces in the two-day Battle of Kritsa in January 1823.'

Rodanthe's head is covered by a scarf, which would have been black and would have veiled her hair and ears. She is remembered as a serene-faced young woman, rather than a youth dying in battle. The bust and its position are appropriate; the house should be suitably restored to commemorate her life and times. Perhaps it will have been when you get there!

26.  Bust of Rodanthe, Melina Mercouri Square, Kritsa,
photographed by the author

## Panagia Kera

Although Rodanthe was our main reason for visiting Kritsa, eleven miles west of Agios Nikolaos, others have different goals. Just before you reach the large village (small town) built into an amphitheatre of rocky hillside, you come across (on your right) the Byzantine church of Panagia Kera which houses important frescoes of the fourteenth and fifteenth centuries; indeed, this is probably the best known about and visited Byzantine church – therefore, choose your time (open daily, 8.30 a.m. to 3.00 p.m.).

For our purposes, the south nave (early fourteenth century) is dedicated to the Virgin's mother, St Anne. The frescoes, largely inspired by the Apocrypha, depict the lives of mother and daughter. The main nave is dedicated to the Assumption of the Virgin. In the north vault is an image of Salome carrying John the Baptist's head. In the north nave (dedicated to St Anthony) you will find the enthroned Virgin, Dance of the Female Martyrs and Saints Entering Paradise, and two panels showing the Wise and Foolish Virgins. On the north-west corner is a portrait of the donor Giorgios Mazezanes with his wife, wearing a wide-bottomed gown and elaborate shawl, and small daughter. These are apparently the only personal portraits from medieval Crete. Copies of some of these frescoes are in the Hagios Markos exhibition centre in Herakleion (see p. 187).

Another reason people visit Kritsa is that it is traditionally a centre for weaving; indeed, looms still rattle away in back rooms. Pat Cameron advises that

The knowledgeable walk the length of the main street before considering a purchase. The most characteristic pieces are either in the natural wool colours of cream, grey and brown, or sometimes dyed to a strong red. Nowadays you may have to persist to find the traditional designs based on geometric patterns or natural variations in the wool.

I hesitate to be negative when women are trying to earn a living, but I found the hard sell a bit off-putting.

One day after my return from that visit to Crete, there dropped through our letter box, from the wife of one of my informants, a slender offprint entitled 'A Late Minoan Figurine from Kritsa'. I was much taken by this gesture and what it told me: it somehow went with Kritsa and Rodanthe and added more substance to Elizabeth Warren who had assisted her husband Peter in the excavation of Myrtos Phournou Koriphi – home of the famous Myrtos Goddess (see pp. 15 and 178). Elizabeth introduces her own little goddess:

At the invitation of Dr Alexiou I am publishing a female figurine ... brought to the Aghios Nikolaos Museum as a chance find from the village of Kritsa, Mirabello, from a spot called [Leonida Chani], by the bakery of Koutoulakis. The body is preserved but the arms and head are missing; height preserved: 14.1 cm; diameter of the skirt: 10.15

cm; thickness of skirt wall: 1.2 cm. The skirt is conical and hollow, made on the wheel, with a thickened everted hem. At the waist the body is flattened and broadens out frontally to the shoulders. The breasts are well-developed. There is no indication of the position of the arms except that they did not touch the breasts or the body.

This figurine has caught my imagination. I have read nothing else of Minoan women in Kritsa, though there was a late Minoan cemetery. She may have originated there, but she was a chance find. Who was she? Elizabeth adds:

The function of the figurine is uncertain. On the evidence of figures like that from the Shrine of the Double Axes at Knossos ours may have been a household goddess or votary, but with missing arms and our ignorance of its original location we have no means of knowing.

The Kritsa figurine is unique, but from its fabric and style it is undoubtedly Late Minoan ...

You can see the figurine in the Agios Nikolaos Museum. As you stroll round Kritsa, evading the demands from nut-brown women to buy their wares, don't forget this Minoan woman and Rodanthe.

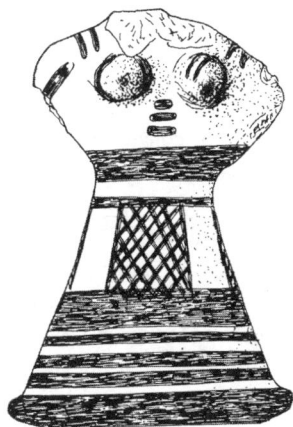

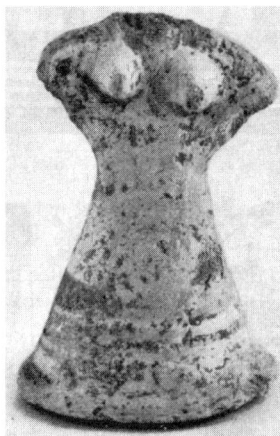

27.   Late Minoan figurine, Kritsa, drawing and photograph, courtesy of Elizabeth Warren

# 24
## From Lato to Myrtos

*Lato, Agios Nikolaos, Myrtos Pyrgos, Myrtos Phournou Koryphi*

Some of the places in this itinerary are best dovetailed logistically with those of the Rodanthe one as Kritsa is only eleven miles west of Agios Nikolaos and Lato only a couple of miles north of Kritsa. But I wanted to make the Rodanthe itinerary – with Kritsa at its centre – self-contained, apart from other things to see in that small town itself. And although this itinerary starts at Lato and ends at Myrtos Phournou Koryphi, the contents are a map-based convenience; you would not attempt to do it all in one day (Lato, Kritsa and Agios Nikolaos might be more than sufficient).

## Lato

Once again, you have to make a decision about whether or not to see objects in a museum before or after you see the site where they were found. It will probably be determined by convenience. Since you may now find yourself in Kritsa, I am going to take you first to Lato. It is well signposted and easy from Kritsa, but remember that it is closed on Mondays (we found out the hard way).

Just outside the drive leading up to the archaeological site, you may well see an old woman in black by the side of the road selling packets of herbs and nuts, her donkey tethered nearby. Do stop and support her enterprise! We enjoyed the oregano for a long time afterwards, and the almonds were sweet and fresh.

Lato dates from Archaic/Classical times (700–330 BC) (see also p. 76). From the seventh to the second century BC, Eileithyia, the goddess of fertility and childbirth, was the patron here, probably inherited from the Minoans. The name of the town was the Doric version of the demi-goddess **Leto**. The relationship of these two women was cemented when Eileithyia attended Leto as she gave birth to Artemis and Apollo. Their father was Zeus and he and his cousin Leto had been lovers before he married Hera (Eileithyia's mother). Hera was not pleased at the news of her husband's dalliance with an old flame, and hounded the pregnant Leto into exile, keeping her constantly on the move until she went into labour on the island of Delos.

Climb up through this site to the top and bear left, through the *agora* (meeting place). Lato was a relatively late discovery for visitors but, although it is now quite popular, you can still think that you're there alone if you go round some rocks to the edge of the mountain side. Perching there, you overlook, far below, Agios Nikolaos, where Lato's ancient port stood, the valley of Kritsa, and the milky Bay of Mirabello.

Back in the *agora*, there is a shrine to Artemis on your left. Stand there and look downwards and then across a little valley to a terrace of fourth century BC temple remains. Although it is called the Temple of Lato, the inscription on the base that would have held the cult statue is so badly damaged that the name of the goddess cannot be read. Sacrifices would have been made in front of the temple. It is easy on top of the world here to conjure up the tangled web of the Olympian deities (see the family tree I have devised on p. 51).

## Agios Nikolaos

This is the administrative and tourist centre of the region. It was not much more than a picturesque fishing village on the Bay of Mirabello when tourists, mostly British, discovered it in the 1960s. Although in times past it was the port for Lato, and was known then as Lato pros Kamara, there is nothing of its past there now except pieces from the Dorian cemetery Potamos in the archaeological museum. The town's immediate seaside attractions for 1960s visitors were enhanced by the strange and very deep little lake Voulismeni in the centre, with its narrow channel to the sea. Inevitably, it has tourist eateries around it, so that it is hard to imagine Athena and Artemis regularly bathing there as they did in legendary times.

If you are there at night, it may still be possible to see the phenomenon observed by the palaeontologist Dorothea Bate in 1904; she wrote in her diary, 'After supper we went down to see a small lake near the harbour which has an inlet to the sea. Has most extraordinary phosphorescent lot of fish in it which dart about looking as if made of fire.' But I haven't seen them mentioned in a travel guide. For all its tourist attractions, if you're a bit of a curmudgeon, you may only visit the town for its archaeological museum.

### Archaeological Museum

Odios Konstantinos Palaeologou; open 8.00 a.m. to 3.00 p.m., closed Mondays

We went to the museum specially for the Myrtos Goddess (see pp. 14, 19 and 330). Even though you are expecting her (in room II), the quirkiness and luminosity of her take you aback as she stands there proudly on display. She may be so much of her time – the Early Minoan II period, c2900–2300 BC – but she could just as easily have won a prize in the twentieth century.

There are eight galleries in the museum and, while exhibits may rotate, the following will give you some guidance:

- **Gallery 1** (Neolithic and Prepalatial): a phallic figure, perhaps an abstract depiction of the deity of fertility.
- **Gallery II** (Prepalatial and Protopalatial): Vasiliki pottery (see pp. 15 and 346); sheet gold jewellery from Mochlos – bracelets, chains, hair ornaments, including a hairpin in the form of a daisy and a remarkable diadem – both adorn the cover of the museum leaflet.

- **Gallery III** (Protopalatial, Neopalatial and Postpalatial): votive offerings from peak sanctuaries, similar to those from Petsophas (see pp. 24–6); naked torso of a woman; female figurine, probably an adorant (a chance find from Myrsini near Siteia), with drum base and joined hands, suggesting worship (see p. 362).
- **Gallery IV** (Postpalatial and early Iron Age): pottery wheel from Kritsa.
- **Gallery V** (Geometric and Orientalising; Archaic and Classical): female figurines and heads with stylised wig-like hair – fine examples of Daedalic style (see pp. 75–6); Archaic busts of female figures, probably representing goddesses, with self-satisfied Archaic smiles and elaborate coiffures (from Elounda, ancient Olous, just north of Agios Nikolaos); maiden-faced bird; goddess or priestess wearing a tall conical headdress; young woman holding a baby to her breast.
- **Anteroom VI:** terracottas from the Siteia area.
- **Gallery VII** (Greco-Roman): Material found in or around Agios Nikolaos, including from Potamos Cemetery, including female clay mask and funerary urn (described below).
- **Gallery VIII** (Hellenistic-Roman): items from Potamos cemetery.

The Myrtos Goddess is an expected treasure in the museum, and she is not likely to disappoint you. Unexpected, though, was the strange, cylindrical funerary urn which caught our attention on a shelf in the penultimate room, with its inscription dating from the first century BC – to the first century AD. Printed out on a stand behind for easier deciphering, and translated, it reads:

> Stranger pass not in noisy haste along this path
> But, pausing, gaze on this stone carved epitaph
> Know that here lies a girl in youth and comeliness
> A mother that two children left alone and motherless

And parents twain to grief and dire distress
For all unyielding was that grim disease
That brought Timonis wise and modest to her resting place
Wherefore, shed tears, O Stranger, as this tomb you pass

The Myrtos Goddess will leave you with a smile; the thought of **Timonis** will make you pause for a moment and think back 2000 or more years. She is all we seem to have left of the women of Lato pros Kamara.

## Towards Myrtos

This itinerary ends at Myrtos Phournou Koryphi, where the Myrtos Goddess lay for 4,500 years. For this second part of it, we chose to drive from Istron the back way, taking the turning to Kalo Chorio and proceeding via Prina, Males and Christos. I wanted to see Christos because it is the maternal home of Emmanuel, my Cretan friend and informant, who lives in London. He had told me about some of the traditions and language of women harvesting olives (see p. 124). It made for a delightfully scenic drive, though we missed the village itself because of inadequate signposting and a dead-end. On those narrow mountain roads you cannot always retrieve your step, but the road was, at least, sealed, which was relatively new. Looking back, we saw the village latched to the mountain side, perhaps more promising from a distance.

We could have added to the drive by visiting the **Panagias Exakoustis** ('Virgin Renowned'; feast day 8 September) Convent which lies 2 km outside the mountain village of Males on the Anatoli road. It was founded in the nineteenth century and was twice dissolved before being revived in the 1960s. Pat Cameron explains that although the original rock-cut chapel is old, the main buildings are no age. But 'the scented garden on a pine-covered hillside offers a memorable view of the Myrtos valley'.

The village of Myrtos itself is an attractive enough tourist centre on the Libyan Sea – good for a pit stop and fresh orange juice, but with one-way streets and difficult to park. But we now have two important archaeological sites to visit, and all through the drive towards the coast and this archaeological area, I was trying to find a likely setting for *Silence in Crete* (1964), the novel by Elisabeth Ayrton (see p. 177). The only hint she gives about location is that the village in which the story starts out is 30 km from Ierapetra. The excavations involved might have been the archaeological site marked on the map near Males, but we could find no sign of it on the ground.

This is a tale, told in the first person, of archaeological skulduggery, of a young Cretan, Arkas, deafened in the Second World War and bitter as a result, but who had worked at Knossos as a boy:

When Mr Lerwick and the women had finished sorting a pile, the shards were taken to another shed and placed in dated trays, in case some hidden piece still lay among them. It was one of my jobs to take them there. I loved pottery – as I still do – I was only thirteen and I used to play with the unwanted shards as I arranged them. The ugly, clumsy Neolithic pottery, blackish grey, of a coarse, gritty texture, I hated. The Minoan pots were all lovely, but the creamy Palace age pots were the best of all.

Arkas got such a taste for what could be dug from the ground that he is unable to resist the lure of an undiscovered Minoan tomb – the unauthorised excavation of which is illegal; he's sure that he will find there a very special goddess figurine.

Arkas has a 'beautiful, elegant and gentle' donkey called Pasiphae whom he found abandoned at birth in a ditch near Lato and who carries his finds. Then there is his sister, 'neat and handsome' Aphaia (named after a nymph of Crete), a teacher, who acts as his ears, his housekeeper and secretary.

Arkas is disappointed that Aphaia ignores her heritage: 'My great-grandmother, my grandmother, even my mother, had taken some part in general affairs and worked and talked on equal terms with men.' Her diffidence was not ordained: their scholar uncle had different expectations. When Arkas was much younger, and Aphaia a tot, he explained why Greece was poor and backward compared with other countries:

'Girls are what we make them. We've held them down like a conquered people for millennia. Now, in the West, they're giving them their freedom, as much freedom as they can learn to take. In Greece, we're beginning too; here on Crete, even, we've made a start. And if I can free Aphaia and make her your equal and mine, or better, perhaps, then I shall feel that my life's been worthwhile, after all.'

Koryne, known as Crow Girl, is the one who loves Arkas and is his salvation; she grows through their adventures.

Somewhere near his precious site, Arkas comes across an old woman, Mme Clerios, who was once the wife of the local mayor; now she spends the winter in Ierapatra but, in the summer, she takes to the hills and lives as a hermit. 'She had done this ever since her husband and two sons were killed in reprisals in the war and a little daughter lost when the women and children fled from the village.' Mme Clerios, too, as a girl, worked at Knossos, 'clearing the earth away'. As she told Arkas, 'On Crete, since then, we are all archaeologists.'

Ever since first reading *Silence in Crete*, I have tried to work out the location of Arkas' archaeological site just above the sea not that far from Ierapetra. If it was not near Males, was it Myrtos Pyrgos, or Myrtos Phournou Koryphi, the excavations of both of which were to start a few years after the publication of this novel? Finally I had a chance to talk to Elisabeth's youngest daughter, Frejä, who was with her and Michael Ayrton in Crete in 1961. Frejä tells me that they travelled all round the island, including the major archaeological sites, at a time when Crete's tourist industry was completely undeveloped and sites almost inaccessible. She is clear that Arkas' village and site are formed from various places – Elisabeth became soaked in the whole of Crete. In spite of that, the clue of Ierapetra sets the story, and my imagination at least, in this itinerary. And Arkas finds his goddess:

She who started us all, who preceded all other gods, was there in her broken splendour. I found her alone, and got her out myself, finding all of her in the earth

28. Elisabeth Ayrton, courtesy of the family

near her altar, except her forearms, and those may still be found when proper digging begins.

She was about fourteen inches high altogether. I found her skirt first, recognised half-ruined ivory and saw the gleam of gold where it still adhered to the skirt flounces. I did not for several moments see that it was her skirt, only recognising the Chryselephantine. Then suddenly I saw. At the waist there was a small round hole, filled solid with yellow earth, into which a peg from the base of her torso would fit, joining her two halves with precision.

But that is by no means the end of the story: others want her too.

## Myrtos Pyrgos

Driving from the village of Myrtos towards the town of Ierapetra along the south coast, the first of the two major archaeological sites you come to, high above the road just outside the village on the east side of the bridge over the Myrtos river, is Myrtos Pyrgos. This is the location of a Minoan villa or country house and provincial settlement dating from the Second Palace period (1700–1450 BC) (see p. 32), though there were important buildings there earlier and later.

The main archaeological attraction is the remains of what was probably a two or even three storey country house. Pat Cameron, for example, will provide you with the archaeological details to help you fully appreciate the site from that point of view; my interest now is in the twentieth-century women who have left their footprints there.

Gerald Cadogan started excavating the site in 1970 and continued on and off until 1982. The best known of his women colleagues was Vronwy Fisher Hankey who joined him there in 1970. Life then was quite tough – no electricity, no proper road, no adequate drainage, no reliable telephone. Most shopping had to be done in bulk in Ierapetra several miles away. The cafe owner in Myrtos slaughtered a pig once a week and donkeys still came down from the Lasithi mountains along the River Myrtos valley with paniers of grapes and potatoes. In its Minoan days, the valley would have provided barley, vetch and olives.

Vronwy was undaunted. Snippets about her in the writings of her colleagues add firm flesh to the biographical details I give you on p. 172. Gerald Cadogan tells us that, as well as the lack of amenities, 'There was also much good company, with singing and dancing and expeditions into the hills to accompany the hard work of the week. Vronwy loved it, and was an example to us all of the best of mixing hard work and hard play, and never complaining.' Another observer noted that 'One of her roles was the *materfamilias* (her rendering of the village style *yiayia* cry could have brought in a whole family from the far-flung fields)'.

**Cressida Ridley** (1917–1998, née Bonham-Carter), the widow of Jaspar Ridley who disappeared as a prisoner of war in Italy, read archaeology as a mature student at the Institute of Archaeology,

London and is best known for her work at Servia in northern Greece. Gerald Cadogan had asked her to join the team for the 1970 season with some trepidation, particularly since she and Vronwy had to share a room. He need not have worried: they became good friends and he describes how, 'A formidable pair of strong-minded women in their early fifties, they kept the young more or less on the straight and narrow.' Paired together on dish-washing duties, it is told how Cressida observed to Vronwy in her deep voice, 'You wash, I'll smash.' They died within months of each other in 1998.

Other women who were to work at Myrtos Pyrgos were **Sara Paton** (St Anne's, Oxford) who ran the pot shed (*apotheke*) – the workshop and storeroom. She was a head of department – her job being similar in status to that of running a trench. She went on to specialise in Roman Crete. It was to Sara that Cressida, mistress of the one-liner, remarked during the Servia excavation: 'Never put lovers in the same trench' – advice that the bush telegraph made sure reached Myrtos and elsewhere. Then there was **Penelope Mountjoy**, a draughtswoman, who also worked in the *apotheke*. And Ruth Padel who was later to make her name as a poet – her poems sometimes drawing on her Cretan experience (see p. 212).

**Eleni Kandaraki**, originally from Athens, had married Petros Petrakis, the star pot mender of the British School at Athens and in Crete for some years. Rachel Hood has written of Eleni's place in Crete's archaeology: 'Eleni contributed her unrivalled gift for providing a sudden culinary treat, her knowledge of the Greek countryside, its herbs and practices and her great kindness, as well as occasional forays into pot-washing with water and acid.' At Myrtos, Eleni's main contribution was helping her husband in pot-washing.

Mostly, archaeological accounts tell us of artefacts and scholars' interpretations of the people thousands of years previously who used them. Insight into the life of the archaeologists themselves are usually only glimpses. That is why *Digging* (1987) by Lucy Cadogan, Gerald's wife, is such fun. The stuffed-shirt scholar is stripped bare, sometimes literally.

**Lucy Cadogan**, an American who read classics at St Anne's, Oxford, met Gerald in Rome where her physicist father was a diplomat. She already had ambitions as a novelist. Landed at Myrtos Pyrgos, she found herself in charge of the commissary. It was autumn. Through rainstorms and along bad roads, it was she who weekly drove to Ierapetra for provisions. Cooking was done on two gas rings by the light of storm lanterns. The headquarters was a one-room house in which cooking was done behind a partition. The others had rooms in or about the village of Myrtos.

Lucy didn't go up the hill to work on the excavation: she and Gerald's cousin, **Monica Cadogan Lewis**, who otherwise cooked directors' lunches in London, ran the social and medical side of the little community. Eventually Lucy realised that she had the material for a novel – the dig was 'an ideal cauldron – characters could act and reveal their true selves'.

We have already met Jenny, wife of the director of the dig, and Laura, her rather vain and lost friend over from London, in the Knossos itinerary (see pp. 211–12). Now they are transferred to an archaeological site – Kallithea ('Beautiful View') – on the south coast. I asked Lucy how far Jenny and her functions in the team coincided with her own. She replied, 'She's tiresome – probably based on me.' For those in the wider archaeological community who read the novel upon publication, the game was disentangling the *roman-à-clef* – 'I recognise that character.' That of Margaret may contain a bit of Lucy too, or other archaeological wives in a similar situation, or Gerald's cousin Monica:

Margaret had cooked a delicious lunch. She'd made a sauce for the pork chops which was light and sharp and delectable; the spinach purée and gratin potatoes went well with it and Christopher tucked in, convinced it was one of Margaret's best meals so far. Everyone enjoyed it, scraping their plates clean, the 'mmmm' sounds of gratified eaters the only talk until all the food was gone. Too tired to talk, and too hungry, the excitement of the day's finds held them all in thrall (except Bill and Christopher of course), a silent satisfaction drifting out through the open door to the newly arrived hippies who chewed at pomegranates in the middle of the street until they were chased off by a woman with three goats, whacking the mulberry trees with a long stick.

Christopher is the stuffed shirt of the enterprise; Annabel, a slightly unstable character – her invitation to him gives a chance to explore character as well as link the story firmly to place:

Annabel cornered Christopher as he was leaving to suggest she walk with him a little before she went to bed. Once outside she suggested they go to Kritsa for the weekend so that he could show her the museum at Ayios Nikolaos and the church at Kera, with its famous frescoes, as well as Gournia and Lato. They were all places she was dying to see. Christopher saw his chance. He jumped at it. He was grateful to Annabel, even if it meant putting up with her flummery.

But however the characters interact with each other, or whatever happens away from the excavation, the real thrill for the participants comes from digging, and the reader learns more about the intricacies of the process:

Laura held the tapes. Susan's small hand made infinitesimal moves of the pencil as she drew the earrings and the pin in their socket of damp earth. Christopher was adjusting his cameras. No one spoke. When Susan finished he crouched with his flash bulb at the entrance to the chamber. Then he reached in and lifted the things, clenching them in his fist as he backed away and straightened up. 'You'd better get an envelope,' he told Susan in a dull voice.

They were beautiful. A pair of gold bull's head earrings and a gold pin. The heads of the bulls were large and elaborately worked, a wide intricately sculpted jaw balanced beautifully with the horns which curved back around the skull to crown the animal. So delicate, so skilful, so sophisticated. Susan held them, then handed them to Laura. The gold shone. They were surprisingly light and yellow as a daisy. Awed, the others gathered round and stared at the three small, priceless objects in Laura's hand, still as brilliant as when they were made thousands of years ago.

Inevitably, the sight of gold, even the prospect of gold being found, arouses the greed of the baddies. 'What is the worst thing that could happen in an excavation?', Lucy had asked when she began to plan her novel. 'Robbery', was the answer.

Lucy Cadogan has not followed up her first novel, but she has photographed and drawn archaeological subjects and only quite recently, in the museum at Herakleion, she realised what the Minoans were about – 'They did make the most beautiful things.'

## Myrtos Phournou Koryphi

Continue now further along that southern highway towards Ierapetra, but be on the qui vive. On your right (seaward), before you get to Nea Myrtos, you will see a sign for the Phournou Koryphi archaeological site pointing across the road up the hill. Best to drive past, turn round and, returning, park in the lee of the hill (facing back the way you have come). There is no proper parking, and only space for one car, and no official approach to the site. We simply scrambled up the gully – almost an adventure (make sure you're wearing walking shoes).

At the top, bear right through the low wild thyme bushes towards the fence which now becomes apparent surrounding the site. I'm not sure that it is open to the public but the gate was unlocked when we were there and we simply went in. We were the only visitors and we were standing on top of the world overlooking the Libyan Sea; we felt that we had discovered the Early Minoan site for ourselves. We set to finding the shrine of the Myrtos Goddess in the south-west corner of the site (I can't say that we necessarily found it, but we had fun looking).

I have written in some detail in the history section about this Early Minoan, Prepalatial settlement (see pp. 14–16) and about the Myrtos Goddess (see pp. 14 and 19) whom you may by now have visited in the Agios Nikolaos museum (see p. 320). The settlement was early destroyed by fire but, as a result, provides archaeologists with a discrete picture of Minoan society at that stage of development, not overlaid by later buildings and artefacts.

Evidence of weaving is one of the most obvious remnants and this probable women's work is engagingly discussed by Elizabeth Wayland Barber in *Women's Work: The First 20,000 Years: Women, Cloth and Society* (1994). The chapter on Crete is called 'Island Fever' and Myrtos Phournou Koryphe is one of the places that most inspired her. Elizabeth has the ability to weave scholarship and experience with textiles with re-creative imagination and the physical attributes of place. She tells us that Myrtos was well-equipped to take the production of cloth from start to finish. Of the dyeing process she writes:

Several dye-producing plants and animals were available in the vicinity of the village, while small pierced stone weights – found in abundance at much later dyeing installations – occurred all over the site. The windiness of the hill could have played a part as well, since dyers always seek a steady wind to help the fabrics dry and to remove the sometimes dreadful stench of the dyestuffs.

Phournou Koryphi also had its husband and wife excavation team – Peter and Elizabeth Warren (see p. 178) – who arrived to dig in 1967. He has described it as a 'shadeless site, sometimes attacked by strong, scorching, gritty winds' and 'temperatures well over 112 degrees'. Elizabeth was more involved than Lucy Cadogan down the road, being not only responsible for cooking, commissariat and relations with villagers, but also the *apotheke*, cataloguing, drawing finds, and taking part in study sessions. She continued to develop her expertise in other excavations with her husband.

However much you read about all the processes involved, you need to sit on that hill in the midst of the dusty remains of a 90-room community that ceased to exist over 4,000 years ago to get the feeling of either a Minoan weaver or a twentieth century woman archaeologist.

From there we drove on to Ierapetra. On a Sunday it is not jumping and I fear we did not do it justice. I had noted nothing about women to take us to the museum; please prove me wrong. We then drove the circle back to Istron, cutting straight northwards past Vasiliki (see p. 345), westwards through Pacheia Ammos (see p. 347) and past Gournia (see p. 338) – not stopping anywhere. You should be careful not to try and cram too much into one day; sites are best appreciated in sips.

# 25

## Harriet Boyd and the Americans

*Kavousi, Gournia, Vasiliki, Pacheia Ammos, Vrokastro, Priniatikos Pyrgos, Halasmenos*

Among the most satisfying of all the itineraries is this one, dominated as it is by the pioneer archaeologist Harriet Boyd (see pp. 160–3). She arrived at Herakleion in April 1900. Passing by Knossos and taking advice from Arthur Evans (see p. 197), she set off on horseback with her friend, the botanist Jean Patten (see p. 162), her trusty right-hand man from the mainland, Aristides **Pappadhias**, and his mother, '**Manna**', to reconnoitre possible sites. After a few days, having travelled as far south and west as the Italian excavations at Gortyn, she crossed the Ierapetra Isthmus and arrived at Kavousi – which is why we start there.

To follow this itinerary – which you will not necessarily do in the order I follow of excavation – you would do as well to spend a few days based in the area. On our first stay in Crete, knowing of the importance only of Gournia, we drove from near Chania and 'did' Knossos and the Herakleion Museum, drove on to the Istron Bay Hotel for one night, visited Gournia first thing in the morning, tried and failed to find Vrokastro, and headed back to Chania (stopping on the way to 'do' Mallia). It was not an ideal itinerary. The following year, we spent two weeks at the hotel, going as far east as Kavousi, as far west as the Lasithi Plateau and down to the south coast (see preceding itineraries pp. 287–308, 309–17 and 318–32). I advise something similar. Further east from Kavousi, you may wish to stay at that end of the island (see pp. 359–80).

## Kavousi

Harriet put the village of Kavousi on the map for visitors to Crete interested in archaeology and the history of excavation. I suppose it is less traditional now than it was then, but it is still rather sleepy, unspoilt and picturesque. You don't have to go into the village to visit the archaeological sites but I wanted to find out where Harriet lived while she was digging.

29.   Harriet Boyd, courtesy of the family

First she had to get permission to dig but, that done, she and her team returned to Kavousi to look for accommodation. Harriet describes her introduction to it in the papers she left which were to have formed part of a popular book about her experiences in Crete. Some of what she had written was published as 'Memoirs of a Pioneer Excavator in Crete' in two parts in *Archaeology* (1965). That material, as well as other papers and letters, was used by her daughter, **Mary Allsebrook**, in the delightful and easy enough to obtain *Born to Rebel: The Life of Harriet Boyd Hawes* (1992). Harriet wrote:

Miss Patten and I rented a small irregularly shaped house which belonged to the chief capitalist and shopkeeper of Kavousi. It is understood on such occasions that the best must be offered strangers, but the best was not too luxurious. I remember well our first impression as our mules scrambled up the rocky path that served for a street, a solid wooden gate swung open, we crouched low in our saddles to avoid striking the wall above our heads, and came to a halt in a narrow courtyard. Three or four small stone sheds used as storerooms stables and kitchen were built around the yard; a flight of stone steps led up to the flat roof of a shed next to the kitchen and from this roof we entered our dwelling-room, which was provided with a wooden floor, one of two in the village.

In the early morning and evening, chairs and table were placed on our terrace roof and as we ate we enjoyed a view never to be forgotten. Across the narrow street stood the little church of Saint George on a cleared space upon a ledge of rock; beyond it was a magnificent outlook over the plain to the sea.

There are four churches in Kavousi, three old, one new. Do not think when you have found Hagios Stelianos (the identity of which you will only deduce by peering through the window and interpreting a painting) that you have found Hagios Giorgios. Start off in the square; then, back to the sea, take the narrow street up to your left. Almost immediately, you will see Hagios Giorgios (fourteenth century) on your right, clearly marked. Just before you reach it, a turning to your left, with a flight of steps going up to the flat roof, after a rough stone wall, suggests Harriet's house. But, re-reading Harriet's description, I wonder if we got that right: shouldn't the house be on the mountain side of the church, with the sea in front of the church? Let me know what you think, and if you can do better. Her granddaughter, **Annie Allsebrook**, after a visit, was equally uncertain.

Settled in her eyrie, Harriet started to collect her team of workers and so appreciated were her methods of employment and working that they were to continue with her for all her seasons of excavation. She did not delegate – dealing in their language directly with her workforce; but she left domestic details (including pottery washing, sorting etc.) to Aristides' organisation, and the cooking to his mother. She did, however, tend the ills of her workers and, indeed, the villagers (she had been a nurse in the Greco-Turkish war of 1897); and she set up a small library in the village, including scientific books on agriculture and historical lives. It was not only the borrowing records which showed its usefulness: in day to day conversation, workers would reveal titbits from their reading.

Harriet wrote up those first excavations in some detail in 'Excavations at Kavousi, Crete, in 1900' (1901), but her daughter's biography will suffice for many readers. I have sketched for you earlier (see pp. 66–7) some of the history and archaeological details of the people who lived in the Kavousi area and that is well supplemented by Pat Cameron. My focus in this itinerary is more on Harriet, those who followed her, and how best you can appreciate them, including some practical hints.

Harriet excavated around Kavousi at St Anthony's, at the Kastro, at Rusty Ridge, at Azoria Hill, at Great Boulder, at Harbour Hill and at Thunder Hill (Vronda). Arriving at Kavousi not knowing what to expect, I thought I should try and find any number of these sites, but it is not that simple. In the end, we found one site, which I recommend to you, more by luck than good management.

Just east of Kavousi village, on the main west–east road, you will see a sign on your right and, beside it, a perfectly clear and carefully constructed map of the archaeological area. Unfortunately, you don't have that in front of you as you proceed and I suspect ability to get to most of the extant sites is for those working on them. Don't do as we did: see what is obviously the Kastro (both mountain peak and citadel site), sticking up and dominating the landscape, and charge up towards it. The road, for a start, requires careful driving: the map said the one we took was 'dirt'; it was rocky, twisting and climbing dirt. We drove on and on until we must have been near the Kastro, found ourselves lodged at a dead-end on a mountain side, sea far below, clouds lowering, and nowhere apparently to turn. (We should never have intruded through that gate.) Do learn from our impetuosity!

As you were, at the bottom of the hill: after a while, a clear sign says 'archaeological site'; a less clear one says 'Vronta' (Vronda). You have not arrived. Bearing right, follow the curves up (past a couple of very small churches) till the olive trees are about to give out and there, on your left, unfenced and apparently un-signposted is Vronda. I should say that once you have left the car (the only other person there had walked up), the presentation panels explaining every aspect of the site are impeccable. Harriet wrote of Thunder (Vronda) Hill:

The campaign of 1900 closed with an exciting incident. Two lads, who were digging at a spot which did not look promising, asked my permission to move a pile of stones that barred their progress. Not to discourage their zeal, I assented and was soon called back to them by frantic cries of 'Lady! Lady!' Other workmen were hurrying toward the excited boys and when I came up, it was to find that by removing the stones, they had made a 'window' in the side of a perfectly undisturbed 'bee-hive' tomb. There it stood, revealed before us as it had been closed three thousand years earlier.

Earlier, she had found the remains of a house nearby and she summed up her finds: 'All indications justify us in assigning the house and tombs on Thunder Hill to the sub-Mycenaean epoch, transitional between the Bronze Age and the Iron Age.' (The term 'sub-Minoan' was not yet coined.)

To get to the Kastro site, I suggest you use Pat Cameron as a (Blue) guide. She even tells you how to cover all this area on foot. If only she had been available to us.

Harriet came back to Kavousi briefly in the 1901 season, but was then lured west to what is now known as Gournia. During the next 75 years, there was sporadic excavation in the Kavousi area. In 1912, for example, Edith Hall spent time there. But in 1978 the 'new Kavousi Project' was formed by the new American team of **Geraldine Gesell**, **Leslie Day** and William Coulson, later joined by **Margaret Mook**. Further excavations were made at Vronda in 1981 and, in 1983 and 1984, the area was cleaned. A small settlement of 12–15 houses dating from twelfth to eleventh centuries BC was revealed. The American team – in which women have predominated (including the human bone, the stone tool and the metallurgical specialists) – found, too, a community shrine which produced the parts (40,000 fragments) of at least 25 large terracotta figures of Minoan goddesses with upraised arms (MGUAs) (see p. 66). Don't feel shy about finding the shrine and sitting there with your arms upraised, looking down over the Gulf of Mirabello. Geraldine Gesell is seen as a major influence in establishing cult places as a specific study.

Continuing excavations have uncovered evidence of habitation in the area as early as Early Minoan times, and as late as Venetian. But, as you stand at Vronda, filling your lungs with fresh air and gazing down to the sea and up to the sharp wedge of the Kastro towering above, it is of Harriet Boyd in 1900 that you think. Geraldine Gesell and her colleagues write of Kavousi in *Crete 2000*:

Harriet Boyd set a new standard for scientific investigation of the ancient environment and the interactions between people and the landscape; the Kavousi Project carried on her ideas with the use of scientific specialists and technologies unknown in her day. Her interest in the transition between the Bronze Age societies and the Greek city-states was far in advance of her times, and is once again a major force of archaeological interest and interpretation.

## Gournia

open Tuesday to Sunday, 8.00 a.m. 2.30 p.m.

When Harriet Boyd returned to Crete in the spring of 1901, she was accompanied by her friend Blanche Wheeler (see p. 163) and they started off where Harriet had left off at Kavousi.

One afternoon a week later, a 'peasant antiquarian' offered to show Harriet broken bits of pottery and old walls at a place called Gournia, four miles west of Kavousi. She tells how, on 19 May, she met her informant and proceeded to

a low hill densely covered with wild carob trees. Here we picked up a few sherds with patterns similar to those from St Anthony's [at Kavousi] and peering with difficulty beneath the thick undergrowth thought we discerned the tops of ancient walls.

In spite of many previous disappointments, we nursed a little hope, and decided to make a thorough exploration of the new site. On the following morning we were up at four o'clock preparing to leave our mountain huts.

Arrived at Gournia, they immediately struck gold or, rather, 'a perfect bronze spear point'. By the end of the day Harriet was ready to pronounce: 'Everything pointed to a prehistoric settlement of some importance, whose existence on that site had remained unsuspected until that day.'

The imagination of their neighbours was caught – they had lived all their lives within walking distance and never realised what was under their feet – and the workers who volunteered were almost as eager as Harriet herself. Work raced ahead. As Harriet wrote it up later:

Within three days we had opened houses, were following paved roads, and had in our possession enough vases and sherds bearing octopus, ivy-leaf, double-axe and other unmistakably Minoan designs as well as bronze tools, seal impressions, stone vases, etc. to make it certain that we had found what we were seeking, a Bronze Age settlement of the best period of Cretan civilization. On the night of May 22, I sent Aristides to Candia to dispatch the following telegram to the Secretary of the American Exploration Society: 'Discovered Gournia Mycenaean site, street, houses, pottery, bronzes, stone jars.'

As her daughter was later to describe it, Gournia was, in fact, 'the oldest town discovered in Europe, and soon became known as the "Cretan Pompeii", even though centuries older than the Roman Pompeii'. Although the name Mycenaean was the only one then available, what Harriet had found was a town from the time of the Minoan Second Palaces (1750–1490 BC) all of which, towns and palaces, had been destroyed in the cataclysm of the end of that period (see p. 48). Her discovery was to expand knowledge of the Minoans beyond the palace – though Gournia, too, was to reveal its own little palace or governor's mansion.

The week after Harriet sent her historic cable, she discovered a small shrine in the centre of Gournia – the first Minoan shrine to be discovered intact. Her daughter, writing in 1992, celebrated how

Slowly there emerged a low altar table, several crude cult vases vaguely reminiscent of Egypt, and a modernistic-looking image of the Earth Goddess, intertwined with snakes. How appropriate that a woman should be the first to find a shrine sacred to the Mother Goddess of the Minoans!

At the time, there was another edge to it: the *Philadelphia Public Ledger* of 5 March 1902 proclaimed:

The results of Miss Boyd's work must be considered as remarkable, not only because of their character, but because she achieved them alone. Other women have made names in the fields of archaeological research, but these have done so in company with their husbands, who shared the glory with them. But Miss Boyd's work is entirely her own.

After the first week at Gournia, Harriet and her team moved their accommodation from Kavousi to the more convenient Pacheia Ammos (see pp. 347–50). And her workforce stabilised – 100 or so men and eleven women who washed the potsherds (eventually numbering tens of thousands). Among the men there were such and such – her 'Firsts' as she called them – but she also set up a democracy. As she explained it:

A form of government invented by the Greeks long before Christ ... Our force was divided into a Senate of the older workmen and an Assembly of the younger men – experience vs numbers. The two voted separately, the Senate first, ... it being understood that both bodies must agree before action could be taken.

This was a useful method for resolving potential disputes – for example, when a stranger proposed opening a cafe near the site, it was voted on and Harriet was pleased that the majority was against, so that hard-earned wages did not go on 'treating'. She had innovated a method of payment, set and regular, rather than depending on what a man found, except for the milk charms – ancient seals which modern women, on finding them, traditionally wore round their necks (see pp. 15 and 144). The method ensured that those doing work where finds might not surface would be satisfied, and the prospect of finding seals would encourage care. This, too, had been voted on.

After a brilliant first season, Harriet was not to return to Gournia until 1903. Then she was joined by the social worker and artist Adeline Moffat (see p. 163) and Richard Seager, a rich young American who would become known as a collector-excavator-historian. Although 33-year-old Harriet was to be 24-year-old Seager's archaeological mentor, when, in 1904, the team was joined by another American, 27-year-old Edith Hall (see p. 163 and pp. 350–7), Edith's letters home show that Harriet and Seager's relations were not always harmonious. Edith wrote of Harriet on 6 March 1904, after receiving a letter from Seager before her arrival at Gournia: 'She is evidently sharp tongued too, judging from what Mr Seager said. The latter seemed bound I should know the seamy side of Gournia life, and wanted me to be prepared for harsh words, etc., from Miss Boyd. I don't think I shall mind ...'

Although it is comforting to have some evidence that Harriet was not perfect, the friction was as likely to be a result of Seager's fragile health, temperament and possible sexual orientation as Harriet's intransigence. There is some evidence that Edith was sweet on Seager (if so, she was to be disappointed); it is equally possible that she saw him as a younger brother. Early on in their work relations, on 1 May 1904, she wrote:

Mr Seager and I have great times jollying each other. He calls me 'youthful enthusiasm' because I am so interested in all he finds, and get excited over each vase that comes out. I get it back on him by teasing him about his laziness. He really has excellent manners, but once or twice he has slipped up, telling me to go to his room (at the hotel) to get a ball of string, and calling out 'handkerchief' once when I dropped mine, instead of picking it up for me. He also mislaid two letters of mine, which he got for me at Chanea, and gave them to me three weeks afterward. It quite reminds me of the cottage and my younger days to have someone to scrap with. I am so sorry for the poor boy's bad health. When he goes swimming, I see that one leg is all purple from varicose veins.

These 1904 letters home from Edith are quoted in *Richard Berry Seager: Pioneer Archaeologist and Proper Gentleman* (Becker and Betancourt, 1997) – a book as interesting about Edith and Harriet as about Seagar. A few week's after Edith's arrival, she was writing to her sister:

[Miss Boyd] and Mr Seager had a petty but very fiery quarrel this week, which nearly killed me off for embarrassment. I couldn't believe that any normal people with a sense of humor could quarrel so ... Mr Seager and I remain good friends. This afternoon to recuperate after two hours of listening to Miss Boyd's fussing, we took a long walk on the beach. The day of the quarrel, we retired behind a rock for an hour's converse, when I tried to bring him round and make him see he was a little to blame.

Harriet, for her part, was to write, 'Mr R.B. Seager and Edith H. Hall (Smith '99) gave valuable help in supervising the excavations.' As well as benefiting from Edith's company (as a chaperone), her equable temperament (Harriet and Edith did not quarrel) and her archaeological experience, Harriet certainly fostered the careers of both her protéges, ensuring, for example, a scholarly approach.

Edith was to excavate her own trench at Gournia and publish its results as her doctoral dissertation – her expertise was pottery and establishing chronology. Harriet's major work *Gournia* – the first monograph on a Minoan site – was published under her married name in 1908. It is a majestic volume, finely illustrated (with contributions by Jean Patten, Blanche Wheeler, Adeline Moffat, Richard Seager and

Edith Hall) but sadly only available in specialist libraries – to own a copy would be a real privilege. A detailed account of Harriet and Edith's life and work is contained in separate chapters in *Breaking Ground: Pioneering Women Archaeologists* (2004, eds Getzel M. Cohen and Martha Sharp Joukowsky) – a fat, rather expensive, but essential book for those interested in the general subject.

There are some archaeological sites that shouldn't be missed if you want to do more than laze. Gournia is among them, partly because of Harriet and the history of archaeology, partly because, apart from the distance from main centres, it is so accessible. Say you are coming from the direction of Ierapetra on the south coast: you cross the isthmus, turn left at the junction when you hit the sea, swing through Pacheia Ammos, round a bend and there is Gournia spread out on a hillside before you. Coming from the west, the entrance to the site is upon you, on your right, before you see the remains. It is almost worth driving on, looking back to your right and seeing it lying there, before doubling back.

You can have fun ambling along the streets that were, imagining where each artisan worked in this town of artisans, including the women weavers and those involved in the pottery processes. The court in front of the 'ruler's palace' is obvious, leading you thus to the shrine. Harriet describes the lie of the land and how the streets and houses had to conform to it in *Crete: The Forerunner of Greece*. Of the wider panorama, the hills swell behind you, Vrokastro sheers upwards to the west, the olive trees, as dark green as citrus, almost intrude on the ancient stones and the sea glitters in front. You could be the only visitors, particularly if you arrived early. The light and the silence then are special.

No wonder that, from 1901, Gournia was to become a magnet for archaeologists, scholars and travellers. May 1904 was to be a particularly busy month, and the 10th was, in retrospect, to be a fateful day. A pleasant-looking anthropologist, Henry Hawes, visited Gournia. Harriet recorded in her irregularly-kept diary:

At about 11 a.m. Mr Hawes appears. Mr H. is an Englishman who has travelled extensively through Asia and has written a book which is much read today in England – about a Russian penal colony.

We show him the site – after lunch he has a sea bath and I arrange shelves for tomorrow. Then we have tea together and he tells me about British India, the native Congress, etc – believes Japan will deal a blow heavy enough to force Russia to allow by treaty Korea to be a Japanese protectorate and Manchuria to be a province of China with open door ...

The following day, that May of 1904, a boatload of archaeologists, mostly German, mostly men, arrived under the leadership of Dr Wilhelm Dörpfeld. Among them was Ellen Bosanquet whose husband was excavating at Palaikastro (see pp. 165 and 367). Ellen later wrote, unfortunately too briefly: 'Harriet Boyd and her friend, Miss Hall, were ... digging at Gournia within a day's ride, and here began another lifelong friendship [with Harriet – Edith was already a friend from Athens].'

The palaeontologist Dorothea Bate arrived at the end of May and made immediate friends with the whole team who were 'charming' to her. She recorded in her unpublished diary:

Went to Kournia the village they have excavated and saw them getting out a lot of pots. In the evening went for a short ride with Mr S on Miss Boyd's pony – went up to a couple of caves in a limestone ridge but found nothing, pudding stone floors. Before breakfast went for a swim with Miss Hall.

Twenty-four years later, when the site had been left to its own devices, Hilda White, John Pendlebury and their companions arrived (see p. 360). Hilda wrote home on 16 February 1928: 'We went back the half hour's walk to Gournia & explored it well. It is a most thrilling spot as one can wander about its narrow streets & in and out of its houses (though they are roofless) & really feel that it is a town – just as one can at Pompeii.' As Hilda implies, the walls of the remains are higher than usual.

That recorded conversation with Henry Hawes in May 1904, unromantic as it seems, was to result in marriage in 1906. Harriet Boyd was to have a family and never to return to her pioneering work in Crete. That is not to say, though, that it was the end of her scholarship, teaching, and humanitarian activities.

Both **Vasso Fotou** and Anne Brown in their Harriet chapter in *Breaking Ground* and **Marina Picazo** in 'Fieldwork is Not the Proper Preserve of a Lady' in *Excavating Women* (1998) suggest neglect of Harriet's contribution in the contemporary public record such as Arthur Evans' *Palace of Minos*, the *Encyclopaedia Britannica* and 'major academic histories of American archaeology'. In recent years, that has been rectified. Marina Picazo adds that

One of the most remarkable aspects of the excavations at Gournia — and indeed something of its uniqueness — lay in the fact that it was the result of a co-operative work of research, mainly carried out by women, and that from this emerged some of the most important reflections on the archaeology of the Minoan Bronze Age.

## Vasiliki

Harriet Boyd was always looking for remains that would give her finds at Gournia more of a context. She and Edith Hall roamed the isthmus looking for likely sites. As her daughter wrote, revealing yet another layer of understanding for our appreciation:

Searching for skeletons was not to Harriet's liking, but ancient burials meant pottery, and pottery was a clue to chronology. A Minoan great aunt might be buried with a childhood treasure and some of the vases in vogue at her death, or perhaps a jar brought from afar. If it chanced to come from Egypt, the advanced dating of styles there could be used as a guide for the Cretan chronology.

One area that Harriet had earlier earmarked was near the village of Vasiliki. When the Dörpfeld party visited Gournia in May 1904, they carried Harriet and Edith off with them to Palaikastro. While they were away, Richard Seager took a party of workmen and started digging at the Vasiliki site. Edith reported how, on their return two days later, they were greeted on the road by some of the workmen. She continued:

Some of our nicest workmen, mostly boys ... crowded around our horses to shake hands with us, and told us of the wonderful luck Mr Seager has had in our absence. We hurried on, and got a warm welcome from him, Aristides and Manna. He has found a lot of early hard polished red and black pottery which was not known in Crete before.

The *New York Times* was to report on 25 September:

This year Miss Boyd and her little army of Cretans discovered three entirely new styles of pottery. One of these styles shows connections with Libya and another with Troy, connections which were unknown before, and the third style is still absolutely unknown ...

This quirky new pottery was to be named Vasiliki ware (see pp. 15 and 320) and is still regarded as one of those styles that defines the Early Minoan period.

The archaeologist Gisela Richter, who became a friend of both Harriet and Edith in 1905, summed up the new appreciation of this period: 'Conditions were by no means as primitive as was once thought. The people were rich and prosperous, lived in comfortable houses, and apparently had communications with the outside world, especially with Egypt.' And you can get some idea of the lifestyle of those early Minoans from the Vasiliki site, with its Red House and evidence of wooden support beams.

There are two ways to get to the site from the north. One is to turn right at the kiosk in Pacheia Ammos and go down a country lane and through today's village of Vasiliki. Time has passed this village by: there are very old women in black carelessly crossing the road and men sitting outside the cafe whom it would clearly be an intrusion to join. Only the odd small truck suggests even the twentieth century. The site is a bit further past the village. Or you can go down the main isthmus highway (turn south just out of Pacheia Ammos). Three kilometres further on is a sign for Vasiliki. There is no designated parking place, but pull in where you can on the edge of an olive grove. A sign on your left leads you to a gate in the fence which is ajar. Unexpectedly, there is a guard in the booth, but there is no entrance fee. Again, if you are lucky, you will have the site to yourself. The tranquillity there is palpable.

## Pacheia Ammos

Harriet Boyd had started her 1901 season living again at Kavousi (see p. 335) but, once excavating at Gournia, the journey each day between the two places proved impractical. She described the solution:

During the first week [at Gournia] the evening ride home to Kavousi, along with our marching workman, was a triumphal procession. But we could not continue to live so far from our excavations. Our new quarters at the little coast-guard station of Pachyammos were even more confined and box-like than a modern New York apartment! One room, reached by an outside staircase, did duty as kitchen and sleeping place for Aristides' mother; the other, narrow and lighted by one small window, accommodated Miss Wheeler and myself. To this we added the luxury of a dining room — a bower of oleanders set up by one of our men on the roof of an adjoining shed — reached in undignified fashion by crawling through the kitchen window!

Those who came later, and even American and British travellers passing by, fared better for in 1909 rich, sickly Richard Seager built himself a fine house on the hill overlooking the sea. Although Seager's private residence, it also served as headquarters and *apotheke* for the future excavations of Seager and Edith Hall in the area. It is still there, just below the modern building housing the headquarters of the American School of Classical Studies at Athens (INSTAP – Institute for Aegean Prehistory). The drive leading to the two places is on your right, coming from the west, before you round the bend and descend to Pacheia Ammos; there might still be a hen-coop there as a landmark. And it is from INSTAP that you can buy the handsome, scholarly (and slightly unwieldy) *Crete 2000: A Centennial Celebration of American Archaeological Work on Crete (1900–2000).* Seager's house, once you have placed it, catches your eye whenever you drive through Pacheia Ammos and, though it is privately owned, if you are lucky, you might see beyond the outside walls – particularly if, as mooted, it becomes a museum.

When Edith Hall came back to Crete in 1910 to excavate (initially at Sphoungaras between Gournia and the sea), it was in Seager's house that she started off. He had thoughtfully provided a chaperone, **Lady Waldron**, who, with her husband, had been a member of a party he joined during a hunting trip to east Africa. Edith described Lady Waldron as exuding 'grandeur'; Seager's description was 'tubby'.

Edith found the house 'nicer than she expected' though photographs of the period show it, from the outside at least, as a concrete block, unredeemed by vegetation. Today it is screened by a stand of cedar trees and a wall and, within that, there is an olive grove and other established trees. Then there were servants, including a professional cook who provided a cooked breakfast after one or other of them had been to supervise the beginning of the day's dig; later there was afternoon tea. There were jugs of hot water in the morning so that Edith could bath in a rubber bath Seager had brought back from East Africa. There were stables to allow riding in the evening and the garden was, from the beginning, planted with seeds Seager had brought from England.

On 1 May, Edith wrote home: 'All goes well here at the house. We wash pottery on days when we don't dig and write. Every evening we play "poker-patience" – a game of cards which I think we would enjoy playing together at home. I am still growing fat and as well as can be.' Edith lived like that from March until 9 May when she started excavating at Vrokastro; then her accommodation, as we shall see, was rather different.

Once she was established at Vrokastro, the museum in Seager's house – which also contained treasures from his travels – became an archaeological resource. In a letter from Vrokastro on 4 June two years later, Edith wrote home of pottery washing perched on her hillside:

That is a task to try the patience of a saint. One sits over a large basin of hydrochloric acid into which the incrusted sherds are put. Of course the gas goes up your nose and the acid bites your fingers when you take the sherds out and when you try to get the last of the mud off, all the paint comes off too. But we are finding a lot of nice pieces as a result of all our pains. I wash them up here and pack them in baskets with newspapers and send them down on packsaddles to Mr Seager, and he arranges them on two long 'picnic tables' in the museum and matches them up.

(The letters of 1910 and 1912 are unpublished.) By 5 July 1912, Edith had finished her last dig in Crete and was based at Seager's house, everyone else having left. She wrote that, although it was dull there alone and she wanted to get home, 'the garden is full of flowers and our museum is full of our finds which look quite imposing now that I see them all together'.

Richard Seager died young but he left the house staffed to receive archaeologists and travellers. Hilda White, John Pendlebury and their companions (see p. 360) arrived there in February 1928. Their car had packed up a few miles before, at Kalo Chorio, and they continued on foot 'a perfect walk over the hills to Pachyammos,' Hilda wrote on 16 February. Of the village and Seager's house, she continued,

Pachyammos is beautiful. It is on a lovely long bay, has range after range of mountains off to the west & the snowy crest of Dicte to the S.W. & on the east a great wall of steep grey mountain cutting off its valley from the East of Crete. A little way up the valley is a house built by Seager an American archaeologist who died in 1925. It is built round a garden & is more Italian than Greek: the garden is walled in by square pillars & in places a wall & in this square is a well & beds of geranium bushes. Round the square outside the pillars & the ivy covered garden wall runs a cobbled path & on to this open all the rooms of the house which is built round the square. On the outer side is another garden or grassy courtyard & on another side a narrow terrace with a view of the bay. It is a most charming & peaceful place.

Returning that way a few days later (after all sorts of accommodation in between), the party got caught in a rainstorm, dried off in Sphaka then, as Hilda continued on 24 February, 'The sun came out and we did that lovely walk back to Pachyammos under delightful conditions … It was a joy to get back to Pachyammos & know that clean beds awaited us. They had only got our telegram just before our arrival, but had a good dinner for us bright & early & so to our comfortable beds & a peaceful night.'

Apart from visiting INSTAP and sticky-beaking at Seager's erstwhile house as far as circumstances allow, there is not much to see in Pacheia Ammos, except to imagine where the boats came in onto which Harriet and Edith stowed their treasures to begin their journey to Herakleion. It is to the left of Zorba's restaurant and seen well as you look back ascending the curve westwards out of the village. If it is lunchtime, you can certainly do worse than eat fresh fish at a taverna on the waterfront, but you probably wouldn't want to swim there.

## Vrokastro

'A week from tomorrow,' Edith Hall wrote home on 1 May 1910, 'I go to Vrokastro to dig an iron-age fortress.' (See pp. 67–8 for its historical context.) On 8 May she left the comfort of Richard Seager's house at Pacheia Ammos and, in an unpublished letter, wrote the following day:

I will write you a word while seated on the hill watching my thirty men. I can see miles and miles away – to the Southwest the great mountains, still-snow-capped of central Crete. To the North the sapphire sea, while straight below us a sheer drop of several hundred feet lies a rich plain with vineyards and olive trees, and at the end of it, in the foothills a white village [Kalo Chorio] with here and there a few red roofs. The place is fragrant with cedar and thyme.

I came yesterday, riding over with George the muleteer, Nikolaos the overseer and Nico the cook and the wheelbarrows and baskets & spades & picks came by caique. The first thing to do was to pitch the tent which took nearly an hour with all hands assisting. Then I could unpack my big canvas bag and put up my bed. There is a little room at the back where I have my rubber tub and portable canvas wash-stand. In the big room I have my bed, a table, a steamer chair and one straight chair. The men built a kitchen behind against a ledge of rock. The men all sleep in little bush huts.

Edith was to excavate at Vrokastro for the rest of that season and for most of the 1912 season under the overall direction of Richard Seager (to whom Harriet Boyd had transferred her permit), but in charge of her own dig. In 1912, she was joined by her friend **Eleanor Rowland**, not an archaeologist but contented to sit and sew or teach their cook new dishes. After her second week, Edith was to amend her first impression: 'It proves to be a late Minoan III town. We had expected it to belong to the Iron Age and not the Bronze Age and there are some indications of Geometric pottery that mark the Iron Age but for the most part it is from the end of the Minoan Age.' The Kastro, indeed, was probably one of the last refuges of the Minoans.

Today, Vrokastro is not an easy site either to track down or to visit. Having failed in 2001, we only succeeded a year later because I had carefully prepared the ground. Our generous informant at the Istron Bay Hotel had set up a friend who, for many reasons, not least his position in the local community, knew not only how to get us to the summit of Vrokastro but also to give us a very special experience. I only wish he were a professional guide who could do the same for you.

Since our visit, the 2003 edition of Pat Cameron's *Blue Guide* has been published, which would have been a help. Let me, at least, tell you about our day, in the hope that it will give some pointers. We were picked up by car, though given the option of doing the outing on foot. I'm glad we started out on wheels; I believe that way we had more energy to see more, though we did much on foot once we had driven out of the hotel and, almost immediately, taken a turning across the road south (upwards) – marked 'Kounenos Apartments'; it's easier to turn right coming from Istron village.

Drive as far as you can towards the obvious wedge of Vrokastro and then, having left the car, follow the sheep's path towards its eastern flank. You will undoubtedly see a flock of sheep being driven timelessly along from the direction of the kastro. (You might also see the shepherd's grandson on a motorbike driving the sheep the modern way.) Edith Hall wrote in her article 'The Cretan Expedition' (1912): 'We had no neighbours save the shepherds who pastured their flocks close by.' The same would apply today.

In the article there is also a photograph captioned 'Cretan methods of threshing' – showing a woman, a man, a donkey and a threshing wheel set into the ground; that, too, is still identifiable – uncanny. Underneath, Edith told the story in words (referring to her second digging season in 1912):

It was now the middle of June and the heat was exceedingly fierce. The women and children no longer returned to the village for the night, but whole families were camping in the fields for the harvesting season. Near every threshing floor a family was encamped under a tree, while men, women and children helped with the work of reaping, threshing and winnowing, all of which is accomplished by the most primitive methods. We were daily visited at our tombs by these neighbors, who brought us fresh almonds, apricots and plums tied up in the corners of their aprons or handkerchiefs, and were delighted to receive in return presents of pins with coloured heads.

Arriving at the base of the kastro wedge, look out for a dead bush which is placed to keep the animals from the 'path' going upwards. This last bit is a proper climb. Our instructions from just behind were 'Hold rock, jump; hold rock, jump [climb]', while ascending and, coming down, '*Siga, siga* [little, little]'. On reaching the top, we realised why we had needed gripping shoes, a jersey, and an anorak: the wind was extraordinary. (Upon our descent, we realised why we needed water – for the raki to steady our nerves.)

The view from the top, where there are the remains of a shrine, is stupendous, assuming you can keep your footing against the wind to appreciate it. To the west, across the Bay of Mirabello is Agios Nikolaos; to the east, across the plain and almost on a level, the imposing white structure of the Faneromeni Monastery (see p. 311).

Once safely down, wander around as we did to rejoice in the vegetation: the wild thyme and sage and the wild almond trees which, when accurately pelted with stones, scatter their nuts. Then there are the carob trees, the fruit of which are a good substitute for chocolate but beware eating them green: as another informant explained, 'they will turn your mouth inside out'. You should also come across a well – perhaps the one Edith describes, though there will not be the same sociological interest:

Every night and morning the well of water near my tent presented a lively scene when the women and children from the village below stopped to water their 'possessions' – generally a donkey, a goat and a pig apiece – on their way to and from their fields. This well of water was, in fact, the social centre of the place, all the more so when the women learned that I would allow them to inspect my tent. Some times at evening when I rode home from work, I would find a dozen waiting for me to show them the wonders of my tent, which consisted of a camp bed, a table, and two chairs.

Somewhere, too, are the remains of one of Edith's best moments, as recounted in a letter of 12 May 1912:

This week nothing matters for we have had a run of luck, the best I ever had. The first day we began work at Vrokastro proper, I sent one of the old trusted workmen ... to a pile of stones which I always wanted to poke in last [time], but which lay just below the guy ropes of my tents so I couldn't get at it. For two days he pried out stones and got only small potsherds and twice he complained that the place I had put him was no good. But we make the rule that when they start to dig, they must always keep on until they reach hard-pan, and so he was made to stay there. He one day sent word that he had found, in addition to quantities of potsherds, a piece of bronze. I at once went to watch, and I have ever since been sitting on the edge of his hole — which proved to be a large rectangular tomb the roof of which had fallen in — watching him knive out all sorts of things. The bronze was from a bronze tripod of which we now have nearly all the pieces, quite enough to set up in a museum. There were quantities of clay vases, iron axe-heads and adzes, and blades galore — all badly corroded — and two or three hundred porcelain beads. But best of all was six seals, five of which have Greek letters and Greek letters in this geometric period are I think quite unknown, so I think it will really be quite a discovery for the history of the alphabet. I can't say for sure until I get to a library, but Mr Seager agrees, and anyway it is something worth coming to Crete for.

To look for Edith's tombs is to court disappointment. Much is overgrown and, as **Barbara Hayden**, who started to work at Vrokastro in 1979, noted in *Crete 2000*, 'many of the tombs Hall excavated in 1912 have not been relocated through intensive survey of the upland area and adjacent to the Vrocastro settlement'. In another report (1991), Barbara Hayden explained: 'Although the site may have been reasonably well excavated according to the standards of her day, the excavation techniques and recording procedures employed have at best provided incomplete data on the chronological limits of the settlement, as well as its nature and external contacts.'

Whatever the limitations of archaeology in the early twentieth century, Edith's 1914 study ' Excavations in Eastern Crete Vrokastro' has recently been reprinted and can be bought via the internet; though a research document with drawings and diagrams of finds, rather than the personal story of her efforts, it is nice to have. And she has been included in *Breaking Ground: Pioneering Women Archaeologists*, alongside her mentor Harriet Boyd.

While the technology and methods may have changed over the years, the human aspects and the links stay strong: asked if she felt that she was following in Edith Hall's footsteps, Barbara Hayden replied: 'Yes, Edith has always been with me, every step, and it was a great help at first, when the steps were very steep and the climbs long and lonely.'

## Priniatikos Pyrgos

On our last evening at the Istron Bay Hotel in 2002, the generous guide and informant who had revealed to us the pleasures of Vrokastro took us down to a little headland between the traditional village of Kalo Chorio and the burgeoning one of Istron. There, half-submerged, and by no means identifiable as an archaeological site, were some scattered remains. We ended up drinking ouzo in an almost deserted stall on the grey beach, and nicking chips off the plate of someone who joined us.

It is only in retrospect that I realise the significance of the place for, in 1912, at the end of her excavations in Crete, having virtually exhausted possibilities at Vrokastro and having money left for two weeks more, Edith Hall did something similar. In telling what happened, she confirmed how far her relations with the local community had deepened and how much she appreciated Crete beyond archaeology. She wrote on 16 June:

We are to devote all the rest of our time to a new place down by the water's edge, which has produced almost the finest Minoan sherds I ever saw and of which I have great hopes. Nikolaos, Eleanor and I have been down there this morning and scolded roundly the woman who has the field for having dug up potsherds by herself. It does seem hard on her that she can't dig in her own field, but when it is a question of antiquities she can't. They were beautiful potsherds though, and even in two weeks we ought to add some good vases to our bag of game. I had told Nikolaos to meet us at the khan (= roadside inn) near this new place, so Eleanor and I rode down the mountain and waited for him at the khan. We dismounted and sat under a mulberry tree with a group of Cretan girls — among them the bride of the recent elopement who has postponed her wedding till next Sunday till she can get her grain harvested — and ate plums and almonds. And then, getting impatient, rode over to the village to find Nikolaos. I had told him to hunt out the people who own the fields where we have been digging and settle with them for damages. Of course we have to destroy some grain and there is more trodden down and wood cut, etc.

The following week, disappointment set in:

Our dig has been very dull all the week. We moved our force down to a little promontory where beautiful sherds had been found, but alas! There were everywhere Roman houses and Roman walls built above Minoan houses and the result was we found nothing whole ... It is trying to feel that one is spending money and not getting much for it, but apart from this bugbear, it has all been very nice. We have had a pretty vine-covered arbor to eat our luncheon in and women and children have been threshing and winnowing in the fields next us. There isn't a day but what I have presents of handkerchiefs full of apricots or plums, of bunches of roses and orange leaves.

The day of the wedding, at which Edith was to be bridesmaid, finally arrived and her horse was needed to collect the licence. On 30 June, Edith describes how they all followed the bride and groom across the

30. Edith Hall, courtesy of the Pennsylvania Museum of Archaeology and Anthropology

beach to a small church on the seashore. Edith was holding 'the hand of the bride's four year old brother who follows me everywhere'. In the chapter 'Edith Hayward Hall Dohan' in *Breaking Ground*, **Katherine Dohan Morrow** writes:

She was also a favourite among the village children. One such child, four years old at the time, remembered her eighty years later when Hall's grand-daughter visited the site and the boy, now the entrance guard, reminisced about 'his lady.' He still had her photograph pasted to the guardhouse wall.

(Which site with a guardhouse this refers to is unclear; by no means all sites are fenced or have guards.)

Barbara Hayden explains in *Crete 2000* how results of the archaeological survey of the whole of this area indicate that Priniatikos Pyrgos spanned most phases of the Bronze Age and later historical periods, lying as it did in a fertile valley, and with port facilities, at the junction of several routes across the island, linking the Lasithi and Mallia region to the Isthmus of Ierapetra and Siteia. There is really nothing to see now, but you can drive down, if you take the track to the sea opposite the road branching off to Pyrgos.

## Halasmenos

Harriet Boyd and her colleagues opened up this whole area to the east and west of the Isthmus of Ierapetra to archaeological investigation. But it was not until 1992 that a joint Greek-American project started excavating at Halasmenos under the direction of Metaxia Tsipopoulou, whom we shall meet in more detail in the next itinerary (see pp. 365–6) and William Coulson (who was part of the team at Kavousi; see p. 338). Up in the mountains, near the village of Monastiraki, and the other side of the highway from Vasiliki, Metaxia and her colleagues found a Minoan public shrine dated twelfth century BC and several goddesses with upraised arms (see pp. 62–3). Halesmenas is fenced but accessible. Metaxia tells me that 'the conservation of the material from the shrine is not completed as yet, so the figures are not exhibited'. But there are similar MGUAs in the Herakleion Museum (see p. 190).

In 1903, Harriet Boyd had sent her trusty Aristides to scale those heights and sniff round and it is thanks to her efforts and example – against all the odds – that the Minoans, from their beginnings to their end, are more familiar now than they were 100 years ago.

# 26
## East Crete

*Sphaka, Tourloti, Myrsini, Mouliana, Siteia, Petras, Palaikastro,*
*Toplou Monastery, Eleonora's Falcon, Itanos, Zakros, Xerokampos,*
*Voila, Praisos*

Both Siteia and Palaikastro are good bases for this itinerary; we
plumped for Palaikastro, staying for a week, in October 2003, at
Glaros ('Seagull') Villas, through Simply Crete. The accommodation
was simple but perfectly adequate, the setting charming, the sea
pleasant (no pool), and the beach nicely walkable. For those with
delicate feet, it is usually a bit pebbly in Crete. We left exploring
Palaikastro and its environs until last, in case we flagged and wanted
to stay close to home (we had had heavy colds earlier in the trip)
but, for the purposes of this itinerary, I shall follow the map, west to
east, then north to Itanos, finally south to Zakros and Xerokampos
and back in a circle.

This is definitely an itinerary to do based in the east – Palaikastro
is a fair stretch from Herakleion; probably best to concentrate on
reaching your accommodation, rather than planning to get stuck
into the meat of the itinerary. The drive from Herakleion to the Bay
of Mirabello has its longueurs, unless you consider stopping at the
archaeological site of Mallia (see pp. 303–8). Past Istron, the scenery
becomes more varied and there are plenty of archaeological sites
(from Gournia to Kavousi; see itinerary 'The Americans', pp. 333–58).
As you get further east, you don't know quite what to expect, and the
distance is deceptive; there is a feeling of anticipation both pleasurable
and, ultimately, a bit fatiguing! But there are some places to note, if

not to stop at on the way. Of course, if you are walking, all is different.

In February 1928 four British archaeological students of the British School at Athens arrived at Herakleion to travel round for a few weeks. Although I have quoted from one of them in previous itineraries, and she was to return to Crete later, this for reasons that emerge is the best place to elaborate on that first visit. John Pendlebury was to write the trip up and it was privately published after his death as 'John Pendlebury in Crete, Comprising his Travelling Hints and His First Trip to Eastern Crete' (1948). But it is his companions who interest us, and the relations between the four. The previous November, Pendlebury had written to his father about his fellow students in Athens. He described **Margaret Rodger** (BA, Somerville) as, 'An efficient South African just down from Oxford'. **Vivian Whitfield** (later Mrs H.T. Wade-Gery, on leave from the University of Reading with various grants) found less favour: 'Miss Whitfield, another of Oxford gems, so conceited she hardly knows what to do with herself.' And of the fourth member of the group, Hilda White (see p. 169), he wrote: ' Miss White ... alone of the lot strikes one as being human ... The rest are definitely sub-human.'

The four headed east, initially by car, past Mallia. Out of the car to allow it to cross a rickety bridge, they fell in with a local man. 'We chatted for a while about the weather,' Pendlebury writes, 'and then he turned and looked at the three ladies who made up the party: he considered for a moment or two and then said to me, "Are you a Turk?" This "mot" gave him the utmost pleasure.' It did to the party, too, it appears. They caused consternation when they reached **Neapoli** (see also p. 130):

And now it happened that we felt the powers of the Neapolis watch committee. For behold, persons of the female sex may not sit in front of cars but modestly behind with the rest of the luggage. This is so that the chauffeur may not be distracted, though what is to prevent him from turning round, and taking his eye right off the road, I do not know. Still I am sure vice has been stamped out in Neapolis. There are no night clubs (any more than there are in the rest of Crete); mixed bathing is not allowed (and private bathing is not much practised); cocktails are unknown (the favourite order being a double methylated).

All this some years after the end of Ottoman (Islamic) rule, and five years after the exchange of populations (see p. 148).

## Sphaka

The car conked out at Kalo Chorio near Istron and they proceeded on foot with a mule for the baggage. Vivian Whitfield left them at Gournia to return to Herakleion (which the British still called Candia). Another local man they met 'employed himself in picking great bunches of anemones for the ladies.' They walked south past Vasiliki (see p. 345) to Ierapetra and back up again, then turned east towards Siteia and Palaikastro, reaching Sphaka. While Hilda White did not publish an account of the journey, happily she did write letters home. She recounts on 24 February:

We didn't have a very good night at Sphaka as the beds were very hard and very fleay: I deserted mine for a couch being less the latter but couldn't sleep because of the bites I already had. I did drop off in the early hours for a bit so felt quite energetic at getting up time and jolly glad to do so.

Once on the road, as Hilda notes, things looked up:

We had a lovely walk from Sphaka to Sitia up over the mountains: I rode a good deal as a matter of fact because my ankle was tired and inclined to turn over. It took about five hours & a half & we arrived in the early afternoon, having picnicked about an hour & a half from our destination. We could see Sitia a long time before we got there, from the hills & then lost sight of it again as we made our way down & rounded a long shoulder of hill before getting to the plain. For the last hour or so the road ran at one side of a most delightful valley with a winding stream and trees.

## Tourloti

But I mustn't get ahead of myself: we are not yet at Siteia. You may well not want to stop at any of these villages, but those passing this way before you in a more leisurely age, and by different transport, did. Then there are the women who lived there. Robert Carr Bosanquet wrote to Ellen on 9 April 1902 of his halt at Tourloti:

Opposite the front door is a quite European dining-room, where we and our host dined at a round table. Our hostess, in un-European fashion, waited on us with her maid to help, and this, though she is an educated woman, sister of the biggest politician and landowner in the province. She was a Phountalides, and that is a great name. There were several sisters; another was my hostess at Pevkous on the South coast, and pleased me immensely by her frankness. We were telling ghost stories and talking about vampires and her husband swung round on his chair and asked ' Do *you* believe in vampires?' – to which she answered rather deliberately 'We women don't believe in vampires, but we're dreadfully afraid of them all the same.'

## Myrsini

The next village on our leisurely ramble is Myrsini, with its lovely views, in the foothills of Mount Ornon. There, in 1961, two other archaeological students – Efi Sapouna (see p. 177) and Yannis Sakellarakis – joined Nicholas Platon in an excavation. Efi, who was to earn her stripes at Zakros (having married Yannis) and to make her name at Archanes (see pp. 377 and 214–25), describes the experience of her first dig in Crete as 'very exciting, very primitive, living with the workers'. You will probably search in vain for the archaeological site today as you pass just below Myrsini, but artefacts from the twelve Postpalatial chamber tombs on a hill north of the village are accessible in Gallery 3 at the Agios Nikolaos Museum. A chance find at Myrsini, on display at the museum, is the homely adorant on a drum base, hands joined between her breasts (see p. 321).

## Mouliana

The next villages, Messa Mouliana and Exo Mouliana, are famous for their wine and raisins. In 1904, the British palaeontologist Dorothea Bate passed through here and wrote in her unpublished 'Journal Kept in Crete' on 29 May, 'Reached Mouliana about 5 pm. Found it was a feast as well as a Sunday. Lots of girls and men dancing in a small house to a lyre and a drum. Atmosphere inside too awful for words! On way got a snake which had not seen previously.' We can only guess at the atmosphere, but behaviour seems to have been more lax than at Neapoli 24 years later. The following day, she continued: 'Left Mouliana 6.30am. Reached Sitia about 1pm. Stopped to get some food and send wire for letters. Country pretty bare here – hilly.'

## Siteia

Between Mouliana and Siteia in 1928, Hilda White and her party had some more badinage with a local man. John Pendlebury wrote:

Before we had gone far our friend with the fresh horse caught us up, and the usual conversation began.

'Where are you from?'
'England.'
'Where are you going?'
'Sitia.'
'Why?'
'To see the place.'
'What are you?'
'Archaeologists.'
'Which of these ladies is your wife?'
'Neither: they are also archaeologists.'

As it happens, Hilda and John were to marry that autumn and return to Crete for some years in 1930 (see p. 203–5).

Hilda and her party arrive in Siteia, and she writes:

Sitia is a little port & quite a busy one I should think. I don't imagine they see many travellers like ourselves for we created quite a sensation. After settling ourselves at the little hotel & dismissing our muleteer we went to the shore & sat in the sun for a bit in the shelter of a breakwater. After a short walk along the sand we went back to the hotel making a few purchases on the way & made ourselves tea with John's little stove.

Siteia, the commercial and export centre for east Crete, is said to be a pleasant place to stay today. To visit it briefly as we did, to go to the Archaeological Museum, it seems a bit touristy: it is clustered around a pretty harbour, the rim of which is a string of tavernas, each with its waiter exhorting you to lunch there. Instead, we took to the back streets, to Fountalidou Street and there, at No. 19, found The Balcony, run by its owner/chef **Tonia Karindinou** who had had restaurants in London and Mexico City, from where she had brought back the stained glass which made the restaurant so unusual and attractive. The cooking was first rate and Tonia a delightful host, but we were the only customers and I fear she may have had to move to greener pastures. Do see if she is still there; you will be rewarded.

Siteia Museum, though small, is worth visiting, particularly for its prize, the famous chryselephantine statuette of a youth or *kouros* from Palaikastro (see pp. 80 and 371). It really is outstanding, especially the rim of gold round its separated waist – a typical Minoan belt. There are also votive terracottas from Petsophas (see pp. 24–6), a bigger collection of which is in the Herakleion Museum (see p. 189).

Of particular interest to us is the exquisite clay Tanagra figurine from the Hellenistic town of Xerokampos (see pp. 83 and 379). She wears a himation, chiton and head-dress; her weight is on her left leg and her head is tilted to the left. She is much smaller than I expected, so be careful you don't miss her in the last section of the museum.

The Daedalic (see pp. 75–6) clay statuette of a woman nursing an infant is also appealing, with her high cylindrical head-dress, official garments and 'Egyptian' coiffure indicating that she represents a goddess. She comes from the Daedalic repository in Siteia. The site of the town was probably inhabited from the Late Minoan period.

There is also a **Folklore Museum** in a restored period house which I'm sorry we missed. The collection concentrates on domestic crafts such as weaving, embroidery, lace making and woodcarving with examples, too, of the technology used. In the bedroom are fine antique, hand-spun and woven silk bed-hangings.

In 1928, Hilda White and her companions only stayed the night in Siteia; she wrote home:

We were very tired so had dinner early as we had arranged to start to Palaicastro at six the next day – I spent the night waking up at odd hours – fleas again – but of course dropped off thoroughly just at the wrong time so that we only wakened at about 5.35. So we had rather a rush getting our breakfast. We'd brought bread from the restaurant the night before – but we were ready just after six. Then no muleteer! We waited until nearly seven with John ramping with fury & then the hotel proprietor produced another, a jolly old Turk (I suspect) with a good little mule.

Things then looked up: 'It was a delightful walk – about 3 hours & ¾ – first along the shore then winding inland upwards through a lovely valley & up hill paths & finally through little lanes & a cultivated plain to the sea once more.'

## Petras

The road east from Siteia runs right by the sea for a short distance. On your right two thirds of the way along that wide inlet of the Bay of Siteia, you should see a signpost to an archaeological site. Persevere along a narrow, ledge-like road until you find parking for only one careful car. Clambering up, you will find the palatial site of Petras.

In the Final Palaces chapter of the historical section (see. p. 56), I have used the excavations at Petras, and the interpretation by its director, **Metaxia Tsipopoulou**, of the of thick walls and ramparts she found, to suggest the debate about the nature of the Minoans: were they as peaceable as previously supposed? Examples of the artefacts from Petras are in the Siteia Museum but no female figurines have been found. Metaxia has also questioned earlier suggestions that Zakros was the only Minoan palace in east Crete. Petras is now included in the growing list of likely palaces (see also Palaikastro, p. 370). It is a pleasing site to visit and has views over Siteia and the bay. You may be alone there.

Where possible I have been interested to establish whether or not Greek women archaeologists are Cretan. When quizzed, Metaxia explains that, though she was born in Athens of an Athenian family, she decided at the age of 12 that she would be a Minoan archaeologist. She visited Crete for the first time after her BA degree and has, since 1978, lived and worked there.

Not long past Petras and where the road leaves the shore, you cannot avoid seeing another sign to an archaeological site – **Anogia Photia**. An unwelcoming track leads down to the seashore. There are artefacts from this Early Minoan cemetery in the Siteia Museum, but the gate to the fence was firmly locked and I have discovered no figurines of Minoan women or goddesses, though, obviously, women were buried there. And Metaxia Tsipopoulou wrote up an archaeological survey of the site (1988) during a year's sabbatical at Bristol University. (Another site on which she worked is in itinerary p. 357.)

## Palaikastro

Drive on now to Palaikastro. Harriet Boyd, in *Crete: The Forerunner of Greece*, sets the scene for us of the archaeological site at Roussolakkos (the red pit) as she saw it in 1904:

A curving bay, lofty headlands, a solitary bluff acropolis ending steeply seawards, and a rich plain of olive groves and corn-land, such is the picturesque setting of Palaikastro. The prehistoric town lay almost on the seashore at the foot of the southern line of hills, and between it and the steep acropolis. Minoan cemeteries dotted the plain.

She compares the Minoan town with her own find at Gournia (see pp. 338–45):

Palaikastro was a flourishing seaport, whereas Gournia was a rural town. The seaport was naturally more cosmopolitan – foreign sailors were seen in her streets; whereas Gournia was more conservative, more typical of Minoan tradition.

These flashes of imaginative reconstruction through words are very helpful to the uninitiated because what you are seeing today are, of course, the veriest remnants of these once flourishing towns, mere stumps of once shining teeth.

We know that Harriet and her colleague Edith Hall visited Robert Carr Bosanquet excavating at Palaikastro on 11 May 1904, leaving Gournia the day after Harriet first met the British anthropologist Henry Hawes, her future husband (and co-author), as he passed by her own archaeological dig pursuing his research.

It's disappointing that Ellen, Bosanquet's wife since 1902, spent so little time at Palaikastro and fails to mention its women or her stay in *Days in Attica*. She was perfectly qualified to give us some insights (see p. 165) and is ready in that book to discuss, though briefly, other places and aspects of Crete (see pp. 198 and 258). I have explained her reasons for staying in Athens (see p. 80), but in her little book *Late Harvest*, she touchingly does it better in the chapter 'Memories 1875–1914':

The best journeys of all were when I was allowed to share CarrB's [Robert Carr Bosanquet] rides up and down the east end of Crete and to settle down with him at the excavations. He was so much beloved by all the country people and so entirely at home in the Cretan dialect that I had nothing to do but sit on my mule and smile and open my saddlebag to receive their presents of flowers or artichokes, salad, olives, and a variety of rather hard fruit; sometimes even dried octopus. The country was so lovely, the sea so blue, the people so friendly, the life so free, I just let myself be carried along without attempting to master the language or the archaeology or the botany – in fact, missing all the opportunities for which other people would have given their eyes [eye teeth? – somewhat different!]. But oh, how

I loved it all! I guess now that my 'smatterings' of modern Greek and prehistoric chronology must often have exasperated CarrB ... but he enjoyed my enjoyment and did not try to make a scholar out of me. I should have been perfectly happy if it had not been for the maternal undercurrent, always wondering what was happening to the child at home.

I have mentioned how in 1904 Ellen joined 'the island cruise' under the archaeologist Wilhelm Dörpfeld and that, after visiting Gournia and having shown off both it and Harriet Boyd (a former student) to his party, he took her and Edith Hall off to Palaikastro (see p. 344). It was soon after they all left, on 25 May, that Bosanquet wrote to Ellen about finding the hymn in honour of Zeus (see p. 79, and room XIX Herakleion Museum) which so influenced the work of the Cambridge classicist Jane Harrison (see p. 80). By Ellen's editing and publishing of her husband's letters from Palaikastro, we learn something of the women of the area. Two years earlier, and before

31.   Ellen Bosanquet as a girl, from Bosanquet, *Late Harvest*

their marriage, Bosanquet wrote to Ellen (23 April 1902), about workers on the dig:

Then there are the four women, who wash pottery and sift earth — three girls under a grave matron. One of them wears an orange-red petticoat which gladdens the eye — try a brilliant bit of orange red against a deep blue sea on a day like to-day and say if it isn't worth 1 franc 20 centimes a day. These are the most prim, industrious young women, and two of them earned their wage to-day by sifting earth and finding two kine [outlines of cattle on shards of pottery] in it.

But all was not hard slog. In the village of Angathia near the site Bosanquet observed his workers relaxing on holy days; he continued on 2 May:

The dance is mainly a boy and girl affair, all looking very serious and decorous: drum and mandoline on low chairs in the middle, and a long string of dancers, boys and girls intermixed in a way one seldom sees in Greece, solemnly footing it round and round them, hands held very high, chins higher, the dance always the same [*Cretico* — Cretan], varying in pace to suit the taste of No. 1 for the time being, who exhausts himself and drops to the tail, when No.2 becomes No.1. On state occasions the chief dancer is always a man, to-night the girls took their turn at the head.

This is not only shades of Ariadne (see p. 53) and the semi-circle of clay dancing women found at Palaikastro (see p. 54 and Herakleion Museum, room X), but it is also still part of every tourist's experience. If you are interested in the way of life of the young women Bosanquet describes, you will get a fair idea from the attractively restored traditional house (**Folklore Museum**) opposite the tourist office in the main street (9.00 a.m. to 1.00 p.m. and 3.30 p.m. to 8.00 p.m.; closed Mondays).

By 1928, the caravan had long moved on – Palaikastro was no longer being excavated, and Hilda White writes:

The excavations at Palaicastro were rather disappointing as parts had been covered over, but the site is lovely. John and I had a bathe before lunch: it was simply glorious

& not a bit cold. We picnicked with our muleteer who sampled everything of ours with great composure but certainly gave us some of his bread in return.

From Palaikastro, Hilda and co. turned back towards Herakleion. It was not until 1962–3 that excavations started again. There is a tantalising glimpse of a Cretan woman's involvement – not a villager but a member of the British School at Athens entourage – in Davina Huxley's *Cretan Quests*: 'The 1962–3 work was overseen by Knossos foreman, Manolis **Markogiannakis**, who with his wife **Ourania** [m.1933] made the long journey to this Cretan "outback", on all dirt roads beyond Ayios Nikolaos.' In a later chapter in that book, Rachel Hood describes how Markogiannakis 'and his wife, Ourania, lived in the rambling servants' quarters of the Villa Ariadne and provided meals for the various excavation parties in the 1950s and 60s.'

Today, the site of Roussolakkos is adequately signposted from the village of Palaikastro (you go through the square as if to Zakros but turn left towards the Hotel Marina Village and the sea). It is among the most pleasing sites to visit. The setting is wide open yet intimate, with an intriguing flat-topped plum pudding hill (Minoan Kastri) at the northern end and the heights of Petsophas rising at the southern.

The site is beautifully maintained, everything carefully marked – this is an unusual and welcome feature. And, in this sizeable Minoan town – 30 hectares, perhaps the largest urban centre after Knossos – there are identifiable separate houses, such that you might like to live in. We chose N – it had good rooms and a bit of privacy. It dates from the last years of the Neopalatial period and Pat Cameron describes which rooms probably had which function, allowing you to play house.

There is still work to be done on the site because it may well be that there is a layer of Minoan habitation still undisclosed underneath and even that Palaikastro may be yet another palace. Then there is the suggestion I have already mentioned (see p. 45) that women and men lived here as equals.

The most recent and most important find, starting with fragments of ivory and gold in 1987, is the chryselephantine *Kouros* that dominates the Siteia Museum (see p. 364). That find associated with Palaikastro is in addition to the Hymn to Zeus (see p. 79 and room XIX of the Herakleion Museum) which suggests a Diktaian (to Zeus) temple dating from the eighth century BC (Geometric period). It also decrees yet another place (see pp. 207, 234 and 295) where Rhea gave birth to the god Zeus and hid him from his jealous father.

I have taken you first to Roussolakkos, the site in the flat plain, because that is the most accessible and your time might be limited but I do recommend that, if you are going to climb up to the Petsophas sanctuary, you do that first, while you are still fresh and it is relatively cool. If you are at all healthy and game – it is an hour's steep climb – do not miss the experience. But do take a water bottle and a hat – there is no shade, even when you reach the top. Having taken neither, I did flag but still didn't regret it.

Pat Cameron says that the short cut to the starting point of the climb should be marked at the Roussolakkos site, but we drove first looking for how to get up and had to use our heads and keep our nerve to find it (you really do not want to climb the wrong way). Once started, along a reasonable path, follow the arrows carefully. The last third, as it curves round the hill, is the flattest and therefore easiest part. Then you go up and, as it were, over the top. The path seems to give out a few yards from the sanctuary (before you can see it) but a sign helps. On your way back, there is a pile of rocks to help you retrieve the path.

The shrine is, of course, special because from it came all those marvellous Petsophas women (votive offerings) (see pp. 24–6 and Herakleion Museum, room II). But then there is also the stupendous view – you are definitely ruler of all your survey – the smell of thyme and sage, the wild flowers, the tinkling of bellwether sheep and the goats standing blackly against the skyline flaunting their ludicrous horns. A supreme Crete moment, even if you are faint with heat exhaustion!

It will take you 20 minutes to get down, taking care not to do so too precipitately. We did Petsophas and Roussolakkos and then had lunch; you might split the two. A delightful lunch is to be had – choose your own fish – at Chiona, sitting over the water, overlooking the bay and beach where you can obviously swim pleasantly. If you only have to tumble back to your accommodation and into the sea, the day is just about perfect.

If you are interested in caves, not Minoan but palaeontological, do take note of Dorothea Bate's visit in 1904. She wrote in 'Search for Pleistocene Mammalia in Crete' (1905):

The only cave deposits found in this part of the island were situated in the rugged limestone cliffs bordering the southern end of the Bay of Kharoumes, not many miles south of Palaikastro. At the foot of these cliffs and only from a few feet to a few yards above the sea were discovered one small bone cave and, on either side, portions of the stalagmitic flooring of two others; all being situated close together and extending for a distance of about a hundred and fifty yards. The most northerly of these deposits, which is at a greater height than, and a little distance from the cave, contained only bones and teeth of the small hippopotamus which also occurs at Melato [Milatos]. The remains in the cave and in the other deposit proved to be those of ruminants similar to those found in the caves of the west of the island.

Dorothea felt these would probably prove to be of an earlier age than Pleistocene (2,000,000–10,000 years old). I'm afraid I must leave you to pursue this site (and perhaps let me know about it). You may be able to spot the area from the top of Mount Petsophas; Karoumes Beach is marked on some maps and there is apparently now a rough track down to the sea (see p. 308 for the Milatos). Dorothea was certainly intrepid, for help that she might have expected could not have been forthcoming: Robert Bosanquet wrote to Ellen on 8 June 1904: 'Miss Bate, courageous as ever, has turned up again, to have another go at the Caroumais Cave near P.K. I'm sorry we are going [leaving] and can't help her.'

## Toplou Monastery

The Temple of Diktaian Zeus at Palaikastro links the Toplou Monastery, the archaeological sites at Itanos and Praisos and today's town of Ierapetra. Although there is no evidence of woman involvement, it might be a sop to throw, as I did, to your patient travelling companion.

Your map will show you that you can either go straight north from Palaikastro to Itanos and, cutting back, turn south-west to Toplou or, if you are coming from Siteia, go to Toplou (turning sharp left) before Palaikastro. The church within the monastery is dedicated to the Panagia Akrotiriani ('Virgin of the Cape' – the Cape of Sideros). Frescoes include the Mother of God enthroned between Adam and Eve, but I liked best the small room behind a velvet curtain on the north side in which women attending services were traditionally confined. Presumably, thus obscured from judgmental eyes, they could gossip, giggle, do their embroidery and swig communion wine. One of them could have been the wife of Demetrios: the family donated the 60-image icon on the stand by the well-known artist Kornaros.

Set into the wall outside the entrance to the church is the inscription, dating to 132 BC, known as the Arbitration of Magnesia. This was the resolution of territorial disputes over control of the Temple at Palaikastro, first between Itanos and Praisos, where the last Minoans (Eteocretans; see pp. 83 and 380) are said to have held out, and, then, when Praisos was defeated by Ierapytna (Ierapetra), between it and Itanos. It is a fascinating document.

As you leave, don't miss the rather good bookshop. At that moment in our visit, I saw a young woman in bathing costume and shorts soundly dispatched by an unsmiling woman custodian.

## Eleonora's falcon

To the north of the monastery is the Dionysades group of islands, interesting to ornithologists as the breeding ground of the rare

Eleonora falcon (*Falco eleonorae*). Who was Eleonora? She was Giudicessa (magistrate or ruler) Eleonora d'Arborea (1350–1404), the Sardinian hero who fought for independence from Aragon and made laws protecting nursing birds of prey. (She was also responsible for a long-lasting and influential law code.) Look out for these birds on the rocky shore of this itinerary, as far south as Xerokampos (see p. 379). From around mid-October they begin to fly south to Madagascar, returning in March and hatching from late August. (They breed late so they can feed their young on other migrating birds!)

## Itanos

On the way north to Itanos, you pass Vai; with its sand and unique palms, it is described as the only proper beach in Crete. As such, sun-worshippers flock to it and it has become over-discovered. We poked a nose down out of mild curiosity but, as soon as we saw the kiosks and rows of deck chairs for hire and, indeed, a kiosk for an entrance fee, we retreated.

Opposite the road leading to it was a more appealing enterprise – a stall selling fresh produce grown in the plantation behind. Stock up on ladies' fingers bananas, honey and olives prepared the traditional way. You may need these comestibles as there is nothing to eat at Itanos.

You may think, when you arrive at Itanos, that there has been a sudden surge in interest in its archaeological sites – there may be many cars. But that is only because these beaches, too, are pleasant enough – with one palm tree – and free. But we went for Cleopatra (see p. 88). And there is a most delightful rocky cove, some distance from the swimming beach, where it is perfectly possible to picture Cleo and Mark Anthony coming ashore with their picnic hamper to inspect her new property, while their galley, oars upended, waits out in the bay. The most obvious remains are of an early Byzantine basilica probably built on the site of a temple to Athena Polias. There is continuing excavation of Minoan occupation but I have been thwarted in finding out more. For the Ptolemaic garrison in Hellenistic times, see p. 82, and for the dispute settled in 132 BC, p. 373.

## Zakros

From Palaikastro, leave the square (with the modern church on your right) and take the signposted turning to your right soon after. It is a good road and interesting though barren scenery. Arriving in Epano (Upper) Zakros, some walk the 9 km through Dead Gorge down to Kato (Lower) Zakros to the main archaeological site. But as you go by road, note for later a bijou archaeological site beside it on your right.

The story of the excavations at Zakros is almost as interesting as the Minoans who lived there thousands of years ago – at least we know more about the people. At much the same time as Arthur Evans started digging at Zakros, another British archaeologist, David Hogarth, did the same at Kato Zakros. Dilys Powell notes: 'He discovered house foundations, pottery, fine seal impressions.' He decided that the site had once been an ancient trading settlement. Hoping to find something more exciting, and failing, in due course he gave up.

In 1939, John Pendlebury published what was to become, because of his untimely death, his chef d'oeuvre, *The Archaeology of Crete*. In the 1930s, he and Hilda, 'Whenever possible,' as Helen Waterhouse explains, 'were walking Crete from end to end, noting sites and routes and collecting the material which went into the making of his book covering all periods.' Seton Lloyd who, with his wife **Joan Firminger**, joined the Pendleburys one year, wrote: 'I still retain a picture of him striding across the Cretan landscape with an occasional glance at his stop-watch, and of his poor wife's brave attempts to keep up with him.' The last part of that remark appears to be in Lloyd's mind, rather than Hilda's – her letters from which I have quoted show her enviably game though, perhaps, as she became a mother, and

John, 13 years her junior, became increasing engrossed in his active research, she flagged.

Zakros was one of the places they visited. Some time after 1962, when renewed excavation at Zakros started to unearth its treasures, and it was known that Hogarth had missed the palace by a few yards, Hilda was to muse to Dilys: 'We must have been sitting on the very site – and saw nothing.'

Until 1962, it had been assumed that all the Minoan palaces had been found; and the right to dig at the others was held onto proprietorally by the Schools – British (Knossos), French (Mallia) and Italian (Phaistos). Then the collectors **Harriet** and Leon **Pomerance** arrived in Herakleion from the United States to study the remains of Minoan art. They read the introduction in the museum catalogue by the senior Greek archaeologist Nicholas Platon suggesting that all sorts of things could still be found in Crete, if only there were the funds. The Pomerances offered them to Platon and he and his wife, Anastasia, known as Sosso (see p. 176), started excavating at Zakros. They were immediately lucky.

The American columnist and writer on archaeology Joseph Alsop, visiting the sites at Zakros in 1966 with the Pomerances, met the Platons for the first time and described Sosso in a long article in the *New Yorker*: 'She is younger than he – an ample Crete lady with thick dark hair, fine features, and the gold satin skin that Cretan women sometimes have.'

The Platons, with their two children, occupied a two-room cottage overlooking the beach, from where they sallied forth to their nearby site. Alsop also describes their methods of working, showing Sosso's involvement:

As I learned that afternoon from Mrs Platon, the organization of such a dig is ... fairly elaborate. Any serious dig, whether major or minor, needs continuous, minute professional supervision, and meticulous records must also be kept of the daily, even hourly, progress. At Kato Zakro, this was mainly done by Dr. and Mrs Platon. One or the other was always walking about the site, now telling a workman to go more slowly, now consulting with the foreman of the dig about next steps, now advising one of the museum technicians who had an especially ticklish job in hand. Both were constantly taking notes and at the end of every day's digging Dr Platon had to spend an hour or two consolidating all these notes into an orderly day-book.

Alsop notes that, in addition to the Platons, the team at the dig included two junior professional archaeologists, Yannis and Efi Sakellarakis. Efi and Yannis had worked with Platon at Myrsini before their marriage (see p. 362) and Efi describes Zakros, where they to started digging in 1962, as their honeymoon. Zakros was a big chance for them and they took it. They were put in charge of a site just outside Epano Zakros and there unearthed the Minoan country house (villa) which I have mentioned. They were called back to the main site, should the need arise.

By the time Alsop met Efi and Yannis in 1966, they were already involved in their excavations at Archanes finding, indeed, another Minoan palace (see pp. 214–25). Alsop, though his article is scholarly, was also writing from a personal point of view, what he saw and what he was told. One of his interests was spotting how modern Greeks or Cretans looked like their ancestors on excavated artefacts; so he wrote of Efi: '[She] looked at though she had stepped straight out of the fresco, from the Mycenaean palace at Tiryns [mainland Greece], of white-robed maidens bringing offerings.'

On the last evening of the digging season, Alsop describes how:

Quite suddenly, Joannis and Effi Sakellarakis emerged from the shadows, both bubbling with gaiety and looking more than ever like a young Byzantine *clarissimus* and a Tirynthian bearer of offerings. A dance was beginning, they announced and they invited us to join the party. At the beachside cafe, sure enough, we found the workmen from the dig energetically doing the athletic Cretan dances. Lee Pomerance and I, as was only proper, made our contribution to the party by buying rounds of the thin red wine of eastern Crete. Harriet Pomerance, who is very light on her feet, took rapid lessons from Andonius, the best of the dancers, and then she and Effi Sakellarakis, already an expert, joined in.

Artefacts from Zakros can be seen in Herakleion (room VII) and Siteia. No women figurines stand out. However, much craftwork went on in the palace, perhaps mostly for export. For example, many looms were in use, chiefly in rooms on the second floor, for the production of woven materials. Dyeing installations suggest rich colours. And there are elaborate examples of embroidery represented on frescoes. Perfumes, too, were apparently produced. Platon suggests, in *Zakros: The Discovery of a Lost Palace in Ancient Crete* (1971), the involvement of 'many women', including 'queens and princesses' (see p. 24). Linear A tablets have been found in what is called the archives room. There is no reason to suppose that some Minoan women were not as literate as some men.

Interpretations of the palace – first built in 1900 BC (Protopalatial), though what you see unearthed dates from the second building phase, about 1600 BC (Neopalatial) – worked on by the Platons' son, Lefteris, are still in flux. Dilys Powell's 1973 comment – 'There is precious little finality in the affairs of archaeology' – was said about Zakros, and still applies. What does seem certain is that life there came to an end in about 1450 BC by some catastrophe (see p. 48). There is evidence of fire and of hurried evacuation. Treasure was left behind and no skeletons have been found. The site is unusual in that many precious artefacts were found, instead of being pilfered over the centuries.

Dilys Powell suggests that the rulers of Zakros perhaps 'felt safe in their valley'. Visiting it in 2003, I had a different feeling; I jotted in my notes: 'The women must have felt a bit cut off from the rest of the world (Crete), though they could get on a boat and go to Egypt, Cyprus or the Levant.'

The palace site is back from the sea; on the beach front there is now a string of tavernas, in one of which we had a pleasant lunch. The woman chef at Nikos Plantanakis made excellent cheese pies. We had planned to swim; indeed, the braver of us ventured in and I was quite alarmed to see him attacked by currents in collusion with violent waves, and hastily begged him to struggle ashore. They say that before and beyond the waterfront tavernas is perfectly safe. I suggest you visit the site early (open 8.00 a.m. to 3.00 p.m.; until 7.00 p.m. in high season) to avoid coach parties, which we just managed.

Don't miss the Neopalatial Epano Zakros site, excavated by Efi and Yannis Sakellarakis, before you leave the area. The finds there showed a luxurious and practical lifestyle – frescoes and an oil and wine press, for example. You will need to park carefully to inspect it; there is only room for one car, perhaps best parked against the hillside facing up the hill towards the village. Then you need to be a bit nippy and alert. The site is slightly below the road, but right up to it; signs of habitation were discovered when the road was improved for the excavation at Kato Zakros.

## Xerokampos

Just past the Minoan villa (as you leave Upper Zakros for Lower), there is a track off to your right. We should have taken it to Xerokampos, but a rough map we had picked up in our accommodation marked it as an unmade road which would take 40 minutes – and that was just going. It is apparently 10 km and I suppose could be sealed in future.

I would have liked to see the Hellenistic site – at the far end of the unspoilt beach – where the exquisite figurine in the Siteia Museum was found (see pp. 83 and 364). Should you be bolder than us, look out, too, for the Eleonora falcon.

## Voila

You don't have to go back via Zakros. Running west from Xerokampos, towards the farming village of Ziros, the road appears to be sealed. North from Chandras, the next village, is a sign on your right to Voila, a ruined medieval village that you can discern at the foot of the hill. The church, Hagios Giorgios, which dominates the village, is still intact and, I gather, usually locked, but it seems to contain the frescoes of the sixteenth century (1518) Venetian family I have used to illustrate the appearance of women then (see p. 112).

## Praisos

Continuing further north towards Siteia, you can turn off to the site of Praisos – the last redoubt of the Eteocretans who probably fled the Dorian encroachment. The city was razed by Ierapytna between 155 and 140 BC. It was never rebuilt and its destruction is said to mark the end of Minoan civilisation (see p. 83). There are remains from the Archaic to the Hellenistic periods. We drove to Zakros direct from Palaikastro and back and obviously missed several interesting villages and sites and a pleasing agricultural landscape. Much depends on where you are staying, the time at your disposal, your companion and your special interests.

The end of the Eteocretans seems all too appropriate a place to end not only this itinerary but all of them, and this book which, inevitably, is dominated by the Minoans. I hope, however, that I have given you enough detail about the women and places of more modern Crete to show that there is more to the island than their alluring forebears.

I ended the historical section with this quotation from Victoria Theodorou about women during the Second World War: 'For the first time in the history of Greece, in the ranks of the Resistance movement women and young people were treated as the equals of adult men at home, at work, in strategic planning and in danger and in sacrifice.' In the women's co-operative at Gavalochori in 2001, I asked Anastasia if Cretan women were as equal today as they appeared to be 4,000 years ago. She replied, 'Yes, and a lot are going into politics.' She also equates the goddess Europa with Crete, which equals Europe and the European Union, which to her means peace. The final irony is that Greece's version of the 2 Euro coin features the 'rape' of Europa.

# Bibliography

## Women's Works (general reader)

Alexiou, Elli, 'The Fountain of Brahim-Baba' in *Greece: A Traveller's Literary Companion*, see Leontis (1997)

Allsebrook, Mary, *Born to Rebel: The Life of Harriet Boyd Hawes* (Oxford, Oxbow Books, 1992, 2002)

Ayrton, Elisabeth, *Silence in Crete* (New York, William Morrow, 1964)

Barber, Elizabeth W., *Women's Work, the First 2000 Years: Women, Cloth and Society in Early Times* (New York, W.W. Norton, 1994)

Bosanquet, Mrs R.C. (Ellen), *Days in Attica* (London, Methuen, 1914)

Boyd, Harriet, 'Excavations at Kavousi, Crete', *American Journal of Archaeology* 5 (1901) 125–57

Boyd Hawes, Harriet, *Crete: The Forerunner of Crete* (London, Harper & Bros., 1909)

Boyd Hawes, Harriet, 'Memoirs of a Pioneer Excavator in Crete', *Archaeology* 18 (1965) 95–101; 268–76

Cadogan, Lucy, *Digging* (London, Chatto & Windus, 1987)

Davies, Scott, *Riding the Minotaur* (Athens, Efstathiadis, 1999)

Finn, Christine, 'A Rare Bird' (Jacquetta Hawkes), *Archaeology* (January/February 2001) 38–43

Fourtouni, Eleni (ed.), *Greek Women in Resistance* (New Haven, Thelphini Press, 1986)

Galanaki, Rhea, *The Life of Ismail Ferik Pasha* (London, Peter Owen, 1996)

Galanaki, Rhea, 'Black and White' in *Greece: A Traveller's Literary Companion*, see Leontis (1997)

Greger, Sonia, *The Village on the Plateau* (Studley, Brewin Books, 1988)

Greger, Sonia, *Ariadne: A Cretan Myth* (Studley, Brewin Books, 1992)

Greger, Sonia, *Letters from Lasithi 1984–1993: A Decade of 'Development' in Cretan Mountains* (Crewe, Gorgona Books, 1993)

Hall, Edith, 'The Cretan Expedition', *The Museum Journal* 3, University of Pennsylvania (1912) 39–44

Hankey, Vronwy, 'A Personal Reminiscence', *Aegaeum* 18 (1989) xxi–xxvii

Hawkes, Jacquetta, *Dawn of the Gods: Minoan and Mycenaean Origins of Greece* (New York, Random House, 1968)

Hawkes, Jacquetta, *A Quest of Love* (London, Chatto & Windus, 1980)

Ivanova, Sabine, *Where Zeus Became a Man: With Cretan Shepherds* (Athens, Efstathiadis, nd)

Leontis, Artemis (ed.), *Greece: A Traveller's Literary Companion* (San Francisco, Whereabouts Press, 1997)

Oulié, Marthe, and de Saussure, Hermine, *La Croisière de la Perlette* (Paris, Hachette, 1926)

Oulié, Marthe, 'To Crete: Four French Girls Sail in a Breton Yawl for the Island of the Legendary Minotaur', *National Geographic Magazine* vol. LV (February 1929) 249–72

Pendlebury, Hilda, 'A Journey in Crete' (1929), *Archaeology* 17 (1964) 162–68

Powell, Dylis, *The Villa Ariadne* (London, Hodder & Stoughton, 1973)

Renault, Mary, *The King Must Die* (London, Vintage, 1958)

Renault, Mary, *The Bull from the Sea* (London, Vintage, 1962)

Rosmini, Emilia De Sanctis, *Dalla Canea a Tripoli* (Rome, Bernado Lux, 1912)

Sakellarakis, Efi and Yannis, *Crete: Archanes* (Athens, Ekdotike Athenon, 1991)

Walker, Mrs (Mary A.), *Eastern Life and Scenery: With Excursions in Asia Minor, Mitilene, Crete and Roumania*, 2 vols (London, Chapman Hall, 1886)

Watson, Betty, *Miracle in Hellas: The Greeks Fight On* (London, Museum Press, 1943)

## Women's Specialised Works

Andreadaki-Vlasaki, Maria, *The County of Khania Through its Monuments* (Athens, Ministry of Culture, Archaeological Receipts Fund, 2$^{nd}$ edition, 2000)

Archer, Léonie J. et al, *Women in Ancient Societies* (New York, Routledge, 1994)

Atchity, Kenneth, & Barber, Elizabeth J.W., 'Greek Princes and Aegean Princesses' in *Critical Essays on Homer*, K. Atchity et al (eds) (Boston, G.K. Hall, 1987)

Bancroft-Marcus, Rosemary E., 'Women in the Cretan Renaissance (1570–1669)', *Journal of Modern Greek Studies* 1 (1983) 19–38

Bancroft-Marcus, Rosemary E. 'Attitudes to Women in the Drama of Venetian Crete' in W*omen in Italian Renaissance, Culture and Society*, Letizia Panizza (ed.) (Oxford, European Humanities Research Centre, 2000)

Bandini, Giovanna, *Lettere dell'Egeo: Archeologhe Italiane fra 1900 e 1950* (Florence, Giunti, 2003)

Banti, Luisa and Pernier, Luigi, *Guida agli Scavi in Creta* (Rome, Libreria dello Stato, 1947)

Banti, Luisa and Pernier, Luigi, *Il Palazzo Minoico di Festos: Scavi e Studi della Missione Archaeologica Italiana a Creta dal 1900 al 1934* (Rome, Libreria dello Stato, 1935)

Barber, Elizabeth J.W., 'Minoan Women and the Challenges of Weaving for Home, Trade and Shrine', see *TEXNH* II (1997) 515–19

Baring, Anne and Cashford, Jules, *The Myth of the Goddesses* (London, Viking Arkana, 1991)

Bate, Dorothea, 'Four and a Half Months in Crete in Search of Pleistocene Mammalian Remains', *The Geological Magazine*, decade V, vol. 11 (May 1905)193–202

Bate, Dorothea, 'The Caves of Crete' in Aubin Trevor-Battye, *Camping on Crete* (London, 1913)

Boyd Hawes, Harriet, *Gournia, Vasiliki and Other Prehistoric Sites etc. 1901, 1903, 1904* (Philadelphia, American Exploration Society, 1908)

Cadogan, Gerald, 'Vronwy Hankey', see Joukowsky (2004)

Claassen, Cheryl, *Women in Archaeology* (Philadelphia, University of Pennsylvania Press, 1994)

Cohen, Getzel M. and Joukowsky, Martha Sharp (eds), *Breaking Ground: Pioneering Women Archaeologists* (Ann Arbor, University of Michigan Press, 2004)

Cullen, Tracey, 'Contributions to Feminism in Archaeology', *American Journal of Archaeology* 100 (1996) 409–14

Cullen, Tracey (ed.), *Aegean Prehistory: A Review* (*American Journal of Archaeology* supplement 1) (Boston, Archaeological Institute of America, 2001)

Eller, Cynthia, *The Myth of Matriarchal Prehistory: Why an Invented Past won't give Women a Future* (Boston, Beacon Press, 2000)

Fiandra, Enrica, 'I Periodi Struttivi de Primo Palazzi di Festos', *Cretalogica* 1 (1962) 112–126

Fitton, Lesley, *The Minoans* (London, British Museum Press, 2002)

Frankfort, Mrs Groenewegen, *Arts of the Ancient World* (New Jersey, Prentice-Hall, 1971)

Gesell, Geraldine C., 'The Place of the Goddess in Minoan Society', see Krzyszkowska (1983)

Gesell, Geraldine C., 'Methods Used in the Construction of Ceramic Objects from the Shrine of the Goddess with Upraised Arms at Kavousi', see *TEXNH II* (1997) 123–5

Gill, David W.J., 'Winifred Lamb' in Cohen and Joukowsky (eds) 2004

Gimbutas, Marija, *Goddesses and Gods of Old Europe* (London, Thames & Hudson, 1974)

Goodison, Lucy and Morrison, Christine, 'Beyond the Great Goddess' in *Ancient Goddesses: The Myths and the Evidence,* Goodison and Morris (eds) (London, British Museum Press, 1998)

Goodison, Lucy, 'From Tholos Tomb to Throne Room: Perceptions of the Sun in Minoan Ritual', see *Potnia* (2001) 77–87

Goodison, Lucy & Hughes-Brock, Helen, 'Helen Waterhouse and her "Priest-King?" Paper', *Cretan Studies* 7 (Amsterdam, Adolf M. Hakkert, 2002)

Greene, Molly, *A Shared World: Christians and Moslems in the Early Mediterranean* (Princeton, Princeton University Press, 2000)

Guarducci, Marguerita, *Inscriptiones Creticae* (Rome, Libreria dello Stato, 1935–50)

Hall, Edith, 'Excavations at Vrokastro, Crete, in 1912', *Art and Archaeology* 1 (1) (1914) 32–36

Hall, Edith, *Excavations in Eastern Crete: Vrokastro* (Philadelphia, University Press, 1914)

Harrison, Jane Ellen, *The Prolegomena to the Study of Greek Religion* (Cambridge, Cambridge University Press, 1903)

Harrison, Jane Ellen, *Themis: A Study of the Social Origins of the Greek Religion* (Cambridge, Cambridge University Press, 1912)

Hayden, Barbara, 'Terracotta Figures, Figurines and Vase Attachments from Vrokastro, Crete', *Hespera* 60 (1991) 103–43

Herrin, Judith, 'Public and Private Forms of Religious Commitment Among Byzantine Women' in *Women in Ancient Societies,* see Archer (1994)

Hughes-Brock, Helen, 'Mycenaean Beads: Gender and Social Contexts', *Oxford Journal of Archaeology* 18, 3 (1999) 277–95

Huxley, Davina (ed.), *Cretan Quests: British Explorers, Excavators and Historians* (London, British School at Athens, 2000)

Jones, Bernice, 'The Minoan "Snake Goddess": New Interpretations of her Costume and Identity', see *Potnia* (2001) 260–5

Joukowsky, Martha Sharp and Lesko, Barbara S. (eds), *Breaking Ground: Women in Old World Archaeology* www.Brown.edu/Research/Breaking_Ground (Brown University, Internet, 2004)

Kopaka, Katerina, 'Women's Arts – Men's Crafts? Towards a Framework for approaching Gender Skills in the Prehistoric Aegean', see *TEXNH II* (1997) 521–31

Kopaka, Katerina, 'A Day in Potnia's Life: Aspects of Potnia and Reflected "Mistress" Activities in the Aegean Bronze Age', see *Potnia* (2001) 15–26

Krzyszkowska O. and Nixon, L. (eds.) *Minoan Society* (Bristol, Classical Press, 1983)

McKee, Sally, 'Greek Women in Latin Households of Fourteenth Century Venetian Crete', *Journal of Medieval History* 19 (1993) 229–49

McKee, Sally, 'Women Under Venetian Colonial Rule in the Early Renaissance: Observations on their Economic Activities', *Renaissance Quarterly* 51 (1998) 34–67

McKee, Sally, *Uncommon Dominion: Venetian Crete and the Myth of Homogeneity* (Philadelphia, University of Pennsylvania Press, 2000)

Maltezou, Chryssa, 'The Historical and Social Context' in *Literature and Society in Renaissance Crete*, see Holton (1991)

Marinatos, Nanno, *Minoan Religion: Ritual, Image and Symbol* (Columbia, University of South Carolinia Press, 1994)

Melena, Elpis (pseud. of Baroness Schwartz), *Die Insel Creta unter der Ottomanischen Verwaltung* (Vienna, 1867)

Melena, Elpis, (ed.) *Kreta-Biene, oder Kretische Volkslieder, Sagen, Liebes-, Denk- und Sittensprüche* (Crete-Bee, or Cretan Folksong, Sayings and Maxims of Love, Thought, and Customs) (Munich, 1874)

*Meletemata: Studies in Aegean Archaeology Presented to Malcolm H. Wiener*, Philip Betancourt et al (eds) *Aegaeum* 20 (1999) (Liège, University of Liège, 1999)

Momigliano, Nicoletta, 'Edith Eccles', see Joukowsky (2004)

Money-Coutts, see Seiradaki

Moody, Jennifer, 'The Minoan Palace as a Prestige Artefact' in *Function of the Minoan Palace*, R. Hägg & N. Marinatos (eds) (Stockholm, Svenska Institutet i Athen, 1987)

Nikolaidou, Mariana, 'Palaces with Faces in Protopalatial Crete' in *Labyrinth Revisited: Rethinking 'Minoan' Archaeology*, Yannis Hamilakis (ed.) (Oxford, Oxbow Books, 2002)

Nixon, Lucia, 'Changing Views of Minoan Society', see O. Krzyszkowska and L. Nixon (1983)

Nixon, Lucia, 'Gender Bias in Archaeology' in *Women in Ancient Societies*, see Archer (1994)

Nixon, Lucia, 'The Cults of Demeter and Kore' in *Women in Antiquity*, Richard Hawley and Barbara Levick (eds) (London, Routlege, 1995)

Nixon, Lucia, 'Women, Children & Weaving', see *Meletemata* (1999) 561–7

Nordfeldt, AnnCharlotte, 'Residential Quarters and Lustral Basins' in *Function of the Minoan Palace*, R. Hägg & N. Marinatos (eds) (Stockholm, Svenska Instituet i Athen, 1987)

Olsen, Barbara B., 'Women, Children and the Family in the Late Aegean Bronze Age', *World Archaeology* 29, 3 (1998) 380–1

Oulié, Marthe, *Les Animaux dans la Peinture de la Crète Préhellénique* (Paris, Librairie Félix Alcan, nd)

Paton, Sara, 'Roman Knossos and the Colonia Julia Nobilis Cnossus' in *Knossos: A Labyrinth of History: Papers in Honour of Sinclair Hood*, Helen Hughes-Brock & Nicoletta Momigliano (eds) (London, British School at Athens, 1994)

Pendlebury, H.W. and J.D.S and M.B. Money-Coutts, 'Excavations in the Plain of Lasithi' reprinted from *The Annual of the British School at Athens*, vol. XXXV1, (1939)

Picazo, Marina, 'Fieldwork is not the Proper Preserve of a Lady' in *Excavating Women: A History of Women in European Archaeology*, A. Diaz-Andreu and M.-L. S. Sørensen (London, Routledge, 1998)

Pomeroy, Sarah B., *Goddesses, Whores, Wives and Slaves: Women in Classical Antiquity* (London, Pimlico, 1975; 1994)

Pomeroy, Sarah B., 'A Classical Scholar's Perspective on Matriarchy' in *Liberating Women's History*, B. Carroll (ed.) (Urbana, University of Illinois Press, 1975)

*Potnia, Deities and Religion in the Aegean Bronze Age*, R. Laffineur & R. Hägg (eds) *Aegaeum* 22 (Liège, University of Liège, 2001)

Sakellarakis, Efi, 'Hair Styles in the Minoan Era' (undated newspaper article)

Sakellarakis, Efi and Yannis, *Archanes: Minoan Crete in a New Light* (Athens, Ammos, 1997)

Saulnier, Françoise, *Anoyia: Un Village de Montagne Crétois* (Paris, Laboratoire d'Anthropologie Sociale, 1980)

Schofield, Elizabeth, 'Mercy Money-Coutts', see Joukowsky (2004)

Seiradaki, Mercy (Money-Coutts), 'Pottery from Karphi', *British School at Athens* 55 (1960) 1–37

Sherratt, Susan, *Arthur Evans, Knossos and the Priest-King* (Oxford, Ashmolean Museum, 2000)

Stawell, Melian, *A Clue to the Cretan Scripts* (London, G. Bell & Sons, 1931)

*TEXNH II: Craftsmen, Craftswomen and Craftsmanship in the Aegean Bronze Age*, R.Laffineur and P. Betancourt (eds) *Aegaeum* 16 (Liège, Université de Liège, 1997)

Tsipopoulou, Metaxia, 'From Local Centre to Palace: The Role of Fortification in the Economic Transformation of the Siteia Bay Area, East Crete' in *Polemos: Le Contexte Guerrier en Egée à l'Age du Bronze*, R. Laffineur (ed.) *Aegaeum* 19 (Liège, Université de Liège, 2003)

van Effenterre, Micheline, 'Le Travail Professionnel des Femmes dans la Crète Antique', *Saitabi*, 49 (1999) 215–22

van Effenterre, Micheline, *Les Minoens: L'Age d'Or de la Crète* (Paris, Armand Colin, 1991)

Warren, Elizabeth, 'A Late Minoan Figurine from Kritsa', *Kretika Chronika*, 22: 2 (1970) 343–6

Warren, Peter and Hankey, Vronwy, *Aegean Bronze Age Chronology* (Bristol, Bristol University Press, 1989)

Waterhouse, Helen, 'Priest Kings?', *Cretan Studies* 7 (Amsterdam, Adolf M. Hakkert, 2002)

Wilde, Lyn Webster, *On the Trail of Women Warriors* (London, Constable, 1999)

Wright, Rita P., 'Women's Labour and Pottery Production in Prehistory' in *Engendering Archaeology: Women and Prehistory*, Joan M. Gero and Margaret W. Conkey (eds) (Oxford, Blackwell, 1991)

## Unpublished Material

Bate, Dorothea, 'Journal Kept in Crete' (1904) Natural History Museum, London

Brock, Ursula, 'Housewife in Crete', obtained privately

Burn, Robin, 'Mary Wynn: Some Passages of her Life', 1989, obtained privately

Evans, Arthur, Correspondence, to and from, Evans Archives, Ashmolean Museum, Oxford

Hall, Edith, Edith Hall papers, Archives, University of Pennsylvania Museum of Archaeology and Anthropology, Philadelphia

Harrison, Jane Ellen, JEH to GM, 21 April 1901, Newnham College Archives, Cambridge

Mackenzie-Young, Rebecca, 'The Role of Women in Minoan Crete: A Historiographic Approach', unpublished doctoral thesis, University College, London (1999)

Pendlebury, Hilda White, Unpublished Letters (1928), British School at Athens, JP/L/293–99

White, Hilda, see Pendlebury

## General Reference

Alexiou, Stylianos, *Minoan Civilization* (translated Cressida Ridley) (Herakleion, V. Kouvidis, nd)

Alastos, Doros, *Venizelos* (London, P. Lund, Humphries, 1942)

Alsop, Joseph, in *New Yorker* (13 August 1966) 32–95

Barnard, Mary, *Sappho* (Berkeley, University of California Press, 1958)

Bauman, Helmut, *Greek Wild Flowers and Plant Lore in Ancient Greece* (London, 1993)

Becker, Marshall J., and Betancourt, Philip P., *Richard Berry Seager: Pioneer Archaeologist and Proper Gentleman* (Philadelphia, University of Pennsylvania Museum of Archaeology and Anthropology, 1997)

Bell, Robert E., *Women of Classical Mythology: A Biographical Dictionary* (Oxford, Oxford University Press, 1991)

Bosanquet, Ellen (ed.), *Robert Carr Bosanquet: Letters and Light Verse* (Gloucester, 1938)

Bosanquet, Ellen, *Late Harvest: Memories, Letters and Poems* (London, nd)

Brock, J.K., *Fortetsa: Early Greek Tombs Near Knossos* (Cambridge, Cambridge University Press, 1957)

Brown, Ann (ed.), *Arthur Evans: Travels in Crete 1884–1899* (Oxford, Archaeopress, 2001)

Butcher, Kevin & Gill, David W.J., 'The Director, the Dealer, the Goddess and her Champions: The Acquisition of the Fitzwilliam Goddess', *American Journal of Archaeology* 97 (1993) 383–401

Cadogan, Gerald, 'Vronwy Hankey', see *Meletemata* (1999)

Cadogan, Gerald, *Palaces of Minoan Crete* (Photographs by Lucy Cadogan) (London, Routledge, 1980)

Cadogan, Gerald, 'The Minoan Distance: The Impact of Knossos upon the Twentieth Century' in *Knossos: Palace, City, State,* Gerald Cadogan, Eleni Hatzaki and Adonis Vasilakis eds. (London, British School at Athens, 2004)

Campanis, Nikos, *Madame Hortense* (Arles, Actes Sud, 1989)

Candy, James, *A Tapestry of Life* (Braunton, Merlin, 1984)

Christ, Carol P., *Odyssey With the Goddess: A Spiritual Quest in Crete* (New York, Continuum, 1995)

Christides, V., *The Conquest of Crete by the Arabs* (Athens, 1984)

Chubb, Mary, *Nefertiti Lived Here* (London, Geoffrey Bles, 1998)

de Bakker, Johan, *Across Crete: From Khania to Herakleion*, part 1 (Amsterdam, Logos Tekstproducties, 2001)

Detorakis, Theochoris E., *History of Crete* (Iraklion, 1994)

Doren, David MacNeil, *Winds of Crete* (Athens, Efstathiadis, 1981)

Duncan, Isadora, *Isadora Duncan* (New York, Henry Holt, 1947)

Elliadi, M.N., *Crete: Past and Present* (London, Heath, Cranton, 1933)

Evans, Arthur, *The Palace of Minos*, 4 vols, (London, Macmillan, 1921–1935)

Evans, Joan, *Prelude and Fugue* (London, Museum Press, 1964)

Evans, J.A.S., *The Empress Theodora: Partner of Justinian* (Austin, University of Texas Press, 2002)

Farnoux, Alexandre, *Knossos: Unearthing a Legend* (London, Thames Hudson, 1996)

(ffennell, Hazel) *Hazel: The Happy Journey* (printed for her friends, nd)

Fielding, Daphne, *Mercury Presides* (London, Eyre & Spottiswood, 1954)

Fielding, Xan, *The Stronghold: An Account of the Four Seasons in the White Mountains* (London, Secker & Warburg, 1953)

Harrison, Jane Ellen, *Reminiscences of a Student's Life* (London, Hogarth, 1925)

Hertzfeld, Michael, *A Place in History: Social and Monumental Time in a Cretan Town* (Princeton, Princeton University Press, 1991)

Hitier, M., 'Appendice sur l'état d'agriculture et des productions de l'île de Crète' in *Les Iles de la Grèce*, L. Lacroix (ed.), (Paris, 1881)

Hoe, Susanna, *Chinese Footprints: Exploring Women's History in China, Hong Kong and Macau* (Hong Kong, Roundhouse, 1997)

Hogarth, David, *Accidents of an Antiquary's Life* (London, Macmillan, 1910)

Holton, David, *Literature and Society in Renaissance Crete* (Cambridge, Cambridge University Press, 1991)

Hood, M.S.F. and Coldstream J.N., 'A Late Minoan Tomb at Ayios Ionnis New Knossos', *British School at Athens* 63 (1968) 205ff

Hood, Sinclair, 'The Mallia Pendant: Wasps or Bees' reprinted from *Tribute to an Antiquary, Essays presented to Marc Fitch*, Emmisson and Stephens (eds) 1976

Hopkins, Adam, *Crete: Its Past, Present & People* (London, Faber & Faber, 1977)

Hughes-Hallet, Lucy, *Cleopatra: Histories, Dreams and Distortions* (London, Pimlico, 1990)

Hutton, Ronald, 'The Neolithic Great Goddess: A Study in Modern Tradition', *Antiquity* 71 (1977) 92–9

James, Edward T. et al, *Notable American Women, 1607–1950: A Biographical Dictionary* (Cambridge MA, Belknap Press, 1971)

Kazantzakis, Nikos, *Zorba the Greek* (London, Faber & Faber, 2000)

Lapatin, Kenneth D.S. 'Snake Goddesses, Fake Goddesses', *Archaeology* (January/February 2001)

Lear, Edward, *The Cretan Journal*, Rowena Fowler (ed.) (Dedham, Essex, Sanctuary, 1984)

Leventhal, F.M., *The Last Dissenter: H.N. Brailsford and his World* (Oxford, Clarendon Press, 1985)

Liszt, Franz, *Letters*, La Mara (ed.) (New York, Greenwood, 1969)

Llewellyn Smith, Michael, *The Great Island: A Study of Crete* (London, Longmans, 1965)

Lloyd, Seton, *The Interval: A Life in Near Eastern Archaeology* (Faringdon, Lloyd Collon, c1986)

Macgillivray, J. Alexander, *Minotaur: Sir Arthur Evans and the Archaeology of the Minoan Myth* (London, Jonathan Cape, 2000)

Maillart, Ella, *Cruises and Caravans* (London, J.M. Dent, 1942)

Matton, Raymond, *La Crète au Cours des Siècles* (Athens, Institut Français d'Athènes, 1957)

Mayor, Adrienne, *The First Fossil Hunters* (Princeton, Princeton University Press, 2000)

Melena, Elpis, *Von Rom nach Creta* (Jena, 1870)

Melena, Elpis, *Garibaldi: Recollections of His Public and Private Life*, trans. Charles Edwards (London, Trübner, 1887)

Melena, Elpis, (assembled and published by) *Garibaldi's Memoirs*, Anthony P. Campanella (ed.) (Sarasota, Florida, International Institute of Garibaldian Studies, 1981)

Momigliano, Nicoletta, *Duncan Mackenzie: A Cautious, Canny Highlander and the Palace of Minos at Knossos* (London, Institute of Classical Studies, 1999)

Muhly, James (ed.), *Crete 2000: A Centennial Celebration of American Archaeological Work on Crete, 1900–2000* (Athens, American School of Classical Studies, 2000)

*Oxford Dictionary of National Biography*

Padel, Ruth, *Summer Snow* (London, Hutchinson, 1990)

Pashley, Robert, *Travels in Crete*, 2 vols (London, John Murray, 1937)

Pendlebury, John, *The Archaeology of Crete* (London, Methuen, 1939)

Pendlebury, John, *John Pendlebury in Crete, Comprising his Travelling Hints and His First Trip to Eastern Crete (1928)*, T.J. Dunbabin (ed.) (Cambridge, Cambridge University Press, privately circulated, 1948)

Prevelakis, Pandelis, *Chronique d'une Cité* (Paris, Gallimard, 1960)

Platon, Nicholas, *Zakros: Discovery of a Lost Palace of Ancient Crete* (New York, Charles Scribner, 1971)

Psilakis, N., *The Monasteries of Crete* (trans.) (Athens, Bank of Crete, 1988)

Rackham, Oliver and Moody, Jennifer, *The Making of the Cretan Landscape* (Manchester, Manchester University Press, 1996)

Ram, Agatha (ed.), *Beloved and Darling Child: Last Letters between Queen Victoria and her Eldest Daughter*, vol. 5 (Stroud, Sutton, 1990)

*Revolution of Therisso* (leaflet at Venizelos Museum, Theriso, nd)

('Cressida Ridley'), obituary, *The Times*, Gerald Cadogan (18 June 1998)

Robinson, Annabel, *The Life and Work of Jane Ellen Harrison* (Oxford, Oxford University Press, 2002)

(Rodanthe) 'The Secret School of the Holy Monastery and the Heroine Rodanthe Kristopoula' leaflet (in Greek) (Faneromeni Monastery, nd)

St Hilda's (College), *Report and Chronicle*, 1973–74 and 1996–97

Sakellarakis, Yannis, *Digging for the Past* (Athens, Amos Publications,1996)

Sanders, Ian, *Roman Crete: An Archaeological Survey and Gazetteer of Late Hellenistic, Roman, Early Byzantine Crete* (Warminster, Aris & Phillips, 1982)

Spratt, T.A.B., *Travels and Researches in Crete* (London, 1865)

Sweetman, David, *Mary Renault: A Biography* (London, Chatto & Windus, 1993)

Tannen, Deborah, *Lalika Nakos* (Boston, Twayne, 1983)

Taylor, Bayard, *Travels in Greece and Russia: With an Excursion to Crete* (New York, Putnam & Sons, 1876)

Tsougarakis, Dimitris, *Byzantine Crete: From the Fifth Century to the Venetian Conquest* (Athens, D. Basilopoulos, 1988)

Unsworth, Barry, *Crete* (Washington D.C., National Geographic, 2004)

van Effenterre, Henri, *Le Palais de Mallia et la Cité Minoenne* 2 vols (Rome, Edizioni Dell'Ateneo, Incunabula Graeca vol. LXXVI, 1980)

Vasilakis, Andonis, *Minoan Crete: From Myth to History* (Athens, Adam Editions, 2000)

Warren, Peter, '16th, 17th and 18th Century British Travellers in Crete', *Kretica Chronika* 24, 9 (1972) 65–92

Warren, Peter, *Myrtos: An Early Bronze Age Settlement* (London, British School at Athens, 1972)

Warren, Peter, 'The Fresco of the Garlands from Knossos' *L'Iconographie Minoenne, Bulletin de Correspondance Hellénique, supplement* XI, P. Darcque & J.-C. Poursat (eds) (1985) 187–208

Warren, Peter, 'Cretan Food Through Five Millennia', *Briciaka: A Tribute to W.C. Brice*, 9, 270–84 (Amsterdam, Adolf M.Hakkert, 2003)

Waterhouse, Helen, *The British School at Athens: The First Hundred Years* (London, The British School at Athens, 1986)

Wharton, Edith, *A Backward Glance* (London, Century, 1987)

Willets, R.F., *Ancient Crete: A Social History From Early Times until the Roman Occupation* (London, Routledge & Kegan Paul, 1965)

Willets, R.F., *Everyday Life in Ancient Crete* (London, Batsford & Son, 1969)

Woolf, Virginia, *A Room of One's Own* (London, Hogarth Press, 1929)

## Guides

Cameron, Pat, *Blue Guide: Crete*, 7th edition (London, A & C Black, 2003)

Castleden, Rodney, *Knossos: Temple of the Goddess* (Athens, Efstathiadis, 1997)

Davaras, Costis, *East Crete* (Athens, Hannibal, nd)

Everyman Guide, *Crete* (London, David Campbell, 1995)

Fisher, John and Garvey, Geoff, *The Rough Guide to Crete*, 5th edition (London, Rough Guides, 2001)

Freely, John, *Crete* (London, Weidenfeld & Nicolson, 1988)

Kanta, Athanasia, *Phaistos, Hagia Triadha, Gortyn* (Athens, Adam Editions, 1998)

Kofou, Anna, *Crete: A Complete Guide* (Athens, Ekdotike Athenon, 2000)

Logiadou-Platonos, Sosso, *Knossos: The Palace of Minos* (Athens, Mathioulakis, nd)

Logiadou-Platonos, Sosso, and Marinatos, Nanno, *Crete* (Athens, Mathioulakis, 1984)

Sakellaraki, Efi, *Minoan Crete: An Illustrated Guide* (Athens, Gnosis, 1994)

Vasilakis, Andonis, *Herakleion Archaeological Museum* (Athens, Adam Editions, nd)

# Index

The following categories are grouped together: caves, convents/monasteries, goddesses, gods, mountains, museums, wars; women, their status and activities are split into several groups under women. Bold numbers indicate main biographical entry.